W9-BYW-114

DATE DUE

DEC 1 9 1979			
MAR 3 1 1982			

HENRY JAMES, Senior

Henry James, Senior

HENRY JAMES, Senior

A SELECTION OF HIS WRITINGS

Edited and with an Introduction by

GILES GUNN

AMERICAN LIBRARY ASSOCIATION
Chicago 1974

Library of Congress Cataloging in Publication Data

James, Henry, 1811-1882.
    Henry James, Senior: a selection of his writings.

    1. Philosophy—Collected works. I. Title.

B921.J21G86   191   74-17313
ISBN 0-8389-0189-1

The recognition of the direction of fulfillment is the
death of the self,
And the death of self is the beginning of selfhood.
All else is surrogate of hope and destitution of spirit.

ROBERT PENN WARREN, *Brother to Dragons*

CONTENTS

vii

PREFACE

As we move closer to America's bicentennial, there is a certain fitness in the desire to revive the memory and repossess the work of Henry James, Senior, by compiling a representative selection of his writings. For not only has James been neglected by most of those critics and historians who in recent years have sought to establish the intellectual contours of the American religious heritage; few religious thinkers in our heritage have reflected more deeply about the problems besetting American democracy, or any other for that matter, and still fewer have adumbrated more thoroughly the vision of a better social order which might transcend them. Yet the fact remains that virtually all of James's books have been allowed to go out of print and that he continues to exist in the minds of most students of American history as no more than a name or, at most, as a disciple of Emmanuel Swedenborg.

The mere fact that Henry James, Senior, was the father of William James the philosopher and Henry James the novelist should have insured him somewhat better treatment at the hands of the past, but his real claim to recognition is not owing solely, or even chiefly, to the deserved reputation of his two more famous sons. The elder James was himself something sui generis in American life, a man of letters, philosopher of religion, and sometime metaphysician who took upon himself the unhappy task of attempting to keep the art of religious writing alive and lively in an age when professional theology, as his son William noted, had long since become a stale, cold conversation. More important than this, however, the elder James grasped, as almost no American thinker before him and few since, that the Christian faith represented in the here and now a call for a new form of social solidarity, a new brotherhood of man—*Society the Redeemed Form of Man* he entitled his last published work—and that, as the herald of this new order, he had no other sacerdotal obligation than to remain a man speaking to men of the divine potentiality resident or incarnate in their own natural humanity.

It was a relatively simple faith which James preached, but one which he never tired of amplifying, refining, complicating, and restating. Part of the reason is that James's faith came to him by way of a process which was intuitive rather than rational, revelatory rather than logical, and he could never be sure that he had captured its essence and significance in words. A larger factor, however, was attributable to its very momentousness: James regarded his faith as the key to life's inmost secret, to the teleological mystery of creation itself, and he could hardly resist attempting to reformulate it, if only because so much depended upon saying it right. Hence he quickly grew to dislike the sight of his own books and was no sooner finished with one before he was well launched into another in an effort to traverse much of the same ground from a slightly different perspective.

This habit of returning again and again to the same core of ideas—one immediately thinks of Emerson in this connection—obviously poses a problem for James's editor: how to present a sufficiently copious sampling of his work without becoming needlessly repetitious. A certain amount of repetition is probably unavoidable in any case, just because James's central ideas were few in number and comparatively uncomplicated in substance; but the frequency of their recurrence in his writing is largely offset by the variety of ways in which he expressed them and the different contexts in which he sought to apply them. Thus I have tried to display the scope of his concerns by dividing the anthology into several distinct sections and to suggest the variousness of his accomplishment by including selections both from some of his more occasional writing (speeches, lectures, book reviews, and character sketches) and also from some of his more polished and theoretical writing (philosophical essays, theological treatises, and the like). Further, I have attempted to balance selections drawn from some of his later, more closely reasoned work with selections drawn from some of his earlier, more exploratory and tentative work, and to include at least one selection from each of his major books while still holding to the principle that each selection should be able to stand by itself, as an independent and unified treatment of a given subject or problem.

Something more should be said about the particular sections into which this anthology is divided. The section headings are designed merely as a way of showing the range of issues and areas of interest which James's "grand scheme," as he called it, touched upon but without presuming to suggest that his thought actually falls into any such neat set of categories. Their intention is purely heuristic: to indicate the reach of his ideas and the extent of their implications without prescribing any clearly differentiable modes of reflection in which he thought about them. In actual fact, James put such notions as the political, the social, the ethical, and the religious to his own very special uses and was constantly mixing one with another, as I indicate in the Introduction. To read him correctly, then, one must finally read him whole, as a man who struggled to involve every one of his major areas of concern with every other, and this often simultaneously.

In preparing this volume for publication, I have made only one basic alteration in the way James presented his own material in book form. In accordance with the custom of the day, James usually offered assistance to his reader by listing the specific theme or issue under discussion at the top of each of his pages. These citations I have here omitted on the grounds that the difference in pagination between this volume and any of his own would only make for confusion if this practice were continued. I have, however, retained the epistolary form of several of the selections I include here in the belief that it is important to realize that James designed several of his books as a collection of letters to a friend, whether real or imagined. The use of this convention was, of course, wholly in character. James depended upon others for his sense of himself and was most fully at ease when he was addressing someone in particular. He was at his best in conversation, which is why all of his richest pages exhibit the earthy directness and cumulative force of good talk.

For assistance in the preparation of this volume, I am indebted to Mr. Herbert Bloom, my sponsoring editor at the American Library Association, whose initial interest and continued support made its conception possible, and to Dean Joseph M. Kitagawa of the Divinity School of the University of Chicago, who arranged for me to have the time and necessary resources to complete it. Thanks are also due to my former student, Mr. James G. Moseley, who shared with me his own broad knowledge of James's work, to my secretary, Mrs. Rehova Arthur, who graciously offered to type and retype various portions of the manuscript, to Sylvia Royt of the American Library Association Publishing Services, who gave me the benefit of her editorial wisdom in preparing the manuscript for publication, and to my wife, Janet, who remained throughout my best critic and chief supporter. I also wish to acknowledge the generosity of Mr. Alexander R. James, who granted me permission to reprint various letters of Henry James, Senior.

My interest in compiling this volume of selections from the writings of Henry James, Senior, was in many ways inspired by the life of my father, Buckingham Willcox Gunn, who lived James's truth without ever knowing his work.

HENRY JAMES, Senior

AN INTRODUCTION

GILES GUNN

1

On May 30, 1850, Edwards Amasa Park of Andover Theological Seminary preached an important sermon in Boston's Brattle Street Meeting House before the Convention of the Congregational Ministers of Massachusetts on "The Theology of the Intellect and That of the Feelings." Though his subject may have been suggested to him two years before when his theological colleague from Hartford, the more famous Horace Bushnell, made use of a similar distinction in an address also delivered at Andover on the relation between "Dogma and Spirit," Park's title reflected an opposition which, in the American tradition, had found its chief exponent a century earlier in the person of Jonathan Edwards and which, in the European tradition, went all the way back through Friedrich Schleiermacher and Martin Luther to the Bible itself. Park was hardly insensible to the importance and magnitude of this legacy, but his chief purpose was less to establish or defend it than to interpret its consequences, to show how each kind of theology needed the other to do full justice to the nature and substance of the Christian truth.

The theology of the intellect, with its preference for evidence over opinion, reason over intuition, precision over intensity, harmony over conflict, the literal over the figural, and the general over the specific was far better suited for dogmatics than for preaching, for dialectics than for confession, for speculation than for narrative. The theology of the feelings, on the other hand, with its opposite tendency to subordinate consistency to assertiveness, logic to feeling, certitude to sensitivity, the discursive to the poetic, and the concrete to the universal, was far more appropriate to the tract than the treatise, the homily than the catechism, the history than the disputation. Park's point was that neither type of theology is sufficient without the other, just as a confusion of either with its complement might destroy the integrity of both:

> It is this crossing of one kind of theology into the
> province of another kind . . . which mars either the
> eloquence or else the doctrine of the pulpit. The
> massive speculations of the metaphysician sink down

into his expressions of feeling and make him appear
cold-hearted, while the enthusiasm of the impulsive
divine ascends and effervesces into his reasonings
and causes him both to *appear*, and to *be* . . . hot-
headed.[1]

Park wanted a recognition of the claims of both kinds of theology so
that he might effect a reconciliation between the intellectual and pietistic
elements not only within his own breast but also within the body of the
Christian faith of his time, between the Evangelicals who made so much
of the heart and what might be loosely called the Unitarians who put such
store in the head, between popular revivalists and Harvard intellectuals.
Park himself was a member of neither radical party. It was the older
orthodoxy of New England that he wanted to repossess, only softened and
made more sensible by an anthropology which acknowledged that man
is at once sentient and rational.

There is no way of knowing if the elder Henry James ever read Park's
sermon—had he done so he would undoubtedly have regarded it as an
expression of what he was fond of calling the "old theology" rather than
the "new"—but there can scarcely be any doubt at all about the relevance
of its presiding differentiation to his own life and work. For anyone who
ever bothered to read the works of Henry James, Senior—a series of books
which, if one includes the unfinished manuscript published posthumously
by his eldest son William, the noted philosopher, comes to well over a
dozen volumes[2]—were likely to be struck by the same kind of confusion
which Park had noted in his sermon: massive metaphysical speculations
which often cast a leaden shadow over an unusually spirited and expressive speaker, thus giving rise to that contradictory set of impressions
which Park evokes with the phrases "cold-hearted" and "hot-headed."

In truth, however, something very nearly the opposite was the case
with the elder James. If his heart suffered from anything, then it was not
from an absence of feeling, but rather from an excess of it, whereas his
speculations and judgments often appeared intemperate or impulsive
only because he viewed his ideas, however universal their scope or implication, as living realities, felt possibilities. James's problem was that
he was clearly a theologian of feeling who tried to express his religious
faith in what most systematic thinkers would regard as a jerrybuilt
theology of intellect. Constantly tempted as well as obliged to convey
what T. S. Eliot once called "the logic of feelings" in "the logic of
concepts," James seems in retrospect to have been caught in the unhappy
situation of a man whose medium frequently constituted a downright
obstacle to, if not parody of, his message. Hence the well-known quip
which Charles Eliot Norton ascribed to William Dean Howells about how
James not only wrote *The Secret of Swedenborg* but "kept it."[3]

There is a certain irresponsibility about the way many have fastened
upon this mischievous but good-natured remark and then used it as an

excuse to dismiss James as an utter eccentric, when, in point of fact, Howells himself could not. Though Howells was a worldly man of letters whose own religious upbringing had been seriously undermined by the new kingdom of forces unleased in the second half of the nineteenth century, he nonetheless believed that James was decidedly worth listening to and that he often made a good deal of sense. Even if Howells was temperamentally indisposed to take any active interest in what James found so important and compelling in Swedenborg's ontology, he had still absorbed enough of his own father's respect for Swedenborg's ethics to respond favorably to James's explication of that "divine natural humanity" to which Swedenborg claimed all men heir, and which in the new dispensation, so James argued, would destroy all those superficial social and political distinctions by which governments had falsely differentiated one man from another.

This conviction, in fact, converged almost precisely with certain underlying assumptions of that emergent progressivism which served to unite Howells with what Daniel Aaron has described as the other "men of good hope" of that era, people such as Edward Bellamy, Henry Demarest Lloyd, and Henry George, whose political faith had a way of turning very quickly into a religion of humanity as well roughly parallel in its convictions to the views of writers as diverse as Mazzini, Victor Hugo, and James himself. Finding Henry Demarest Lloyd the most eloquent spokesman of this "secular religion," Professor Aaron has defined it as follows:

> The religion of progressivism conceived of the mediator between God and man not as an individual Christ but as a universalized Christ, Christ as a symbol of humanity itself. It broke with the orthodox Protestant assumption that "God's redemptive operation," to quote Gronlund, is "confined to the isolated individual bosom" and refused to make religion a private affair between one man and his God. For the progressives, God appeared to man through men and revealed himself in human history and institutions. Men were damned or saved collectively. They entered into communion with God when they shed their selfish personalities and united with one another in a confederation of love. According to this religion, social evil was not confirmed by individual criminal acts but by what the elder Henry James called "our organized inclemency of man to man." And in turn, social good could not be attained through individual acts of charity but through the organized clemency of man to man.[4]

Except for the omission of the assumption that religion has its tragic side, entailing the death of the old egoistic self to make way for the rebirth of a new social self, this summary of the faith of the progressives

could also stand as a fairly accurate, brief statement of the thought of
the elder Henry James. True, he differed with the later progressives, just
as he had with the earlier Transcendentalists, over the question of the
reality and governance of evil, but his view of salvation was still as equal-
itarian as that of the first and as infused with a spirit of optimism—albeit
a very much more tempered one—as that of the second. As William James
summarized his father's view of the world, it flowed from two basic perceptions: "In the first place, he felt that the individual man, as such, is
nothing, but owes all he is and has to the race nature he inherits, and to
the society into which he is born. And, secondly, he scorned to admit,
even as a possibility, that the great and loving Creator, who has all the
being and the power, and has brought us as far as *this*, should not bring
us *through*, and *out*, into the most triumphant harmony."[5]

Yet few people, then or now, have perceived the depth of James's
relationship either to the Transcendentalists or to the progressives, or,
for that matter, to any other major group of thinkers and writers in the
American tradition. Instead, the impression which with certain notable
exceptions has continued to prevail is the one most vividly conveyed by
E. L. Godkin, that fearlessly independent former Irish immigrant destined to become one of America's most liberal and distinguished journal-
ists, who from 1875 to 1881 was a resident in Cambridge and frequent dinner guest at the James's—the impression of an interesting and, in his own
terms, formidable eccentric with no very clear intellectual outline who
was alienated from and disavowed by the only sect or group, in this case
the Swedenborgians, to whose cause he professed any allegiance at all:

> Henry James, the elder, was a person of delightful
> eccentricity, and a humorist of the first water. When in
> his grotesque moods, he maintained that, to a right-
> minded man, a crowded Cambridge horse-car "was the
> nearest approach to heaven upon earth!" What was
> the precise nature of his philosophy, I never fully
> understood, but he professed to be a Swedenborgian,
> and carried on a correspondence full of droll incidents
> with anxious inquirers, in various parts of the
> country. Asking him one day about one of these, he
> replied instantly, "Oh, a devil of a woman!" to my great
> astonishment, as I was not then thoroughly familiar
> with his ways. One of his most amusing experiences
> was that the other Swedenborgians repudiated all
> religious connection with him, so that the sect to which
> he belonged, and of which he was the head, may be
> said to have consisted of himself alone.[6]

Oddly enough, Godkin closed this recollection with the final observation that James "was a writer of extraordinary vigor and picturesqueness, and I suppose there was not in his day a more formidable master of English style."[7]

This almost parenthetical remark from one who was closely associated with James Russell Lowell and Charles Eliot Norton in the founding and editing of the *Nation* was no mean compliment; yet it only deepens the mystery of obscurity to which James fell victim almost immediately after his death and from which he has never fully recovered, in spite of the efforts of such scholars as Austin Warren, Ralph Barton Perry, F. O. Matthiessen, Frederick Young, Leon Edel, Quentin Anderson, R. W. B. Lewis, and Richard Poirier.[8] Clearly part of the reason derives from James's turn toward theology (and an abstruse form of it at that!) just at a time when this mode of reflection was rapidly going out of fashion among those with whom James most wanted to communicate. Recognizing the need for new religious wine to revive the spirit of those who had long since lost a taste for the old, James made the mistake of not replenishing his stock of wineskins, and this, in turn, tended to give his product a flat, sometimes even brackish, flavor. For all the originality and prescience of many of his insights, his stubbornly metaphysical cast of mind, together with the esoteric and untraditional framework of thought in terms of which he chose to express it, frequently made his insights appear too recondite and vague to his contemporaries.

Then, too, he lived in an age which was somewhat indifferent to, even impatient with, particular kinds of thinkers, at least those like James who refused to permit their interest in and sympathy for concrete problems from obscuring their still more fervent vision of what transcends and resolves them. Though James was as absorbed with the individual and the concrete as the next man—indeed, his son Henry observed at one point in his *Notes of a Son and Brother* (1914) that there was in his father, for all his love of the abstract, not the least embarrassment of the actual about him—he remained steadfast in his belief that the key to all particular issues lay in reconstituting our conception of the whole. A philosophical monist by inclination, if not always by practice, James suffered the same fate of incomprehension which befell those other two metaphysical visionaries of the age, Herman Melville and Walt Whitman.

But there were also other, more personal reasons why the elder James's work disappeared so quickly from public view, reasons having to do both with the remarkable development of certain members of his family and also with a particular, rarely mentioned element of his own style as thinker and writer. To begin with, James's work was very quickly overshadowed by that of his two more gifted and famous sons. Henry, Junior, had already published six books before his father finished his own most mature work, *Society the Redeemed Form of Man,* and by the time the elder James died three years later, his novelist son had added seven more titles to that list. William's productive outflow of books and essays did not commence in earnest until several years later with the publication of his two-volume study entitled *The Principles of Psychology* (1890); but he had already begun teaching at Harvard as early as 1872, had established his pioneering laboratory in psychology and started to work on the massive *Principles* by 1876, and had acquired many of his most durable convictions by 1884, when he edited his father's last work in progress entitled "Spiritual Creation" and then published it, together with his father's "Autobiographical Sketch" and an introduction of his own, as *The Literary Remains of the Late Henry James.*

What is most relevant to observe at this point is that, had the elder James lived long enough to witness the full measure of this ultimately staggering achievement of his two sons which so thoroughly eclipsed his own, he would neither have been alarmed nor displeased. On the contrary, to him their accomplishment would have constituted an eloquent vindication of the principles by which he had sought to educate them, or, more accurately, by which he had sought to permit them the freedom to educate themselves. Further, and this leads to the second personal reason that James's work was relegated to obscurity so rapidly: there was about virtually all of his writing a certain elusive, even ineffable, quality which resisted any sort of systematic intellectual analysis. Stated negatively, it was not that James didn't mean every word that he wrote, only that, by his own admission, he could never quite express exactly what he meant. One can lay part of the blame for this on the deficiencies of his chosen medium and the limitations of his own intellectual gifts, but it really involved something more. In one corner of his mind, at least, James knew that his truth was deeper than his philosophy, than any philosophy perhaps, and that he could only bridge the gap between them with his own sensibility, with the personal authority of his own faith. To put the matter more positively, James was less interested in his theories than his truths, truths which, as William said after his father's death, were inseparable from his life. Hence James's profound integrity of being tended to prevail even where the integrity of his ideas could not, making for that marked discrepancy between the letter and the spirit of his writing which is evident even in some of his most abstract and unwieldy passages. Either way, his son Henry was right: "His tone . . . always so effectually looks out, and the living parts of him so singularly hung together, that one may fairly say his philosophy *was* his tone."⁹

But this is only another way of explaining why his books failed either to attract or to hold any very large audience. Being more an expression of sentiment than of science, of convinced feeling rather than clearheaded reasoning, his writing lacked those characteristics of straightforward exposition, sound logic, and ready classifiability which help insure preservation in the memory of the past. As one who was better at living the truth he wanted to express than at expressing the truth he lived, James didn't quite seem to fit anywhere, and so was dismissed by some and neglected by the rest.

2

Yet if one actually takes the time to read James carefully, one soon discovers that he appeared out of step with his time only because in many ways he lived so far in advance of it. His close relation to the progressives who came after him, with their belief that the reformation of society depends upon the social rebirth of the individual, has already been remarked. What has not been so fully appreciated is that James also perceived the kind of criticism to which this secularized religion of the progressives could become vulnerable, as when their visionary dream of the redemption of society gave way to a kind of benevolent social idealism and was then exposed by a generation of thinkers following the lead of Reinhold Niebuhr to be but another mask of egoistic self-approbation.

Like the neoorthodox theologians whom Niebuhr represented, James had realized long before that man is most culpable when he thinks himself most virtuous, that man's ideals, as James would have put it, tempt him to commit the greatest "spiritual evil," that moralism, in short, is an expression of self-love. But James would also have acknowledged the necessity not only of the neoorthodox theological critique of religious liberalism but also of the neoliberal theological critique of religious neo-orthodoxy, or at least of its doctrine of God and its view of creation. For he was at one both with the process theologians of our own day and also with their more radical, occasional fellow travelers, the so-called "Death-of-God" theologians, in finding it inconceivable to think of divinity in the terms popularized by the neo-Reformation theologians—as One who is "wholly other," unchanging, and impassible but for that single moment in history when, in the person of Jesus Christ, He undertook a divine rescue operation in behalf of a creature who bore almost no discernible trace of the image in which he was made and who was absolutely undeserving of this completely unmerited act of grace. To James, on the contrary, if God was not closer to us than we are to ourselves, if God did not need us as much as we need Him, if God did not take His stripes with the rest of us and thus demonstrate how suffering and death could be the way to truth and new life, then the religion of the Incarnation made no sense to him and he wanted no part of it. Further, if life was not process, if nature was not illustrative of change, if history did not exhibit some measure of creative progress, then the Deity, to paraphrase one of James's most colorful figures, must be like some immense duck that has continued to emit the same unchanged, unimproved quack which it first uttered on the day it was born.

Instead, James conceived of God as the perfect man, as what is divine in our natural humanity when it is raised to the level of absolute perfection, and he made no bones about what this amounts to in terms of traditional theological conceptions of God. As he said with characteristic belligerence and verve in the Advertisement appended to the front matter of what, paradoxically, is one of his more thickly metaphysical volumes:

I find myself incapable, for my part, of honoring the pretension of any deity to my allegiance, who insists upon standing eternally aloof from my own nature, and by that fact confesses himself personally incommensurate and unsympathetic with my basest, most sensuous, and controlling personal necessities. It is an easy enough thing to find a holiday God who is all too selfish to be touched by the infirmities of his own creatures—a God, for example, who has naught to do but receive assiduous court for a work of creation done myriads of ages ago, and which is reputed to have cost him in the doing neither pains nor patience, neither affection nor thought, but simply the utterance of a dramatic word; and who is willing, accordingly, to accept our decorous Sunday homage in ample quittance of obligations so unconsciously incurred on our part, so lightly rendered and so penuriously sanctioned on his. Every sect, every nation, every family almost, offers some pet idol of this description to your worship. But I am free to confess that I have long outgrown this loutish conception of deity. I can no longer bring myself to adore a characteristic activity in the God of my worship, which falls below the secular average of human character. In fact, what I crave with all my heart and understanding—what my very flesh and bones cry out for—is no longer a Sunday but a weekday divinity, a working God, grim with the dust and sweat of our most carnal appetites and passions, and bent, not for an instant upon inflating our worthless pietistic righteousness, but upon the patient, toilsome, thorough cleansing of our physical and moral existence from the odious defilement it has contracted, until we each and all present at last in body and mind the deathless effigy of his own uncreated loveliness.[10]

Such convictions as these might lead one to suspect that James's modernity consisted merely in his desire to throw over the entire theological inheritance of Calvinism, but this is decidedly incorrect. Indeed, while James anticipated certain theological and philosophical developments of the future, he also preserved and transmitted much of the Calvinist-Puritan legacy of the past, so much of it, in fact, that he often struck many of his liberated contemporaries as a holdover from some earlier age of faith. It is no accident, I think, that comparatively early in his career, James confided in a letter to Emerson his belief that "Jonathan Edwards *redivivus* in true blue" would still make the best reconciler and critic of the kind of philosophy which had grown up since the middle of the eighteenth century.[11] For, in spite of James's attraction to currents of thought emanating from writers like Swedenborg and Fourier, who could only appeal to a later and very different era than that of Edwards's, what James wanted was not to overthrow Calvinism but rather to *humanize* it. His beliefs, having been derived from the precepts of Calvinism, continued to retain its sense of man's utter dependence on God for his very being, to underline its insistence that nature, life, and history exist only for the glorification of the Creator, to stress its belief in the inevitability and universality of man's involvement with sin and death, and to reemphasize its conviction of man's need for deliverance from evil and rebirth to new life, but not at the expense of allowing Calvinism's insistence upon the doctrine of God's sovereignty to obscure what James perceived to be the equally important fact of God's immanence, His living presence both among and within us as the source and center of what is common and natural to the humanity of all men.

This perception of necessity involved some basic modification of the traditional Calvinist scheme of salvation; the philosopher Ralph Barton Perry later went so far as to describe it as a complete inversion. Where Calvinism, for example, assumed that men fall collectively, as a result of the natural imperfection of human nature as such, and then are saved only as God elects certain individuals who through faith have exhibited their readiness to receive what they cannot earn or acquire of themselves, James postulated to the contrary that men fall individually, precisely as a result of believing themselves personally meritorious of Divine solicitude, and then are saved only when they relinquish their pride in themselves and learn to identify their own lives with the collective nature and destiny of their fellow human beings.[12] This was probably the most profound of James's revisions of cherished Calvinist assumptions. But from this basic modification emanated several others as well which had the effect, if not of turning the entire system upside down, at least of radically revising it according to James's own more humane and optimistic sentiments.

The most famous of James's proposals for a renovation of the orthodox scheme of salvation—though one in which he unknowingly received tacit support from certain of his contemporaries[13]—was his positive or affirmative interpretation of the Fall. According to the view he put forward so emphatically in *The Nature of Evil* and several of his other books, the Fall was neither the result of some accident or unintentional mistake on God's part, as certain liberal Unitarians proposed, nor the result of some primal act of disobedience on man's part, as traditional Calvinists were wont to claim, but rather a necessary and wholly salutary step in God's beneficent plan for man's redemption. In awakening Adam from his state of sensuous slumber to a knowledge of good and evil, Eve had merely precipitated in him the development of that moral conscience identical with conscious selfhood or *proprium,* as James termed it, which he considered the requisite stepping stone to salvation. Without a moral sense of himself, man could not discover what a spiritual liability it was, and how, therefore, he could obtain new life, not through repentance merely, but only by committing what James called "moral suicide, or inward death to self in all its forms. . . ."[14]

Yet this, in turn, suggested another departure from traditional formulas of regeneration. One was brought to the state of preparation for moral suicide and then subsequently underwent that act, "not by learning," as James suggested in a letter to one of his favorite female correspondents, but "only by *unlearning*."[15] The actual process of regeneration of the self into full awareness of its divine sociality could only be conceived as a kind of "demolition" or "undoing," to quote from the same letter, a process of decreation leading to that moment of spiritual rebirth where the individual discovers "his object a *life* within him, and no longer a *law* without him."[16] Human redemption still implied reunion with God, then, but the spatial conception of this transaction had changed: man was no longer lifted up and out of himself into communion with the God who exists, as it were, above, but was rather lifted out of himself and into relation with his neighbors for communion with the God who exists nowhere more completely than in the universally human. Further, Jesus Christ, in this view, was neither a substitutionary victim compelled to satisfy the affront made to God's sense of honor by man's original act of disobedience, nor a propitiatory sacrifice intended to mitigate the punishment rightly due to man by a God whose just demands had been betrayed, but rather a representative figure who demonstrated that the only way to achieve reunion with the Creator is by dying to self and becoming one with mankind.

The upshot of all this was a revised conception of the purpose of creation and a severely restricted view of the role of the church and organized religion in general. The elder James could still say with Jonathan Edwards that God is glorified in man's dependence and that all things created exist for the joyous expression of the Creator, but only after having dissociated the word *dependence* from all connotations of the word *subservience* and then relocating the realm of God's creative operation in man's very being. God glorified Himself, then, only by completely emptying Himself, by giving up all special claims to Himself, by showing through the Incarnation that the chief end of creation was the perfect realization of God Himself in the universal humanity of others.

In this scheme of things, the church was obliged to play a decidedly subordinate role, serving, as James said in *Substance and Shadow,* a wholly purgative rather than nutritive function. At best, organized religion was merely a way station on the road to salvation, an institution whose sole purpose was to awaken in its followers a sense of death rather than life, "to reveal to them the dearth of life they have in themselves as morally and finitely constituted, in order to prepare them for that fulness of life they shall find in each other as socially constituted."[17] For this reason James could conclude, and not without a certain measure of Biblical precedent, that "the sinner . . . and not the sin is as yet God's best achievement in human nature: when this achievement becomes somewhat universalized by society itself coming to the consciousness of its shortcomings, we shall at last have a righteousness and a health and wealth which shall never pass away, which shall be for the first time on earth Divine and permanent."[18]

This last observation may serve as a way of gauging James's relationship to his age. Coming to maturity just as the Transcendental era was dawning in America, James could hardly avoid participating in what F. O. Matthiessen, following William Ellery Channing, termed "the moral argument against Calvinism."[19] Yet what differentiates James from Emerson, and especially from the company of humanitarian optimists and perfectionists which Emerson trailed after him, is that though he was willing to dispense with many of the outmoded and (to him) repellant formulations of Calvinism, he was not willing to dispense with all the substance underneath. Even if James detested the "New Divinity men" just as much as any good Transcendentalist might—probably not realizing the degree to which he shared common cause with them on several crucial issues—James never meant to found a new religion but only to pump fresh life and significance into the old one. And in this, it might be said, his relation both to Calvinism and also to his age bore a strong resemblance to that of another native New Yorker's, the novelist Herman Melville. Each man rebelled violently against the rigid and rigidified letter of New England Calvinism while still preserving a vital sense of its underlying spirit. Yet this ambivalence was more than their countrymen could comprehend. Melville's novels were quickly relegated to the status of children's books, while James's volumes, when they were read at all, were typically regarded merely as footnotes to Swedenborg and mysticism generally. In Melville's case this oversight has now been handsomely rectified; in James's case it has yet to be even widely noticed.

But the affinities between James and Melville do not stop here. If both writers suffered the same historical fate because of their ambivalent feelings toward the unconscious metaphysic which their age was attempting to overthrow, so in almost equal measure both found their chief spiritual resource in what might be termed the new irregular metaphysic which their age professed to put in its place. For what do all of James's books represent, from *Moralism and Christianity* to *Society the Redeemed Form of Man,* if not an exhaustive—and, at times, exhausting—attempt to give flesh and blood to that democratic conception of Deity which Melville articulated in the "Knights and Squires" chapter of *Moby Dick*—of "the great God absolute! The centre and circumference of all democracy!," as Melville called him, whose "omnipresence" is "our divine equality"? This is clearly not to suggest that James derived from Melville himself any of his own ideas about Melville's "just Spirit of Equality" who, as the novelist went on to say, "hast spread one royal mantle of humanity over all my kind!" It is simply to reiterate that the sole object of James's entire life work, like the implicit aim of Melville's passage, was to fuse Christianity and democracy into what might be called a new religion of "the kingly commons," and that this new religion of "the kingly commons," even if Melville himself could never place an abiding faith in it, required a displacement of the old Calvinistic sense of the God above by a more modern and egalitarian sense of the God within and without.

In this, of course, James and Melville were hardly alone. One sees intimations and foreshadowings of this marked shift in theological emphasis as early as William Ellery Channing, and by the time one reaches Emerson, one finds it realized in a form which would later typify much of the progressive social and political thought of the later decades of the nineteenth century. But where Emerson subordinated the community to the individual and then raised the individual to a level coequal with God Himself, James and Melville held on to the older and wiser perception that the individual finds his completion only in relation to others and thus discovered Divinity neither in the Over-Soul nor in society but rather, if anywhere, in that "abounding dignity," as Melville referred to it, which is common to the acutal humanity of all men.

3

Henry James, Senior (1811–1882), was the fourth of ten children born to William James (1771–1832) of County Cavan, Ireland, who emigrated to this country at the age of eighteen, and his third wife, the former Catharine Barber (1782–1859). Though the last Mrs. James (the first died in childbirth and the second two years after her marriage) came from a family with deep roots in the American past—her grandfather was a judge and her father, a highly respected farmer, fought in the Revolutionary War with two more illustrious uncles who were personal friends of Washington's and Lafayette's—it was her husband who established the solid American reputation and then came to epitomize the native tradition which subsequently was passed on to their children.

According to family legend, William of Albany, as he came to be known, arrived in this country in 1789 with little more than "a very small sum of money, a Latin grammar in which he had already made some progress at home, and a desire to visit the field of one of the revolutionary battles."[20] By the time he died, only a little more than forty years later, he had acquired a name second only to that of Stephen Van Renssalaer, the last of the old patroons, and amassed an estate valued at approximately $3,000,000. His was a career which later set the pattern for the typical American success story, parlaying through keen business intelligence and rigorous spiritual self-discipline his half-interest in a small tobacconist concern into one of the great American fortunes of his day. In the course of his extraordinary career, William was led into such various pursuits as real estate, banking, public utilities, and philanthropy, became a major backer of the construction of the Erie Canal, was elected a trustee of Union College in Schenectady, and played a prominent role in various civic affairs throughout the Hudson River Valley. Yet in spite of his great worldly success, he never permitted his business prowess to overshadow his strong religious convictions. Indeed, his brilliant display of the former seemed to follow almost as a kind of reward for his plentiful supply of the latter, encouraging him to pass on to his children the same strict form of Presbyterianism which seemed to support his own life so beneficently.

Oddly enough, of the fourteen children he sired in all, only two among those who survived exhibited any real interest in theological matters, and both eventually rebelled against their father's brand of orthodoxy. The first to fall away was "the Rev. William." After being converted in 1815 during one of the many revivals which swept the Eastern seaboard where he was attending college, he was ordained in 1820 and then drifted from one charge to another for another decade or so until he finally abandoned the parish ministry altogether to devote the rest of his life to "philosophical and theological research." The second was Henry himself, whose resistance to his father's strict Presbyterianism surfaced at a much earlier age than his half-brother's and shaped the whole of his life more consistently.

Whether or not the event had any direct influence on Henry's religious thinking, there can be no doubt that his terrible accident at the age of thirteen, when he was badly burned in a gallant attempt to stamp out a fire caused by a boy's balloon and suffered a double amputation of one leg above the knee, determined much of the temper, if not the substance, of his life to come. The two long years of recuperation in bed, together with the prospect of remaining a cripple for the rest of his life, could not fail to leave an indelible mark upon a boy who was full of animal spirits and who could say of himself, years later, "I lived in every fibre of my body. . . ."[21] Though this calamity apparently did little to diminish his extraordinary fund of energy and left his confidence in himself and the universe intact, the long period of convalescence, as well as the restriction of his physical mobility afterwards, gave inevitable encouragement to his tendencies to introspection, heightened the sensitivity of his powers of observation, and clearly predestined him to a life of thought rather than action. It is interesting to note that one of his own most vivid memories of the incident concerned his father's reaction to his suffering. His father was apparently so deeply moved by the sight of his son's agony during surgery made without the benefit of anaesthesia that Henry's mother had the greatest difficulty in restraining her husband from making too excessive a display of his feelings. This spontaneous outpouring of sympathy from a parent who was otherwise careful to keep his emotions under prudent check could hardly fail to make a lasting impression on a child who was, then as later, never able to control his own rich veins of feeling.

But William of Albany's sympathy was quickly dampened when young Henry set off for Union College in 1828. By this time his wound had completely healed and his zest for life returned. Though Henry could no longer indulge, as he had once done, in "the sports of the river, the wood, or the field,"22 he was perfectly free to enjoy the liberal religious atmosphere at the home of the Reverend Eliphalet Nott, the president of Union College, with whom he lodged and to take part in some of the more fashionable aspects of Schenectady's social life. It was not long before an old habit acquired in younger days, of snitching pennies from the cache of change his father kept in his dresser drawer, encouraged Henry to run up a series of fairly heavy debts to his father's account. To this the parental reaction was immediate and severe. Convinced that his son was on the verge of moral and spiritual ruin—charges of Henry's "progress in arts of low vileness," his "unblushing falsehood," and his newly developed taste "for segars and oysters" were duly noted—William dispatched a friend to warn young Henry to mend his ways or suffer the consequences. Rather than submit or reform, however, Henry decided to run away to Boston instead, where for a time he became a proofreader and translator with the firm of Jenks and Palmer and continued to indulge himself by enjoying the company of some of the city's first families. But it was not long before he decided to return to Union College, where he graduated in 1830, and then, in an effort to placate his irate father, came home to Albany to begin a study of law while working as an editor for a local publication.

Yet Henry was clearly ill at ease during this period of his life. Because of his strong but unconventional religious cast of mind, legal study did not satisfy him and theological study did not attract him. It was only when his father died in 1832 and Henry found himself independent of parental censure or restriction that he finally decided upon a course of action. Partly in deference to his father and partly because he wanted to resolve some of his own nagging questions, he took it upon himself in 1835 to enroll in Princeton Theological Seminary. The choice of Princeton over some other school was a natural one. His half-brother William had prepared for the ministry there twenty years earlier; his former tutor and life-long friend, the physicist Joseph Henry, had recently accepted a professorship in natural history in the college; and the seminary itself, founded as recently as 1812, had already acquired a distinguished reputation as a bastion of Protestant orthodoxy. The Princeton theology, as it was soon to be called, a mixture of strict Reformed confessionalism and Biblical conservatism, had now been given distinct shape and form under the influence of the seminary's first professor, Archibald Alexander, and by 1822 his more famous pupil, colleague and, later, successor, Charles Hodge, had joined the faculty and was quickly taking on all comers, from the "New Divinity men" under Nathaniel William Taylor at Yale to the Congregational conservatives at Andover.

To Henry's religious sensibility, all of this seemed quite foreign and barbarous. Though his religious conscience had always been an intensely living one, Henry was constitutionally repelled by the thought of a God such as the "Old School" men at Princeton described—whose only purpose seemed to be the self-abasement of His creatures—and could in no way admit the distinction so dear to the Princeton theology itself between the church and the world. As James described himself at the time in his fictionalized *Autobiographical Sketch,* through the eyes of a friend who was meant to serve the function of a neutral observer:

> he contrasted signally with the entire mass of student life in the Seminary, by the almost total destitution which his religious character exhibited of the dramatic element,—that element of unconscious hypocricy which Christ stigmatized in the religious zealots of his day, and which indeed seems to be inseparable from the religious *profession.* The ordinary theological student, especially, has a fatal professional conscience from the start, which vitiates his intellectual integrity. He is personally mortgaged to an institution—that of the pulpit—which is reputed sacred, and is all the more potent in its influence upon his natural freedom on that account; so that even the free sphere of his manners is almost sure to lose whatever frank spontaneous flavor it may by inheritance once have had, and become simply servile to convention. My friend was an exception to the rule. His reverence for the Divine name was so tender and hallowed as to render him to a very great extent indifferent to the distinction so loudly emphasized throughout the Seminary between the church and the world. . . . All his discourse betrayed such an unconscious, or at all events unaffected, habit of spiritualizing secular things and secularizing sacred things, that I was erelong forced to conclude that for *his* needs at all events the outward or figurative antagonism of "the church" and "the world" had more than fulfilled its intellectual uses, whatever these may have been; and that any attempt on the part of the Church to perpetuate and especially to exaggerate such antagonism would infallibly expose it to permanent divine ignominy.[23]

With such sentiments as these, it is not surprising that Henry finally decided to leave Princeton in 1838 before taking his degree. His experience there had only confirmed the depth of his alienation from the pretentions of organized religion, and, in any event, faith to him was not a matter of the dogmatic interpretation of tradition but rather an experience, a new sense of the heart, a revelation. Thus he removed himself to New York City to begin a life-long career dedicated to the discovery and expression of his own truth, his own spiritualized version of the good news reported in the Christian scriptures. When in later years his children were to ask him to define his vocation, he merely suggested half-whimsically: "Say I'm a philosopher, say I'm a seeker for truth, say I'm a lover of mankind, say I'm an author of books if you like; or, best of all, just say I'm a student."[24]

By the time James had taken up residence in New York, he was financially independent. The restrictions his father had originally placed upon the disposition of his estate now had been more equitably arranged after his children had decided to take the matter to court, and, as a result, Henry had received a considerable piece of property in Syracuse which yielded him some $10,000 per year. Being "leisured for life" as he later put it, he was now in a position to acquire a family, and so, in 1840, he took as his wife Mary Robertson Walsh (1810–1882), the sister of a fellow seminary student, who herself came from a staunch Presbyterian family. The marriage ceremony, however, was, according to the bridegroom's wishes, a strictly civil one, performed by the Mayor of New York in the parlors of the bride's parents. It was not until two years later that the couple was finally installed at 21 Washington Place, just a block off Washington Square, where they were to reside, except when traveling, until they moved to Cambridge in 1866; but even before they were settled the children began to arrive. William was born in January 1882; Henry, a year later; Garth Wilkinson and Robertson followed in 1845 and 1846; and then Alice finally appeared two years later, in 1848.

During these years of domestic settlement and the growth of his family, Henry, Senior's, religious and intellectual life remained anything but dormant. As early as 1837, in fact, even before he had abandoned his seminary training or become a husband and father, Henry had felt the influence of one of three interrelated currents of thought which were eventually to shape so decisively the very idiom as well as substance of his writing. The first of these derived from the writings of Robert Sandeman (1718–1771) to which James was exposed during a trip in the same year to England with his friend Joseph Henry.

Robert Sandeman was a former medical student and later linen manufacturer in Scotland before he turned to preaching under the influence of his father-in-law, the Reverend John Glas (1695–1773). Glas led a small reform movement within the Church of Scotland which accentuated a restoration of certain practices of the Apostolic Church, such as the kiss of peace, the ritual cleansing of the feet, and the weekly celebration of the Eucharist as a common meal or love feast—this he called the *Agape*. Glas also emphasized the Reformation doctrine of justification by faith rather than works and did much to democratize the polity of his small sect by making the offices of elder, pastor, and bishop elective rather than appointive and abolishing all qualifications to such offices on the basis of education or lay occupation.

His son-in-law, Robert Sandeman, accepted the principles of the Glasites almost in toto but carried one or two of them much further.

Justification, he insisted, for example, is not a matter of the priority of faith to works but rather of faith alone, and the only difference between the faith we invest in any common report, he went on to contend, and the faith by which we accept the report of the Gospel has solely to do with the different nature of that which constitutes its substance. This anti-nomian strain in Sandeman, which undercut the works-righteousness basis of every form of moralism, held strong appeal for James. So did the Sandemanian emphasis on the democratic solidarity of primitive Christianity. Hence to acknowledge the debt he owed Sandeman, James brought out an edition of Sandeman's *Letters on Theron and Aspasio* (1757) in 1838, introducing it with an unsigned two-page preface.

But Sandeman's influence upon James's later thought was relatively slight compared with the more massive impact which the writings of Emanuel Swedenborg (1688–1772) and Charles Fourier (1772–1837) had on him. His exposure to the work of the first may have been initiated by an article published in the *Monthly Magazine* in 1841 by a young English physician named J. J. Garth Wilkinson, a recent convert to Swedenborgianism who in later years, as Swedenborg's editor, translator, and interpreter, became one of James's closest intellectual friends and the namesake of his third child. But James's decisive introduction to Sweden-borg did not take place until five years later, while he was still recovering from an emotional and spiritual crisis which had taken place almost two years before. The circumstances attending that crisis, and the part which Swedenborg's writing played in helping to resolve it, are among the better known facts of the James family history.

James's spiritual crisis occurred during one of his family's extended periods of residence in England. James, his wife, Mary, and their first two children, William and Henry, were comfortably settled in a small house near the Great Park of Windsor. In the intervening years between his withdrawal from Princeton Seminary and his establishment in Eng-land, James had continued to work away in leisured independence on certain metaphysical questions which had vexed him almost from late adolescence—the reconciliation of science and religion, the question of nature's meaning and unity, and the purpose of creation as revealed by a mystical and symbolic interpretation of the Book of Genesis. James had now begun to suspect that he was close to some major theological discoveries, but as yet all he had to show for his effort were the moun-tainous piles of manuscript on his desk. Still, he had excellent reasons to feel pleased with himself: his health was good, his circumstances were congenial, his family was coming grandly along, and he was excited about his work.

As he lingered at the dinner table one afternoon in late May of 1844, the fire burning quietly in the grate seemed to confirm the sense of well-being and contentment he felt within. But then, suddenly, and for no apparent reason, his composure abruptly abandoned him, and he found himself face to face with an invisible terror. It was as though some deathly presence were squatting at the other end of the table, "raying out from his fetid personality influences fatal to life."[25] In the space of a few seconds, he was reduced "from a state of firm vigorous joyful manhood to one of almost helpless infancy."[26] It was all he could do to keep from bolting from the room, and when he finally did quit his chair to seek the protective sympathy of his wife, his sense of self was utterly shattered. As he interpreted the event many years later:

> It was impossible for me . . . to hold this audacious
> faith in selfhood any longer. When I sat down to dinner
> on that memorable chilly afternoon in Windsor, I held
> it serene and unweakened by the faintest breath of
> doubt. Before I rose from the table it had inwardly
> shrivelled to a cinder. One moment I devoutly thanked
> God for the inappreciable boon of selfhood; the next
> that inappreciable boon seemed to me the one thing
> damnable on earth, seemed a literal nest of hell within
> my own entrails.[27]

James's collapse was no doubt owing partly to physical and spiritual exhaustion which left him vulnerable to a severe attack of depression. But he was later to insist that it was actually the result of something else, something which could only be understood as a part of God's plan for his life and which provided direct evidence of his own spiritual regeneration. Intelligence concerning these last matters came quite by accident, as a result of James's wholly fortuitous meeting with a certain Mrs. Chichester, a kindly Englishwoman who lived in the neighborhood of one of the water cures to which James repaired from time to time to work his way out of his depression. When Mrs. Chichester learned of his collapse, she informed him that he was probably suffering from what Swedenborg called a *vastation*, one of the necessary stages in the process of man's spiritual redemption, leading through awakening, purgation, and illumination to that rebirth of the individual in all his "Divine Natural Humanity" which for Swedenborg was the sole purpose and destiny of creation. James needed to hear little more. In spite of medical warnings about overtaxing himself, he quickly hurried to London to purchase one or two of the master's volumes—he actually bought *Divine Wisdom* and *Love and Divine Providence*—and once he had opened them, his reaction was immediate:

> I read from the first with palpitating interest. My heart
> divined, even before my intelligence was prepared to
> do justice to the books, the unequalled amount of truth
> to be found in them. . . . imagine a subject of some
> petty depotism condemned to die, and with—what is
> more and worse—a sentiment of death pervading all

> his consciousness, lifted by a sudden miracle into felt
> harmony with universal man, and filled to the brim
> with the sentiment of indestructible life instead, and
> you will have a true picture of my emancipated
> condition.[28]

Almost before James had put these first two volumes down, disputes were to arise over whether or not his Swedenborg, the Swedenborg he claimed to have read, bore any relation to the original. After nearly thirty years of correspondence and close personal friendship, J. J. Garth Wilkinson was reluctantly to conclude that the only term James and Swedenborg shared in common was the *Divine Natural Humanity,* a concept which, from Wilkinson's orthodox point of view, James did not really understand. "Swedenborg's Divine Natural," Wilkinson reminded him in a revealing letter written after receipt of a copy of *Society the Redeemed Form of Man* and dated 20 May 1879,

> is Jehovah triumphant in Jesus Christ over his infirm
> humanity, and over all the hells which had access to it:
> transforming his natural into the Divine Natural.
> Swedenborg goes to this end, and to the consequences
> of a new and everlasting Church proceeding from this
> Divine Natural. Your Divine Natural, unless I
> misunderstand you, is diffused in all men, giving, or
> to give, them infinitude of some kind, and abolishing
> heavens and hells as mere preparations for the Godhead
> of Humanity. . . . And at last, the Christ Himself
> seems to disappear into Humanity, as God has
> disappeared into Christ; and Man is all in all.[29]

What Wilkinson could not accept was James's eagerness to make Christ fully incarnate in humanity, thus blurring His uniqueness and under-cutting the necessity of the Church as the New Jerusalem. But this, of course, is exactly what James intended. James was opposed to Christo-centrism in theology on the same grounds that he was opposed to ecclesi-asticism among Christians—first, because they both encouraged sectari-anism and were therefore destructive of that sense of human solidarity which for him was the ground-base of all religious experience; and, second, because their inevitable claims to special favor and their conse-quent promotion of such distinctions as believer and nonbeliever, elect and inelect, the saved and the damned, only served to encourage pre-cisely that form of self-righteousness which, again for James, was the root of all evil.

It is no accident that James found confirmation of these views in the one other thinker who seems to have influenced him decisively during these years, the social theorist, reformer, and utopian, Charles Fourier. James had started reading Fourier while he was still recovering from his collapse in 1844, but he was quickly to find himself in a large and disparate company. By 1846 the Fourierist enthusiasm had swollen from a small group of disciples converted by Albert Brisbane four years earlier— George Ripley, Horace Greeley, and Parke Goodwin becoming the most famous American exponents—to a movement with approximately 200,000 followers. But the popularity of Fourierism was hardly an isolated phenomenon. Closely related in spirit to the idealistic ethos of such sister phenomena as the Free Soil movement, the Owenite movement, Transcendentalism, and Abolitionism, members of one group frequently belonged to, or were sympathetic with, the goals of one or more of the others. All partook of that reformist spirit, often strongly utopian, even millennial, in character, which swept across the northern part of the country in the years following Jackson's tenure in the White House, and each called for some great renovation in the laws of society binding man to man and individuals to institutions.

Fourier was important because he offered the blueprint for such a renovation, all carefully worked out according to scientific principles. The result was a kind of transcendental social science which served as a perfect complement to that sort of spiritual science which James had already acquired from Swedenborg. Swedenborg had provided James with a way of understanding how the emerging social sentiment of the era, the new feeling of human fellowship and solidarity, could be interpreted as evidence of God's redeeming and transforming work in nature; Fourier then produced a concrete outline of the way that new social sentiment might achieve visible shape and form in the actual social order.

Beyond this, however, James was also attracted to Fourier because, as Ralph Barton Perry has pointed out, he supported two of James's firmest convictions. In the first place, Fourier confirmed his view of man's social solidarity, man's unity with his kind, which was then reflected in James's religious belief that God works not in isolated individuals but rather in the very stuff of human nature itself, employing as His chief field of operations the most natural and universal of our affections and appetites. This led Wilkinson to charge that James was guilty of a form of pantheism, what he called "pananthropism,"[30] but to James himself, who had long since decided that Wilkinson was "eaten up with spirits and all that,"[31] he was proposing nothing more radical than a development of the logic of the Incarnation: by showing what followed with perfect consistency from God's taking upon Himself not merely the image but the very being of His creature and thus displaying the life of Divinity in the incarnate form of perfect humanity.

What did not follow, however, with any consistency at all from James's fully developed view of the religion of the Incarnation was the second idea he found attractive in Fourier, the idea of human innocence. Fourier assumed that man was created good rather than evil and that whatever evil man subsequently committed was therefore due not to anything inherently wrong with his own nature but rather to external restraints placed on him by society. Redesign society in such a way that the restrictions on man's freedom are removed, Fourier argued, and we would once again discover that when man can act spontaneously, according to his own nature, he is truly innocent and in his innocence good. "Make society do its duty to the individual," James declared in the same mood, "and the individual will be sure to do his duties to society."[32]

The problem was that James's own religious experience proved otherwise. If the blame for human evil could be laid solely at the door of the social order, then the Transcendentalists and their idealist friends were right: simply remove the restrictions to man's spontaneity and freedom and each individual, when he can be made to accept it, will realize the divine infinitude of his own soul. As James matured in the knowledge of his own experience, however, he became more and more certain that this would not do. The redemption of the individual required something more profound than a readjustment of the social order; it required a rebirth and regeneration of the individual himself.

This alteration in James's thought about the nature of human innocence, and the development of his contrasting view of man's inevitable but not wholly contemptible corruptibility, can be discerned quite readily from his changing relations with two of his more famous correspondents and friends, Ralph Waldo Emerson and Thomas Carlyle. James first met Emerson in the early spring of 1842, after James attended one of Emerson's New York lectures and then invited him to call. James was immediately attracted to Emerson because he could recognize so easily in his Concord acquaintance the marks of one who was seeking out the very reality of things with no regard for anything but the truth; yet almost from the very beginning of their ripening friendship, one can discern the seeds of James's later disillusionment.

At first it was simply the problem of drawing Emerson out, of dissociating the speaker who charmed with his words and uplifted by his example from the man who thought and questioned and felt. Emerson impressed James from first to last as a kind of divine presence who was so serenely composed within himself and so magnanimous and tender in his relations with others that it was all but impossible to resist being captivated by him. But James wanted to be instructed as well as inspired, to be challenged as well as enlightened, and on this score Emerson could not help him. The older man seemed temperamentally incapable of explanation and dispute, while the younger man not only thrived on such things but could not live without them.

As the years wore on, however, and the relations between them, at least after the middle of the century, began to cool, the problem ceased being merely temperamental and became intellectual and religious as well. From James's point of view, Emerson simply could not be brought to see the potential evil as well as good in the kind of self-consciousness he was always preaching, and, as a consequence, Emerson was inevitably disposed to promote as cure for the human situation what James took to be the disease itself. The question was whether Emerson's blindness on this point, his refusal to take into his purview any evidence supplied by consciousnesses other than his own, was not itself symptomatic? Wasn't Emerson's sublime indifference to any arguments challenging his position and questioning his optimism indicative of the presence, or at least the potential, of that very evil of egotism which James wanted to point out to him?

If it were, then James could not bring himself to hold Emerson in any way personally responsible for it, as the Scotsman Thomas Carlyle might have done. James first met Carlyle in 1843 and then resumed their acquaintance during another visit to England in 1855. Carlyle supplied precisely what Emerson lacked, a mind which had reasons for everything and a crochety skepticism about the sincerity of all human motives to go along with it. Carlyle fed James's love for argument and contentiousness but went beyond them to a cynicism so prevasive and relentless that it hardly left room for anything else. James had to admire and respect Carlyle for the trenchancy of his social criticism, for his deadly aim in unmasking every form of human folly, but he could not follow Carlyle when the latter used his eye for human weakness to support his pessimism about the whole human race. On occasion James was able to assume a light attitude of amused disapproval toward Carlyle, as when he referred to him in a letter to Emerson as "the same old sausage, fizzing and sputtering in his own grease";[33] but he was also capable of drawing very accurate aim himself, as when he noted in the "Personal Recollections" he published after Carlyle's death:

> His own intellectual life consisted so much in
> bemoaning the vices of his race, or drew such inspiration
> from despair, that he could not help regarding a man
> with contempt the instant he found him reconciled to
> the course of history. Pity is the highest style of
> intercourse he allowed himself with his kind. . . .
> "Poor John Sterling," he used always to say; "poor John
> Mill, poor Frederick Maurice, poor Neuberg, poor
> Arthur Helps, poor little Browning, poor little Lewes"
> and so on; as if the temple of his friendship were a
> hospital, and all its inmates scrofulous or paralytic.[34]

James could enjoy Carlyle's declamations but not his wholesale condemnations. Though he himself frequently used the abstract as a kind of club to beat the actual, he could still never forget, as Ralph Barton Perry has said, "the Man in men."[35] Nor, for that matter, could he overlook the element of good amidst all the ill. For James was fundamentally reconciled to the divine Providence which guides men's affairs in a way that Carlyle clearly was not, and this made all the difference. However pointed

and stinging his criticism of his fellows, and however frontal and slash-
ing his assaults on various ideas, James's invective was never cruel or
sardonic. For all of his noisy thunder and bombast, there was always a
generous dose of the Quixotic knight-errant about him, one who, whether
he knows it or not, inevitably ennobles both himself and his windmills by
tilting at them with such gusto.

For this reason alone, many people cultivated James's friendship, his
society, even when they lacked sympathy with or interest in his ideas.
There was an elemental humanity in him very like the substance he kept
imputing to the nature of his fellow mortals. Even when he baited Bronson
Alcott for being "an egg half hatched . . . [with] the shells . . . yet
sticking about your head,"[36] or railed out against a conception of the Deity
as absolute, irrelative, and unconditionally perfect, on the grounds that
"any mother who suckles her babe upon her own breast, any bitch in fact
who litters her periodical brood of pups, presents to my imagination a
vastly nearer and sweeter Divine charm,"[37] there was a brightness, a
color, a robust vigor to his polemics which tempered censure with concern, judgment with humor. "To exalt humble and abase proud things
was ever the darling sport of his conversation," his son William reported,
"which, when he was in the *abasing* mood, often startled the good people
of Boston, who did not know him well enough to see the endlessly genial
and humane intuition from which the whole mood flowed."[38] Yet genial
and humane the intuition always was, because James seemed to embody
in himself what he imputed to his God—a sense of insufficiency rather
than self-sufficiency, springing from his intuitive grasp of the fact that
man, like God, is incapable of realizing himself except in others.

4

It was this singular unity of sensibility in their father—what Henry,
Junior, described as "a passion peculiarly his own" by which he "kept
together his stream of thought, however transcendent and the stream of
life, however humanized"[39]—which so impressed his two sons when they
looked back upon his life, and which partially accounts for the surpris-
ingly strong impact he was to have on both of them long after he was
dead. Indeed, it would not be too much to say that while James made
little impression on his contemporaries either in the world of letters or
in the theological community, he still left an indelible imprint upon American culture. And that imprint came by way of his influence on his two
sons, who subsequently then divided between them so much of that
intellectual and spiritual heritage of the nineteenth century which was
passed on to the twentieth.

At first glance such a claim may sound exaggerated. After all, did not
William differentiate himself from his father in the most explicit of terms
when he pointed out in his "Introduction" to *The Literary Remains* that
the elder James was a philosophical and theological monist who would
brook no compromise with ethical and philosophical pluralists; and did
not Henry, in his turn, then confess, in a letter acknowledging the receipt

of this volume, that for all his love and admiration for his father's person, he could never make head nor tail of his ideas? The answer is inevitably yes, but there is also important evidence on the other side of this question. One could cite, for example, the letter William wrote to the elder James four days before the latter's death, in which he confessed that no matter how different their expressions of it, he derived virtually the whole of his intellectual life from his father; or, again, one could refer to comments Henry, Junior, made thirty years later, in *Notes of a Son and Brother,* where he suggests that none of the children could really escape being affected by "Father's ideas," as his wife referred to them, just because they constituted so large a part of the "daily medium" in the James household.

Yet the question of influence cannot be resolved through personal testimony of this kind, because the process of its occurrence is always more subtle and indirect. The elder James himself described its more probable form of operation among the members of his own household when he observed in a letter to Emerson "that a vital truth can never be transferred from one mind to another, because life alone appreciates it. The most one can do for another is to plant the rude formula of such truth in his memory, leaving his own spiritual chemistry to set free the germs whenever the demands of his life exact it."[40] The rude formulas of their father's truth, his ideas, clearly made little or no impression upon William and Henry, either when those ideas were first uttered in their presence, or long after when both men tried to remember them; it was the germs of "vital truth" which were transmitted, but which were not set free until their own individual lives demanded it and which then developed only as the "spiritual chemistry" of their own natures permitted it. Henry, Junior's, trust in moments of vision and his equally strong interest in the sensuous or felt qualities of thought, no less than his intense absorption with the sin of self-culture and his emphasis on the virtue of self-denial and self-renunciation; William's theory of knowledge as a kind of action and his stress on the element of change, no less than his firm insistence on having a say about the deepest reasons of the universe and his criticism of the blindness which human beings practice on each other—all show the unmistakable influence of their father, even though both men found support for these views in many other sources as well.

But the evidence of a paternal legacy is even more striking if one examines that core of values which, despite their more obvious differences, William and Henry shared in common. Consider, for example, the common emphasis both placed on the virtue of intellectual sympathy. In Henry this surfaced in his obsession with the singular point of view of specific, individual consciousnesses and beyond this, in his insistence that the only way to appreciate a work of art, as he suggested in his famous analogy of the Persian rug and its complex design, is by imaginatively penetrating into the pattern of the whole before attempting to define its controlling figure. In William this was reflected in his belief that the only way to understand another man's ideas is by placing yourself at the center of his philosophical vision, where you can then understand all the different observations which flow from it. "But keep outside," he warned in *A Pluralistic Universe,* "use your post-mortem method, try to build the philosophy up out of the single phrases, taking first one and then another and seeking to make them fit, and of course you fail. You crawl over the thing like a myopic ant over a building, tumbling into every microscopic crack or fissure, finding nothing but inconsistencies, and never suspecting that a centre exists."[41] What were such sentiments as these but an extension of their father's belief that the virtue of trying to put yourself in the position of another owes its authority to Divine precept and example, an example which the elder James perfectly emulated himself, according to his novelist son, "there being no human predicament he couldn't by a sympathy more *like* direct experience than any I have ever known enter into . . ."?[42]

Or, to take another example, there is the stress each placed on the sacredness of the individual and the life that is in him, a belief which evoked, supported, and confirmed their equally brilliant gifts of personal observation and psychological insight. Again, what was this but a re-appropriation, according to their own lights, of their father's conviction that every fibre of a person's humanity is resident with divinity, a conviction which, again like his sons, explained his own powers of observation? Indeed, it was precisely because of his father's theological convictions, Henry, Junior, reports, that "no element of character, no spontaneity of life, but instantly seized his attention and incurred his greeting and comment, which things could never possibly have been so genially alert and expert—as I have, again, superabundantly recorded—if it had not fairly fed on active observation and contact."[43] The elder James "fairly fed" on such matters because he thereby conceived himself to be trafficking with the incarnate form of God Himself. His two sons clearly had less explicitly theological reasons for nourishing themselves on such matters, but both still took no fewer pains to evoke the appropriately religious emotions of awe and wonder when, through careful observation, each found himself in their presence.

Such observations as these do not add up to the conclusion that either of the sons was a covert disciple of his father. At most they merely suggest the existence of a more intimate relationship among all three members of the James family than has heretofore been perceived. Neither William nor Henry took any of his father's ideas at face value and simply re-expressed them in a different medium. What they were receptive to instead was the element of "vital truth" underneath, which they both then worked to complement or comment upon according to their own taste and genius. The point is that such "vital truths," and not the ideas which are but rude formulas of them, are precisely what a culture consists of; and, in this sense, we can say that Henry, Senior, and his two sons belonged to the same one.

To say this is to suggest the necessity of a fresh reassessment of the elder James's whole relation to the American tradition. Where until now he has usually been regarded merely as an American eccentric, more careful study will reveal, I think, that he was closer to being something like an American original and one we can scarcely afford any longer to ignore, since, in the history of American philosophy and religion, we have had, comparatively, so very few of them.

NOTES

1. Edwards A. Park, "The Theology of the Intellect and That of the Feelings," in *Memorial Collection of Sermons by Edwards A. Park*, comp. by Agnes Park (Boston, 1902), p. 108.

2. The following comprises a list of his chief titles: *What Constitutes the State* (New York, 1846); *Tracts for the New Times. No. I., Letter to a Swedenborgian* (New York, 1847); *Moralism and Christianity: or, Man's Experience and Destiny* (New York, 1850); *Lectures and Miscellanies* (New York, 1852); *Love, Marriage, and Divorce; A Discussion between Henry James, Horace Greeley, and Stephen Pearl Andrews* (New York, 1853); *The Church of Christ not an Ecclesiasticism; A Letter of Remonstrance to a member of the "soi-distant" New Church* (New York, 1854); *The Nature of Evil* (New York, 1855); *Christianity the Logic of Creation* (New York, 1857); *The Social Significance of our Institutions* (Boston, 1861); *Substance and Shadow: or, Morality and Religion in Their Relation to Life: An Essay on the Physics of Creation* (Boston, 1863); *The Secret of Swedenborg: Being an Elucidation of his Doctrine of the Divine Natural Humanity* (Boston, 1869); *Society the Redeemed Form of Man, and the Earnest of God's Omnipotence in Human Nature* (Boston, 1879); and *The Literary Remains of the Late Henry James*, ed., with an intro., by William James (Boston, 1884).

3. *Letters of Charles Eliot Norton*, with biog. comment by Sara Norton and M. A. De Wolfe Howe (2 v., Boston, 1913), 2:379.

4. Daniel Aaron, *Men of Good Hope* (Galaxy Books Edition, New York, 1961), p. 133.

5. *Literary Remains*, p. 15.

6. *Life and Letters of Edwin Lawrence Godkin*, ed. by Rollo Ogden (2 v., New York, 1907), 2:117–18.

7. Ibid., 2:118.

8. *See* Austin Warren, *The Elder Henry James* (New York, 1934); Ralph Barton Perry, *The Thought and Character of William James* (2 v., Boston, 1935), 1:3–169; F. O. Matthiessen, *The James Family* (New York, 1947), p. 3–69; Frederick Harold Young, *The Philosophy of Henry James, Sr.* (New York, 1951); Leon Edel, *Henry James, The Untried Years: 1843–1870* (New York, 1953), p. 19–56; R. W. B. Lewis, *The American Adam* (Chicago, 1955), p. 54–63; Quentin Anderson, *The American Henry James* (New Brunswick, N. J., 1957), p. 3–28, 51–124; Richard Poirier, *A World Elsewhere* (New York, 1966), p. 22–26, 111–13.

9. Henry James, *Notes of a Son and Brother* (New York, 1914), p. 230. Cited hereafter as *Notes*.

10. *The Secret of Swedenborg*, p. vi–vii.

11. *Quoted in* Perry, *William James*, p. 47.

12. Ibid., p. 13.

13. *See* R. W. B. Lewis's discussion of "the fortunate Fall" and "the party of Irony" in *The American Adam*, p. 54–73.

14. *Literary Remains*, p. 216.

15. *Notes*, p. 234.

16. *Literary Remains*, p. 391.

17. *Substance and Shadow*, p. 220.

18. Ibid., p. 222.

19. Matthiessen, *James Family*, p. 6.

20. Ibid., p. 4.

21. *Literary Remains*, p. 183.

22. Ibid.

23. Ibid., p. 124, 127.

24. *Notes*, p. 69.

25. *Society the Redeemed Form of Man*, p. 45.

26. Ibid.

27. Ibid., p. 74.

28. Ibid., p. 53.

29. *Quoted in* Perry, *William James*, p. 27.

30. Ibid.

31. Ibid., p. 84. Quoted from one of James's letters to Emerson.

32. Edel, *Henry James*, p. 35.

33. Perry, *William James*, p. 83.

34. *Literary Remains*, p. 424.

35. Perry, *William James*, p. 64.

36. Ibid., p. 133–34.

37. *Society the Redeemed Form of Man*, p. 333–34.

38. *Literary Remains*, p. 75–76.

39. *Notes*, p. 229.

40. Perry, *William James*, p. 71.

41. Matthiessen, *James Family*, p. 680.

42. *Notes*, p. 229.

43. Ibid., p. 172.

Autobiographical Writings

1

AUTOBIOGRAPHICAL
SKETCH

James's "Autobiographical Sketch" or, as he entitled
it himself, *"Immortal Life: Illustrated in a Brief
Autobiographic Sketch of the Late Stephen Dewhurst,
edited, with an introduction by Henry James,"*
represented something of a concession to the members
of his family who had been after him for years to
express his religious philosophy in the form of a
personal narrative. Because of his deep aversion to
self-advertisement, James sat down to undertake this
task a good many times before attaining any concrete
results, and was then, finally, able to proceed only
after he had invented the wholly fictitious character of
Stephen Dewhurst behind whom he could hide. It is
not that James was reluctant to use the personal
pronoun or fearful of self-exposure—his published
writing is crowded with the most intimate and
revealing confessions on every manner of subject—but
only that his commitment to man rather than to men,
to humanity rather than to individual persons, made
this kind of analysis distasteful to him. Yet James's
singular capacity for candor and his by turns richly
vascular and robust manner of speaking about himself
leave one disappointed that this "Sketch" was not
extended to cover the later periods of his life. For
personal observations of his later experience, one has
to rely upon various fragmentary comments James
interspersed throughout his books and essays, a
generous portion of which are reprinted in many of
the selections which follow.

This autobiographical fragment was originally
published together with a preface, in which James,
now adopting the role of a neutral observer, provided
an impression of his fictionalized friend, Stephen
Dewhurst, as he purportedly knew him during their
student days in seminary.

What follows is the "Autobiographic Sketch" which

our "reader's friend" claims to have found among
Dewhurst's effects after the latter's supposed death.
William James, who finally published this fictionalized
version of his father's autobiography, supplied the
necessary items of personal and geographic facts in
the notes which accompany it. This selection is taken
from *The Literary Remains of the Late Henry James*,
edited, with an introduction, by William James
(Boston, 1884), 145–91.

My Earliest Recollections

I will not attempt to state the year in which I was born,[1] because
it is not a fact embraced in my own knowledge, but content myself with
saying instead, that the earliest event of my biographic consciousness
is that of my having been carried out into the streets one night, in the
arms of my negro nurse, to witness a grand illumination in honor of
the treaty of peace then just signed with Great Britain. From this circumstance I infer of course that I was born before the year 1815, but it
gives me no warrant to say just how long before. The net fact is that my
historic consciousness, or my earliest self-recognition, dates from this
municipal illumination in honor of peace. So far, however, as my share
in that spectacle is concerned, I am free to say it was a failure. That is,
the only impression left by the illumination upon my imagination was
the contrast of the awful dark of the sky with the feeble glitter of the
streets; as if the animus of the display had been, not to eclipse the darkness, but to make it visible. You, of course, may put what interpretation
you choose upon the incident, but it seems to me rather emblematic of
the intellect, that its earliest sensible foundations should thus be laid in
"a horror of great darkness."

My father[2] was a successful merchant, who early in life had forsaken
his native Somerset County,[3] with its watery horizons, to settle in Balti-
more;[4] where on the strength of a good primary education, in which I was
glad to observe some knowledge of Latin had mingled, he got employment
as a clerk in a considerable mercantile house, and by his general intelligence and business sagacity erelong laid the foundations of a prosperous
career. When I was very young I do not remember to have had much
intellectual contact with my father save at family prayers and at meals,
for he was always occupied during the day with business; and even in the

frank domestic intercourse of the evening, when he was fond of hearing his children read to him, and would frequently exercise them in their studies, I cannot recollect that he ever questioned me about my out-of-door occupations, or about my companions, or showed any extreme solicitude about my standing in school. He was certainly a very easy parent, and I might have been left to regard him perhaps as a rather indifferent one, if it had not been for a severe illness which befell me from a gun-shot wound in my arm, and which confined me for a long time to the house, when his tenderness to me showed itself so assiduous and indeed extreme as to give me an exalted sense of his affection.[5] My wound had been very severe, being followed by a morbid process in the bone which ever and anon called for some sharp surgery; and on these occasions I remember— for the use of anaesthetics was still wholly undreamt of—his sympathy with my sufferings was so excessive that my mother had the greatest possible difficulty in imposing due prudence upon his expression of it.

My mother[6] was a good wife and mother, nothing else,— save, to be sure, a kindly friend and neighbor. The tradition of the house, indeed, was a very charitable one. I remember that my father was in the habit of having a great quantity of beef and pork and potatoes laid by in the beginning of winter for the needy poor, the distribution of which my mother regulated; and no sooner was the original stock exhausted than the supply was renewed with ungrudging hand. My mother, I repeat, was maternity itself in form; and I remember, as a touching evidence of this, that I have frequently seen her during my protracted illness, when I had been greatly reduced and required the most watchful nursing, come to my bedside fast asleep with her candle in her hand, and go through the forms of covering my shoulders, adjusting my pillows, and so forth, just as carefully as if she were awake. The only other thing I have to remark about her is, that she was the most democratic person by temperament I ever knew. Her father,[7] who spent the evening of his days in our family, was a farmer of great respectability and considerable substance. He had borne arms in the Revolutionary War, was very fond of historic reading, had a tenacious memory, and used to exercise it upon his grandchildren at times to their sufficient *ennui*. I never felt any affectionate leaning to him. Two of his brothers had served throughout the war in the army,— one of them, Colonel F. B.,[8] having been a distinguished and very efficient officer in various engagements, and a trusted friend of Washington; the other, Major W. B.,[9] who, if my memory serve me, was an aid of General Lafayette. These of course are never ungratifying facts to the carnal mind; and when accordingly we children used to ask our mother for tales about her uncles, she gave us to be sure what she had to give with good-will, but I could very well see that for some reason or other she never was able to put herself in our precise point of view in reference to them. She seemed someway ashamed, as well as I could gather, of having had distinguished relations. And then I remember I used to feel surprised to see how much satisfaction she could take in chatting with her respectable sewing-women, and how she gravitated as a general thing into relations of the frankest sympathy with every one conventionally beneath her. I should say, indeed, looking back, that she felt a tacit quarrel with the fortunes of her life in that they had sought to make her a flower or a shrub, when she herself would so willingly have remained mere lowly grass.

But I must say one word of my mother's mother, whose memory I cherish much more than that of my grandfather. She came to us at times in winter, and as long as she lived we spent a month of every summer with her in the country, where I delighted to drive the empty ox-cart far afield to bring in a load of fragrant hay, or gather apples for the cider-press, refreshing myself the while with a well-selected apricot or two. She was of a grave, thoughtful aspect, but she had a most vivacious love of children, and a very exceptional gift of interesting them in conversation, which greatly endeared her society to me. It was not till I had grown up, and she herself was among the blessed, that I discovered she had undergone a great deal of mental suffering, and dimly associated this fact somehow with the great conscience she had always made of us children. She had been from youth a very religious person, without a shadow of scepticism or indifference in her mental temperament; but as life matured and her heart became mellowed under its discipline, she fell to doubting whether the dogmatic traditions in which she had been bred effectively represented Divine truth. And the conflict grew so active erelong between this quickened allegiance of her heart to God, and the merely habitual deference her intellect was under to men's opinions, as to allow her afterwards no fixed rest this side of the grave. In her most depressed condition, however, she maintained an equable front before the world, fulfilled all her duties to her family and her neighborhood, and yielded at last to death, as I afterwards learned, in smiling confidence of a speedy resolution of all her doubts. I never failed to contrast the soft flexibility and sweetness of her demeanor with the stoicism of my grandfather's character, and early noted the signal difference between the rich spontaneous favor we children enjoyed at her hands, and the purely voluntary or polite attentions we received from him. Nor could I doubt when in after years my own hour of tribulation sounded, and I too felt my first immortal longing "to bathe myself in innocency," that this dear old lady had found in the ignorance and innocence of the grandchildren whom she loved to hug to her bosom a truer gospel balm, a far more soothing and satisfactory echo of Divine knowledge, than she had ever caught from the logic of John Calvin.

I have nothing to say of my brothers and sisters, who were seven[10] in number, except that our relations proved always cordially affectionate; so much so, indeed, that I cannot now recall any instance of serious envy or jealousy between us. The law of the house, within the limits of religious decency, was freedom itself, and the parental will or wisdom had very seldom to be appealed to to settle our trivial discords. I should think indeed that our domestic intercourse had been on the whole most innocent as well as happy, were it not for a certain lack of oxygen which is indeed incidental to the family atmosphere, and which I may characterize as the lack of any ideal of action but that of self-preservation. It is the curse of the worldly mind, as of the civic or political state of man to which it affords a material basis; it is the curse of the religious mind, as of the ecclesiastical forms to which it furnishes a spiritual base,— that they both alike constitute their own ideal, or practically ignore any ulterior Divine end. I say it is their curse, because they thus conflict with the principles of universal justice, or God's providential order in the earth, which rigidly enjoins that *each particular thing exist for all, and that all things in general exist for each.* Our family at all events perfectly illustrated this common vice of contented isolation. Like all the other families of the land it gave no sign of a *spontaneous* religious culture, or of affections touched to the dimensions of universal man. In fact, religious truth at that day, as it seems to me, was at the very lowest ebb of formal remorseless dogmatism it has ever reached, and offered nothing whatever to conciliate the enmity of unwilling hearts. When I remember the clergy who used to frequent my father's house, which offered the freest hospitality to any number of the cloth, and recall the tone of the religious world generally with which I was familiar, I find my memory is charged with absolutely no incident either of manners or conversation which would ever lead me to suppose that religion was anything more in its votaries than a higher prudence, or that there was anything whatever in the Divine character as revealed in the gospel of Christ to inflame in common minds an enthusiasm of devotion, or beget anything like a passionate ardor of self-abasement.

Thus the entire strain of the Orthodox faith of the period was at fault, and restricted the motions of the divine life in us to the working out at most of a conventionally virtuous and pious repute. It was eminently respectable to belong to the church, and there were few insatiate worldlings, I suspect, who did not count upon giving in a prudent adhesion to it at the last. We children of the church had been traditionally taught to contemplate God as a strictly *super*natural being, bigger personally than all the world; and not only therefore out of all sympathy with our pigmy infirmities, but exceedingly jealous of the hypocritical homage we paid to his contemptuous forbearance. This dramatic homage, however, being of an altogether negative complexion, was exceedingly trying to us. Notoriously our Orthodox Protestant faith, however denominated, is not intellectually a cheerful one, though it is not so inwardly demoralizing doubtless as the Catholic teaching; but it makes absolutely no ecclesiastical provision in the way of spectacle for engaging the affections of childhood. The innocent carnal delights of children are ignored by the church save at Christmas; and as Christmas comes but once a year, we poor little ones were practically shut up for all our spiritual limbering, or training in the divine life, to the influence of our ordinary paralytic Sunday routine. That is, we were taught not to play, not to dance nor to sing, not to read story-books, not to con over our school-lessons for Monday even; not to whistle, not to ride the pony, nor to take a walk in the country, nor a swim in the river; nor, in short, to do anything which nature specially craved. How my particular heels ached for exercise, and all my senses pined to be free, it is not worth while to recount; suffice it to say, that although I know my parents were not so Sabbatarian as many, I cannot flatter myself that our household sanctity ever presented a pleasant aspect to the angels. Nothing is so hard for a child as *not-to-do;* that is, to keep his hands and feet and tongue in enforced inactivity. It is a cruel wrong to put such an obligation upon him, while his reflective faculties are still undeveloped, and his senses urge him to unrestricted action. I am persuaded, for my part at all events, that the number of things I was conventionally bound *not-to-do* at that tender age, has made Sunday to my imagination ever since the most oppressive or least gracious and hallowed day of the week; and I should not wonder if the repression it riveted upon my youthful freedom had had much to do with the habitual unamiableness and irritability I discover in myself.

My boyish Sundays however had one slight alleviation. The church to which I was born occupied one extremity of a block, and sided upon a public street. Our family pew was a large square one, and embraced in part a window which gave upon the street, and whose movable blinds with their cords and tassels gave much quiet entertainment to my restless fingers. It was my delight to get to church early, in order to secure a certain corner of the pew which commanded the sidewalk on both sides of the street, and so furnished me many pregnant topics of speculation. Two huge chains indeed extended across the street at either extremity of the church, debarring vehicles from passing. But pedestrians enjoyed their liberty unimpeded, and took on a certain halo to my imagination from the independent air with which they used it. Sometimes a person would saunter past in modish costume, puffing a cigar, and gayly switching ever and anon the legs of his resonant well-starched trousers; and though I secretly envied him his power to convert the sacred day into a festivity, I could not but indulge some doubts as to where that comfortable state of mind tended. Most of my *dramatis personae* in fact wore an air of careless ease or idleness, as if they had risen from a good night's sleep to a late breakfast, and were now disposing themselves for a genuine holiday of delights. I was doubtless not untouched inwardly by the gospel flavor and relish of the spectacle, but of course it presented to my legal or carnal apprehension of spiritual things a far more perilous method of sanctifying the day, than that offered by men's voluntary denial of all their spontaneous instincts, of all their aesthetic culture.

I may say, however, that one vision was pretty constant, and left no pharisaic pang behind it. Opposite the sacred edifice stood the dwelling-house and office of Mr. O——r, a Justice of the Peace; and every Sunday morning, just as the sermon was getting well under way, Mr. O——r's housemaid would appear upon the threshold with her crumb-cloth in hand, and proceed very leisurely to shake it over the side of the steps, glancing the while, as well as I could observe, with critical appreciation at the well-dressed people who passed by. She would do her work as I have said in a very leisurely way, leaving the cloth, for example, hanging upon the balustrade of the steps while she would go into the house, and then returning again and again to shake it, as if she loved the task, and could not help lingering over it. Perhaps her mistress might have estimated the performance differently, but fortunately she was in church; and I at all events was unfeignedly obliged to the shapely maid for giving my senses so much innocent occupation when their need was sorest. Her pleasant image has always remained a fixture of my memory; and if I shall ever be able to identify her in the populous world to which we are hastening, be assured I will not let the opportunity slip of telling her how much I owe her for the fresh, breezy, natural life she used to impart to those otherwise lifeless, stagnant, most unnatural Sunday mornings.

----·•·----

Conflict Between My Moral and My Spiritual Life

The aim of all formal religious worship, as it stood impressed upon my youthful imagination, was to save the soul of the worshipper from a certain liability to Divine wrath which he had incurred as the inheritor of a fallen nature, and from which he could only get relief through the merits of Christ imputed to him, and apprehended by faith. I had been traditionally taught, and I traditionally took for granted, that all souls had originally forfeited the creative good-will in the person of Adam, their attorney or representative, even if they should never have aggravated that catastrophe subsequently in their own persons; so that practically every man of woman born comes into the world charged with a weight of Divine obstruction or limitation utterly hopeless and crushing, unless relieved by actual faith in the atoning blood of Christ. I ought not to say that I actually believed this puerile and disgusting caricature of the gospel, for one believes only with the heart, and my heart at all events inmostly loathed this dogmatic fouling of the creative name, even while it passively endured its authoritative imposition. I accepted it in short only as an Orthodox tradition,—just as all the world does,—commended to my unquestioning faith by the previous acceptance of those I loved and honored.

And so accepting it, its inevitable effect was, I may say, perpetually to inflame a self-love and love of the world in me which needed everything but inflaming.

My boyish animal spirits, or my excessive enjoyment of life, allowed me no doubt very little time for reflection; yet it was very seldom that I lay down at night without a present thought of God, and some little effort of recoil upon myself. My days bowled themselves out one after another, like waves upon the shore, and as a general thing deafened me by their clamor to any inward voice; but the dark silent night usually let in the spectral eye of God, and set me to wondering and pondering evermore how I should effectually baffle its gaze. Now I cannot conceive any less wholesome or innocent occupation for the childish mind than to keep a debtor and creditor account with God; for the effect of such discipline is either to make the child insufferably conceited, or else to harden him in indifference to the Divine name. The parent, or whoso occupies the parent's place, should be the only authorized medium of the Divine communion with the child; and if the parent repugn this function, he is by so much disqualified as parent. Men have their instructed reason and their experience to guide them in Divine things, and guard them from false teaching; but nothing can be so fatal to the tender awe and reverence which should always sanctify the Divine name to the youthful mind and heart, as to put the child in a bargaining or huckstering attitude towards God, as was done by the current religious teaching of my early days. I was habitually led by my teachers to conceive that at best a chronic apathy existed on God's part towards me, superinduced by Christ's work upon the active enmity he had formerly felt towards us; and the only reason why this teaching did not leave my mind in a similarly apathetic condition towards him was, as I have since become persuaded, that it always met in my soul, and was practically paralyzed by, a profounder Divine instinct which affirmed his stainless and ineffable love. I should never indeed have felt my intellectual tranquility so much as jostled by the insane superstition in question, if it had not been that my headlong eagerness in the pursuit of pleasure plunged me incessantly into perturbations and disturbances of conscience, which had the effect often to convert God's chronic apathy or indifference into a sentiment of acute personal hostility. Whenever this experience occurred, I was down in the dust of self-abasement, and then tried every way I possibly could to *transact* with God—on the basis of course of his revealed clemency in Christ—by the most profuse acknowledgments of indebtedness, and the most profuse promises of future payment. Obviously I could not be expected at that early age to entertain problems which my elders themselves were unable to solve. Thus I never stopped to ask myself how a being whose clemency to the sinner wears so flatly commercial an aspect,— being the fruit of an actual purchase, of a most literal and cogent *quid pro quo* duly in hand paid,—could ever hope to awaken any spiritual love or confidence in the human breast, or ever pretend consequently to challenge permanent Divine honor. In short, I was incapable as a child of accepting any theologic dogma as *true*, and received it simply on the authority of the Church; and whenever accordingly I had pungently violated conscience in any manner, I was only too happy to betake myself to the feet of Christ, to plead his healing and gracious words, and pray that *my* offences also might be blotted out in his atoning blood.

But I must guard against giving you a false impression in respect to these devotional exercises of my childhood. I have always in looking back been struck with the fact, and used at first to be somewhat disconcerted by it, that my conscience, even in my earliest years, never charged itself with merely literal or ritual defilement; that is to say, with offences which did not contain an element of active or spiritual malignity to somebody else. For example, there was a shoemaker's shop in our neighborhood, at which the family were supplied with shoes. The business was conducted by two brothers who had recently inherited it of their father, and who were themselves uncommonly bright, intelligent, and personable young men. From the circumstance that all the principal families of the neighborhood were customers of the shop, the boys of these families in going there to be fitted, or to give orders, frequently encountered each other, and at last got to making it an habitual rendezvous. There were two apartments belonging to the shop, — one small, giving upon the street, which contained all the stock of the concern, and where customers were received; the other, in which the young men worked at their trade and where we boys were wont to congregate, much larger, in the rear, and descending towards a garden. I was in the habit of taking with me a pocket full of apples or other fruit from home, on my visits to the shop, for the delectation of its occupants, several of the other lads doing the same; and I frequently carried them books, especially novels, which they were fond of reading, and their judgments of which seemed to me very intelligent. The truth is, that we chits were rather proud to crony with these young men, who were so much older than ourselves, and had so much more knowledge of the world; and if their influence over us had been really educative, almost any beneficial results might have been anticipated. I do not know exactly how it came about, but one step probably led to another, until at last we found ourselves providing them an actual feast, some of us supplying edibles and other potables from our own larders and cellars. I used, I recollect, to take eggs in any number from the ample, uncounted, and unguarded stores at home, cakes, fruits, and whatever else it was handy to carry; and I do not know to what lengths our mutual emulation in these hospitable offices might not have pushed us, when it was brought to a sudden stop. Among the urchins engaged in these foraging exploits were two sons of the governor of the State, who was a widower, and whose household affairs were consequently not so well looked after as they might have been. By the connivance of their father's butler, these young gentlemen were in the habit of storing certain dainties in their own room at the top of the house, whence they could be conveniently transported to the shop at their leisure without attracting observation. But the governor unfortunately saw fit to re-marry soon after our drama opened, and his new wife took such good order in the house, that my young friends were forced thereafter to accomplish their ends by profounder strategy. And so it happened that their step-mother, sitting one warm summer evening at her open but unilluminated chamber-window to enjoy the breeze, suddenly became aware of a dark object defining itself upon the void between her face and the stars, but in much too close proximity to the former to be agreeable, and naturally put forth her hand to determine the law of its projection. It proved to be a bottle of Madeira, whose age was duly authenticated by cobwebs and weather-stains; and from the apparatus of stout twine connected with it there seemed to be no reasonable doubt that some able engineering was at the bottom of the phenomenon. Search was made, and the engineers discovered. And to make a long story short, this discovery did not fail of course to propagate a salutary rumor of itself, and eke a tremor, to the wonted scene of our festivities, begetting on the part of the *habitués* of the place a much more discreet conduct for the future.

But this is not by any means the only or the chief immorality that distinguished my boyish days. My father, for example, habitually kept a quantity of loose silver in a drawer of his dressing-table, with a view I suppose to his own and my mother's convenience in paying house-bills. It more than covered the bottom of the drawer, and though I never essayed to count it, I should judge it usually amounted to a sum of eight or ten dollars, perhaps double that sum, in Spanish sixpences, shillings, and quarters. The drawer was seldom locked, and even when locked usually had the key remaining in the lock, so that it offered no practical obstacle to the curiosity of servants and children. Our servants I suppose were very honest, as I do not recollect to have ever heard any of them suspected of interfering with the glittering treasure, nor indeed do I know that they were at all aware of its exposed existence. From my earliest days I remember that I myself cherished the greatest practical reverence for the sacred deposit, and seldom went near it except at the bidding of my mother occasionally, to replenish her purse against the frequent domestic demands made upon it, or the exaction of my own weekly stipend. My youthful imagination, to be sure, was often impressed on these occasions with the apparently inexhaustible resources provided by this small drawer against human want, but my necessities at that early day were not so pronounced as to suggest any thought of actual cupidity. But as I grew in years, and approached the very mundane age of seven or eight, the nascent pleasures of the palate began to alternate to my consciousness with those of my muscular activity,—such as marbles, kite-flying, and ball-playing; and I was gradually led in concert with my companions to frequent a very tempting confectioner's-shop in my neighborhood, kept by a colored woman, with whom my credit was very good, and to whom accordingly, whenever my slender store of pocket money was exhausted,

I did not hesitate to run in debt to the amount of five, ten, or twenty cents. This trivial debt it was, however, which, growing at length somewhat embarrassing in amount, furnished the beginning of my moral, self-conscious, or distinctively human experience.

It did this all simply in making me for the first time think with an immense, though still timorous sigh of relief, of my father's magical drawer. Thus my country's proverbial taste for confectionery furnished my particular introduction to "the tree of knowledge of good and evil." This tragical tree, which man is forbidden to eat of under pain of finding his pleasant paradisiacal existence shadowed by death, symbolizes his dawning spiritual life, which always to his own perception begins in literal or subjective darkness and evil. For what after all is spiritual life in sum? It is the heartfelt discovery by man that God his creator is alone good, and that he himself, the creature, is by necessary contrast evil. But this life in man, being divine and immortal, is bound to avouch its proper grandeur, by thoroughly subjugating evil or death to itself; that is, absorbing it in its own infinitude. Hence it is that man, constitutionally requiring the most intimate handling of evil, or the intensest spiritual familiarity with it, actually finds *himself provisionally identified* with that principle, and so far furthered consequently on his way to immortal life.

The sentiment of relief which I felt at the remembrance of this well-stocked drawer, remained a sentiment for a considerable time however before it precipitated itself in actual form. I enjoyed in thought the possibility of relief a long time before I dared to convert it into an actuality. The temptation to do this was absolutely my first experience of spiritual daybreak, my first glimpse of its distinctively moral or death-giving principle. Until then, spiritual existence had been unknown to me save by the hearing of the ear. That is to say, it was mere intellectual gibberish to me. Our experience of the spiritual world dates in truth only from our first unaffected shiver at guilt. Our youthful innocence, like every other divine-natural endowment of humanity, dwells in us in altogether latent or unconscious form, and we never truly recognize it until we have forever forfeited it to the exigencies of a more spiritual and living innocence. It is sure, for example, never to come to direct consciousness in us until we are seriously tempted to do some conventionally opprobrious thing, and have incontinently yielded to the temptation; after that, looking back at ourselves to see what change has befallen us, we become aware of our loss, and immediately, like the inapprehensive spiritual noodles we are, we bend all our energies to recover this fugacious innocence, and become henceforth its *conscious* guardians!—as if man were ever capable by *consciousness* of embracing anything good! As if the human *conscience* were *ever* open to anything else but evil in some of its myriad-fold modulations!

I doubtless relieved myself of debt, then, by two or three times borrowing freely from my father's drawer, without any thought of ever making restitution. But it is idle to pretend that my action in any of these cases was spiritually criminal. It was clandestine of course, as it could hardly help being if it were destined ever to take place at all, and was indeed every way reprehensible when judged from the established family routine or order. I had no idea at the time, of course, that the act was not sinful, for no one existed within my knowledge capable of giving me that idea. But though I should have felt excessively ashamed of myself, doubtless, if my parents had ever discovered or even suspected my clandestine operations, yet when my religious conscience became quickened and I had learned to charge myself with sin against God, I practically never found that acts of this sort very heavily burdened my penitential memory. I did not fail, I presume, to ventilate them occasionally in my daily litany, but I am sure they never any of them gave me a sense of spiritual defilement, nor ever cost me consequently a pang of godly sorrow. The reason why they did not spiritually degrade me in my own esteem was, I suppose, that they were at worst offences committed against my parents; and no child as it seems to me with the heart of a child, or who has not been utterly moralized out of his natural innocency and turned into a precocious prig, can help secretly feeling a property in his parents so absolute or unconditional as to make him *a priori* sure, do what he will, of preserving their affection. It would not have seemed so in ancient days, I grant. The parental bond was then predominantly paternal, whereas of late years it is becoming predominantly maternal. At that period it was very nearly altogether authoritative and even tyrannous with respect to the child; while in our own day it is fast growing to be one of the utmost relaxation, indulgence, and even servility. My father was weakly, nay painfully, sensitive to his children's claims upon his sympathy; and I myself, when I became a father in my turn, felt that I could freely sacrifice property and life to save my children from unhappiness. In fact, the family sentiment has become within the last hundred years so refined of its original gross literality, so shorn of its absolute consequence, by being practically considered as a rudiment to the larger social sentiment, that no intelligent conscientious parent now thinks of himself as primary in that relation, but cheerfully subordinates himself to the welfare of his children. What sensible parent now thinks it a good thing to repress the natural instincts of childhood, and not rather diligently to utilize them as so many divinely endowed educational forces? No doubt much honest misgiving is felt and much honest alarm expressed as to the effect of these new ideas upon the future of our existing civilization. But these alarms and misgivings beset those only who are intellectually indifferent to the truth of man's social destiny. For my own part, I delight to witness this outward demoralization of the parental bond, because I see in it the pregnant evidence of a growing spiritualization of human life, or an expanding *social* consciousness among men, which will erelong exalt them out of the mire and slime of their frivolous and obscene private personality, into a chaste and dignified natural manhood. This social conscience of manhood is becoming so pronounced and irresistible that almost no one who deserves the name of parent but feels the tie that binds him to his child outgrowing its old moral or obligatory limitations, and putting on free, spiritual, or spontaneous lineaments. Indeed, the multitude of devout minds in either sex is perpetually enlarging who sincerely feel themselves unfit to bear, to rear, and above all to educate and discipline, children without the enlightened aid and furtherance of all mankind. And it is only the silliest, most selfish and arrogant of men that can afford to make light of this very significant fact.

But to resume. What I want particularly to impress upon your understanding is that my religious conscience in its early beginnings practically disowned a moral or outward genesis, and took on a free, inward, or spiritual evolution. Not any literal thing I did, so much as the temper of mind with which it was done, had power to humble me before God or degrade me in my own conceit. What filled my breast with acute contrition, amounting at times to anguish, was never any technical offence which I had committed against established decorum, but always some wanton ungenerous word or deed by which I had wounded the vital self-respect of another, or imposed upon him gratuitous personal suffering. Things of this sort arrayed me to my own consciousness in flagrant hostility to God, and I never could contemplate them without feeling the deepest sense of sin. I sometimes wantonly mocked the sister who was nearest me in age, and now and then violently repelled the overtures of a younger brother who aspired to associate himself with me in my sports and pastimes. But when I remembered these things upon my bed, the terrors of hell encompassed me, and I was fairly heartbroken with a dread of being estranged from God and all good men. Even now I cannot recur to these instances of youthful depravity in me without a pungent feeling of self-abasement, without a meltingly tender recognition of the Divine magnanimity. I was very susceptible of gratitude, moreover, and this furnished another spur to my religious conscience. For although I abounded in youthful cupidity of every sort, I never got the satisfaction of my wishes without a sensible religious thankfulness. Especially rife was this sentiment whenever I had had a marked escape from fatal calamity. For I was an ardent angler and gunner from my earliest remembrance, and in my eagerness for sport used to expose myself to accidents so grave as to keep my parents in perpetual dread of my being brought home some day disabled or dead. I distinctly remember how frequently on these occasions, feeling what a narrow escape I had had from rock or river. I was wont to be visited by the most remorseful sense of my own headlong folly, and the most adoring grateful sentiment of the Divine long-suffering.

To sum up all in a word: my religious conscience, as well as I can recall it, was from infancy an intensely *living* one, acknowledging no ritual bonds, and admitting only *quasi* spiritual, that is natural, satisfactions. There was of course a certain established order in the house as to coming and going, as to sleeping and waking, as to meal-times and morning prayers, as to study hours and play hours, and so forth. I certainly never exhibited any wilful disrespect for this order, but doubtless I felt no absolute respect for it, and even violated it egregiously whenever my occasions demanded. But at the same time nothing could be more painful to me than to find that I had wounded my father's or mother's feelings, or disappointed any specific confidence they had reposed in me. And I acutely bemoaned my evil lot whenever I came into chance personal collision with my brothers or sisters. In short, I am satisfied that if there had been the least spiritual Divine leaven discernible within the compass of the family bond; if there had been the least recognizable subordination in it to any objective or public and universal ends,—I should have been very sensitive to the fact, and responsive to the influences it exerted. But there was nothing of the sort. Our family righteousness had as little felt relation to the public life of the world, as little connection with the common hopes and fears of mankind, as the number and form of the rooms we inhabited; and we contentedly lived the same life of stagnant isolation from the race which the great mass of our modern families live, its surface never dimpled by anything but the duties and courtesies we owed to our private friends and acquaintances.

The truth is, that the family tie,—the tie of reciprocal ownership which binds together parent and child, brother and sister,—was when it existed in its integrity a purely legal, formal, typical tie, intended merely to *represent* or symbolize to men's imagination the universal family, or household of faith, eventually to appear upon the earth. But it never had the least suspicion of its own spiritual mission. It was bound in fact in the interest of self-preservation to ignore this its vital representative function, to regard itself as its own end, and coerce its children consequently into an allegiance often very detrimental to their future spiritual manhood. For any refining or humanizing influence accordingly which the family is to exert upon its members, we must look exclusively to the future of the institution, when it will be glorified for the first time into a natural or universal bond. It is a denial of order to demand of the subterranean germ what we expect of the full corn in the ear. If for example the family as it once existed had ever been conscious of its strictly *representative* virtue; if it had for a moment recognized that spiritual Divine end of blessing to *universal* man which alone inwardly consecrated it,—it would have incontinently shrivelled up in its own esteem, and ceased thereupon to propagate itself; so defeating its own end. For the only spiritual Divine end which has ever sanctified the family institution and shaped its issues, is the evolution of a free society or fellowship among men; inasmuch as the family is literally the seminary of the race, or constitutes the sole Divine seed out of which the social consciousness of man ultimately flowers. Thus the only true Divine life or order practicable within the family precinct, the only sentiment truly spiritual appropriate to the isolated family as such, would have been fatal to its existence, as it would have taken from it its proper pride of life; for it would have consisted in each of its members freely *disowning* all the rest in the faith of a strictly unitary *spiritual* paternity or being to all men, and a strictly universal *natural* maternity or existence.

We seem in fact only now becoming qualified to realize the spiritual worth of the family considered as a *representative* economy. For unquestionably we do *as a people* constitutionally reject—in the symbols of priest and king—the only two hitherto sacred pillars upon which the ark of man's salvation has rested, or which have based his public and private righteousness; and it is very clear that we could not have rejected the symbol unless the substance had first come empowering us so to do. That is to say, we as a people are without any proper political and religious life or consciousness which is not exclusively generated by the *social* spirit in humanity, or the truth of an approaching marriage between the public and private, the universal and the particular interests of the race; so that our future welfare, spiritual and material, stands frankly committed to the energies of that untried spirit. Happy they who in this twilight of ever-deepening spiritual unbelief within the compass of the old symbolic Church, and hence of ever-widening moral earthquake, confusion, and desolation within the compass of the old symbolic State, intelligently recognize the serene immaculate divinity of the social spirit, feel their souls stayed upon the sheer impregnable truth of human society, human fellowship, human equality, on earth and in heaven! For they cannot fail to discern in the gathering "clouds of heaven," or the thickening obscuration which to so many despairing eyes is befalling the once bright earth of human hope, the radiant chariot-wheels of the long-looked-for Son of Man, bringing freedom, peace, and unity to all the realm of God's dominion. But these persons will be the promptest to perceive, and the most eager to confess, that the family bond with us, as it has always been restricted to rigidly literal dimensions, and never been allowed the faintest spiritual significance, so it must henceforth depend for its consideration wholly and solely upon the measure in which it freely lends itself to reproduce and embody the distinctively social instincts and aspirations of the race.

Same General Subject

Considering the state of things I have been depicting as incident to my boyish experience of the family, the church, and the world, you will hardly be surprised to hear me express my conviction that the influences —domestic, ecclesiastical, and secular—to which I was subjected, exerted a most unhappy bearing upon my intellectual development. They could not fail to do so in stimulating in me as they did a morbid doctrinal conscience.

The great worth of one's childhood to his future manhood consists in its being a storehouse of innocent natural emotions and affections, based upon ignorance, which offer themselves as an admirable Divine mould or anchorage to the subsequent development of his spiritual life or freedom. Accordingly in so far as you inconsiderately shorten this period of infantile innocence and ignorance in the child, you weaken his chances of a future manly character. I am sure that my own experience proves this truth. I am sure that the early development of my moral sense was every way fatal to my natural innocence, the innocence essential to a free evolution of one's spiritual character, and put me in an attitude of incessant exaction—in fact, of the most unhandsome mendicancy and higgling—towards my creative source. The thought of God in every childish mind is one of the utmost awe and reverence, arising from the tradition or rumor of his incomparable perfection; and the only legitimate effect of the thought, accordingly, when it is left unsophisticate, is to lower his tone of self-sufficiency, and implant in his bosom the germs of a *social* consciousness,—that is, of a tender, equal regard for other people. But when the child has been assiduously taught, as I was, that an essential conflict of interests exists between man and his Maker, then his natural awe of the Divine name practically comes in only to aggravate his acquired sense of danger in that direction, and thus preternaturally inflame all his most selfish and sinister cupidities. Our native appreciation of ourselves or what belongs to us is sufficiently high at its lowest estate; but you have only to dispute or put in peril any recognized interest of man, and you instantly enhance his appreciation of it a hundred-fold.

Our selfhood, or *proprium*, is all we have got to dike out the inflowing tides of the spiritual world, or serve as a barricade against the otherwise overwhelming influence of heaven and hell. My body isolates me from the world, or separates between me and the outward or finite; but I should be literally stifled in my own inward genesis, actually suffocated in my creative substance, were it not for this sentiment of selfhood,—the sentiment of a life *within* so much nearer and dearer to me than that of the world, so much more intimately and exquisitely *my own* than the life of the world is, as spiritually to guarantee me even against God or the infinite. The world gives me sensible constitution or existence, and if consequently you put yourself between me and the world, you doubtless inflict a sensible but not necessarily a vital injury upon me. But my selfhood, or *proprium*, is all I know of spiritual life or inward immortal being, is all I am able consciously to realize of God himself, in short; and whenever therefore you impinge upon that,—as when you assail my vital self-respect, when you expose me to gratuitous contumely or contempt, when you in any manner suppress or coerce my personal freedom to your own profit,—you put yourself as it were between me and God, at all events between me and all I thus far spiritually or *livingly* know of God; you darken my life's sun at its very centre, and reduce me to the torpor of death. You fill my interiors in short with an unspeakable anguish, and a resentment that knows no bounds; that will stickle at absolutely nothing to give me relief from your intolerable invasion.

Now, I had been thoroughly disciplined as a child in the Christian doctrine. My juvenile faith as enforced upon me at home, at church, and at Sunday-school, amounted substantially to this: that a profound natural enmity existed from the beginning between man and God, which however Christ had finally allayed, and that I ought therefore gratefully to submit myself to the law of Christ. I never had a misgiving about my absolute duty in the premises, but practically the thing was impossible. For this law of Christ, as it was authoritatively interpreted to my imagination, revolted instead of conciliating my allegiance, inasmuch as it put me at internecine odds with my own nature, or obliged me to maintain an ascetic instead of a spontaneous relation to it. If there be any pretension more absurd philosophically than another, it is that any person or anything *can* act contrarily to their own nature. And if there be any pretension more immoral practically than another, it is that any person or thing *ought* to act in that manner. No higher obligation is incumbent upon any man in respect to the demands either of honesty or honor, than to act according to his nature; and if his action prove to be vicious or disorderly, we may be sure that his nature is still imperfectly developed, or is not allowed fair play. Of course I never actually framed the thought to myself that Christ's law as interpreted by the church was essentially burdensome, nor should I have dared to confess it, if my intellect had been ripe enough to suggest such a thing; but I instinctively felt it to be so, simply because it represented Christ as sequestrating to himself henceforth that personal allegiance on our part which is the due exclusively of our nature. For this according to the church is precisely what Christ does. All men have forfeited their natural title to God's favor; Christ pays the forfeit in his proper person, and so confiscates to himself ever after the debt which men once owed exclusively to their nature.

This doubtless was the reason—at least I can imagine none other so potent—why I began very early to discover disorderly tendencies, or prove rebellious to religious restraints. I cannot imagine anything more damaging to the infant mind than to desecrate its natural delights, or impose upon it an ascetic regimen. For nature is eternal in all her subjects, and when the child's natural instincts are violently suppressed or driven inwards by some overpowering outward authority, a moral feverishness is sure to result, which would finally exhaust or consume every possibility of his future manhood, if nature did not incontinently put him to seeking a clandestine satisfaction of her will. I felt this impulse very strongly; I doubt whether ever any one more so. I had always had the keenest savor and relish of whatsoever came to me by nature's frank inspiration or free gift. The common ore of existence perpetually converted itself into the gold of life in the glowing fire of my animal spirits. I lived in every fibre of my body. The dawn always found me on my feet;

and I can still vividly recall the divine rapture which filled my blood as I pursued under the magical light of morning the sports of the river, the wood, or the field. And here was a law which frowned—nay, scowled—upon that jocund unconscious existence; which drew a pall over the lovely outlying world of sense, and gave me to feel that I pursued its pleasures only at the imminent risk of immortal loss. Just conceive the horror of leading the tender mind of childhood to believe that the Divine being could under any circumstance grudge it its natural delights; could care, for example, for the holiness of any stupid day of the seven in comparison with the holiness of its innocent mind and body! Herod's politic slaughter of the innocents were mercy itself beside this wanton outrage to nature.

This, accordingly, is the offence I charge upon my early religious training,—that it prematurely *forced* my manhood, or gave it a hot-bed development, by imposing upon my credulous mind the fiction of a natural estrangement between me and God. My sense of individuality, my feeling of myself as a power endowed with the mastery of my own actions, was prematurely vitalized by my being taught to conceive myself capable of a direct—that is, of a personal or moral—commerce with the most High. I do not mean of course that my individuality was perfectly hatched, so to say, while I was thus subject to parental authority; but only that it was altogether unduly stimulated or quickened, by my having been led at that very tender age to deem myself capable of maintaining good and evil relations with God. It is amazing to me how little sensitive people are to the blasphemy of this pretension, whether in the child or the man. That the stream should reproduce in its own sinuous self the life of the fountain, and rejoice in it the while as its own life,—nothing can be better or more orderly. But that the stream should pretend actually to revert to the creative source whence all its life and motion are instantly derived, and affect to deplore the tortuous career which alone gives it phenomenal identity, as an absolute defect of nature or wrong done to the parent fount,—can anything be imagined more flagrantly audacious and impudent, if it were not first of all so supremely stupid?

But be this abstractly as you please, my own experience profoundly avouches its concrete truth. The thought of God as a power foreign to my nature, and with interests therefore hostile to my own, would have wilted my manhood in its cradle, would have made a thoughtful, anxious, and weary little slave of me before I had entered upon my teens, if it had not been for Nature's indomitable uprightness. It aroused a reflective self-consciousness in me when I ought by natural right to have been wholly immersed in my senses, and known nothing but the innocent pleasures and salutary pains they impart. I doubt whether any lad had ever just so thorough and pervading a belief in God's existence as an outside and contrarious force to humanity, as I had. The conviction of his supernatural being and attributes was burnt into me as with a red-hot iron, and I am sure no childish sinews were ever more strained than mine were in wrestling with the subtle terror of his name. This insane terror pervaded my consciousness more or less. It turned every hour of un-allowed pleasure I enjoyed into an actual boon wrung from his forbear-ance; made me loath at night to lose myself in sleep, lest his dread hand should clip my thread of life without time for a parting sob of penitence, and grovel at morning dawn with an abject slavish gratitude that the sweet sights and sounds of Nature and of man were still around me. The terror was all but overpowering; yet not quite that, because it called out a juvenile strategy in me which gave me as it were a new *proprium*, or at all events enabled me *bel et bien* to hold my own. That is to say, Nature itself came to my aid when all outward resources proved treacherous, and enabled me to find in conventionally illicit relations with my kind a gospel succor and refreshment which my lawful ties were all too poor to allow.

There was nothing very dreadful to be sure in these relations, and I only bring myself to allude to them by way of illustrating the gradual fading out or loss of *stamina* which the isolated family tie is undergoing in this country, and indeed everywhere, in obedience to the growing access of the social sentiment. Man is destined to experience the broadest conceivable unity with his kind,—a unity regulated by the principle of spontaneous taste or attraction exclusively; and it is only our puerile civic *régime*, with its divisions of rich and poor, high and low, wise and ignorant, free and bond, which keeps him from freely realizing this des-tiny: or rather let us say that it is the debasing influence which this civic *régime* exerts upon the heart and mind of men, that keeps them as yet strangers even in thought to their divine destiny. Now, the isolated family bond is the nucleus or citadel of this provisional civic economy; and prac-tically, therefore, the interest of the isolated family is the chief obstacle still presented to the full evolution of human nature. Accordingly, even in infancy the family subject feels an instinct of opposition to domestic rule. Even as a child he feels the family bond irksome, and finds his most precious enjoyments and friendships outside the home precinct. I do not say that the family in this country *consciously* antagonizes the social spirit in humanity, or is at all aware, indeed, of that deeper instinct of race-unity which is beginning to assert itself. For the family with us is not an institution, as it is and always has been in Europe, but only a transmitted prejudice, having no public *prestige* in any case but what it derives from the private worth of its members. Still, it is a very rancorous and deep-rooted prejudice, and speculatively operates every sort of vexa-tious hindrance to the spread of the social spirit. The "rich" family looks down upon the "poor" family, the "cultivated" family upon the "unculti-vated" one,—the consequence being that this old convention which we have inherited from our European ancestry still profoundly colors our practical ethics, and blights every effort and aspiration towards race-harmony.

I have no desire, either, to intimate that I myself suffered from any particularly stringent administration of the family bond. My intercourse with my parents was almost wholly destitute of a moral or voluntary hue. Whether it was that the children of the family were exceptionally void in their personal relations of malignity or not, I do not know; but, strive as I may, I cannot remember anything but a most infrequent exhibition of authority towards us on my father's part. And as to my mother, who was all anxiety and painstaking over our material interests, she made her own personal welfare or dignity of so little account in her habitual dealings with us as to constitute herself for the most part a law only to our affections. I presume, however, that our childish intercourse with one another was unusually affectionate, since it incessantly gave birth to relations of the most frankly humoristic quality, which would have been repugnant to any tie of a mere dutiful regard.

Nevertheless, I was never so happy at home as away from it. And even within the walls of home my happiest moments were those spent in the stable talking horse-talk with Asher Foot, the family coachman; in the wood-house talking pigeons, chickens, and rabbits with Francis Piles, the out-door servant; in the kitchen, in the evenings, hearing Dinah Foot the cook, and Peter Woods the waiter, discourse of rheumatism, methodism, and miracle, with a picturesque good faith, superstition, and suavity that made the parlor converse seem insipid; or, finally, in the bedrooms teasing the good-natured chambermaids till their rage died out in convulsions of impotent laughter, and they threatened the next time they caught me to kiss me till my cheeks burnt crimson. These were my purest household delights, because they were free or imprescriptible; that is, did not appeal to my living heart through the medium of my prudential understanding. But sweet as these "stolen waters" were, they were not near so refreshing as those I enjoyed outside the house. For obviously my relation to the household servants, however democratic my youthful tendencies might be, could not be one of true fellowship, because the inequality of our positions prevented its ever being perfectly spontaneous.

I was indebted for my earliest practical initiation into a freer sentiment to the friendly intimacy I chanced to contract with my neighbors the shoemakers, whom I have described in a former chapter. Unfortunately, these plausible young men had really no more moral elevation than if they openly cultivated some form of dubious industry; and they were willing, I think, to take advantage of our boyish frankness and generosity to an extent which, on the whole, rendered their acquaintance very harmful to us. I cannot in the least justify them, but on the contrary hand their memory over to the unfaltering Nemesis which waits upon wronged innocence. But at the same time I must say that their friendship for awhile most beneficially housed my expanding consciousness, or served to give it an outward and objective direction. They had, to begin with, such an immense force of animal spirits as magnetized one out of all self-distrust or timidity, barely to be with them. And then they were so utterly void of all religious sensibility or perturbation that my mental sinews relaxed at once into comparative ease and freedom, so that the force of nature within me then felt, I may say, its first authentication. They gave me, for example, my earliest relish of living art and art criticism. There was no theatre at that time in the city, but its place was held by an amateur Thespian company, whose exhibition they assiduously attended; and the delight they manifested in the drama, and the impassioned criticism they indulged in upon its acting, made me long for the day when I too should enter upon the romance of life. They were also great admirers of the triumphs of eloquence, and I used to bring collections of speeches from our own library to read to them by the hour. It was a huge pleasure to be able to compel their rapt attention to some eloquent defence of liberty or appeal to patriotism which I had become familiar with in my school or home reading. There was an old workman in the shop, an uncle of the principals, who sacrificed occasionally to Bacchus, and whose eyes used to drip very freely when I read Robert Emmet's famous speech, or the plea of the prisoner's counsel at the trial scene in "The Heart of Midlothian." He even went so far in his enthusiasm as to predict for the reader a distinguished career at the bar; but apparently prophecy was not my friend's strong point.[11]

NOTES

1. June 2, 1811.
2. William James.
3. County Cavan, Ireland.
4. Albany, N. Y.
5. At the age of thirteen, Mr. James had his right leg so severely burned while playing the then not usual game of fire-ball that he was confined to his bed for two years, and two thigh amputations had to be performed.
6. Catharine Barber.
7. John Barber, of (then) Montgomery, Orange Co., N. Y. (near Newburgh).
8. Francis Barber.
9. William Barber.
10. My grandfather married three times, and had in all eleven children. The seven of whom my father speaks were his *own* brothers and sisters, born of the third marriage.—[W. J.]
11. The Autobiography was interrupted by Mr. James at this point, and never finished.—[W. J.]

2

VASTATION AND THE USES
OF SWEDENBORG

The experience which gave rise to James's conversion
to a new faith in the divinity of man's nature and in
what he called society as its redeemed form did not
become intelligible to him until he was led to the works
of Emmanuel Swedenborg and there found a name for
and a description of the spiritual experience that had
occurred to him. The name James gave to his experience was Swedenborg's word *vastation*, and the significance he eventually came to attach to that word was
closely allied with the way he used all of Swedenborg's
writings. Hence there is no coincidence in the fact that
when James, towards the very end of his life, set out
to record the specific details of his religious experience,
he found it necessary to yoke his report of its exact
nature and circumstances to a more general discussion
of the way Swedenborg's writing could serve as a
resource for determining its precise meaning.

It should be clear from what follows that James had
no desire to become enslaved to the specific letter of
Swedenborg's formulations; it was the spirit of those
formulations which chiefly interested him and which
he then went on to interpret in the most liberal and
personal of ways. It should also become apparent that
James had no desire to become an apologist for
Swedenborg himself and continually regarded those
who were as betrayors of the master's cause.
Swedenborg's books were important to James precisely
because they subordinated everything else to the glory
and majesty of the Divine Name. Thus to transform
Swedenborg himself into a great religious prophet or
seer, or to erect various cults in his honor, seemed a
perversion of the very intention of his writing. All
Swedenborg purported to be, according to James, was a
kind of reporter who was interested in recording, as
faithfully and modestly as humanly possible, certain
facts of spiritual experience which might then produce
the same redemptive effects in others which they had
already produced in himself. To ask Swedenborg to do
anything more than this—either to give reasons for the

way he perceived these facts, or to claim any special
authority of his own because of his knowledge of
them—was completely to misunderstand the nature of
his achievement and to destroy his relevance to the
present day.

The following selection is taken from *Society the
Redeemed Form of Man* (Boston, 1879), 43–76.

———•·•·•———

My Dear Friend:—

I will introduce what I have to say to you in regard to the genesis of my
religious faith, by reciting a fact of experience, interesting in itself no
doubt in a psychological point of view, but particularly interesting to my
imagination as marking the interval between my merely rationalistic interest in Divine things, and the subsequent struggle of my heart after a more
intimate and living knowledge of them.

In the spring of 1844 I was living with my family in the neighborhood
of Windsor, England, much absorbed in the study of the Scriptures. Two
or three years before this period I had made an important discovery, as I
fancied, namely: that the book of Genesis was not intended to throw a
direct light upon our natural or race history, but was an altogether mystical or symbolic record of the laws of God's *spiritual* creation and providence. I wrote a course of lectures in exposition of this idea, and delivered
them to good audiences in New York. The preparation of these lectures,
while it did much to confirm me in the impression that I had made an
interesting discovery, and one which would extensively modify theology,
convinced me, however, that a much more close and studious application
of my idea than I had yet given to the illustration of the details of the
sacred letter was imperatively needed. During my residence abroad, accordingly, I never tired in my devotion to this aim, and my success seemed so
flattering at length that I hoped to be finally qualified to contribute a not
insignificant mite to the sum of man's highest knowledge. I remember I
felt especially hopeful in the prosecution of my task all the time I was at
Windsor; my health was good, my spirits cheerful, and the pleasant sce-
nery of the Great Park and its neighborhood furnished us a constant temptation to long walks and drives.

One day, however, towards the close of May, having eaten a comfortable
dinner, I remained sitting at the table after the family had dispersed, idly
gazing at the embers in the grate, thinking of nothing, and feeling only the
exhilaration incident to a good digestion, when suddenly—in a lightning-
flash as it were—"fear came upon me, and trembling, which made all my
bones to shake." To all appearance it was a perfectly insane and abject
terror, without ostensible cause, and only to be accounted for, to my perplexed imagination, by some damnèd shape squatting invisible to me
within the precincts of the room, and raying out from his fetid personality

influences fatal to life. The thing had not lasted ten seconds before I felt myself a wreck, that is, reduced from a state of firm, vigorous, joyful manhood to one of almost helpless infancy. The only self-control I was capable of exerting was to keep my seat. I felt the greatest desire to run incontinently to the foot of the stairs and shout for help to my wife,—to run to the roadside even, and appeal to the public to protect me; but by an immense effort I controlled these frenzied impulses, and determined not to budge from my chair till I had recovered my lost self-possession. This purpose I held for a good long hour, as I reckoned time, beat upon meanwhile by an ever-growing tempest of doubt, anxiety, and despair, with absolutely no relief from any truth I had ever encountered save a most pale and distant glimmer of the Divine existence,—when I resolved to abandon the vain struggle, and communicate without more ado what seemed my sudden burden of inmost, implacable unrest to my wife.

Now, to make a long story short, this ghastly condition of mind continued with me, with gradually lengthening intervals of relief, for two years, and even longer. I consulted eminent physicians, who told me that I had doubtless overworked my brain, an evil for which no remedy existed in medicine, but only in time, and patience, and growth into improved physical conditions. They all recommended by way of hygiene a resort to the water-cure treatment, a life in the open air, cheerful company, and so forth, and thus quietly and skilfully dismissed me to my own spiritual medication. At first, when I began to feel a half-hour's respite from acute mental anguish, the bottomless mystery of my disease completely fascinated me. The more, however, I worried myself with speculations about the cause of it, the more the mystery deepened, and the deeper also grew my instinct of resentment at what seemed so needless an interference with my personal liberty. I went to a famous water-cure, which did nothing towards curing my malady but enrich my memory with a few morbid specimens of English insularity and prejudice, but it did much to alleviate it by familiarizing my senses with the exquisite and endless charm of English landscape, and giving me my first full rational relish of what may be called England's pastoral beauty. To be sure I had spent a few days in Devonshire when I was young, but my delight then was simple enthusiasm, was helpless aesthetic intoxication in fact. The "cure" was situated in a much less lovely but still beautiful country, on the borders of a famous park, to both of which, moreover, it gave you unlimited right of possession and enjoyment. At least this was the way it always struck my imagination. The thoroughly disinterested way the English have of looking at their own hills and vales,—the indifferent, contemptuous, and as it were *disowning* mood they habitually put on towards the most ravishing pastoral loveliness man's sun anywhere shines upon,—gave me always the sense of being a discoverer of these things, and of a consequent right to enter upon their undisputed possession. At all events the rich light and shade of English landscape, the gorgeous cloud-pictures that forever dimple and diversify her fragrant and palpitating bosom, have awakened a tenderer chord in me than I have ever felt at home almost; and time and again while living at this dismal water-cure, and listening to its endless "'strife of tongues" about diet, and regimen, and disease, and politics, and parties, and persons, I have said to myself: *The curse of mankind, that which keeps our manhood so little and so depraved, is its sense of selfhood, and the absurd abominable opinionativeness it engenders. How sweet it would be to find oneself no longer man, but one of those innocent and ignorant sheep pasturing upon that placid hillside, and drinking in eternal dew and freshness from nature's lavish bosom!*

But let me hasten to the proper upshot of this incident. My stay at the water-cure, unpromising as it was in point of physical results, made me conscious erelong of a most important change operating in the sphere of my will and understanding. It struck me as very odd, soon after my breakdown, that I should feel no longing to resume the work which had been interrupted by it; and from that day to this—nearly thirty-five years—I have never once cast a retrospective glance, even of curiosity, at the immense piles of manuscript which had erewhile so absorbed me. I suppose if any one had designated me previous to that event as an earnest seeker after truth, I should myself have seen nothing unbecoming in the appellation. But now—within two or three months of my catastrophe—I felt sure I had never caught a glimpse of truth. My present consciousness was exactly that of an utter and plenary destitution of truth. Indeed an ugly suspicion had more than once forced itself upon me, that I had never really wished the truth, but only to ventilate my own ability in discovering it. I was getting sick to death in fact with a sense of my downright intellectual poverty and dishonesty. My studious mental activity had served manifestly to base a mere "castle in the air," and the castle had vanished in a brief bitter moment of time, leaving not a wrack behind. I never felt again the most passing impulse, even, to look where it stood, having done with it forever. Truth indeed! How should a beggar like me be expected to discover it? How should any man of woman born pretend to such ability? Truth must *reveal itself* if it would be known, and even then how imperfectly known at best! For truth is God, the omniscient and omnipotent God, and who shall pretend to comprehend that great and adorable perfection? And yet who that aspires to the name of man, would not cheerfully barter all he knows of life for a bare glimpse of the hem of its garment?

I was calling one day upon a friend[1] (since deceased) who lived in the vicinity of the water-cure—a lady of rare qualities of heart and mind, and of singular personal loveliness as well—who desired to know what had brought me to the water-cure. After I had done telling her in substance what I have told you, she replied: "It is, then, very much as I had ventured from two or three previous things you have said, to suspect: you are undergoing what Swedenborg calls a *vastation;* and though, naturally enough, you yourself are despondent or even despairing about the issue, I cannot help taking an altogether hopeful view of your prospects." In expressing my thanks for her encouraging words, I remarked that I was not at all familiar with the Swedenborgian technics, and that I should be extremely happy if she would follow up her flattering judgment of my condition by turning into plain English the contents of the very handsome Latin word she had used. To this she again modestly replied that she only read Swedenborg as an *amateur*, and was ill-qualified to expound his philosophy, but there could be no doubt about its fundamental postulate, which was, that a new birth for man, both in the individual and the universal realm, is the secret of the Divine creation and providence: that the other world, according to Swedenborg, furnishes the true sphere of man's spiritual or individual being, the real and immortal being he has in God; and he represents *this* world, consequently, as furnishing only a preliminary theatre of his natural formation or existence in subordination thereto; so making the question of human regeneration, both in grand and in little, the capital problem of philosophy: that, without pretending to dogmatize, she had been struck with the philosophic interest of my narrative in this point of view, and had used the word *vastation* to characterize one of the stages of the regenerative process, as she had found it described by Swedenborg. And then, finally, my excellent friend went on to outline for me, in a very interesting manner, her conception of Swedenborg's entire doctrine on the subject.

Her account of it, as I found on a subsequent study of Swedenborg, was neither quite as exact nor quite as comprehensive as the facts required; but at all events I was glad to discover that any human being had so much even as proposed to shed the light of positive knowledge upon the soul's history, or bring into rational relief the alternate dark and bright—or infernal and celestial—phases of its finite constitution. For I had an immediate hope, amounting to an almost prophetic instinct, of finding in the attempt, however rash, some diversion to my cares, and I determined instantly to run up to London and procure a couple of Swedenborg's volumes, of which, if I should not be allowed on sanitary grounds absolutely to read them, I might at any rate turn over the leaves, and so catch a satisfying savor, or at least an appetizing flavor, of the possible relief they might in some better day afford to my poignant need. From the huge mass of tomes placed by the bookseller on the counter before me, I selected two of the least in bulk—the treatise on the *Divine Love and Wisdom*, and that on the *Divine Providence*. I gave them, after I brought them home, many a random but eager glance, but at last my interest in them grew so frantic under this tantalizing process of reading that I resolved, in spite of the doctors, that, instead of standing any longer shivering on the brink, I would boldly plunge into the stream, and ascertain, once for all, to what undiscovered sea its waters might bear me.

My Dear Friend:—

I read from the first with palpitating interest. My heart divined, even before my intelligence was prepared to do justice to the books, the unequalled amount of truth to be found in them. Imagine a fever patient, sufficiently restored of his malady to be able to think of something beside himself, suddenly transported where the free airs of heaven blow upon him, and the sound of running waters refreshes his jaded senses, and you have a feeble image of my delight in reading. Or, better still, imagine a subject of some petty despotism condemned to die, and with—what is more and worse—a sentiment of death pervading all his consciousness, lifted by a sudden miracle into felt harmony with universal man, and filled to the brim with the sentiment of indestructible life instead, and you will have a true picture of my emancipated condition. For while these remarkable books familiarized me with the angelic conception of the Divine being and providence, they gave me at the same time the amplest *rationale* I could have desired of my own particular suffering, as inherent in the profound unconscious death I bore about in my *proprium* or selfhood.

—Here let me interpose a few words of caution. I have not the least ambition to set myself up as Swedenborg's personal attorney or solicitor. Swedenborg himself is not the least a fascinating personality to my regard, and if I were able by skilful palaver to reason you out of an unfavorable into a favorable estimate of his personal genius and worth, I should prefer no to do it; because just in proportion as you concede any personal authority to a writer you are unlikely to be spirtually helped by him. You are sure in fact, to be spiritually enfeebled by him. Besides, I am persuaded that notwithstanding Swedenborg's personal limitations as measured by the taste of our day, his amazing books will suffer by no man's neglect, were he the most considerable man of his time in religion, in science, and in philosophy. And I should think myself very ill employed, therefore, in drumming up a regiment of raw recruits to dim their patient lustre, or degrade it to the glitter of the gutters. His books invite the most opposite appreciation, for they have all the breadth and variety of nature in their aspect—now smiling with celestial peace, now grim with infernal storm and wrath. But they have always a light above nature, that is to say, not only above this realm of *mixed* good and evil which we call the natural world, but also above that realm of *divided* good and evil to which we give the name of the spiritual world; and in this Divine light we may discern, if we are attentive, an objective reconciliation of infinite and finite, which shall finally blot all memory, either of a mixed or a divided good and evil, forever out of mind.

At the moment I am speaking of—the moment of my first encounter with Swedenborg's writings—my intellect had been so completely vastated of every semblance of truth inherited from the past, and my soul consequently was in a state of such sheer and abject famine with respect to Divine things, that I doubt not I should have welcomed "the father of lies" to my embrace, nor ever have cared to scrutinize his credentials, had he presented himself bearing the priceless testimony which these books bear to the loveliness and grandeur of the Divine name. Nor should I counsel any one, who is not similarly dilapidated in his intellectual foundations— any one who is still at rest in his hereditary bed of doctrine, orthodox or heterodox—to pay the least attention to them. For on the surface they repel delight. They would seem to have been mercifully constructed on the plan of barring out idle acquaintance, and disgusting a voluptuous literary curiosity. But to the aching heart and the void mind—the heart and mind which, being sensibly famished upon those gross husks of religious doctrine whether Orthodox or Unitarian, upon which nevertheless our veriest swine are contentedly fed, are secretly pining for their Father's house where there is bread enough and to spare—they will be sure, I think, to bring infinite balm and contentment. I am confident that no such readers will ever care to discuss any question which is properly personal to Swedenborg.

I disdain to argue, then, with you or anybody else, in regard to Swedenborg, on general or *à priori* principles. Think what you will, and say what you will, of his dogmatic pretensions—make him out if it please you, in the abundance of your self-satisfaction, either a knave or a fool or both—the judgment it is true may give out a stronger subjective flavor, but I have something better to do than to argue it on its objective merits. Besides, I take it that no man is eager to argue a question about which he himself has not at least some secret misgiving. And I have no more misgiving, either secret or open, in regard to Swedenborg's teaching, than the new-born babe has in regard to its mother's milk. He has moreover so effectually vulgarized to my mind the inmost significance of heaven and hell by exposing their purely *provisional* character and contents, that I should feel myself wanting both in proper self-respect and proper homage to the Divine name, if I continued to cherish anything but a strictly scientific curiosity with regard to angel or devil; or viewed it as the consummation of my being to be eternally associated with the one and eternally separated from the other.

In thus avowing my free conviction of the immortal services Swedenborg has rendered to the mind, I confess I should be greatly mortified if you looked upon this avowal as a "profession of faith" in him, or as an ascription on my part of any more dogmatic authority to him than I should ascribe in their various measure to Socrates or John Mill.[2] He reports himself as interviewing, by special Divine appointment, spirits and angels and devils in respect to what they could attest each in their degree, whether consciously or unconsciously, of the principles of the world's administration. Thus he is at best a mere informer or reporter, though an egregiously intelligent one, in the interest of a new evolution of the human mind, speculative and practical; and his testimony, therefore, to the spiritual truth of the case, however much it may attract your confidence both in respect to its general competence and its palpable veracity, is not for an instant to be regarded as a revelation, or confounded with living Divine truth. The sphere of Revelation is the sphere of life exclusively, and its truth is addressed not to the reflective understanding of men, but to their living perception. Truth, to every soul that has ever felt its inward breathing, disowns all outward authority,—disowns, if need be, all outward *prob-*

ability or attestation of Fact. The only witness it craves, and this witness it depends upon, is that of good in the heart; and it allows no lower or less decisive attestation. Swedenborg, at all events, is incapable of the effrontery thus imputed to him. Nothing could have awakened a blush of deeper resentment on his innocent brow, if he could have foreseen the outrage, than the base spirit of sect, which in the face of his honest denunciations of it ventures to renew its unhallowed empire by clothing him with Divine authority.

The pretension to authority in intellectual things belongs exclusively to the Romish Church; and it has of late grown so reckless and wanton even in that hysterical suburb, as to show that it has no longer any faith in itself, but is clung to only as a desperate commercial speculation. If, accordingly, any taint of this spiritual dry-rot attached to these transparent books, I should advise you to send author and books, both alike, into the land of forgetfulness. It is not conceivable that the Divine providence should deliberately endow a quack to further his wise designs towards the intellect of the race. And every man in this day of restored spiritual liberty, and with the doomed papacy before him, who yet apes its blasphemy, so far as to claim either for himself or another a delegated Divine authority over the reason and conscience of men, must be a double-distilled quack; that is, knave and fool both; though he may not have perspicacity enough to suspect himself of either obliquity. Indeed, none but a truly wise man ever suspects himself of being a fool, and none but a truly good man has courage to avow himself a knave; so that if the world could once get fairly defecated of its unconscious knaves and fools, we should have only good men and wise left behind.

At all events, Swedenborg is conspicuously free of this vulgarity. His own faith is vowed unaffectedly and exclusively to the one sole and consummate revelation of the Divine name, made in the gospel of Jesus Christ; and he is not such a silly and vicious he-goat, accordingly, as to go about peddling a rival revelation. His sole intellectual pretension is to emphasize the eternal lustre of the gospel to men's regard, by disclosing its interior or spiritual and philosophic contents, as they became known to him through the opening of his spiritual senses. Take particular notice, therefore: what any honest mind goes to these sincere books for is, not to find any Divine warrant there either for his faith or his practice, for every man's own heart alone is competent to that question; much less to discover in them any new deodorizing substance which will disguise the stale fetor of ecclesiasticism or sacerdotalism, and so commend it anew to men's revolted nostrils; but all simply to find light upon the philosophy of the gospel, or ascertain what its internal or universal and impersonal contents are, of the truth of which contents he himself is all the while his own sole and divinely empowered arbiter.

And here a proper caution must be used, lest one run headlong into an exaggerated or superstitious estimate of Swedenborg's books, even from their own point of view. For it is past all dispute that Swedenborg himself

had at best only a most general and obscure notion of the benefit which
was to accrue to the mind of man, on earth and in heaven, from the last
Judgment whose operation in the world of spirits he so minutely describes.
The immediate chaotic or revolutionary effects of the Judgment apparently so absorbed his attention as to leave him neither leisure nor inclination, even if he had had the power, to prognosticate its redeeming virtue
upon the progress of the human mind. But he had no such prophetic faculty, even in reference to the events he was daily witnessing in the world
of spirits, much less, therefore, in reference to the contingencies of God's
order in this lower or universal world. Indeed, he tells us that when he
asked the angels what *their* judgment was, as to the specific effects which
would follow upon earth from the events occurring in the world of spirits,
they were completely unable to satisfy his curiosity in that behalf. They
replied, in effect, that *they* knew just as little of the specific future as he
did—future events being present only to the Divine mind—and that all they
felt sure of *in general* was, that the old spiritual tyranny under which the
human mind had been so helplessly stifled, being now at last effectually
dissipated by the breaking up of the ecclesiastical heavens, Popish and
Protestant alike, freethinking in religious things would be henceforth the
divinely guaranteed basis of the Church on earth. And if freethinking or
scepticism in religious things—the things of the intellect—be henceforth the
normal attitude of the natural mind as a consequence of the last Judgment,
surely nothing could have well seemed more preposterous to Swedenborg
than to think of ever again elevating the discredited banner of Authority.

Conceive of Swedenborg then, personally, as you will, and welcome.
What alone I care about is not to interest your intelligence in anything that
is personal to the devout and estimable old seer, but in his performances.
I feel, indeed, a perfect indifference to all his private claims upon attention.
But my gratitude and admiration are immense for what he has done to
flood the human mind with light out of inscrutable darkness, upon the
question of our human origin and destiny; upon every question, in fact,
involved in a true cosmology, or permanent science of the relations which
exist between the world of thought and the world of substance. But then,
remember, there is no access to this light but through honest research,
guided by the felt needs of your intellect, and not by any idle literary curiosity, or mere silly ambition to know what other people know, and to be
able to talk about what they talk about. Above all, let me counsel you to
avoid, as you would avoid a fog, every flippant jackanapes who is ecclesiastically ordained (or unordained by the holy Ghost) to minister truth to
you. The ecclesiastical spirit, and the civic spirit bred of it, are now the
only evil spirits upon earth, and they are no longer compatible with any
living knowledge of truth. Indeed, no man can outwardly communicate
truth to his neighbor, much less any whose profession it is to do so, however skilled he may be to communicate scientific information. For truth is
living, spiritual, Divine, being shaped to every one's intelligence only by
what he has of celestial love in his heart. Thus Swedenborg will doubtless

give you any amount of interesting and enlightening information about the spiritual world, and its principles of administration. And this knowledge taken into your memory, or mental stomach, will constitute so much nutritive material to be intellectually assimilated by you, when the living truth itself has begun to germinate and sprout in your heart. But as to actually communicating the truth to you—or making it literally over to your understanding—Swedenborg is of course just as flatly incompetent to that function as every other man of woman born, and even more incapable morally, if that be possible, than he was intellectually, of making any such blasphemous claim.

My Dear Friend:—

I have not lost sight of my subject, as you doubtless by this time suspect, and we shall soon return to it. But, as I told you in my first letter, my nervous force is very much abated at present, and I am obliged to write not exactly as I would, but as my defective energy permits me. Besides, even if my nerves were unimpaired, it would be within the strict logic of my theme to hold a little discourse with you about Swedenborg and the relation of my thought to his books, since he is the only man, as it seems to me, in human history who has shed any commanding or decisive light on the physiology of the soul. That is to say, his books set before you, as no other books have the least pretension to do, *certain* FACTS *of spiritual observation and experience* which must, if you read them with interested attention, very soon convince you that you, like all other men, have hitherto utterly misconceived the function of selfhood in man, and hence have attributed an original or causative influence, instead of a purely ancillary or ministerial one, to morality in human affairs. Observe what I say. *It is exclusively these facts of spiritual observation and experience,* recounted by Swedenborg, *which produce the effect in question,* and not the least any reasoning of his own in regard to the facts. For this is what Swedenborg never does, namely, reason about the things he professes to have learned from angels and spirits. It may betoken great wisdom or great imbecility in him to your mind that he does not; but such, nevertheless, is the fact. He never once, so far as I have observed, has attempted to throw a persuasive light upon the things he professes to have heard and seen among his angelic acquaintance.

Indeed, his own intellectual relation to the facts is left altogether undetermined in his books. There can be no doubt that the things he learned diffused an atmosphere of great peace and sweetness in his breast, and this makes his books the most heavenly reading I know; but there is no sign extant, that I can see, of any intellectual quickening being produced by them, on his part, in regard to the history or the prospects of the race. I am not going to be so dull, therefore, as to promise you the very same intellectual results that I get from Swedenborg's books, even if you yourself actually have recourse to them. Indeed, multitudes of people are said to read his books and bring away almost no intellectual result,—multitudes who resort to them with great apparent complacency, and get, no doubt, much incidental entertainment and instruction from them, and yet are quite blind to their proper intellectual significance, to the extent, I am told, many of them, of seeming acutely hostile to it when it is brought before them. All this, of course, because of the more or less vacant mind they bring to the reading of him; or rather, their more or less unsympathetic hearts. Most of them come to the banquet of facts and observations Swedenborg spreads before them with an obvious gross hankering after ecclesiastical righteousness, and make the most, accordingly, of every crumb they can pick up adapted to gratify that unmanly and dyspeptic relish. But if you bring human sympathies to the banquet in question, I can assure you, you will find no speck of that base, unworthy nutriment. For it cannot be too much insisted on, that no books address the reader's intellect so much through the heart as these of Swedenborg do, all in confining themselves to giving him spiritual information merely.

This is no doubt an endless stumbling-block to the mass of readers, who regard Swedenborg as a sort of intellectual tailor, whose shop they have only to enter, to find whatsoever spiritual garments their particular nakedness craves, all made to hand. And when they find, as every one among them is sure to do who has any faculty of spiritual discernment, that there are absolutely no garments made up, but only an immense sound of the shearing of sheep and the carding of wool and the whirling of wheels and the rattling of looms and the flying of spindles, and that every forlorn wight who would be spiritually clad must actually turn to and become his own wool-grower, weaver, and tailor, the great majority of course go away disgusted, and only those remain whose vocation for Truth is so genuine as to make any labor incurred in her service welcome if not pleasant. The case of course is far more hopeless when one goes in with absolutely no conscious nakedness to cover, but only to satisfy a vague outside curiosity about intellectual novelties, and make, perchance, a handsome addition to an already luxurious literary wardrobe. But Swedenborg is not now, and probably never will be, so much the mode as greatly to attract this style of customer.

In fact, the whole existing conception of the man and his aims is a mistake. He is not at all the intellectual craftsman or quack the world takes him for. He is no way remarkable as a man of original thought, or even as a reasoner, unless it be negatively so, while as a man of experience, or a seer, his worth is of the very highest grade, as imposing no kind of obligation upon your belief. His judgments doubtless in regard to this world's affairs were those of his day and generation, and strike one as grown very antiquated; but there is almost no fact of spiritual observation and experience he recounts which does not seem of really priceless worth to my imagination, *as illustrating and enforcing a new mind in man*. If his books seem interesting to you also in this point of view, if they tend to enlighten you upon very many things which have puzzled you in your own mental pathway, or in respect to our race-origin and destiny, well and good; no doubt you too are bound to an ultimate profitable commerce with them. And in this event you will find it unquestionably true that their main advantage to the intellect is, that they furnish it with truths which really nourish and quicken it, or irresistibly compel it to function for itself, and independently of foreign stimulus. His books, in fact, amount to nothing so much as to an intellectual wheat-field, of no use to any one who does not enter in to gather and bind his own golden sheaves, and then proceed to thresh and grind his grain, to bolt his flour, to mix his bread, to build it up and bake it in such shapely and succulent loaves as his own intellectual bread-pan alone determines. . . .

I have said that the main philosophic obligation we owe to Swedenborg lies in his clearly identifying the evil principle in existence with selfhood. The Christian truth somewhat prepares us for this; but the church theology so overlays and systematically falsifies the truth, that we practically get little good of it. This theology, for example, identifies evil with a person called the *Devil* and *Satan*, outside the pale of human nature, but intimately conversant with its secret springs, and both able and disposed to use his knowledge with the malign purpose of corrupting all its subjects. Of course this conception was originally due to a very immature scientific condition of the mind, when men had not the least idea of good and evil as having an exclusively spiritual or subjective source. It befits, in fact, a strictly mechanical or material conception of the soul's relation to God, and only deepens the mystery it attempts to explain; for if the good and evil of human life acknowledge no inward root, but betray a purely moral, voluntary, or personal genesis, it can only be because the creative relation to man is primarily in fault, being the power of an external, not an internal, life. And if God were the power primarily of an external life in man, and *not altogether mediately through an internal one,* neither creature nor creator would ever invite, as they assuredly would never reward, the homage of an intellectual appreciation.

My Dear Friend:—

Without doubt I had suffered intellectually from the same or similar unworthy views of the creative relation to man, as those I adverted to in my last letter. I had always, from childhood, conceived of the Creator as bearing this outside relation to the creature, and had attributed to the latter consequently the power of provoking His unmeasured hostility. Although these crude traditional views had been much modified by subsequent reflection, I had nevertheless on the whole been in the habit of ascribing to the Creator, so far as my own life and actions were concerned, an outside discernment of the most jealous scrutiny, and had accordingly put the greatest possible alertness into His service and worship, until my will, as you have seen—thoroughly fagged out as it were with the formal, heartless, endless task of conciliating a stony-hearted Deity—actually collapsed. This was a catastrophe far more tragic to my feeling, and far more revolutionary in its intellectual results, than the actual violation of any mere precept of the moral law could be. It was the practical abrogation of the law itself, through the unexpected moral inertness of the subject. It was to my feeling not only an absolute decease of my moral or voluntary power, but a shuddering recoil from my conscious activity in that line. It was an actual acute loathing of the moral pretension itself as so much downright charlatanry. No idiot was ever more incompetent, practically, to the conduct of life than I, at that trying period, felt myself to be. It cost me, in fact, as much effort to go out for a walk, or to sleep in a strange bed, as it would an ordinary man to plan a campaign or write an epic poem. I have told you how, in looking out of my window at the time at a flock of silly sheep which happened to be grazing in the Green Park opposite, I used to envy them their blissful stupid ignorance of any law higher than their nature, their deep unconsciousness of self, their innocence of all private personality and purpose, their intense moral incapacity, in short, and indifference. I would freely, nay, gladly have bartered the world at the moment for one breath of the spiritual innocence which the benign creatures outwardly pictured, or stood for to my imagination; and all the virtue, or moral righteousness, consequently, that ever illustrated our specific human personality, seemed simply foul and leprous in comparison with the deep Divine possibilities and promise of our common nature, as these stood symbolized to my spiritual sight in all the gentler human types of the merely animate world. There seemed, for instance—lustrously represented to my inward sense—a far more heavenly sweetness in the soul of a patient overdriven cab-horse, or misused cadger's donkey, than in all the voluminous calendar of Romish and Protestant hagiology, which, sooth to say, seemed to me, in contrast with it, nothing short of infernal.

You may easily imagine, then, with what relish my heart opened to the doctrine I found in these most remarkable books, *of the sheer and abject phenomenality of selfhood in man;* and with what instant alacrity my intellect shook its canvas free to catch every breeze of that virgin unexplored sea of being, to which this doctrine, for the first time, furnished me the clew. Up to this very period I had lived in the cheerful faith, nor ever felt the slightest shadow of misgiving about it—any more, I venture to say, than you at this moment feel a shadow of similar misgiving in your own mind—that my being or substance lay absolutely in myself, was in fact identical with the various limitations implied in that most fallacious but still unsuspected quantity. To be sure, I had no doubt that this being or self of mine (whether actually burdened, or not burdened, with its limitations, I did not stop to inquire, but unquestionably with a capacity of any amount of burdensome limitation) came originally as a gift from the hand of God; but I had just as little doubt that the moment the gift had left God's hand, or fell into my conscious possession, it became as essentially independent of Him in all spiritual or subjective regards as the soul of a child is of its earthly father; however much in material or objective regards it might be expedient for me still to submit to His external police. My moral conscience, too, lent its influence to the same profound illusion;

for all the precepts of the moral law being objectively so good and real, and intended in the view of an unenlightened conscience to make men righteous in the sight of God, I could never have supposed, even had I been tempted on independent grounds to doubt my own spiritual or subjective reality, that so palpably Divine a law contemplated, or even tolerated, a wholly infirm and fallacious subject; much less that it was, in fact, altogether devised for the reproof, condemnation, and humiliation of such a subject. I had no misgiving, therefore, as to the manifest purpose of the Law. The Divine intent of it at least was as clear to me as it ever had been to the Jew, namely, to serve as a ministry of plain moral life or actual righteousness among men, so constructing an everlasting heaven out of men's warring and divided personalities: and not at all, as the apostles taught, a ministry of death, *to convince those who stood approved by it of* SIN, thereby shutting up all men, good and evil alike, but especially the good, to unlimited dependence upon the sheer and mere mercy of God.

It was impossible for me, after what I have told you, to hold this audacious faith in selfhood any longer. When I sat down to dinner on that memorable chilly afternoon in Windsor, I held it serene and unweakened by the faintest breath of doubt. Before I rose from table it had inwardly shrivelled to a cinder. One moment I devoutly thanked God for the inappreciable boon of selfhood; the next that inappreciable boon seemed to me the one thing damnable on earth, seemed a literal nest of hell within my own entrails. Whatever difficulties then stood in the way of a better faith, they were infinitely milder and more placable than those inherent in the old one. In fact the old faith was itself the only obstacle in the path of the new. Take the one away, and the other becomes inevitable. If you admit the intrinsic or essential phenomenality of selfhood—its utter unreality or non-existence out of consciousness—you are logically forced upon the truth of the creative incarnation in the created nature—or the Divine Natural Humanity—as the sole possible method of creation, as the only truth capable of explaining nature and history. When I say *forced,* I take for granted that you have some rational interest in the subject; I take for granted that you deem nature and history worthy to be explained, and are not a mere sensualist so intent upon your own pleasure as to feel no capacity for inward satisfactions. In that case, I repeat, the only existing obstacle to your belief in the necessary incarnation of the Creator in the created nature in order to the redemption and salvation of the human race from the empire of evil and falsity, will be dissipated by your coming to acknowledge the pure phenomenality of consciousness, or to disbelieve in the spiritual reality of selfhood. Nothing hinders one believing in spiritual truth but the limitary influence of falsity. And so, conversely, nothing hinders a man succumbing to spiritual falsity but the liberating influence of truth. So that the only possible way for men to arrive at the spiritual or living knowledge of truth, is by unliving their natural prejudices and prejudices of education. Now the deepest and most universal of these prejudices is that which makes selfhood the greatest of realities, and consequently inflates the heart of man with all manner of spiritual pride, avarice, and cruelty. And it is accordingly the conquest of this fundamental prejudice which best promotes our spiritual rectitude, or living conjunction with God. . . .

NOTES

1. A woman whose name has been preserved for posterity only as Mrs. Chichester.—Editor's note.

2. The reference is to John Stuart Mill (1806–1873) who was a great favorite of James's because of the broad human sympathies which were expressed in his famous essay, "On Liberty."—Editor's note.

3

THE SWEDENBORGIAN INHERITANCE

Throughout the course of his career, James kept
returning again and again to the writings of Emmanuel
Swedenborg in an effort to clarify and restate what
he thought he had learned from him. Swedenborg was
an inexhaustible source of interest to James only
because he believed that Swedenborg's books held the
key to an inexhaustible truth. James's obsession with
Swedenborg was not quieted until he devoted a full-
length book to this remarkable spiritualist, and even
then James's very title, *The Secret of Swedenborg*,
suggested with unintentional irony some essence of
his subject which might prove forever elusive.

The following selection is important as, perhaps,
the most succinct and personal summary of those
crucial ideas which Swedenborg made accessible to
James. It is taken from *The Secret of Swedenborg*
(Boston, 1869), 170–80.

———————

It would be difficult to express the exquisite peace which flowed into
my intellect, when this great discovery began to shape itself out of the
multitudinous but accordant details of Swedenborg's marvellous yet most
veracious *audita et visa* ["revelations," literally, "things heard and seen"].
If there had been anything habitually unquestioned to my conviction, it
was the indefeasible sovereignty of conscience on the one hand, or the
literal finality of its judgments in all the field of a man's relations to God,
and the truth on the other hand of every man's complete personal ade-
quacy to all the demands of its righteousness, provided he were only actu-
ated by good-will; and I spared no pains accordingly to cultivate such
good-will, and so conciliate its austere regard. I never questioned the absoluteness of all the *data*, good and evil, of my moral experience. I never
doubted the infinite and eternal consequences which seemed to me to be
wrapped up in my consciousness of personality, or the sentiment I habitually cherished of my individual relations and responsibility to God. I had
never, to my own suspicion, been arrayed in any overt hostility to the
divine name. On the contrary, I reckoned myself an unaffected friend of
God, inasmuch as I was a most eager and conscientious aspirant after

moral perfection. And yet the total unconscious current of my religious life was so egotistic, the habitual color of my piety was so bronzed by an inmost selfishness and indifference to all mankind, save in so far as my action towards them bore upon my own salvation, that I never reflected myself to myself, never was able to look back upon any chance furrow my personality had left upon the sea of time, without a shuddering conviction of the abysses of spiritual profligacy over which I perpetually hovered, and towards which I incessantly gravitated. And I have accordingly no hesitation in expressing my firm persuasion that nothing kept me in this state of things from lapsing into a complete despair, and a consequent actual loathing and hatred of the divine name, but the infinite majesty of Christ; that is to say, a most real and vital divine presence *in my nature* deeper than my *self*, deeper than consciousness, deeper than any and every fact of my moral or personal experience, which was able, therefore, to rebuke and control even the pitiless rancor of conscience itself, and say with authority to its tumultuous waves, Peace, be still!

I do not mean to say that I had any clear idea of this truth at the time. Familiar as my intellect had always been with the letter of revelation, it was—not indeed altogether, but—comparatively blind to its spiritual scope, until I found in Swedenborg all the light it was possible to crave in that direction. My traditional faith bound me to look upon Christ as a mere succedaneum to Moses, or practically subordinated the gospel in my estimation to the law; so that the only use I ever made of the christian facts —whenever the voice of conscience was loud in my bosom, proclaiming the inextinguishable difference of good and evil, or God and man—was to worry out of them some more or less plausible pretext of consolation against the wrath of God, still presumably impending upon all manner of unrighteousness. I do not think I overstate my intellectual obligations to Swedenborg, when I say that his spiritual disclosures put an effectual end to this insane worry and superstition on my part forever. For these disclosures made plain to my understanding, what the Scriptures themselves had long before made plain to my understanding, what the Scriptures themselves had long before made plain to my heart, namely, that the law, with whatever pomp it had been sometimes administered, boasted of no independent worth, that its total sanctity lay in its negatively adumbrating to sense a coming righteousness in our nature so truly divine or infinite as to forbid all positive anticipation of it without instant wreck to the mind's freedom. Swedenborg showed me, in fact, in the discovery he for the first time makes to the intellect of spiritual laws, the laws of the divine creation, that the conception of law or conscience as a basis of intercourse between God and the soul is no longer tenable in philosophy, but must give place at once to the truth of a present or actual divine life in the very heart of human nature. He shows the empire of law, of conscience, of religion in human affairs, to be superseded henceforth by the christian truth, the truth of God's NATURAL humanity, and he allows the soul no permanent refuge against spiritual illusion and insanity but what it finds

in that supreme verity. What renders this lapsed *régime* of law or conscience or religion spiritually odious and intolerable to me, is that it proves
a sheer and invariable ministration of death to all my personal hopes God-
ward; it proves this, and cannot help proving it, because its ends are primarily public or universal, and mine are primarily private or individual.
What I crave with the whole bent of my nature is that God should be pro-
pitious to me personally, whatever he may be to all the rest of mankind. I
have naturally a supreme regard to myself, although I habitually conceal
that fact both from my own sight and that of other people under a flowing
drapery of professional benevolence; and what conscience or the law—
regarded as a literal divine administration—does, is to inflame my cupidity
towards God to such a pitch, as that the thick scales fall at last from my
eyes, and I am ready not only to perceive what an unclean and beggarly
lout I have always spiritually been in his sight, but also to agree that it
were better there were no God at all, than that he should be capable of
lending a benignant ear to my hypocritical or dramatic worship.

Understand me here, I beg. I have not the least idea of representing
myself as ever having been especially obnoxious to the rebuke of conscience. On the contrary, I am willing to admit that I have been tolerably
blameless in all the literal righteousness of the law. It is probable, no
doubt, that I have borne actual false-witness on occasion, or committed
here and there actual theft, adultery, and murder. I am not in the least
interested either to admit or deny any literal imputations of this sort. But
the habitual tenor of my life has been undeniably contrary to these practices; and it is only in my spiritual aspect accordingly, that I find myself
a reprobate. For example, I have been living all my days in great comfort
and plenty, when the great mass of my fellow-men are sunken in poverty,
and all the ills physical and moral which poverty is sure to breed. From
the day of my birth till now I have not only never known what it was to
have had an honest want, a want of my nature, ungratified, but I have
also been able to squander upon my mere fantastic want, the will of my
personal caprice, an amount of sustenance equal to the maintenance of
a virtuous household. And yet thousands of persons directly about me, in
all respects my equals, in many respects my superiors, have never in all
their lives enjoyed an honest meal, an honest sleep, an honest suit of
clothes, save at the expense of their own personal toil, or that of some
parent or child, and have never once been able to give the reins to their
personal caprice without an ignominious exposure to severe social penalties. It is, to be sure, perfectly just that I should be conveniently fed and
lodged and clad, and that I should be educated out of my native ignorance
and imbecility, because these enjoyments on my part imply no straitening
of any other man's social resources, and are indeed a necessary condition
of my own social worth. But it is a monstrous affront to the divine justice
or righteousness, that I should be guaranteed, by what calls itself society,
a life-long career of luxury and self-indulgence, while so many other men
and women every way my equals, in many ways my superiors, go all their

days miserably fed, miserably lodged, miserably clothed, and die at last in the same ignorance and imbecility, though not, alas! in the same inno- cence, that cradled their infancy. It is our wont, doubtless, to submit more or less cheerfully to this unholy social muddle or chaos, and many of us indeed are to be found rejoicing in it as the fit opportunity of their own lawless aggrandizement, material and moral. But be assured that no one, be he preacher or philosopher, statesman or churchman, poet or philan- thropist, artist or man of science, can reconcile himself in heart to it, can reflectively justify it on grounds either of reason or necessity, either of principle or expediency, without *ipso facto* turning out an unconscious but most real abettor of spiritual wickedness in high places, and reaping a spiritual damnation so deep that he will himself be the very last to feel or suspect its reality.

Now I had long felt this deep spiritual damnation in myself growing out of an outraged and insulted divine justice, had long been pent up in spirit to these earthquake mutterings and menaces of a violated conscience, without seeing any clear door of escape open to me. That is to say, I perceived with endless perspicacity that if it were not for the hand of God's providence visiting with constant humiliation and blight every secret aspiration of my pride and vanity, I should be more than any other man reconciled to the existing most atrocious state of things. I knew no outward want, I had the amplest social recognition, I enjoyed the converse and friendship of dis- tinguished men, I floated in fact on a sea of unrighteous plenty, and I was all the while so indifferent if not inimical in heart to the divine justice, that save for the spiritual terrors it ever and anon supplied to my lethargic sympathies, to my swinish ambition, I should have dragged out all my days in that complacent sty, nor have ever so much as dreamed that the out- ward want of my fellows—their want with respect to nature and society— was in truth but the visible sign and fruit of my own truer want, my own more inward destitution with respect to God. Thus my religious conscience was one of poignant misgiving towards God, if not of complete practical separation, and it filled my intellect with all manner of perplexed specula- tion and gloomy foreboding. Do what I might I never could attain to the least religious self-complacency, or push my devout instincts to the point of actual fanaticism. Do what I would I could never succeed in persuading myself that God almighty cared a jot for me in my personal capacity, i.e. as I stood morally individualized from, or consciously antagonized with, my kind; and yet this was the identical spiritual obligation imposed upon me by the church. Time and again I consulted my spiritual advisers to know how it might do for me to abandon myself to the simple joy of the truth as it was in Christ, without taking any thought for the church, or the interests of my religious character. And they always told me that it would not do at all; that my church sympathies, or the demands of my religious character, were everything comparatively, and my belief in Christ com- paratively nothing, since devils believed just as much as I did. The retort was as apt as it was obvious, that the devils believed and trembled, while

I believed and rejoiced; and that this joy on my part could not be helped, but only hindered, whenever it was allowed to be complicated with any question about myself. But no: the evidently foregone conclusion to be forced upon me in every case was, that a man's religious standing, or the love he bears the church, takes the place, under the gospel, of his moral standing, or the love he bore the state, under the law; hence that no amount of delight in the truth, for the truth's sake alone, could avail me spiritually, unless it were associated with a scupulous regard for a sancti- fied public opinion.

Imagine, then, my glad surprise, my cordial relief, when in this state of robust religious nakedness, with no wretchedest figleaf of ecclesiastical finery to cover me from the divine inclemency, I caught my first glimpse of the spiritual contents of revelation, or discerned the profoundly philo- sophic scope of the christian truth. This truth at once emboldened me to obey my own regenerate intellectual instincts without further parley, in throwing the church overboard, or demitting all care of my religious char- acter to the devil, of whom alone such care is an inspiration. The christian truth indeed—which is the truth of God's incarnation in our nature, and hence of the ineffable divine sanctity of our natural bodies, not only in all the compass of their appetites and passions, but down even to their literal flesh and bones—teaches me to look upon the church's heartiest malison as God's heartiest benison, inasmuch as whatsoever is most highly esteemed among men—namely, that private or personal righteousness in man, of which the church is the special protagonist and voucher—is abomination to God. The church maintains a jealous profession of the divinity of Christ, and fills the earth with the most artfully reiterate and melodious invocation of his name; but when it comes practically to interpret this divinity, and apply it to men's living needs, the result turns out a contemptible quackery, inasmuch as this alleged union of the divine and human natures endows us helpless partakers of the latter nature with no privilege towards God, but leaves us, unless we are consecrated by some absurd ecclesiastical usage, as far off from the sheltering divine arms, as any worshipper of Jupiter or the Syrian Astarte. Revelation, on the contrary, teaches me that Christ's divinity is an utterly insane pretension, in so far as it implies any personal antagonism on his part with the rest of mankind, or claims to have been exerted on his own proper behalf, and not on behalf exclusively of universal man, good and evil, wise and simple, clean and unclean. In other words, spiritual christianity means the complete secularization of the divine name, or its identification henceforth only with man's common or natural want, that want in which all men are absolutely one, and its con- sequent utter estrangement from the sphere of his private or personal ful- ness, in which every man is consciously divided from his neighbor: so that I may never aspire to the divine favor, and scarcely to the divine tolerance, save in my social or redeemed natural aspect; i. e. as I stand morally iden- tified with the vast community of men of whatever race or religion, culti- vating no consciousness of antagonist interests to any other man, but on the contrary frankly disowning every personal hope towards God which does not flow exclusively from his redemption of human nature, or is not based purely and simply upon his indiscriminate love to the race.

Such, as I have been able to apprehend it, is the intellectual secret of Swedenborg; such the calm, translucent depths of meaning that underlie the tormented surface of explication he puts upon the spiritual sense of scripture. In spite of my reverence for the christian letter, perhaps to a great extent because of it, I had never enjoyed the least rational insight into the principles of the world's spiritual administration, until I encountered this naïve, uncouth, and unexampled literature, and caught therein, as I say, my first clear glimpse of the vast intellectual wealth stored up in its new philosophy of nature, or its doctrine of the divine *natural* humanity. The obvious disqualification of my intellect, no doubt, spiritually viewed, lay in my habitually identifying nature, to my own thought, with the created rather than the creative personality. That is to say, inasmuch as the creature to my sensuous imagination appeared to exist absolutely or in himself, and not exclusively in and by the creator, I could not logically help making him responsible for his nature, or whatsoever is legitimately involved in himself. By the *nature* of a thing we mean whatsoever the thing is in itself, and apart from foreign interference; and so long consequently as we ascribe real and not mere phenomenal personality or character to the creature, we cannot possibly help saddling him with the responsibility of his own nature. The only way to evade this necessity is to deny him all real, and allow him a purely phenomenal, existence, by making his actual life or being to inhere, not in himself, but exclusively in his creator. But who, before Swedenborg, ever dreamt of such a thing? The moral pretension in existence has always been regarded outside of the church as altogether absolute and unquestionable; and inside the church no machinery exists for its confutation or exhaustion, but the two initiatory rites of Baptism and the Lord's Supper, upon which alone the church was founded: the one rite inferring its subject's complete purgation from any amount of moral defilement his conscience may have contracted, the other his consequent free impletion with any amount of spiritual divine good.

No more than any one else, however, had I compassed the least spiritual apprehension of the church, or divined save in the dimmest manner the endless philosophic substance wrapped up in its two constitutive ordinances. Thus, although I rendered faultless ceremonial homage in my soul to the supreme lordship of Christ (as traditional God-man, or God in our nature), I yet all the while had no distinct conception that the divinity thus ascribed to him implied any really creative or comprehensive relation on his part to our immortal destiny. In fact I utterly ignored his pretension to constitute an utterly new and final—because spiritual—divine advent upon earth, nor ever for a moment therefore supposed it to be pregnant with hostility and disaster to all that our natural understanding has been wont to conceive of under the name of God, and our natural heart has been wont dramatically to worship under that specious and grandiose appellation.

Along with the entire christian world, on the contrary, I always conceived of Christ's divinity as an eminently personal and restrictive one, based upon his conceded moral superiority to all mankind, whereas in truth it is a purely spiritual or impersonal one, based upon his actual and undisguised moral inferiority to the lowest rubbish of human kind that faithfully dogged his footsteps, and hung enchanted upon his lips.

The world has had gods many and lords many, but they are one and all eternally superseded and set at naught by the christian revelation of the divine name as being essentially inimical and repugnant to the moral hypothesis of creation, or the existence of any personal relations between the soul and God. It is true that the christian church has never been just to the idea of its founder, has been indeed anything but just to the altogether spiritual doctrine of the divine name he confided to it. From the day of the apostle John's decease down to that of our modern transcendentalism, a midnight darkness has rested upon the human mind in regard to spiritual things—a darkness so palpable at last, so utterly unrelieved by any feeblest starshine of faith or knowledge, that a church has recently set itself up among us which claims to be nothing if not spiritual, and yet, forsooth, excludes Christ from a primacy in its regard, because it can get no conclusive proof of his having been *morally* or *personally* superior to certain other great men, of whom history preserves a memorial! This indeed has been the animus of the church throughout history, to naturalize rather than spiritualize,—to moralize rather than humanize,—the creative name, by identifying it with certain personal interests in humanity rather than those of universal man; by showing it instinct in short with a sectarian or selfish rather than a social or loving temper. It could not possibly have done otherwise in fact, without violating its function as a literal or a ritual economy, which has always been to represent or embody in itself the instincts of the purely natural mind, of the strictly unregenerate heart, towards God.

The church has thus spiritually or unconsciously crucified the divine name, while intending literally or consciously to hallow it. For no man by nature has any other idea of God than that of an almighty and irresponsible being creating all things—not out of his own infinite love and wisdom yearning to communicate their own potencies and felicities to whatsoever is simply not themselves—but out of stark and veritable naught, and merely to subserve his own personal pleasure, his own selfish and vainglorious renown. The conception we naturally cherish of God in his creative aspect is that of an unprincipled but omnipotent conjuror or magician, who is able to create things—i. e. to make them *be* absolutely or in themselves, and irrespectively of other things—by simply willing them to be; and to unmake them therefore, if they do not happen to suit his whim, just as jauntily as he has made them. Now there is no such unprincipled and almighty power as this, nor any semblance of such a power, on the hither side of hell. And the church, accordingly, by massing or embodying in its own distinctive formulas this superstition of the carnal heart, and affording it a *quasi* divine authentication, only succeeds in furnishing the creative spirit in our nature the very imprisonment or appropriation it needs—the identical crucifixion or assimilation it demands—in order finally to transfuse our natural veins with the blood of its own resurgent and incorruptible life. But in spite of all this—in spite of the church's owning only a negative worth, only a representative sanctity—we cannot too gratefully appreciate its proper historic use, which has been to induct the common mind into a gladsome recognition of God's NATURAL HUMANITY, by gradually disgusting or fatiguing it with the conception of an abstract—i. e. an idle, unemployed, or unrelated—divine force in the world.

Deism, as a philosophic doctrine, enjoys only a starveling existence. To be sure, nothing is more congruous with the uncultivated instincts of the heart, than the conception of a self-involved or self-contained deity,—a deity who is essentially sufficient unto himself, and who is therefore a standing discredit, reproach, and menace to whatsoever is not himself. For we who are by nature finite and relative can contrive no other way of honoring God than by making him intensely opposite to ourselves, or projecting him in imagination as far as possible from our personal limitations, from our own finite experience. We do not hesitate to attribute simple or absolute—which is sheerly idiotic—existence to him, an existence-in-himself, or before the world was, and utterly irrelative to his creature; we endow him with all manner of passive personal perfection, such as infinitude of space and eternity of time; and by way of conclusively establishing his subjection to nature, while at the same time avouching his personal superiority to ourselves, we call him omniscient, omnipresent, and omnipotent, or suppose him literally cognizant of every event in time, literally present in every inch of space, and literally doing whatsoever he pleases, while we do only what we can. No doubt this proceeding is none the less useful for being inevitable on our part. No doubt we thus adequately objectify the divine being to our regard, or get him into conditions at once of such generic nearness to us, and at the same time of such specific remoteness, as to constitute a very fair basis of evolution to any subsequent spiritual intercourse which may take place between us. But this is the sole justification we can allege of the devout natural habit in question. For God has really no absolute but only a relative perfection, no passive but a purely active infinitude. His perfection is no way literal, but a strictly spiritual or creative one, being entirely inseparable save in thought from the work of his hands; his infinitude a wholly actual or living one, standing in his free communication, or spontaneous abandonment, of himself to whatsoever is not himself. He has in truth no absolute or personal and passive worth, such as we ourselves covet under the name of virtue; no claim upon our regard but a working claim; a claim founded not upon what he is in himself, but upon what he is relatively to others. Our native ignorance of divine things to be sure is so dense, that we cannot help according him a blind and superstitious worship for what he presumably is before creation, or in-himself and out of relation to all other existence. But this nevertheless is sheer stupidity on our part. His sole real claim to the heart's allegiance lies in the excellency of his creative and redemptive name. That is to say, it consists, first, in his so freely subjecting himself to us in all the compass of our creaturely destitution and impotence, as to endow us with physical and moral consciousness, or permit us to feel ourselves absolutely to be; and then, secondly, in his becoming by virtue of such subjection so apparently and exclusively objective to us—so much the sole or controlling aim of our spiritual destiny —as to be able to mould our finite or subjective consciousness at his pleasure, inflaming it finally to such a pitch of sensible alienation from—or felt *otherness* to—both him and our kind, as to make us inwardly loathe ourselves, and give ourselves no rest until we put on the lineaments of an infinite or perfect man, in attaining to the proportions of a regenerate society, fellowship, brotherhood of all mankind.

Social and Political Writings

4

SOCIALISM AND CIVILIZATION

During the early part of his career, in the late
eighteen forties and fifties, James gave considerable
thought to the social and political implications of his
ideas. This was owing chiefly to the temper of the
times, being the era of the Brook Farm experiment, the
Harbinger magazine, increased abolitionist agitation,
and a host of other reform activities. The air was thick
with social proposals of one kind or another, and
political consciousness of a noticeably idealistic cast
was very high. The ideas of Robert Owen, Charles
Fourier, and St. Simon enjoyed widespread currency
among many intellectuals, and lecture societies and
literary clubs devoted to their discussion and
dissemination were plentiful and influential.

Oddly enough, James was particularly anxious about
delivering the address which follows. In a letter to
Emerson, who had arranged the invitation for him to
speak at Boston's Town and Country Club on
November 1, 1849, James expressed concern that his
topic, a discussion of socialism "from the highest point
of view," might prove offensive to his audience. His
intention was to argue in favor of socialism and against
civilization, as he defined them, on the grounds that
from his point of view the one rendered unconscious
service to the divine life in man whereas the other did
not; but he suspected that the very word *socialism*
constituted "a stench in the nostrils of all the devout
and honourable." Yet James's apprehension was not
unmixed with a little of his characteristic contempt for
this kind of occasion. As he stated with typical candor
a few lines later, "There is nothing I dread so much as
literary men, especially *our* literary men. Catch them
out of the range of mere personal gossip about authors
and books, and ask them for honest sympathy with
your sentiment or an honest repugnancy of it, and you
will find the company of stage-drivers sweeter and
more comforting to your soul."

The lecture which follows was originally entitled "Socialism and Civilization in Relation to the Development of the Individual Life" and is reprinted from *Moralism and Christianity* (New York, 1850), 39–42, 61–67, 80-94.

———•-•-•-———

Gentlemen:

I propose to discuss the relative bearing of Socialism and Civilization on human destiny, or the development of the individual life.

By Socialism, I mean not any special system of social organization, like that of Fourier, Owen, or St. Simon,[1] but what is common to all these systems, namely, the idea of a perfect fellowship or society among men. And by Civilization, of course, I mean the present political constitution of the nations. Between the fundamental idea of Socialism, which affirms the possibility of a perfect life on earth, or the insubjection of man both to nature and his fellow-man, and the fundamental idea of Civilization, which affirms the perpetual imperfection of human life, or the permanent subjection of man to nature and society, a great discrepancy exists; and I hope to interest my audience in a brief examination of its features. I am sure you cannot bestow your spontaneous attention upon the subject without the greatest advantage.

The differences of detail which characterize the systems of St. Simon, Owen, Fourier, and other societary reformers, are of very little present account to us. What is of great present account is the signal agreement of these men in point of principle. They agree in holding our present social condition to be not only vicious, which every one will admit, but also stupid, which is not so universally obvious. They declare that it is entirely competent to us at any time to organize relations of profound and enduring harmony among men, and thus to banish crime, vice, and suffering from the earth; and that nothing but an ignorance of the true principles of human nature stands between us and this most desirable consummation. Crime, vice and suffering, they allege, are not essential to human society, but are merely incidental to its infancy or nonage, and are sure to disappear before the advancing wisdom of its majority. Thus the socialist maintains the inherent righteousness of humanity, and resolves all its disorders into imperfect science.

Here, then, we have the fundamental difference between Socialism and Civilization. The socialist affirms the inherent righteousness of humanity, affirms that man is sufficient unto himself, and needs no outward ordinances for his guidance, save during his minority. The conservative, on the other hand, or the advocate of the present, affirms the inherent depravity of man, affirms that he is insufficient unto himself, and requires the dominion of tutors and governors all his appointed days upon the earth. This accordingly is the quarrel which has first to be settled–the quarrel between Socialism and Civilization, before men will care in any considerable numbers to balance the claims of rival socialists. Let it first of all be made plain to us that Socialism is true in idea, is true as against Civilization; then we shall willingly enough discuss the relative superiority of St. Simon to Owen, or of Fourier to both.

How then shall this grand preliminary quarrel be settled? Of course, historically or actually, it will be settled only by the march of events. But how shall it be settled meanwhile, intellectually, or to your and my individual satisfaction? Each of us, doubtless, will judge it in the light of his own ideas and aspirations. If, for example, Socialism appear to promise better things than Civilization to the highest life of man, we cannot fail, of course, to bid it God-speed, and predict its speedy triumph. If the reverse judgment should ensue, we shall, equally of course, execrate it, and leave it to the contempt of mankind. . . .

I have no hesitation in affirming, that society, as at present, or rather as heretofore, constituted, arrays the lower interest in conflict with the higher, and debases man into subject slavery to itself. Society affords no succor to the divine life in man. Any culture we can give to that life, is owing not to society, but to our fortunate independence of it. For the incessant action of society is to shut up all my time and thought to the interests of my mere visible existence, to the necessity of providing subsistence, education, and social respect for myself and my children. To these narrow limits society confines all my passion, all my intellect, all my activity; and so far denies me self-development. My true or divine selfhood is completely swamped in transient frivolous cares. Indeed so rigorous is our social tyranny, so complete a servitude does society impose upon the individual, that we have almost lost the tradition of our essential freedom, and scarcely one in a million believes that he has any individuality or sacredness apart from his natural and social ties. He who constitutes our private and distinctive individuality, He who ceaselessly pants to become avouched and appropriated to every man as his nearest and most inseparable self, is for the most part banished from the glowing heart of humanity, into frigid and extramundane isolation, so that we actually seem to have no life above the natural and social spheres.

But this appearance is fallacious. It is a correspondence of that fallacy of the senses which makes the earth central, and the heavens circumferential. I will not deny that the most genial relations bind God and my body, bind God and my neighbor; but I will deny *totis viribus* ["vigorously": literally, "with all my might"] that either my body or my neighbor forms the true point of contact between God and me. He is infinitely nearer to me than my own body; infinitely nearer to me also than my neighbor. In short He is with me not only finitely but infinitely, not only by the medium of the physical and moral life, but also in my spontaneous attractions and tendencies. Here pre-eminently do I find God. Here alone do I behold the infinite Beauty. Here alone do I perfectly lose myself and perfectly find myself. Here alone, in short, do I feel empowered to say, what every true creature of God is bound to say: I and my father are one.

I repeat that the whole strain of society is adverse to this spontaneous and divine life in man. It relegates his whole energy to the service of his physical and moral interest, that is to its own direct advantage, and beyond this point takes no cognizance of him. It utterly ignores his proper, God-given, and aesthetic life, the life whose supreme law is the good pleasure of the subject; or recognises it only to profane and corrupt it. It is melancholy to see the crawling thing which society christens Art, and feeds into fawning sycophancy. It has no other conception of Art than as polished labor, labor stripped of its jacket and apron, and put into parlor costume. The Artist is merely the aboriginal ditcher refined into the painter, poet, or sculptor. Art is not the gush of God's life into every form of spontaneous speech and act; it is the talent of successfully imitating nature—the trick of a good eye, a good ear, or a good hand. It is not a really infinite life, consubstantiate with the subject and lifting him into ever new and unpremeditated powers and achievements; it is an accomplishment, a grace to be learned, and to be put off and on at one's convenience.

Accordingly society establishes academies of Art, gives out rules for its prosecution, and issues diplomas to the Artist, by which he may be visibly discriminated from ordinary people. But always on this condition, that he hallow, by every work of his hands, its existing prejudices and traditions; that he devote his perfectly docile genius to the consecration of its morality. If he would be truly its child, let him confine himself to the safe paths of portraiture and bust making, to the reproduction of the reigning sanctities in church and state, their exemplary consorts and interesting families. By this door many of our aspiring "artists" have entered the best society. But if the disciple be skittish, and insist on "sowing the wild oats" of his genius, let him, at most, boldly allegorize the Calvinistic divinity or the Unitarian morality into Voyages of Life and similar contrivances, or dash off ineffectual brigands and Magdalens that should find no forgiveness in this world or the next. But these things are trivial. If society did no greater harm to God's life in man than to misconceive the nature and misapply the name of Art, it would be foolish to complain. But the evil it does is positive and profound, and justifies a perfectly remorseless criticism.

For the true complaint against society is not the little it does actually to promote the divine life in man, but the much it does actually to hinder that life by giving him a conscience of sin against God, and so falsifying the true relation between them. If I fail in my allegiance to society, if I violate any of its enactments, in forcibly taking, for example, the property of my neighbor, society is not thereupon content to visit me with the penalty provided for the case: it has the hardihood also to proclaim me a sinner against God, and threaten me with His wrath. Society has the presumption to identify its own will with the will of God. It assumes that whatsoever it declares to be property, or to belong to A., B. and C., is also viewed as such property, or as so belonging, on the part of God; and that hence in violating this property I offend God no less than itself. Certainly it is contrary to the divine will that any man should violate his neighbor's property. We may say that such a thing is *absolutely* contrary to the divine will, and cannot therefore be done. It would be an aspersion of the divine power to say that He gave me a property which any other man had power to take away from me. Or it would be an aspersion of His goodness to suppose Him giving me a certain property, and at the same time giving another power to deprive me of it. The whole conception of a man really sinning against God is intolerably puerile.

The error of society herein lies in its giving man what Swedenborg calls a *false proprium*, that is a property which God does not give him. Society does all it can to finite man, to include or shut up his proprium, his selfhood, within itself, and so render him its abject vassal or dependent. The more external property it gives him, the more houses, lands, flocks, and perishable goods of all sorts, the more it finites him and renders him dependent on itself. For society alone confers and guarantees this property. Abstract the protection of society, and no man could keep it a day. God, on the contrary, seeks incessantly to aggrandize His child, and render him *in-finite*. He strives to insinuate a proprium, which shall lift him above all outward limitation. He makes Himself over to him in an inward and invisible way, and so endows him with a property both incorruptible and inviolable, which no moth can corrupt, and no thief break through and steal. . . .

If the evils I have described be real, if civilization be fraught with these and all other forms of hindrance to the divine life, then clearly civilization stands condemned by its fruits, and has no title to prejudice the promise of Socialism. Socialism claims to be nothing more than a remedy for the physical and moral ills which inhere in civilization, which result from its very genius. The whole promise of Socialism may be thus summed up.—It promises to lift man out of the harassing bondage which he is under to nature and society, out of that crushing responsibility which he is under to his own body and his fellow-man, and so leave him subject forever to God's unimpeded inspiration, leave him, in fact, the very play-thing of God, a mere pipe for the finger of Deity to play what stops it pleases. It proceeds upon a double postulate, namely, that every creature of God, by virtue of his creation, is entitled, 1, to an ample physical subsistence, that is, to the satisfaction of all his natural appetites; 2, to an ample social subsistence, that is, to the respect and affection of every other creature of God. Whatever institution violates these principles by nonconformity, it pronounces tyrannous and void.

Thus Socialism condemns, after a certain stage of human progress, the institution of limited property. It demands for man an infinite property, that is to say a property in universal nature and in all the affections and thoughts of humanity. It is silly to charge it with a tendency to destroy property. It aims indeed to destroy all merely limited and conventional property, all such property as is held not by any inward fitness of the subject, but merely by external police or convention; but it aims to destroy even this property only in the pacific way of superseding it, that is, by giving the subject possession of the whole earth, or a property commensurate with his inward and essential infinitude.

This, I confess, is what attracts me in the programme of Socialism, the unconscious service it renders to the divine life in me, the complete inauguration and fulfilment it affords to the Christian hope of individual perfection. Christianity is a virtual denial of all mystery to Deity, and an affirmation of His essential intelligibility. It denies to Deity any mere passive or inoperative perfection, and affirms His existence exclusively within human conditions. It reveals a perfect harmony between God in His infinitude and man in his lowest natural and social debasement, even when devoid of all physical grace and comeliness, and when despised, cast out, and rejected of the best virtue of his time. In short it affirms the unity of God and Man. Two things hinder the consciousness of this unity on the part of man—nature and society, the one by limiting his power, the other by limiting his sympathies; the one by finiting his body, the other by finiting his soul. Accordingly, the Christ, or representative Divine Man, is seen warring with and subjugating both nature and society, making time and space so fluent and plastic to his desires as to avouch his actual bodily infinitude, and exerting so wholly genial an influence upon the opposite extremes of society—saint and sinner, Jew and Gentile,—as to avouch his equal spiritual infinitude.

Now what is here typically reported of the Christ is to be actually fulfilled in universal humanity, in every man, according to the promise, "What things ye see me do, ye shall do also, and greater things than these." Nature and society are to be glorified into the footstool of Almighty God, enshrined in every human bosom. I have no idea that man will ever be able literally to change water into wine, or to feed his body upon inadequate food, or to pass through stone walls at pleasure, or to satisfy the tax-gatherer out of the mouth of fishes. But I believe that the various internal reality of these symbols will be fully accomplished in us, that nature and society will become in the progress of science so vivid with divine meaning, that the infinite desire of man will receive a complete *present* satisfaction, and that instead of our relegating the vision of God, as now, to an exclusively *post-mortem* experience, He will become revealed to the natural senses with such an emphasis as to make the most frolicsome sports of childhood more worshipful than all piety.

Now Socialism alone supplies the science of this great consummation. It reveals the incessant operation of laws by which man's physical and social relations will be brought into the complete subjection of his inward or divine personality. It is the demonstration of a plenary unity between man and nature and man and man. It convinces me of infinitely more extended relations to nature than those which now define me, and of infinitely sweeter ties with man than those which bind me to the Tom, Dick and Harry of my present chance acquaintanceship.

Let this unity then become visible, become organized, and I shall instantly realize the divine freedom, realize my true and infinite selfhood. For then I shall become released from this finite and false *proprium* which now enslaves me and keeps me grovelling in the dust. If I am one with nature and my fellow-man, if there be a sovereign unity and not enmity pervading all our reciprocal relations, then clearly every appetite and affection both of my physical and moral nature become instantly legitimated, and I stand henceforth absolved from all defilement, a new creature of God triumphant over death and hell, nay more, taking death and hell into friendly subjection, and suffusing their hitherto dusk and dejected visages with the roseate flush of omnipresent and omnipotent Life.

I repeat that the curse of our present ties, that which eliminates all their poetry, is our limited property in men and things, is the finite selfhood imposed on us by the present evil world. My internal property or selfhood, that which God gives me, is nothing short of infinite, is Himself in truth. To match this divine internal, nature gives me my feeble body, society gives me a petty score of relatives and friends. Whilst I accept this niggardly service from nature and society, whilst I strive to compel my internal aspirations within these outward bounds, I suffer torments which are appeased only to be renewed. This body is incompetent to the subjugation of nature which my spirit demands. I may battle stoutly for a while, but I accomplish after all only a grave. But suppose the battle to have been never so successful in a material point of view, suppose me to have realized any amount of superfluous potatoes, yet after all how mere a potato-cask do I remain, destitute of inward pith and riches! The battle with nature, the battle for animal subsistence, leaves us merely animal, leaves us actually unvivified of God, leaves us only the dimmest and most fluctuating hope of God in realms beyond the grave.

But society imposes the most torturing disability. Affiliating me to one man, and that man incapable seven times out of eight of supplying my bare necessities; restricting me to the fraternity of two or three persons whom probably the penury of our joint resources converts into mutual rivals and foes; committing my profoundest passional interests to the keeping of one frail will; turning the most sacred depths of passion within me into an arena of public traffic, into material of habitual and vulgar gossip; society does its utmost to ensure me a daily profanation, and turn God's otherwise joyful force in me into the force of a giant despair, into the force of an eventual deadly retribution.

Let any one consider for a moment the best endowment he gets from present society, or the extent of limitation it imposes upon him, and then reply whether it can be long tolerable to God.

In the first place, we have the tie of the insulated family, which enjoins a superior affection to all involved in it than to any others. Let my father's interests clash with his neighbors; let my mother and the mother of any body else, come into rivalry; let my brother or sister conceive a quarrel with any unrelated person: you know that in all these cases I am a natural partisan, and that if I should practically disown the obligation, that blissful home which furnishes the theme of so much sincere as well as dishonest sentimentality, would become on the instant a very hell incapable of pacification. Conduct so unnatural on my part, no matter how just it might be in the abstract, would convert these natural brethern into my envenomed foes, and even disqualify me for any very cordial welcome from their original antagonist, the person for whose cause I had forsaken theirs. Take the tie of township or country, that which generates the old-fashioned virtue called patriotism, and you see it to be full of the same iniquitous bondage.

In fact there exists no tie either natural or social, as society is now constituted, which does not tend to slavery, which does not cheat man's soul of its fair proportions. I love my father and mother, my brother and sister, but I deny their unconditional property in me. Society having been incompetent hitherto to fulfill its duties to me, has deputed the care and sustenance of my tender years to them. I acknowledge gratefully the kindness I have received at their hands. But if they ask any other reward for this kindness than the satisfaction of seeing me a man, if they expect me to continue their humble satellite and partisan, instead of God's conscript and votary solely, I am bound to disappoint them. I will be the property of no person, and I will accept property in no person. I will be the son of my father, and the husband of my wife, and the parent of my child, but I will be all these things in a thoroughly divine way, or only as they involve no no obloquy to my inward righteousness, only as they impose no injustice on me toward others.

You all remember those grand mystic sayings of the Christ, "whoso will lose his life in this world shall keep it unto life eternal," and "whoso will leave father or mother, or brother or sister, or wife or child, for my sake, shall find all these relations multiplied a hundredfold." Now what is the great spiritual burden of these divine words, for you know every divine word is so mainly from within. Is it not that our primary dignity is divine, and flows from God within us instead of from our outward relations? Is it not that each of us is under paramount allegiance to his own spontaneous life, and that if we insist first on the fulfillment of this allegiance, all these secondary or derivative relations will fall of themselves into harmony?

But you know this truth experimentally also. You know that you never find perfect peace or contentment in your outward and finite *proprium.* You know by experience that you cannot set your life's happiness upon any outward possession, be it wife or child, or riches, without an incessant and shuddering dread of betrayal. The infinite faculty within you steadfastly refuses these limited satisfactions. But when you rejoice first of all in that infinite faculty, when you seek above all things to give it development by the medium of appropriate action, by the medium of Art, then the house of your peace is built upon a rock, against which the windows of heaven are opened in vain. Let a man then renounce all enforced property in persons and things, accepting only such things and persons as actually gravitate to him; let him renounce all tale-bearing and recourse to the police, and come into universal candor, into complete whiteness of soul towards all men and things, how instantly would every heart expand to him as to God's melting sunshine, and the earth swarm with fragrant kisses for his feet!

To become possible, however, in any great degree for the individual man, this quality of manhood must first become universal, and to make it universal is the function of Socialism, is the aim of social science. Socialism lifts us out of these frivolous and pottering responsibilities we are under to man, and leaves us under responsibility to God alone, or our inmost life. The way it does this, is by revealing the existence and operation of laws, which shall provide every man, woman, and child, the orderly and ample satisfaction of their natural appetites and affections, the unlimited expansion of their intellect, and the complete education of their faculty of action, however infinitely various that faculty may be. In short it reveals the method of man's perpetual re-creation, a re-creation so complete that every day shall come clad to him with all the freshness of God's dewy hand, stifling both memory and hope in the amplitude of a present bliss. Suppose Socialism then to have attained its end, suppose the Divine Life to have become by its means universalized, what a temple of enchantment this lacerated earth would become! For when all things and persons become free, become self-pronounced, then a universal reverence and truth spring up, every manifestation of character claiming and enjoying the homage we now pay only to unmanifested Deity.

Besides we degrade and disesteem whatsoever we absolutely own. We degrade by owning and just in the degree of our owning. It is a proverb, that no man values the good he has in hand, but only that which is to come. This is signally true in respect to persons. We degrade and disesteem every person we own absolutely, every person bound to us by any other tenure than his own spontaneous affection. Of course one values one's brothers and sisters in the present state of things, if from nothing else, then from self-love, for society is so unfriendly and torpid to us that the domestic hearth gathers a warmth not wholly its own. But who is ever found idealizing a brother or sister? Our instinct of Friendship is profaned where a brother is the claimant, and Love expires of sheer self-loathing in the presence of a sister.

It is the indispensable condition of a perfect respect, that a person be inwardly individualized, that is, possess the complete supremacy of his own actions. Then all his relations are of an inevitable dignity. When the wife of Quisquis declined his merely dutiful or voluntary allegiance, when she insisted upon erasing the marriage-bond as a stain upon his truth, and giving to their relation the sole sanction of spontaneity, her husband found that relation instantly glorified, or purged of its abundant meanness. His home became henceforth a livelier sanctuary than the church, and his wife a diviner page than all the prophets. So also one's child, how tiresome he grows when he does nothing morning, noon or night, but reflect the paternal dullness, when he is sedulous to do all the father prescribes and avoid all the mother condemns! Yet how beautiful he becomes, when he ever and anon flashes forth some spontaneous grace, some self-prompted courtesy!

Why is it esteemed disgraceful for the mature man to consult his natural father and mother in every enterprise, and be led by their advice? The cause of this judgment is spiritual, and lies in the truth that man is destined by the fact of his divine genesis to self-sufficiency, to self-government, that he is destined to find all guidance within him and none whatever without him, and that he cannot persist accordingly in the infantile habit of seeking help beyond himself without flagrant detriment to his manhood, to his destiny. All our natural and social phenomena, in fact, are symbolic, and have no worth apart from the spiritual verities they embalm and typify.

To conclude, Socialism promises to make God's great life in man possible, promises to make all our relations so just, so beautiful and helpful, that we shall be no longer conscious of finiteness, of imperfection, but only of life and power utterly infinite. I am not able to satisfy any one's reasonable curiosity on this subject. Every one who trusts in a living and therefore active God, in that God who is quite as active and original in our day as He was six thousand years ago, in short every one whose hope for humanity is alert, behooves to acquaint himself forthwith with the marvellous literature of Socialism, above all with the writings of CHARLES FOURIER. You will doubtless find in Fourier things of an apostolic hardness to the understanding; you will find many things to startle, many things perhaps to disgust you; but you will find vastly more both in the way of criticism and of constructive science to satisfy and invigorate your understanding, while such glimpses will open on every hand of God's ravishing harmonies yet to ensue on earth, that your imagination will fairly ache with contentment, and plead to be let off.

These are what you will find in Fourier, provided you have no secret interest dogging your candor and watching to betray it. Let me also tell you what you will *not* find there. You will find no such defaming thought of God as makes His glory to depend upon the antagonism of His creature's shame. You will find no allegation of an essential and eternal contrariety between man and his creative source. Whatever be Fourier's errors and faults, this crowning and bottomless infamy by no means attaches to him. On the contrary, if the highest homage paid to Deity be that of the understanding, then Fourier's piety may safely claim pre-eminence. For it was not a traditional piety, that piety of habit which keeps our churches open— and cheerless; nor was it a selfish piety, the piety which springs from jail-bird conceptions of Deity, and paints him as a colossal spider bestriding the web of destiny and victimizing with fell alacrity every heedless human fly that gets entangled in it; but a piety as broad as human science, co-extensive in fact with the sphere of his senses, for its prayers were the passions or wants of the universal human heart, its praises the laws or methods of the human understanding, and its deeds the innumerable forms of spontaneous human action.

NOTES

1. James is referring here to Charles Fourier (1772–1837), a French social reformer who proposed the development of a utopian society based on the voluntary association of producers in units he called phalanxes; to Robert Owen (1771–1858), a pioneer in industrial reform and considered the father of English socialism, who finally came to America to test his social and educational theories

by founding an experimental community at New Harmony, Indiana; and to Claude-Henri de Rouvroy, Comte de Saint-Simon (1760–1825), another of the founders of modern socialism who proposed a social system which would abolish inheritance, socialize the means of production, and distribute goods and services on the basis of need and merit rather than privilege.—Editor's note.

5

DEMOCRACY AND ITS USES

James delivered this lecture along with several others ("Property as a Symbol," "The Principle of Universality in Art," "The Old and New Theology," and "The Scientific Accord of Natural and Revealed Religion") in New York City during the winter of 1850–1851 and then published them all in expanded form, together with certain fugitive essays, as *Lectures and Miscellanies* in 1852. In "Democracy and Its Uses" he continues his reflections on the relation between the social order and human destiny, arguing passionately that the function of democracy is largely propaedeutic— "to prepare the way," as he puts it, "by a disorganization of the political life of men, for their perfect society or fellowship." Here, as before, James's political convictions are derived strictly from his religious convictions; the value of the essay is that both sorts of commitment achieve an unusual clarity of expression just because James perceives so vividly the nature of their mutual interpenetration.

This selection is taken from Lecture 1, "Democracy and Its Uses," in *Lectures and Miscellanies* (New York, 1852), 1–28.

———•••———

It is my design to offer a few observations on the genius of Democracy, and the peculiar bearing it exerts upon the destiny of humanity.

Our institutions are Democratic. That is to say, the idea which they more or less incorporate, is the sovereignty of the people. The entire import of this idea may be best gathered from a brief reference to the ideas which have hitherto borne rule in the political earth, and against which Democracy is a protest.

The ideas which under one form or another have hitherto borne rule in the political world, are two, monarchy and aristocracy. Monarchy asserts the right of one person or one family to govern others. Aristocracy asserts the right of one class of persons to govern other classes. Against these two claims, Democracy is a protest. It denies the claim of any one man to govern other men, and the right of any one class to govern other classes. It asserts that the people are rightfully sovereign, and possess the exclusive claim to the governing function.

Thus the Democratic idea exhibits a purely negative development. It is revolutionary, not formative. It is born of denial. It comes into existence in the way of denying established institutions. Its office is rather to destroy the old world, than fully to reveal the new. You have only to fix your thought upon it for a moment, to perceive that is is not directly constructive. Thus it alleges the people's exclusive right to govern themselves. Now, when it speaks of the people, it means the people. It does not mean any special portion of the people, as, for example, a numerical majority in contradistinction to a minority, or the male portion in contradistinction to the female, but the whole people without difference. But now, if you regard the people as a unit, if you regard their polity as expressing their united interests—the interests of the minority as well as of the majority—you instantly perceive that their polity can, in no proper sense of the word, be pronounced governmental, but simply administrative. The government in that case simply utters or carries out the entire will of the people. It has no will but to do the will of the whole people. Consequently, its function is purely ministerial or servile.

Thus the Democratic idea, in affirming the people's sovereignty, does in effect reduce government into a mere public ministry or service. It utterly explodes the old conceptions of government, as having an authority derived from some other source than the people. It is only while imperfectly evolved as in this country, in which not the whole people, but an ill-defined majority, rules, that it tolerates institutions which exhibit some faint remnant of authority. Our institutions do not, as yet, by any means, perfectly incorporate the Democratic idea. They exhibit a far more advanced development of it than has been attained anywhere else, but still fall very far short of giving it perfect expression. The great advantage, as it appears to me, which our position claims, is this: that we publicly recognise the worth of the Democratic idea, and stand committed by our past history, and our present tendencies, to allow it a complete evolution. It cannot be doubted by any attentive observer of our national and state legislation, that the tendency among us, from the beginning, has been to curtail the force of government, to reduce its legislative branches into a complete docility to the popular will, and make the executive branch more and more purely executive. And if this be undeniable, if such be the continual operation of the Democratic idea, you will readily admit that its tendency is to destroy all absolute authority over men, all such authority as is not authenticated by the welfare of the people, and, consequently, to convert our political institutions into social ones.

Now why do I allege these things? Is it from any dissatisfaction with our institutions? Is it with a view to suggest distrust of the Democratic tendency? God forbid! I have no such dissatisfaction or distrust. I see nothing in our future but hope and abundant cheer, and I see these things only as the direct offspring of our unfaltering allegiance to the principle of Democracy. No, I allege them only for the purpose of proving to you what you, perhaps, may not have fairly considered, that Democracy is not so much a new form of political life, as a dissolution or disorganization of the old forms. It is simply a resolution of government into the hands of the people, a taking down of that which has before existed, and a re-commitment of it to its original sources, but is by no means the substitution of anything else in its place. It signalizes the period of puberty in the race, the period which separates the child from the man, a period of dissonance presenting very often a disagreeable commingling of the two extremes. If you recollect, that period in the history of the individual is often extremely unhandsome. The urchin has outgrown the jacket and dickey of infancy, but is still a world too small for the standing collar and long-tailed coat of manhood. His actual powers are small, but his instincts are unlimited. He has the thoughts of boyhood, but he utters them with a voice more hoarse than the adult man's. He has the sentiment of freedom, but he knows no positive or manly methods of demonstrating it. He attempts it chiefly by rudeness towards his progenitors, calls his father the old man, and his mother the old woman, and gives out, on every occasion, a suspicion that they have been over-estimated. He renounces the customs and statutes of the paternal mansion, bullies the servants and his younger brothers, and hastens to involve himself in courses which afflict the older people with the saddest auguries of the future man.

It is so with our own nation, arrived at Democracy. We are greatly more estimable for our criticism than for our performance, for the judgment and execution we have wrought upon vicious forms of government, than for the realization of any final and perfect form for ourselves. We have aroused the people to self-respect, by leading them out from under the burdensome yoke of kings and nobles, but we have not shown them how to be at peace and unity among themselves. We are good by comparison, not by position. When compared with the polities of the Old World, we present the auroral beauty of the morning emerging from the thick night; but the glowing morning does not always ensure an unclouded noon. I see in our present political attainments everything to love and admire, when I contrast them with those of the Old World, because our polity recognises on all its front, the great truth that the *true* ruler of the people, in all time, must be the *servant* of the people. But when I look to see how this truth is practically administered, I confess my enthusiasm somewhat subsides. For the ruler, when closely regarded, turns out to be the servant, not of the whole people, but a majority of them, and I find so eager a rivalry for political supremacy going on among the people, as proves that the interests of the whole are not chiefly studied.

Democracy, then, is still imperfectly embodied even among us. Monarchy asserts the rule of one man; aristocracy the rule of a minority. Our institutions assert the rule of a majority. These latter consequently exhibit a very decided advance upon the old institutions, but are by no means conclusive. They indicate the progress of the democratic idea, but are very far short of giving it a complete expression. If the rule of a majority be valid as against that of a minority, much more must the rule of the whole be valid as against that of a mere majority; and so far, accordingly, our institutions sustain and subserve the sentiment of Democracy. But when the sentiment becomes fully acknowledged, or attracts the universal homage of mankind, it will disown our present political institutions no less than all past ones. It will disown, in fact, all merely *political* forms, and claim a purely social manifestation.

For the Democratic idea, the idea of the people's sovereignty, implies above all things their exemption from arbitrary rule, implies that they recognise no authority which the interests of their own welfare do not confer. And this pretension, you will observe, is directly fatal to all merely political or national existence. Political or national existence is based upon the sacredness or perpetuity of certain institutions. The nation is represented by these institutions, so that if you destroy these latter, you at the same time destroy the nationality they embody. If, for example, you could destroy the institutions of monarchy and nobility in England, and establish republican institutions in their place, you would completely change the existing nationality, the present political life of that country. Or if you should simply remove its existing institutions, without substituting any other, you would utterly destroy its nationality, or reduce it to political nonentity. The people would still exist, of course, but not as a nation cognizable to other nations. Its peculiar institutions alone give it national form, or political unity, and render it intelligible to other nations.

This being the case with every nation, with every form of political life known to the world, it is manifest that the Democratic idea, in affirming the sovereignty of the people, or their responsibility to their own welfare alone, vacates every mode of national or political existence, by vacating the sacredness of the institutions on which such existence is based. In affirming the sovereignty of the people, the Democratic idea denies institutions any intrinsic or absolute sanctity, any sanctity save that which they derive from reflecting the popular well-being. It avouches the sole sacredness of humanity, and allows no sanctity to institutions underived from that source. Thus it has hitherto seemed good to our people to entrust their executive administration to a President, eligible every four years, and their legislative action to the two Houses of Congress. But should the people now deem it good to abolish the Presidency, transferring its functions to the Senate, or to abolish the Senate also, leaving the House of Representatives alone chargeable with the political interests of the country, Democracy would ratify the step, because the institutions in question possess no intrinsic authority, but derive their force wholly from the popular will. Thus Democracy everywhere proclaims the superiority of man to institutions, allowing the latter no respect, however consecrated by past worth, save in so far as they also reflect the present interests of humanity. It allows no usage nor recorded statute whatever, any binding obligation which is underived from the instincts of the universal human heart.

It is clear, then, that the promise we behold in Democracy has not a primary regard to our political destiny. National aggrandizement or glory, which was the aim of the kingdoms of the Old World, is not what we are specially to look for. Our glory is to be an inward, rather than an outward one. Our geographical position and immense territorial resources will, doubtless, secure us a long career of political prosperity. But our political institutions do not, of themselves, inspire enthusiasm and exert no authority. They are felt to be the expression or symbol of something more sacred than themselves, which is the interests of humanity; and they possess, therefore, no absolute sanctity. Every institution descended to us from the past, descends to us upon trial. If it do not secure to us the benefits it secured to its inventors, it possesses no claim to our observance, but must give way to new institutions adapted to the new wants.

The principle of Democracy, which legitimates this result, is enthroned in our polity, and what is more, vivifies the newest affections and thoughts of all people. It is not a conventionality of man. It is an actual tendency of the Divine Providence, felt all along the progress of human history, and marching now in open day to a complete and triumphant evolution. Happy are they, therefore, who no longer think of resisting or impeding it. But, above all, happy are they who betimes joyfully accept it with all the merely political changes it induces, believing that the paternal Wisdom, whose instrument it is, designs only good and no evil from it, and that in lieu of every edifice removed, He will build up another so glorious that the former will never again come into mind.

But now you will reasonably ask me, what positive or constructive results I anticipate from Democracy? You will ask me what *is* the nature of the benefits, if they are not political, which Democracy is going to introduce? The question admits of an easy, and, I cannot doubt, a completely satisfactory reply.

The positive or constructive results, then, which I anticipate from Democracy, are of a moral or social character, rather than political. The benefits which it heralds for humanity, will lie not in the increased external splendor of a nation, but in the increase of just, amicable, and humane relations amongst all its members. In short, I look upon Democracy as heralding the moral perfection of man, as inaugurating the existence of perfectly just relations between man and man, and as consequently preparing the way for the reign of infinite Love.

This hope or confidence in Democracy is justified, you will perceive, by the fundamental meaning of the word. For Democracy means nothing more than the self-government of the people. Now, a capacity of self-government supposes in its subject a wisdom proportioned to his needs, and Democracy, therefore, implicitly attributes such wisdom to humanity. It supposes that men are capable of so adjusting their relations to each other, as that they will need no police or external force to control them, but will spontaneously do the right thing in all places and at all times. Thus Democracy really does contemplate a time when all coercion and restraint shall be disused in the conduct of human affairs, and when, consequently, every man will *freely* do unto others as he would have others to do unto him.

It is precisely here that we discern the difference between the Old World and the New, and perceive how Democracy silently prepares a new triumph for humanity. The fundamental conviction of the Old World—the conviction which lay at the bottom of all its stringent theories of government—was a distrust of humanity. This distrust was doubtless justifiable, because humanity had not yet fully manifested itself, nor proved the righteousness of its instincts. The immense mass of mankind was enslaved both physically and intellectually, and the fruits of slavery, in either sphere, are not such as reflect credit upon humanity. Human nature was thus unfairly dealt with, being asked to bring forth the fruits of freedom while it was itself in bondage, and being condemned because it did not obey the absurd requisition. Yet men do not plant a peach tree in the rock, and then ask it to bring forth its proper fruit. They place it in a congenial soil, and amidst favorable skiey influences, and so leave it to justify itself.

But times have changed since these conceptions of humanity were begotten. The mass of mankind has been gradually working upwards into comparative freedom, and silently enforcing a profound modification of the old judgments. This has been the case all over the world; but in this country the moral lesson accruing from the changed condition of the masses, is especially irresistible. The great lesson which this country teaches, has not been set forth, it seems to me, with that distinctness which it claims. Our true glory, in my opinion, is not that we enjoy, by means of our institutions, an unequalled material prosperity. It is that we, being our own rulers, having no government but one of our own creation, with no army to overawe us, have yet exhibited in all things the most orderly tendencies, and so refuted forever the old despotic theories of the essential corruption of human nature.

This lesson can never be gainsaid. When you tell me of the ineradicable evil of human nature, I point you to these United States for an illustration on the largest scale of its uncontrolled tendencies. Here you will doubtless see individual corruption and disorder as well as elsewhere, because society here, as well as elsewhere, is not scientifically adjusted by the reconciliation of the private and public interests of its members. But you will not see, in the associated action of the people at large, any of that wilfulness, disorderliness, and ferocity which the theories in question charge upon humanity when left to itself. You find, on the contrary, a general urbanity and fellow-feeling, a proverbial deference for the female sex, enlarged sympathy for the distressed and destitute, ample provision for the interests of science and education, a lively enthusiasm for the progress of the arts, a boundless hope in the future, and a complete acquiescence in the power of peaceful legislation.

This it is which constitutes the primary claim of these United States to the reverence of the world, that they have thus far vindicated humanity from the charge of essential depravity. It is indeed a grateful recollection, when one is in foreign countries, amidst the enormous machinery there at work to keep the people in what is called order, to remember that in his own country this machinery scarcely exists at all, and, where it does exist, possesses no tenure apart from the popular will. But even then the grand charm of the recollection is the gratification it offers to an enlarged humanitary sentiment, rather than a shallow and conceited patriotism; for no one is foolish enough to suppose that American human nature differs radically from European, or that the people will not one day justify themselves on the one continent as fully as they are now doing on the other.

It may very well be that some of my hearers have not fully considered the moral bearings of Democracy, and are not prepared therefore to yield a perfect assent to my claims for it in that behalf. I would like accordingly to occupy the remainder of this lecture with a fuller elucidation of that point. First of all, let me re-state my exact position.

I say, then, that the inevitable result of the Democratic tendency will be such an improvement of the moral or social relations of men, as will completely obviate the necessity of coercive institutions, or exhaust the function of a restrictive police.

The powers that be are ordained of God. That is to say, government represents the unitary interests of society, those interests which are paramount to every other. Every governmental institution has been a standing testimony to the harmonic destiny of society, a standing proof that the life of man is destined for peace and amity, instead of disorder and contention. No one can doubt that such has been the origin and meaning of government among mankind. No one can doubt that if human life had been perfect in the infancy of the race, that is to say, if just social relations had existed from the beginning, government would never have been thought of as a necessity of human society. Its existence is simply a confession of the *immaturity* of society. Because the true fellowship of man with man is imperfectly realized, therefore the magistrate is bound to bear the rod, symbol of that sovereign unity before which all private differences are bound to disappear.

Now, if government could have rightly discerned its function from the beginning, and remained true to it, by continually expanding as the wants of society demanded its expansion, men could never have quarrelled with it. But government, in the infancy of human culture, could, of course, entertain only the narrowest conceptions of its real function. It indeed claimed a personality at that time quite distinct from its function, and identified its interests with certain families and classes of the people, instead of the entire mass. Hence the efforts which are making at this day in the Old World, to overthrow established governments, and remit royal families into the shade of private life. It is very idle to expect any but a successful issue to these attempts. They may fail for a while, but in the long run they must succeed, because governments are merely the instruments or lieutenants of humanity, and are therefore essentially responsible to it. They are liable to be summoned to their audit at any moment, and if any chronic infidelity to their trust be found attaching to them, they are sure to be cashiered.

This identification of human interests with certain personal interests, is the plague of man in every sphere. It involves a certain practical atheism, and so contradicts the deepest instincts of the heart. How absurd the idea that the universal Father cares one whit more for Queen Victoria, personally, than he does for the scullion who removes the ashes from her grate! It is her function only which is divine. It is her glory to sit in the seat she does, at the head of her glorious people. That seat confers upon her all the honor she enjoys, and receives not one particle from her. If, then, she claim any personal superiority to other men, any consideration apart from the humanitary function she wields, she puts herself in conflict with destiny, and is sure, sooner or later, to provoke a righteous retribution.

I say a righteous retribution, because nothing is truer than that man's loyalty is at bottom never due to persons. The brute is essentially servile. He obeys a will superior and foreign to his own. And before man has been elevated out of brute conditions, before he has been lifted out of the bondage of his nature, by a beneficent social culture, into the obedience of divine ideas, persons also dominate his imagination, and receive his allegiance. But, clearly, this is a transient state of man, his rudimental and lowest state. For, as culture dawns upon him, he perceives that persons are worthy only in so far as they represent something higher than themselves—only in so far as they represent a goodness which is infinite or divine. This is the glory of Christianity, in this consists its spirituality, that it makes a man's loyalty due only to humanitary truth and goodness, and never to persons, save as representing these. If, then, a person truly represent a humanitary good, if he seek no covert personal gain by the representation, there need be no fear of the decline of loyalty. But if the person cease merely to represent, and assume himself *to be* the reality, to be the good to which man's homage is due, then loyalty itself is outraged, and demands his instant overthrow. Rebellion, in this case, seems a divine necessity, and the memories of those who successfully organize it, remain a cherished possession to the race.

The truth is, that you miss the whole meaning—the whole humanitary worth—of both the regal and sacerdotal office from history, unless you look upon them as claiming a purely representative sacredness. Both the king and the priest severally symbolize that divine or perfect man whose life descends to him from within, or from God, and whom nature and society shall therefore perfectly obey. Hence you find the king and the priest placed above all physical and social subjection. You find them not merely exempted from servile labor, put above the reach of want, and adorned with luxury and power, but invested also with moral sanctity, or such a superiority to merely secular men, as absolves them from the responsibility the latter are under to civil law for their actions. If you will look at the state of Europe, previously to the democratizing of the Church in the Protestant Reformation, you will observe that both the king and the priest were exempt from secular jurisdiction. "The king can do no wrong," was a maxim of political ethics, never practically gainsaid before the Reformation. And the immunity of the clergy from civil penalty, in case of any flagrant offense against good morals, stands still expressed in the now almost purely traditional phrase, "benefit of clergy."

This conventional superiority of the king and the priest to the ordinary lot of man, arose, I say, out of their symbolic character, was due exclusively to their representative worth. Both of them officially symbolized that perfected aspect of man in nature, which, so far from having been then historically achieved, had not even been confessed as an idea by the most advanced intelligences, but which nevertheless was infallibly bound in the fulness of time to cover the earth with the knowledge of God, as amply as the waters cover the sea. Neither functionary, of course, had any private worth above other men, but both were often, on the contrary, owing to the inevitably corrupting influence of their privileged position, men of signally bad morality. But their public worth was so great—their worth to humanity considered as representing the Lord, or man of destiny, to whom nature and society owe an unlimited allegiance—that we willingly shroud their private vices in oblivion. These vices prove, of course, that they were *not* the man whom they represented; prove that they were only the unconscious instruments, the emptiest and most superficial symbols of his crowded and intimate sanctity. In a word, the intrinsic baseness of the representative served, of itself, to glorify the principal.

It seems to me that any Christian king or Christian priest who should now manifest a slight perception of the true *spirituality* of his function, would be honored of all men, as no king or priest had ever been honored before. No human being would object to Queen Victoria's state or emoluments, provided that she admitted her purely representative character—provided that she admitted her complete responsibility to that perfect or divine man whose eventual glory she prefigures. On the contrary, every one would then feel a common interest in cherishing her, in aggrandizing her state, and making it lustrous with all the splendor of romance. So should all men bow to-morrow to the crozier of the pope, if he would confess its purely prophetic or symbolic significance—if he would confess that he stands forth only to avouch that inmost purity which shall one day consecrate universal man, and repugn accordingly every private lust which brings him into conflict with human destiny.

Government, then, has a purely humanitary or representative basis. Its whole end and intention is to proclaim the unity of man, and guard the interests of that unity. Its function is to reconcile the interests of the individual with those of the mass, to see that the utmost possible harmony prevail between each and all of its subjects. Of course the restrictive or coercive service of government is needed only so long as the forms of society do not fulfil this unity or harmony, only so long as the fellowship of man with man is incompletely realized. Because the moment society becomes perfect, the moment all legalized privilege ceases among its subjects, and every man becomes the equal of every other in the public care, that moment you make it the interest of the individual to cherish the good of the whole, because his own advantage is identified with it; and if you can make it the *interest* of man to be orderly, of course you need no machinery of police to ensure that result. It will take place of itself, without any compulsion.

Now this is precisely what Democracy tends to produce, a reconciliation of the public and private interests of men. It designs to give all men, women, and children exact equality before the law, or in the public regard, and precisely in proportion to the degree in which this tendency is realized, does it become the interest of every man to maintain public order. The reason why evil exists among mankind, is that their outward life, their life as determined by institutions, does not fully accord with their inward or essential life, the life they have in God. God is infinite goodness, infinite truth, infinite power. If, therefore, the institutions of human society are not careful to serve this essential infinitude of man; if they do not incessantly endeavor to lift *all* men up out of the slough of natural destitution, and equalize culture, refinement and comfort among them, they are not faithful to the divine intent, and must fall into disuse. It is nothing but this legalized injustice among men, this organized and chronic inequality among them, which begets what are termed the "dangerous classes" in the European communities. These communities tolerate a privileged class; that is to say, they will ensure a child born of one parentage, a good education, good manners, a graceful development in every respect, sumptuous lodging, sumptuous food, sumptuous clothing; and they will ensure another child, born of an opposite parentage, the complete want of all these things: and yet they wonder at the existence of a dangerous class among them. Let them change these institutions; let them ensure all the children born among them a precisely equal social advantage and estimation, and they will soon see the dangerous classes disappear. They will soon destroy the sole existing motive to crime; for crime is always directed against mere arbitrary advantage. I admit that a man whose passions have been wounded by another, even without any blame on the part of that other, may be tempted, in the anguish of disappointment, to blaspheme his innocent rival, and even take his life on occasion. But this is not the criminality society chiefly suffers from. Men willingly bear with the injury springing out of a wounded self-love, knowing their own liability to need the same forgiveness. It is deliberate, systematic crime from which society suffers, crime that gives name to large classes and localities; and this criminality is the product exclusively of vicious legislation, of institutions which insist upon distributing the bounties of Providence unequally.

Man has derived no original boon from legislation. The service it has rendered him has been purely ministerial, consisting in a very slow denial of the chance supremacy of one race over others, or of one class over others. The utmost it has done, has been to clothe the instinct of human unity in progressive but temporary formulas. It has by no means *created* the unity it has acknowledged. It has merely developed the essential unity which all men have in God, their infinite source. Even in so far as the old legislation has recognised the unity of humanity, it has been without any wide awake assent, without any clear perception of the sublime issues involved in its action. In fact, a certain instinct of danger to itself renders the legislative power slow to look the truth fully in the face. For the moment human unity becomes broadly organized, or what is the same thing, the moment class legislation ceases and privilege becomes a thing of naught; the legislator will have no function but to serve laws higher than himself, laws of God, revealed by God's true minister, science.

The world waits for nothing else, in order to begin its eternal Sabbath, than this legislative recognition of human unity by the destruction of the last remnant of privilege. No argument can be needed on this subject, with the beautiful analogy of the human body before us. You never find a man wilfully cheating himself. Why? Because there are no antagonistic interests in his body, but each member thrives by the active concurrence of all the rest. Undoubtedly there is a hierarchy in the body, just as there is in all true society or fellowship; but this hierarchy is organized by use, the highest in function only being highest in honor. But notwithstanding this essential unity of the body, in fact *because* of it, it is manifest that if you could contrive some authentic legislation by which the nose should be declared, without reference to its intrinsic power or faculty, the most honorable member of the body, and entitled to the amplest measure of life or enjoyment, you would instantly prompt a conspiracy amongst the other interests, mouth, ears, eyes, legs and arms, to cheat this privileged member on all occasions, and stint it of its unhallowed revenues.

I beg to be fairly understood. I am very far from deficient in a feeling of respect to the past. I could not dare to wish that a single feature of past legislation had been omitted; for I believe in God, or in the infinite goodness and wisdom which embed human destiny, and which therefore prevent any disaster befalling it; which therefore, in fact, make all events equally tributary to it. Thus vicious legislation was anything but vicious when it took place. Privilege was a great and benign fact when the whole race was swamped in natural impotence; when mere physical might would otherwise have dominated in human affairs, and man have been reduced infinitely below the brute, by the very energy which, when properly recognised, raises him infinitely above it. The strong man, the man of immense thews and sinews, the man of gigantic will, how he would have swept the earth before him, had it not been for the institution of private property, and for the strenuous assertion on the part of society of every man's right to the undisturbed possession of his property, no matter how inordinate its bulk might be. Property has been the ægis and palladium of humanity—of human freedom, the symbol of all righteousness. Wherever it planted its foot, it said to the raging waves of brute force: Peace, be still! It proclaimed a higher fact in man than nature, even God; it proclaimed a higher fact than community of nature, the fact of incommunicable or sacred individuality. The whole force of society was originally dedicated to the service of this fact. The vindication of it was the original meaning of all our existing police, whether civil or ecclesiastical. Why has not the law of society, the law of property, been communistic from the beginning?

It has been because society has overruled nature, or subjected it to the needs of man's ultimate destiny; because it has recognised a truly infinite life in man, and devoutly kept itself for the service and vindication of that. Society has no objection to the communism which flows from the free individuality of man, has no objection to the freest communication of outward goods which at the same time consists with individual good-will. On the contrary, society rather applauds me when I, out of the abundance of my spiritual wealth or generosity, make you, and you, and every one sharers of my material goods. It has no objection, but on the contrary the greatest good-will towards the extremest possible communism which dates from the spiritual freedom, from the unforced consent, of the parties. But this previous basis it will exact at all hazards. It will first have the divine element in man recognised above all things, the principle of individual sacredness or freedom: then organize as you please, no possible detriment can ensue to the interests which society guards.

Let us therefore not condemn, let us thoroughly justify society in the past. What though her stringent legislation on behalf of persons has become, in the course of time, a shelter for the greatest inhumanity, yet remember the distance between our present position and the chaos out of which we sprang. For all that we now enjoy of goodness, and knowledge, and power, for all the benefits which flow from our intercourse with nature and our kind, we are indebted to past legislation, to past society, and far be it from me accordingly to attempt the slightest disparagement of it. By all the difference between myself and the Hottentot, between my children and his children, I am prevented cherishing any feeling towards *the past* but gratitude.

But the past is only *in order to* the future. It must no more pretend to dominate the future, than the foundation of a house should pretend to dominate the superstructure, than the egg should pretend to dominate the chick of which it is totally unconscious. These similitudes accurately reflect the relation of the past to the future. The past is the foundation of the future; it is the unhandsome and concealed but still massive and adequate basis upon which the superb columns of our future manhood shall rest. It is the egg which houses and nourishes for a time a life superior to itself. But who ever heard of the foundation giving law to the house, prescribing its rooms, determining its architecture? The foundation is laid, on the contrary, with reference exclusively to the wants of the superstructure: it is the house which fashions the foundation. And whoever heard of the egg giving law to the chick, prescribing its form, determining its faculties? The egg, on the contrary, is formed with reference to the needs of its tenant exclusively: it is the chick which fashions the egg.

The true worth of the past, then, to a rational regard, lies in its use to the future, just as to a rational regard the true worth of a foundation lies in its suitableness to the superstructure, or the true worth of an egg in its use to the future life which it embosoms. To prize the foundation for its own sake, would virtually be to keep oneself houseless forever: to prize the egg for its own sake, would virtually be to prevent incubation, and finally, of course, to deprive oneself even of eggs. Just so to prize the past for its own sake, and seek to perpetuate its institutions because they once have been, is forever to exclude the lustrous and divine future of humanity: it is, figuratively, to live always in cellars and cultivate addled eggs: which truly were an unhandsome destiny! . . .

6

THE SOCIAL SIGNIFICANCE
OF OUR INSTITUTIONS

On 4 July, 1861, James was invited by the residents
of Newport, Rhode Island, to deliver their annual
Independence Day address; "The Social Significance of
Our Institutions" was his response. The occasion was
made more dramatic by the recent outbreak of the
Civil War only three months before, and James lost no
time in availing himself of the opportunity this crisis
afforded. Taking the Declaration of Independence as
his inevitable text, James spoke with great feeling
about the nature and meaning of equality, pointing out
that the Declaration insisted not that men are *born*
equal but only that they are *created* equal. This then
enabled him to argue that all men are worthy of each
other's respect and good will not because of their
personal differences, which are, of course, plentiful and
obvious, but solely because of their common human
needs, wants, and affections.

Assuming that the Civil War was precipitated by the
argument over slavery, James refused to believe that
the eruption of hostilities between the states was a mere
accident. Instead, he contended, this terrible conflict
was in fact the inevitable consequence of the expanding
social consciousness of the race, a result of an
increased sense of the breadth and depth of human
unity. James's address, which often swells to great
emotional crests, is therefore a moving expression of
his invincible faith in man's essential solidarity and
brotherhood, and he wastes no words in pointing out
that any institution which opposes the realization of
that solidarity constitutes an offense to God and a
diminishment of the life of all men everywhere.

*The Social Significance of Our Institutions; an
oration delivered by request of the citizens at Newport,
R.I., July 4th, 1861* was originally published by Ticknor
and Fields (Boston, 1861), and is here reprinted from
American Philosophic Addresses, 1700–1900, edited by
Joseph L. Blau (New York, 1946), 234–46, 250–56.

A friend observed to me a few days since, as I accepted the invitation with which your Committee of Arrangements has honored me, to officiate as your orator on this occasion, that I could hardly expect, under the circumstances, to regale my auditors with the usual amount of spread-eagleism. I replied, that that depended upon what he meant by spread-eagleism. If he meant what was commonly meant by it, namely, so clearly defined a Providential destiny for our Union, that, do what we please, we shall never fall short of it, I could never, under any circumstances, the most opposed even to existing ones, consent to flatter my hearers with that unscrupulous rubbish. No doubt many men, whose consciences have been drugged by our past political prosperity, do fancy some such inevitable destiny as this before us,—do fancy that we may become so besotted with the lust of gain as to permit the greatest rapacity on the part of our public servants, the most undisguised and persistent corruption on the part of our municipal and private agents, without forfeiting the Providential favor. From that sort of spread-eagleism I told my friend that I hoped we were now undergoing a timely and permanent deliverance. But if he meant by that uncouth word an undiminished, yea, a heightened confidence in our political sanity and vigor, and in the fresh and glowing manhood which is to be in yet larger measure than ever the legitimate fruit of our institutions, I could assure him that my soul was full of it, and it would be wholly my fault if my auditors did not feelingly respond to it.

I never felt proud of my country for what many seem to consider her prime distinction, namely, her ability to foster the rapid accumulation of private wealth. It does not seem to me a particularly creditable thing, that a greater number of people annually grow richer under our institutions than they do anywhere else. It is a fact, no doubt, and like all facts has its proper amiable signification when exposed to the rectifying light of Truth. But it is not the fact which in a foreign land, for example, has made my heart to throb and my cheeks to glow when I remembered the great and happy people beyond the sea, when I thought of the vast and fertile land that lay blossoming and beckoning to all mankind beyond the setting sun. For there in Europe one sees this same private wealth, in less diffused form, it is true, concentrated in greatly fewer hands, but at the same time associated in many cases with things that go every way to dignify it or give it a lustre not its own,—associated with traditional family refinement, with inoffensive unostentatious manners, with the practice of art and science and literature, and sometimes with the pursuit of toilsome and honorable personal adventure. Every one knows, on the other hand, how little *we* exact from our rich men; how meagre and mean and creeping a race we permit our rich men to be, if their meanness is only flavored with profusion. I have not been favored with a great many rich acquaintance, but still I have known a not inconsiderable number, and I have never found them the persons to whom one would spontaneously resort in his least personal moments, or communicate with the most naturally in his hours of the purest intellectual elation or despondency. Of course I have known exceptions to this rule, men whose money only serves to illustrate their superior human sweetness, men of whose friendship everybody is proud. But as a general thing, nevertheless, one likes best to introduce one's foreign acquaintance, not to our commercial nabobs, who aggravate the price of house-rent and butcher's meat so awfully to us poor Newporters; not to our fast financiers and bank cashiers, who on a salary of three thousand a year contrive to support in luxury, beside their proper wife and offspring, a dozen domestic servants and as many horses; but to our, in the main, upright, self-respecting, and, if you please, untutored, but at the same time unsophisticated, children of toil, who are the real fathers and mothers of our future distinctive manhood.

No; what makes one's pulse to pound when he remembers his own home under foreign skies, is never the rich man, nor the learned man, nor the distinguished man of any sort who illustrates its history, for in all these petty products almost every country may favorably, at all events tediously, compete with our own; but it is all simply the abstract manhood itself of the country, man himself unqualified by convention, the man to whom all these conventional men have been simply introductory, the man who—let me say it—for the first time in human history finding himself in his own right erect under God's sky, and feeling himself in his own right the peer of every other man, spontaneously aspires and attains to a far freer and profounder culture of his nature than has ever yet illustrated humanity.

Shallow people call this pretension of ours the offspring of national vanity, and stigmatize it as implying the greatest immodesty in every one who asserts it. Is it not the same as saying, they ask, that ignorance is as good as experience, weakness as good as skill, nature as good as culture, the crude ore as good as the polished metal which is extracted from it? I will show you the absurdity of this criticism in a few moments, when I show you the peculiar foundation which the sentiment in question, the sentiment of human equality, claims in our historic evolution and growth. For the present, I have a word more to say in regard to the contrasts of European and American thought and aspiration.

No American, who is not immersed in abject spread-eagleism,—that is to say, no American who has had the least glimpse of the rich social promise of our institutions, or of the free play they accord to the spiritual activities of our nature,—values the mere political prestige of his nation, or the repute it enjoys with other nations, as the true ground of its glory. Much less, of course, does he esteem the mere *personnel* of his government as conferring any distinction upon him. Loyalty, which is a strictly personal sentiment, has long given place even in the English bosom where it was native, to patriotism, which is a much more rational sentiment. Loyalty bears to patriotism the same relation that superstition bears to religion. The zealot worships God, not as an infinite Spirit of Love, but as a finite person: not for what He is inwardly in himself, but for what He may outwardly be to the worshipper. He adores him, not for what alone renders him worthy of adoration, namely, his essential humanity, that infinitely tender sympathy with his infirm creature which leads him forever to humble himself that the latter may be exalted, but simply because he is eminent in place and power above all beings, and so is able to do all manner of kindness to those who please him, and all manner of unkindness to those who displease him. Exactly so the loyalist worships his king or his queen,—not for their radiant human worth; not for the uses their great dignity promotes to the common or associated life; in short, not from any rational perception of their inward adjustment to the place they occupy; but simply because they do occupy that eminent place, simply because they happen to be crowned king and crowned queen, traditional sources of honor and dishonor to their subjects. In both cases alike, the homage is purely blind or instinctive, and, though befitting children, is unworthy of adult men. Religion, on the contrary, clothes the Divine supremacy with essentially spiritual attributes, makes His perfection the perfection of character, the perfection of love and wisdom, and of power thence alone energized, so that no religious man worships God from choice or voluntarily, but spontaneously, or because he cannot help himself, so much does the overpowering loveliness constrain him. That is to say, every man truly worships God in the exact measure of his own unaffected goodness, purity, and truth. And it is thus precisely that the patriot loves his king or queen,— not for their traditional sanctity, not for their exalted privilege, not for their conventional remoteness, in short, from other men,—but for their willing nearness to them, that is, for their positive human use or worth, and consequent fitness to lead the great honest hearts they represent. In one word, what the patriot sees and loves in his king is his country and his country only; and he serves him, therefore, as the spiritually enlightened man serves God, not with a ceremonial or ritual devotion, but with a cordial or living one, with a service which only exalts, instead of any longer degrading, either of the parties to it.

No wonder, then, that the sentiment of loyalty should have utterly died out of our blood, when even that higher sentiment of country, to which alone it ministered in the bosom of our English ancestry, has in its turn given place in *our* bosoms to a sentiment still higher, that of humanity. We are the descendants, not of English loyalists by any means, but of English patriots exclusively; that is, of men who valued royalty only so long as it served the common life, and when it grew tired of that service, and claimed only to be served in its turn, unhesitatingly suspended it by the neck, and sent its descendants skipping. And this English patriotism, which was itself a regenerate loyalty, or a love of country purified of all personal allegiance, has itself become glorified in our veins into a still grander sentiment,—that is, from a love of country has become exalted into a love of humanity. It is the truest glory any nation may boast, that the love it enkindles in the bosom of its children is the love of man himself; that the respect it engenders there for themselves is identical with the respect which is due to all men. As Americans, we love our country, it is true, but not because it is *ours* simply; on the contrary, we are proud to belong to it, because it is the country of all mankind, because she opens her teeming lap to the exile of every land, and bares her hospitable breast to whatsoever wears the human form. This is where the ordinary European mind inevitably fails to do us any justice. The purblind piddling mercenaries of literature, like Dickens, and the ominous scribes and Pharisees of the Saturday Review, have just enough of cheap wit to see and caricature the cordial complacency we feel in our virgin and beautiful mother; but it takes an acumen bred of no London police-courts, and an education of the heart which all the studies of Oxford will never yield, to see the rich human soul that vivifies that complacency, that burns away all its dross, and makes it laughable only to literary louts and flunkies who live by pandering to the prejudices of the average human understanding.

The American misses in European countries and institutions this exquisite human savor, this exquisite honor which is due to man alone, and this exquisite indifference which is due to persons. In European institutions,—I do not say in existing European *sentiment*, for that, no doubt, is greatly in advance of the institutions,—but in European institutions persons are everything and man comparatively nothing. It is always the skilled man, or the learned man, or the mighty man, or the noble man, in short the propertied or qualified man of some sort, that is had in reverence; never our common humanity itself, which, on the contrary, is starved in garrets in order that the man of quality may live in plenty, is ground to powder by toil in order to keep up his iniquitous state, is butchered in crowds to maintain his peace, and rots in prisons to avouch his purity. Abroad every American sees, of course and accordingly, any amount of merely political energy and efficiency, sees governments flourishing by the permanent demoralization of their people. He sees every appliance of luxurious art, all manner of imposing edifices, of elaborate gardens and pleasure-places, the deadliest arsenals of war, armies innumerable, and natives disciplined with infernal force, all consecrated to the sole purpose of keeping up the purely *political* status of the country, or aggrandizing its own selfish aims and repute to the eyes of other nations and its own people. And he cries aloud to his own heart, May America perish out of all remembrance, before what men blasphemously call public order finds itself promoted there by this costly human degradation! Disguise it as you will in your own weak, wilful way, in no country in Europe has the citizen as yet consciously risen into the man. In no country of Europe does the government consciously represent, or even so much as affect to represent, the unqualified manhood of the country, its lustrous human worth, the honest unadulterate blood of its myriad beautiful and loving bosoms, its fathers and mothers, its brothers and sisters, its sons and daughters, its husbands and wives, its lovers and friends, every throb of whose life is sacred with God's sole inspiration; but only the adulterate streams which course through the veins of some insignificant conventional aristocracy. Take England itself for an example of the perfect truth of my allegations. We may easily do injustice to England just now; may easily forget the shining and proud pre-eminence which belongs to her political development among all the polities of the earth. Another nation so great, so vowed in its political form to freedom, so renowned for arms, for art, for industry, for the intelligence of its scholars, for its public and private morality, does not illustrate human annals; and yet, because she now thinks of herself before she thinks of us, because she listens to the prayer of her starving operatives before she listens to the demands of our betrayed nationality, we are ready to forget her glorious past, and pronounce her a miracle of selfishness. But no truly human virtue is compatible with an empty stomach; and England, like everybody else, must be allowed first of all to secure her own subsistence before she bestows a thought upon other people. I will not blame England, then, for her present timidity. I will never forget the inappreciable services she has rendered to the cause of political progress. But just as little can I be blind to the immense limitations she exhibits when measured by American humanitary ideas. She claims to be the freest of European nations; and so she is, as I have already admitted, so far as her public or political life is concerned. But viewed internally, viewed as to her *social* condition, you observe such a destitution of personal freedom and ease and courtesy among her children as distinguishes no other people, and absolutely shocks an American. Conventional routine, a wholly artificial morality, has so bitten itself into the life of the people, into the national manners and countenance even, that the kindly human heart within is never allowed to come to the surface, and what accordingly is meant among them for civility to each other is so coldly and grudgingly rendered as to strike the stranger like insult. The intensely artificial structure of society in England renders it inevitable in fact, that her people should be simply the worst-mannered people in Christendom. Indeed, I venture to say that no average American resides a year in England without getting a sense so acute and stifling of its hideous class-distinctions, and of the consequent awkwardness and *brusquerie* [literally, "abruptness"] of its upper classes, and the consequent abject snobbery or inbred and ineradicable servility of its lower classes, as makes the manners of Choctaws and Potawatamies sweet and christian, and gives to a log-cabin in Oregon the charm of comparative dignity and peace.

For, after all, what do we prize in men? Is it their selfish or social worth? Is it their personal or their human significance? Unquestionably, only the latter. All the refinement, all the accomplishment, all the power, all the genius under heaven, is only a nuisance to us if it minister to individual vanity, or be associated with a sentiment of aloofness to the common life, to the great race which bears us upon her spotless bosom and nourishes us with the milk of her own immortality. What is the joy we feel when we see the gifted man, the man of genius, the man of high conventional place of whatever sort, come down to the recognition of the lowliest social obligations,—what is it but a testimony that the purest personal worth is then most pure when it denies itself, when it leaps over the privileged interval which separates it from the common life, and comes down to identify itself with the commonest? This sentiment of human unity, of the sole original sacredness of man and the purely derivative sanctity of persons, no matter who they are, *is what we are born to,* and what we must not fail to assert with an emphasis and good-will which may, if need be, make the world resound. For it is our very life, the absolute breath of our nostrils, which alone qualifies us to exist. I lived, recently, nearly a year in St. John's Wood in London, and was daily in the habit of riding down to the city in the omnibus along with my immediate neighbors, men of business and professional men, who resided in that healthy suburb, and fared forth from it every morning to lay up honest, toilsome bread for the buxom domestic angels who sanctified their homes, and the fair-haired cherubs who sweetened them. Very nice men, to use their own lingo, they were, for the most part; tidy, unpretending, irreproachable in dress and deportment; men in whose truth and honesty you would confide at a glance; and yet, after eight months' assiduous bosom solicitation of their hardened stolid visages, I never was favored with the slightest overture to human intercourse from one of them. I never once caught the eye of one of them. If ever I came nigh doing so, an instant film would surge up from their more vital parts, if such parts there were, just as a Newport fog suddenly surges up from the cold remorseless sea, and wrap the organ in the dullest, fishiest, most disheartening of stares. They took such extreme pains never to look at one another, that I knew they must be living men, devoutly intent each on disowning the other's life; otherwise I could well have believed them so many sad well-seasoned immortals, revisiting their old London haunts by way of a nudge to their present less carnal satisfactions. I had myself many cherished observations to make upon the weather, upon the lingering green of the autumn fields, upon the pretty suburban cottages we caught a passing glimpse of, upon the endless growth of London, and other equally conservative topics; but I got no chance to ventilate them, and the poor things died at last of hope deferred. The honest truth is what Dr. Johnson told Boswell, that the nation is deficient in the human sentiment. "Dr. Johnson," says Boswell, "though himself *a stern, true-born* Englishman, and fully prejudiced against all other nations, had yet discernment enough to see, and candor enough to censure, the cold reserve among Englishmen toward strangers (of their own nation). 'Sir,' said he, 'two men of any other nation who are shown into a room together, at a house where they are both visitors, will immediately find some conversation. But two Englishmen will probably go each to a different window and remain in obstinate silence. Sir, we do not, as yet,' proceeded the Doctor, 'understand the common rights of humanity.'"

These common rights of humanity of which Dr. Johnson speaks are all summed up in the truth of man's social equality; that is, every man's joint and equal dependence with every other man upon the association of his kind for all that he himself is or enjoys. These common rights of humanity have got political ratification in England, as they have got it nowhere else in Europe out of Switzerland; but the private life of England, as Dr.

Johnson charges, is shockingly indifferent to them. The moral sentiment, the sentiment of what is exceptionally due to this, that, or the other *person*, utterly dominates in that sphere the social sentiment, the sentiment of what is habitually due to every man as man. It is this unchallenged primacy of the moral life over the social life of England, this intense sensibility among her scholars to personal claims over human claims, which so exalts her Pharisaic pride and abases her true spirituality, which leaves her outwardly the greatest and inwardly the poorest of peoples, and makes the homesick because better-nurtured foreigner feel, when exposed to it, how dismal and dingy the very heaven of heavens would become if once these odiously correct and lifeless white-cravatted and black-coated respectabilities should get the run of it.

You see at a glance that this penury of England in all spiritual regards is owing to the simple fact that not *man*, but *English*-man, is the key-note of her aspirations. European thought generally and at best is peninsular,— that is, *almost* insular,—in that it regards European culture as constituting the probable limits of the human mind. But English thought is absolutely insular, in that it makes England the actual measure of human development. Every Englishman who lives and dies an Englishman, that is to say, who has not been made by God's grace a partaker in heart of the *commonwealth* of mankind, or a spiritual alien from the mother that bore him, believes that no Europe, but England itself, one of the smallest corners of Europe, as Judæa was one of the smallest corners of Asia, furnishes the real *Ultima Thule* ["outermost limits"] of human progress. This being the key-note of English thought, the pitch to which all its tunes are set, you are not surprised to see the sentiment dominating the whole strain of English character, till at last you find the Englishman not only isolating himself from the general European man, but each individual Englishman becoming a bristling independent unapproachable little islct to every other Englishman, ready, as Dr. Johnson describes them, to leap out of the windows rather than hold that safe and salutary parley with each other which God and nature urge them to; so that probably a huger amount of painful plethoric silence becomes annually accumulated under English ribs than befalls the whole world beside, and an amount of spiritual numbness and imbecility generated which is not to be paralleled by anything this side of old Judæa. And it is exactly the rebound of his thought from all this social obstruction and poverty which causes the American wayfarer's heart to dance with glee when he remembers his own incorrect and exceptionable Nazareth, his own benighted but comfortable and unsuspecting fellow-sinners, who are said to sit sometimes with their tired feet as high as their head, who light their innocent unconscious pipes at everybody's fire, and who occasionally, when the sentiment of human brotherhood is at a white heat in their bosom, ask you, as a gentleman from Cape Cod once asked me at the Astor House table, the favor of being allowed to put his superfluous fat upon your plate, provided, that is, the fat is in no way offensive to you. That the forms in which human freedom expresses itself in these latitudes are open to just criticism in many respects, I cordially admit, and even insist; but he who sees the uncouth form alone, and has no feeling for the beautiful human substance within it, for the soul of fellowship that animates and redeems it of all malignity, would despise the shapeless embryo because it is not the full-formed man, and burn up the humble acorn because it is not yet the branching oak. But the letter is nothing, the spirit everything. The letter kills, the spirit alone gives life; and it is exclusively to this undeniable spiritual difference between Europe and America, as organized and expressed in our own constitutional polity, that all our formal differences are owing. Our very Constitution binds us, that is to say, the very breath of our political nostrils binds us, to disown all distinctions among men, to disregard persons, to disallow privilege the most established and sacred, to legislate only for the common good, no longer for those accidents of birth or wealth or culture which spiritually individualize man from his kind, but only for those great common features of social want and dependence which naturally unite him with his kind, and inexorably demand the organization of such unity. It is this immense constitutional life and inspiration we are under which not only separate us from Europe, but also perfectly explain by antagonism that rabid hostility which the South has always shown towards the admission of the North to a fair share of government patronage, and which now provokes her to the dirty and diabolic struggle she is making to give human slavery the sanction of God's appointment.

When I said awhile ago that an American, as such, felt himself the peer of every man of woman born, I represented my hearers as asking me whether that claim was a righteous one; whether, in fact, he whose conscience should practically ratify it in application to himself would not thereby avouch his own immodesty,—confess himself devoid of that humility which is the life of true manhood. To this question I reply promptly, No! for this excellent reason,—that the claim in question is by no means a distinctive personal claim, but a claim in behalf of every man. When, by virtue of our national genesis and genius, I claim before God and man a rightful equality with every other man, what precisely is it that I do? Do I claim for myself an equality of wit, of learning, of talent, of benevolence, with this, that, or the other special person whom you may name as remarkable for those endowments? Do I mean to allege my private personal equality with all other persons; my equal claim, for example, to the admiring or sympathetic homage of mankind, with Shakespeare, with Washington, with Franklin? No man who is not an ass can believe this; and yet you perpetually hear the paid scribes of old-fogyism repeating the slander throughout the world, as if it were the most indisputable of truths. Nothing is more common than to hear persons who are disaffected to the humane temper of our polity affecting to quote the Declaration of Independence as saying that all men are *born* equal, and under cover of that audacious forgery exposing it to ridicule. The Declaration is guilty of no such absurdity. It does not say that all men are born equal, for it is notorious that they are born under the greatest conceivable inequalities,—inequalities of heart and head and hand,—inequalities even of physical form and structure; but it says that, notwithstanding these inequalities, they are all *created equal*,—that is, are all equal before God, or claim no superior merit one to another in his sight, being all alike dependent upon his power, and possessing a precisely equal claim, therefore, each with the other, to the blessings of his impartial providence. The inequalities under which men are born, or which they inherit from their forefathers, are the needful condition of their individuality, of their various personal identity. The framers of the Declaration saw this as well as anybody, but they also saw, and so in effect said, that however much men may differ among themselves, it was yet not these personal differences which commend them to each other's true respect, but rather that common human want which identifies them all in the Divine regard by making them all equal retainers of His sovereign bounty. No man not a fool can gainsay this, and no man not a fool, consequently, can pretend that when I urge this constitutional doctrine of human equality I have anything whatever to say of myself personally regarded, or *as discriminated from other persons*, but only as SOCIALLY regarded,—that is, as *united* with all other persons. In short, it is not a claim urged on my own behalf alone, but in behalf of every other man who is too ignorant or too debased by convention to assert it for himself.

Our political Constitution, like every other great providential stride in human affairs, was intentionally educative; was designed to gather us together under the discipline of well-disposed but often sorely tried and disheartened political guides, in order finally to draw us fully forth out of the land of darkness and the house of bondage. The sole great aim of our political Constitution has been gradually to induct us out of errors and evils, which no Pagan Jew was ever more slow and reluctant to suspect than we are, into a new and far more grandly human consciousness into a land of everlasting righteousness and peace. Not one of its literal framers ever had the faintest foresight of its ultimate scientific destination, any more than Moses had of the Messiah whom he prefigured; any more than Isaiah or Jeremiah had of the tremendous spiritual scope of the prophecies which uttered themselves through their rapt and dizzy imaginations. The scientific promise of our polity is only to be understood by watching its practical unfolding, by observing the expansive influence it has hitherto exerted, and is now more than ever exerting, upon the popular mind and upon the popular heart. View it either positively or negatively, its influence is the same. In its negative aspect,—its aspect toward Egypt, which is the European conception of man's true state on earth,—it denies all absoluteness both to persons and institutions, by boldly resolving what is the highest of personalities, namely, the king, and what is the most sacred of institutions, namely, the Church, both alike from a power into the servant of a power, from a righteousness into the symbol of a righteousness, from a substance into the shadow of a substance; this substance itself being those great disregarded instincts of human unity or fraternity which all along the course of history have been patiently soliciting scientific recognition, in order to put on organic form and cover the earth with holiness and peace. In its positive aspect,—the aspect it bears toward Canaan,— which means the supremacy of man's associated life over his individual one, it makes my private righteousness, or that which inwardly relates me to God, utterly posterior to, and dependent upon, my public righteousness, or that which relates me to my fellow-man. How is it possible, therefore, that its practical effect should be otherwise than educative,—educative, too, in the very profoundest manner, that is, out of all evil into all good? Its direct influence is to modify or enlarge my private conscience, the consciousness I have of myself as a moral being, a being independent of my kind and capable of all manner of arrogant presumptuous private hope toward God, into a public conscience, into a consciousness of myself as above all things a *social* being most intimately and indissolubly one with my kind, and incapable therefore of any blessing which they do not legitimately share. It laughs at the pretensions of any person however reputable, and of any institution however venerable, to claim an absolute divine sanctity,—that is, a sanctity irrespective of his or its unaffected human worth; and it gradually so inflames the mind with its own august spiritual meaning, so quickens it with its own vivid and palpitating divine substance, that the conscience which is governed by it of necessity finds itself regenerating, finds itself expanding from a petty drivelling and squeaking witness of one's own righteousness, into the clear and ringing and melodious testimony of God's sole righteousness in universal man. . . .

Such, my friends, I conceive to be our undeniable inward significance as a nation. Such the bright consummate flower of manhood, which is spiritually disengaging itself from the coarse obscuring husks of our literal Democracy, consisting in the gradual but complete subjugation of the selfish instinct in our bosoms to the service of the social instinct. Such is the great and righteous temper of mind to which we are Divinely begotten; such the paternal animating spirit that shapes our constitutional polity, that originally gave us birth as a nation, and that even now, in this day of seeming adversity, gives us a conscience of rectitude and invincible might which is itself incomparably richer than all prosperity. It is idle to talk,— as silly people, however, will talk, as all people will talk whose gross grovelling hearts go back *to the flesh-pots of Egypt, when they eat bread to the full,*—it is idle to talk of our political troubles as springing up out of the ground, as having no graver origin than party fanaticism or folly. These troubles, on the contrary, are the inevitable fruit of our very best growth, the sure harbingers, I am persuaded, of that rising Sun of Righteousness whose beams shall never again know eclipse. They are merely an evidence, on a larger scale and in a public sphere, of the discord which every righteous man perceives at some time or other to exist between his essential human spirit and his perishable animal flesh. For every nation is in human form, is in fact but an aggregate or composite form of manhood, greatly grander and more complex than the simple forms of which it is made up, but having precisely the same intense unity within itself, and claiming, like each of them, a quickening controlling spirit, and an obedient servile body. This animating controlling spirit of our national polity, like that of our own private souls, is Divine, comes from God exclusively, and is only revealed never exhausted, only embodied or empowered never belittled or enfeebled, by the literal symbols in which human wisdom contrives to house it. That part of the letter of our Constitution which best reveals the majestic human spirit that animates our polity is of course its preamble. But the real divinity of the nation, its vital imperishable holiness, resides not in any dead parchment, but only in the righteous unselfish lives of those who see in any constitution but the luminous letter of their inward spiritual faith, but the visible altar of their invisible worship, and rally around it therefore with the joyous unshrinking devotion not of slaves but of men.

Now, such being the undoubted spirit of our polity, what taint was there in its material constitution, in our literal maternal inheritance, to affront this righteous paternal spirit and balk its rich promise, by turning us its children from an erect sincere hopeful and loving brotherhood of men intent upon universal aims, into a herd of greedy luxurious swine, into a band of unscrupulous political adventurers and sharpers, the stink of whose corruption pervades the blue spaces of ocean, penetrates Europe, and sickens every struggling nascent human hope with despair?

The answer leaps at the ears; it is Slavery, and Slavery only. This is the poison which lurked almost harmless at first in our body politic, and to which its righteous soul is an utter stranger; this is the curse we inherited from the maternal English Eve out of whose somewhat loose lascivious lap we sprung. But of late years the poison has grown so rank and pervasive, making its citadel, indeed, the very heart of the commonwealth, or those judicial and legislative chambers whence all the tides of its activity proceed, that each successive administration of the country proves more recreant to humanity than its predecessor, until at last we find shameless God-forsaken men, holding high place in the government, become so rabid with its virus as to mistake its slimy purulent ooze for the ruddy tide of life, and commend its foul and fetid miasm to us as the fragrant breath of assured health. It is easy enough to falsify the divinity which is shaping our constitutional action, wherever a will exists to do so. Men whose most cherished treasure can be buttoned up in their breeches pocket, and whose heart, of course, is with their treasure, are doubtless panting to convince the country that we have already done enough for honor, and the sooner a sham peace is hurried up the better. It only needs a wily wolf of this sort to endue himself here and there in sheep's clothing, and bleat forth a cunning pathetic lament over the causeless misfortunes which have befallen our bread-and-butter interests, to see dozens of stupid sheep taking up in their turn the sneaking hypocritical bleat, and preparing their innocent fleece for his dishonest remorseless shears. The friends of Mammon are numerous in every community; but, blessed be God, they nowhere rule in the long run. They are numerous enough to give an odious flavor to the broth; but they never constitute its body. It is impossible that we should err in this great crisis of our destiny, a crisis to which that of our national birth or independence yields in dignity and importance, as much as body yields to soul, flesh to spirit, childhood to manhood. For this is the exact crisis we are in; the transition from youth to manhood, from appearance to reality, from passing shadow to deathless substance. Every man and every nation of men encounters somewhere in its progress a critical hour, big with all its future fate; and woe be to the man, woe be to the nation, who believes that this sacred responsibility can be trifled with. To every man and to every nation it means eternal life or eternal death; eternal liberty or eternal law; the heaven of free spontaneous order, or the hell of enforced prudential obedience. There is no man who hears me who does not know something of this bitter sweat and agony; whose petty trivial cares have not been dignified and exalted by some glimpse of this hidden inward fight; who has not at times heard the still small voice of truth on the one hand counselling him to do the right thing though ruin yawn upon his hopes,— counselling him *to force himself* to do the honest thing though it cost him tears of blood,—and the earthquake voice of hell on the other, or the fiery breath of passion infuriated by long starvation, doing its best to drown and devour it. Our national life, believe me, is at that exact pass in this awful moment, and nowhere else. It is the hour of our endless rise into all beautiful human proportions, into all celestial vigor and beatitude, or of our endless decline into all infernality and uncleanness, and into the inevitable torments which alone discipline such uncleanness. And we must not hesitate for a moment to fight it manfully out to its smiling blissful end, feeling that it is not our own battle alone, that we are not fighing for our own country only, for our own altars and firesides as men have fought hitherto, but for the altars and firesides of universal man, for the ineradicable rights of human nature itself. Let bloated European aristocracies rejoice in our calamities; let the mutton-headed hereditary legislators of England raise a shout of insult and exultation over our anticipated downfall; the honest, unsophisticated masses everywhere will do us justice, for they will soon see, spite of all efforts to blind them, that we occupy in this supreme moment no petty Thermopylae guarding some paltry Greece, but the broad majestic pass that commands the deathless wealth and worth of human nature itself, the Thermopylae of the human mind; they will soon see, in fact, that our flags are waving, our trumpets sounding, our cannon showering their deathful hail, not merely to avenge men's outraged political faith and honor, but to vindicate the inviolable sanctity of the human form itself, which for the first time in history is Divinely bound up with that faith and honor.

This is the exact truth of the case. The political tumble-down we have met with is no accident, as unprincipled politicians would represent it. It is the fruit of an inevitable expansion of the human mind itself, of an advancing social consciousness in the race, an ever-widening sense of human unity, which will no longer be content with the old channels of thought, the old used-up clothes of the mind, but irresistibly demands larger fields of speculation; freer bonds of intercourse and fellowship. We have only frankly to acknowledge this great truth in order to find the perturbation and anxiety which now invade our unbelieving bosoms dispelled; in order to hear henceforth, in every tone of the swelling turbulence that fills our borders, no longer forebodings of disease, despair, and death, but prophecies of the highest health, of kindling hope, of exuberant righteousness, and endless felicity for every man of woman born. "I was once," says an old writer, "I was once in a numerous crowd of spirits, in which everything appeared at sixes and sevens: they complained, saying that now a total destruction was at hand, for in that crowd nothing appeared in consociation, but everything loose and confused, and this made them fear destruction, which they supposed also would be total. But in the midst of their confusion and disquiet, I perceived a soft sound, angelically sweet, in which was nothing but what was orderly. The angelic choirs thus present were within or at the centre, and the crowd of persons to whom appertained what was disorderly were without or at the circumference. This flowing angelic melody continued a long time, and it was told me that hereby was signified how the Lord rules confused and disorderly things which are upon the surface, namely, *by virtue of a pacific principle in the depths or at the centre; whereby the disorderly things upon the surface are reduced to order, each being restored from the error of its nature.*" The pacific and restorative principle which in the same way underlies all our political confusion and disorder, and which will irresistibly shape our national life to its own righteous and orderly issues, is the rising sentiment of human society or fellowship, the grand, invincible faith of man's essential unity and brotherhood. The social conscience, the conscience of what is due to every man as man, having the same divine origin and the same divine destiny with all other men, is becoming preternaturally quickened in our bosoms, and woe betide the church, woe betide the state, that ventures to say to that conscience, Thus far shalt thou go, and no further!

Slavery has this incredible audacity. Slavery, which is the only institution of our European inheritance we have left unmodified, confronts and spits upon this rising tide of God's righteousness in the soul of man. Slavery boldly denies what all our specific culture affirms, namely, the inviolable sanctity of human affection in every form, the inviolable freedom of human thought in every direction. The cultivated intelligence of the race abhors the claim of any human being to possess an *absolute* property in any other being, that is, a property unvivified by the other's unforced, spontaneous gift. Slavery affirms this diabolic pretension,—affirms the *unqualified* title of the master to outrage, if need be, the sacredest instincts of natural affection in the slave, and to stifle at need his feeblest intellectual expansion. Accordingly, the heart of man, inspired by God and undepraved by Mammon, pronounces slavery with no misgiving an unmitigated infamy; and the intelligence of man, thence enlightened, declares that its empire shall not be extended. We have no right to say that evil shall not exist where it already does exist without our privity; but we have not only all manner of right, both human and divine, to say that its existence shall not be promoted by our active connivance; it is our paramount wisdom as men, and our paramount obligation as citizens, to say so. Such, at all events, is our exact social attitude with respect to slavery. Every unsophisticated soul of man feels it to be what it actually is, namely, the ultimate or most general form and hence the king of all evil pent up in human nature; so that when *it* once disappears by the clear indignant refusal of the human mind any longer actively to co-operate with it, all those interior and subtler shapes of evil which now infest us, and are held together by it as the viscera of the body are held together by the skin, will be dissipated along with it. We know not when the hour of this great salvation shall strike. We only know that as God is just and sovereign it must strike erelong, and that when it does strike the morning stars of a richer creation than has yet been seen on earth will sing together, and all the sons of God in every subtlest ineffable realm of his dominion shout for joy. Our government itself is waking up from its long trance; is beginning to perceive that there is something sacreder than commerce on earth,—that the interests of this very commerce, in fact, will best be promoted by first of all recognizing that there are depths in the human soul, demands of immaculate righteousness and assured peace, which all the pecuniary prosperity of the world can never satisfy. In short, the government is fast coming, let us hope, to a consciousness of its distinctively social or human function, by practically confessing that its supreme responsibility is due only to man, and no longer to persons, or infuriated sectional exactions. Of course, in pursuing this career, it will become gradually converted from the mere tool it has hitherto been for adroit political knaves to do what they please with, into a grandly social force, reflecting every honest human want, fulfilling every upright human aspiration. What matters it, then, if we forfeit the empty political prestige we have hitherto enjoyed with European *statesmen*? Let us only go on overtly to inaugurate that promised perfect society on earth, all whose officers shall be *peace*, and its sole exactors *righteousness*, by practically acknowledging on all occasions the infinite Divine Good enshrined in man's heart, the infinite Divine Truth enthroned in his understanding, and we shall fast attain to a social standing in the eyes of European *peoples* which shall grandly compensate our mere political disasters, and do more to modify the practice of European statesmen themselves than anything else we could possibly do.

In this state of things, how jealously should we watch the Congress to-day assembling at Washington! How clear should be the watchword we telegraph to guide their deliberations! Have *we* indeed no higher monition for our legislature than old heathen Rome supplied to hers, namely, *to see that the Republic suffer no damage?* The body is much, but it is not the soul. The Republic is much, but it is not all. It is much as a means, but nothing as an end. It is much as a means to human advancement, but nothing as its consummation. It is much as an onward march of the race, it is nothing whatever as its final victory and rest. Let us be sure that, so far as we are concerned, our legislators understand this. Let them know that we value the Republic so much, only because we value man more; that we value peace, prosperity, and wealth not as ends, but as means to an end, which is justice, truth, and mercy, in which alone man's real peace, his true prosperity, and his abiding wealth reside, and which will be ours so long as we are faithful to the gospel of human freedom and equality. For my part, if I thought that our rulers were going to betray in this agonizing hour the deathless interest confided to them,—if I thought that Mr. Lincoln and Mr. Seward were going at last to palter with the sublime instincts of peace and righteousness that elevated them to power and give them all their personal prestige, by making the least conceivable further concession to the obscene demon of Slavery,—then I could joyfully see Mr. Lincoln and Mr. Seward scourged from the sacred eminence they defile, yea more, could joyfully see our boasted political house itself laid low in the dust forever, because in that case its stainless stars and stripes would have sunk from a banner of freemen into a dishonored badge of the most contemptible people on earth; a people that bartered away the fairest spiritual birthright any people ever yet were born to, for the foulest mess of material pottage ever concocted of shameless lust and triumphant fraud.

Moral and Ethical Writings

7

THE PERFECT MAN

In the following essay, whose full title is "A Scientific Statement of the Christian Doctrine of the Lord, or Divine Man," James seeks to answer the question as to who the divine or perfect man really is. His answer is somewhat astonishing: the divine or perfect man is none other than the artist or aesthetic man, by which James did not mean those who pursue a specific vocation such as painting, music or writing, but rather those who, whatever their specific vocation, fulfill it by following the inspiration of their own individual genius, the inward life of their own nature. The artist or aesthetic man, then, is the very opposite of the artisan or craftsman. Where the first obeys only his own internal taste and attraction, the second is controlled strictly by physical necessities or social obligations. "The artisan," James claims, "seeks to gain a livelihood or secure an honorable name. He works for bread, or for fame, or for both together. The Artist abhors these ends, and works only to show forth that immortal beauty whose presence constitutes his inmost soul."

In proclaiming this theory of the divine man as one who is "a law unto himself, and [who] ignores all outward allegiances, whether to nature or society," James could easily have been misunderstood as espousing a crude doctrine of individualism when, in point of fact, his was a diametrically opposed view. Indeed, nothing was more loathsome to him than the Transcendentalist preoccupation with the individual soul, and nothing could have been further from his mind on this particular occasion than the idea of becoming a spokesman for this doctrine. Hence to understand his theory of the divine man correctly, it is absolutely necessary to realize that the law which James imputed to the single divine individual was the same law which he regarded as common to all men, the law of their universal nature as human beings, which had its source in, and was an explicit expression of, the very life of God Himself. It was for this reason that James took such pains at the beginning of his lecture to develop a theory of personality out of his beliefs about the nature of creation. Without an understanding of the latter, his comments about the former made no sense.

This selection is taken from Lecture 1, "A Scientific Statement of the Christian Doctrine of the Lord, or Divine Man," in *Moralism and Christianity* (New York, 1850), 1–14, 19–30, 32–35.

———•-•-•-•———

The Christian doctrine of the Lord, or Divine Man, rests upon this fundamental axiom, that God alone is being, or life in Himself. Man is not being, but only a subject of being, only a form or image of being. His being is not absolute, but phenomenal, as conditioned in space and time. But God's being is utterly unconditioned either in space or time. It is infinite, not as comprehending all space, but as utterly excluding the bare conception of space; and eternal, not as comprehending all time, but as utterly excluding the bare conception of time. He is not a subject of being, but being itself, and therefore the sole being.

Consistently with this fundamental axiom, we are bound to deny that the creature of God has any being or substance in himself. The substantial being or life of every creature is God, while the creature is but a form or image of God. The creature is not another being than God, nor yet is he an identical being with God; because the creature is not being at all, but only a shadow or reflection of being. You would not call the shadow of the tree on the ground another substance than the tree itself, nor yet the same substance, for the reason that the shadow is not any substance at all, but merely the image of a substance. So man, the shadow or image of God, is neither a different being from God, nor yet an identical being, because he is not any being whatever, but only the reflection of being. Thus God's creature is without any being or substance in himself, his selfhood being nothing more than an image or reflection of the only and universal being, which is God. The internal of every man is God. The external, or that which defines the man, defines his self-consciousness, is only a shadow or reflection of this internal.

These things being granted, which they must be as it seems to the writer, unless one prefers to deny the fact of creation, it follows from them that the universe of creation is a vast theatre of imagery or correspondence. If God be the sole and therefore universal being, his universal creature can be nothing more and nothing less than His image or shadow. And if the creature be only the image or shadow of God, then creation itself is not the origination of any new being or substance on the part of God, but only the revelation or imaging forth of a being which is eternal and unchangeable. Thus in the light of the principles here stated, the created universe resolves itself both in whole and in part into an imagery or correspondence of God, and the universal science consequently, or the science of sciences, becomes the science of correspondence.

If now all this be true, if it be true that creation can be nothing more and nothing less than the revealing or imaging forth of God, then some momentous results immediately ensue to our theology and philosophy. Primarily it results that the true creature of God is not finite, cannot be comprehended within the laws of space and time. For as the creature is only an image or reflection of God, and as God being eternal and infinite is utterly ignorant both of time and space, so His true creature cannot be finited by these conditions. Thus the life of nature, or that life which lies within the laws of space and time, does not image God. The only life which does image Him consequently is one that transcends these laws, being a spiritual life, and this life belongs exclusively to man.

But in order to justify this affirmation, it is necessary to state what we mean by spirit as distinguished from sensible nature. In speaking of the spirit of a thing in contradistinction to the sensible thing itself, nothing else is meant than its distinctive genius, or faculty of operation. For example, the horse is an outward form discernible by my senses from all other natural forms. But there is something more in the horse than meets my eye, namely, a certain faculty or capacity of use, which constitutes his distinctive spirit or genius, and is cognizable only by the eye of my understanding. Thus what is spiritual about the horse is what lies within his material form, and constitutes his power or faculty of use. This faculty is different in the horse from what it is in every other animal, the cow, the sheep, the ox, the lion, the elephant, etc. Take another example from the sphere of the arts. My hat is an artificial form sensibly distinct from all other forms. But this outward or sensible form of the hat does not exist by itself. It embodies a certain use or function, namely the protection of my head, which use or function constitutes its spirit. In short the spirit of a thing is the end or use for which it exists. Thus you may take the whole range either of nature or the arts, and you will find everything existing for a certain use beyond itself, which use is the spiritual ground or justification of its existence. Nature is properly nothing more than the robe or garment of spirit. It is only the tabernacle or house of spirit, only the subservient instrument or means by which spirit subsists and becomes conscious. Every thing in nature, without any the most insignificant exception, embodies an internal use or capacity of operation, which constitutes its peculiar spirit. Deprive it of this internal use or capacity, not only actually or for a limited time, but potentially or for ever, and you deprive it of life. Exhaust the power of the horse to bear a burden and draw a load, of the cow to produce milk, of the sheep to produce wool, of the tree to produce fruit or seed, and you at the same time consign them all to death. For death, or the departure of the spirit from the body, means in every case the cessation of the subject's capacity of use. Thus nature in all its departments is merely the vehicle or minister of spirit. Its true sphere is that of entire subjection to spirit, and never since the world began has an instance occurred of its failing to exhibit the most complete acquiescence in this subjection.

But if this spiritual force reside in Nature, what hinders any natural form being a true revelation or image of God? If, for example, the horse possess a spiritual substratum, why does not the horse image God? The reason is obvious. The spirit of the horse is not his own spirit. He is entirely unconscious of it. He performs incessant uses to man, but does not perform them *of himself*. His end is external to himself. The object of his actions does not fall within his own subjectivity. The spirit of universal nature is a spirit of subjection to some external power. It never manifests itself spontaneously, but always in obeisance to some outward constraint. Thus the horse does not spontaneously place himself in the harness. The cow does not come to your dairy, to make a spontaneous surrender of her milk. The sheep feels no spontaneous impulsion to deposit his fleece at your door. Nor does the tree inwardly shake itself in order to supply you with apples. In short there is no such thing as a spiritual horse—cow—sheep—or apple tree. . . .

No, all these performances are for the benefit of man. The whole realm of nature is destitute of a spiritual consciousness, of such a consciousness as elevates any of its forms to the dignity of a person. No animal is conscious of a selfhood distinct from its outward or natural limitations. No animal is capable of suicide, or the renunciation of its outer life, on the ground of its no longer fulfilling the aspiration of its inner life. Thus nature is destitute of any proper personality. The only personality it recognizes is man. To him all its uses tend. Him all its powers obey. To his endowment and supremacy it willingly surrenders itself, and finds life in the surrender. Take away man accordingly, and nature remains a clod, utterly spiritless —impersonal—dead.

Thus nature does not image or reveal God. For God's activity is not imposed. It is spontaneous, or self-generated. It flows from Himself exclusively, and ignores all outward motive. Hence God's true creature or image is bound above all things to exhibit that power of self-derived or spontaneous action which constitutes our idea of the divine personality.

Accordingly it is man alone who fulfills this requisition. Man alone possesses personality, or the power of self-derived action. Personality, the quality of being a person, means simply the power of self-derived or supernatural action, the power of originating one's own action, or, what is the same thing, of acting according to one's own sovereign pleasure. It means a power of acting unlimited by any thing but the will of the subject. Thus, in ascribing personality to God, we do not mean to assert for him certain bodily limitations palpable to sense, which would be absurd; we mean merely to assert His self-sufficiency or infinitude—His power to act according to his own sovereign pleasure. We mean, in plain English, to assert that He is the exclusive source of His own actions. So also, in ascribing personality to man and denying it to the horse, we mean to assert that man possesses the power of supernatural or infinite action, the power of acting independently of all natural constraint, and according to his own individual or private attraction, while the horse has not this power. Man's action, when it is truly personal, has its source in himself, in his own private tastes or attractions, as contra-distinguished on the one hand from his physical necessities, and on the other from his social obligations; therefore we affirm man's personality, or his absolute property in his actions. Nature's action has not its source in any interior self, but in some outward and constraining power; therefore we deny nature any personality, any absolute property in its actions. When the fire burns my incautious finger, I do not blame the fire, and why? Because I feel that the fire acts in strict obedience to its nature, which is that of subjection to me, and that I alone have been in fault, therefore, for reversing this relation and foolishly subjecting myself to it.

But now, if personality imply the power of self-derived or spontaneous action, then it is manifest that this power supposes in the subject a composite self-hood. It supposes its subject to possess an internal or spiritual self as the end or object of the action, and an external or natural self as its means or instrument. For clearly, when you attribute any action to me personally, or affirm my exclusive property in it, you do not mean to affirm that it was prompted by my nature, that nature which is common to me and all other men, but by my private taste or inclination. You hold that I have some internal end, some private object to gratify by it, and thereupon you declare the action mine. I repeat, then, that personality, or the power of self-derived action, supposes a dual or composite selfhood in the subject, a selfhood composed of two elements, one internal, spiritual, or private, the other external, natural, or public.

But this is not all. Personality, or the power of self-derived action, not only supposes this composite selfhood in the subject, not only supposes him to possess an internal self, and an external self, but it also supposes that these two shall be perfectly united in every action which is properly called his. For example, I perform a certain action which you pronounce mine, on the ground of its having visibly proceeded from my hand. Now I say, this is not sufficient to prove the action absolutely mine. In order to prove it absolutely mine, you must not only show that it was done by my hand or my external self, but also that this external self did not at the time dominate or overrule my internal self. If the two elements of my personality were not perfectly united, perfectly concurrent, in the action; if the internal self were overruled by the external, or *vice versa;* then the action is not truly mine, is not a legitimate progeny of my will and understanding, but a bastard or *filius nullius* [literally, "nobody's son"], abhorred of God and man. . . .

Here let us pause a moment to survey the ground we have traversed. We have seen that creation is but the revelation or imaging forth of the divine personality. We have consequently seen that nature is incompetent to this revelation, because nature is destitute of personality, destitute of power to originate its own action. And finally we have seen that man is the only competent revelation or image of God, because man alone possesses personality. So far we have attained.

But now, from the definition given of personality, it is manifest that it is to be ascribed to man only in his very inmost or highest development, and not at all in his physical or social relations. For personality, when applied to any subject, affirms the subject's infinitude or perfection, affirms, in other words, the subject's entire sufficiency unto himself. It affirms his self-sufficiency or perfection, because it implies the power of originating his own action. He who has power to originate his own action is sufficient unto himself, and to be sufficient unto oneself is to be infinite or perfect. Infinitude or perfection means self-sufficiency. I admit the words are often used by rote, or without any definite intention. But whenever they are used intelligently, they are designed to express the subject's self-sufficiency. We can form no conception of the divine infinitude or perfection other than is expressed by saying that He is sufficient unto Himself. And if we further ask ourselves what we mean by His being sufficient unto Himself, we reply instinctively that we mean to express His power to originate his own action. This power, which is inherent in God, is the basis of His personality or character, is that thing, without which to our conception He would not be God, that is, would not be infinite or perfect. Had He not this power He would be finite or imperfect. His power, like that of nature, would be limited by something external to Himself.

If, therefore, personality, when applied to any subject, expresses his infinitude or perfection, expresses his self-sufficiency, it is manifest as was said before, that it cannot be applied to man in every aspect of his subjectivity, namely, as a subject either of nature or of his fellow-man, but only in his very highest aspect, which is that of a divine subject. For man's highest or inmost subjection is a subjection to God, which lifts him entirely beyond the sphere of necessity or duty, and indeed enables him, if need be, to lay off the bodily life and the friendship of men as easily as he lays off his garments at night. This subjection of man to God is involved in the very relation of Creator and creature. For the Creator being essential life, life in itself, cannot communicate life, save by communicating Himself to the creature. And He cannot communicate Himself, save in so far as the creature be made receptive, which receptivity becomes effected by means of the creature's natural and moral experience, the issue of which is to exalt him above nature and above society, endowing him with the lordship or supremacy of the external universe. Man's natural activity degrades or obscures his personality. It is not spontaneous—does not originate in his internal self, but in a mere necessity of his nature common to all its partakers. Instead of expressing his distinctive personality, therefore, it expresses a common property of all men. Regarded as a subject of nature, therefore, man lacks personality, lacks at least all such personality as reflects the divine.

His moral subjectivity presents a similar fatal defect. Morality covers my relations to society or my fellow-man. Thus, as my natural action is conditioned upon a law of necessity, or of subjection to nature, so my moral action is conditioned upon a law of duty, or of subjection to my fellow-man. I act morally only in so far as I act under obligation to others, being morally good when I practically acknowledge, and morally evil when I practically deny, this obligation. Thus morality displays me in subjection not to God, but to society or my fellow-man, and thus equally with nature denies me proper personality. For personality implies the subject's absolute property in his action, which property is impossible unless the subject constitute also the object of the action, or, in other words, unless the object of the action fall *within,* be internal to, the subject's self, and this condition is violated when I act not to please myself, but to please my fellow-man. Hence neither man's natural nor his moral action confers a divine or perfect personality on him. The former does not, because it displays him in subjection to nature. The latter does not, because it displays him in subjection to his fellow-man. Both the moral and natural man are imperfect. Both fail to exhibit that balanced or self-centred action, which is the exclusive basis of personality, and both alike consequently fail to express the DIVINE MAN, or accomplish the divine image in humanity.

But here it may be asked whether benevolence does not confer personality. Decidedly not, for the reason that benevolent action is not spontaneous but purely sympathetic. Personal action—all action which warrants the ascription of personality to the subject—is of necessity spontaneous, or inwardly begotten. I say of necessity, because action which is outwardly begotten, or originates in something foreign to the subject, does not pertain to him absolutely but only partially, pertains to him only as he stands involved in nature or society. Now sympathetic action evidently falls under this latter category, being begotten not from within but from without the subject's self, as the etymology of the word indicates. It supposes a want on the part of somebody not the subject, disposing the latter to relieve it. If, therefore, you take away suffering from all others, you take from the benevolent subject all power of action. And surely no one will consider that as a divine or perfect personality, whose power of action is controlled by circumstances foreign to itself.

Thus the fundamental requisite of personality, namely, that it attest the subject's self-sufficiency or perfection by exhibiting in him the power of self-derived action, is necessarily made void in all purely benevolent action. And the inevitable conclusion therefore is, that the benevolent man, as such, does not possess true personality, or is incompetent to image God.

Who, then, *is* the true divine man? Who of all mankind possesses personality, and thus constitutes the image of God in creation? Evidently it must be some one who unites in himself, or harmonizes, all these finite or imperfect men. For the divine man does not exclude the natural man, nor the moral man, nor the sympathetic man, nor any other phasis of humanity. These are all constituent elements of the human nature, and the perfect man is bound not to exclude but accept them, blending and reconciling all in his own infinite manhood, in his own unitary self. These men are the geometric stones of the divine edifice of humanity; they are by no means the edifice itself, but its indispensable *material*, and he therefore who should attempt to construct the edifice to their exclusion, would necessarily have his work about his ears.

Who, then, is the perfect or divine man, the man who actually reconciles in himself all the conflicting elements of humanity? Is any such man actually extant? If so, where shall we find him?

We find him in the aesthetic man, or Artist. But now observe that when I speak of the aesthetic man or Artist, I do not mean the man of any specific function, as the poet, painter, or musician. I mean the man of whatsoever function, who in fulfilling it obeys his own inspiration or taste, uncontrolled either by his physical necessities or his social obligations. He alone is the Artist, whatever be his manifest vocation, whose action obeys his own internal taste or attraction, uncontrolled either by necessity or duty. The action may perfectly consist both with necessity and duty; that is to say, it may practically promote both his physical and social welfare; but these must not be its animating principles, or he sinks at once from the Artist into the artisan. The artisan seeks to gain a livelihood or secure an honorable name. He works for bread, or for fame, or for both together. The Artist abhors these ends, and works only to show forth that immortal beauty whose presence constitutes his inmost soul. He is vowed to Beauty as the bride is vowed to the husband, and beauty reveals herself to him only as he is true to his inmost soul, only as he obeys his spontaneous taste or attraction.

The reason accordingly why the painter, the poet, the musician, and so forth, have so long monopolized the name of Artist, is, not because Art is identical with these forms of action, for it is identical with no specific forms, but simply because the poet, painter, and so forth, more than any other men, have thrown off the tyranny of nature and custom, and followed the inspirations of genius, the inspirations of beauty, in their own souls. These men to some extent have sunk the service of nature and society in the obedience of their own private attractions. They have merged the search of the good and the true in that of the beautiful, and have consequently announced a divinity as yet unannounced either in nature or society. To the extent of their consecration, they are priests after the order of Melchisedec, that is to say, a priesthood, which, not being made after the law of a carnal commandment, shall never pass away. And they are kings, who reign by a *direct* unction from the Highest. But the priest is not the altar, but the servant of the altar; and the king is not the Highest, but the servant of the Highest. So painting, poetry, is not Art, but the servant and representative of Art. Art is divine, universal, infinite. It therefore exacts to itself infinite forms or manifestations, here in the painter, there in the actor; here in the musician, there in the machinist; here in the architect, there in the dancer; here in the poet, there in the costumer. We do not therefore call the painter or poet, Artist, because painting or poetry is a whit more essential to Art than ditching is, but simply because the painter and poet have more frequently exhibited the life of Art by means of a hearty insubjection to nature and convention.

When, therefore, I call the divine man, or God's image in creation, by the name of Artist, the reader will not suppose me to mean the poet, painter, or any other special form of man. On the contrary, he will suppose me to mean that infinite and spiritual man whom all these finite function-aries represent indeed, but whom none of them constitutes, namely, the man who in every visible form of action acts always from his inmost self, or from attraction, and not from necessity or duty. I mean the man who is a law unto himself, and ignores all outward allegiance, whether to nature or society. This man may indeed have no technical vocation whatever, such as poet, painter, and the like, and yet he will be none the less sure to announce himself. The humblest theatre of action furnishes him a plat-form. I pay my waiter so much a day for putting my dinner on the table. But he performs his function in a way so entirely *sui generis,* with so exquisite an attention to beauty in all the details of the service, with so symmetrical an arrangement of the dishes, and so even an adjustment of every thing to its own place, and to the hand that needs it, as to shed an almost epic dignity upon the repast, and convert one's habitual "grace before meat" into a spontaneous tribute, instinct with a divine recognition.

The charm in this case is not that the dinner is all before me, where the man is bound by his wages to place it. This every waiter I have had has done just as punctually as this man. No, it is exclusively the way in which it is set before me, a way altogether peculiar to this man, which attests that in doing it he is not thinking either of earning his wages, or doing his duty towards me, but only of satisfying his own conception of beauty with the resources before him. The consequence is that the pecuniary relation between us merges in a higher one. He is no longer the menial, but my equal or superior, so that I have felt, when entertaining doctors of divinity and law, and discoursing about divine mysteries, that a living epistle was circulating behind our backs, and quietly ministering to our wants, far more apocalyptic to an enlightened eye than any yet contained in books.

The reader may deem the illustration beneath the dignity of the subject. The more the pity for him in that case, since it is evident that his eyes have been fixed upon the shows of things, rather than upon the enduring sub-stance. It is not indeed a dignified thing to wait upon tables. There is no dignity in any labor which is constrained by one's necessities. But still no function exists so abject or servile as utterly to quench the divine or per-sonal element in it. It will make itself manifest in all of them, endowing them all with an immortal grace, and redeeming the subject from the dominion of mere nature and custom.

But whether the illustration be mean or not, it is fully to the point. The divine life in every man, the life which is the direct inspiration of God, and therefore exactly images God, consists in the obedience of one's own taste or attraction, where one's taste or attraction is uncontrolled by necessity or duty, by nature or society. I know that this definition will not commend itself to the inattentive reader. But let me leave my meaning fully expressed. I say, then, that I act divinely, or that my action is perfect, only when I follow my own taste or attraction, uncontrolled either by my natural wants or my obligations to other men. I do not mean that I act divinely when I follow my attractions to the denial of my physical wants and my social obligations; but only in independence of them. If these things control my action, it will not be divine. . . .

A man, then, does not truly act at all, does not act in any such sense that the action may be pronounced absolutely *his*, so long as his personality remains undeveloped; so long as he remains in bondage to nature or society. Before he can truly act or show forth the divine power within him, he must be in a condition of perfect outward freedom, of perfect insubjection to nature and society; all his natural wants must be supplied, and all social advantages must be open to him. Until these things are achieved his action must be more or less imperfect and base. You may, indeed, frighten him into some show of decorum, by representations of God as an infallible policeman intent always on evil-doers, but success in this way is very partial. The church itself, in fact, which authorizes these representations, incessantly defeats their force by its doctrine of absolution, or its proclamation of mercy to the most successful villany, if only repentant at the last gasp. Not only the church, but the whole current of vital action defeats these safeguards. Thus our entire system of trade, as based upon what is called "unlimited competition," is a system of rapacity and robbery. A successful merchant like Mr. A. or B., is established only on the ruins of a thousand unsuccessful ones. Mr. A. or B. is not to be blamed individually. His heart is destitute of the least ill-will towards the men whom, perhaps, he has never seen, but whom he is yet systematically strangling. He acts in the very best manner society allows to one of his temper or genius. He feels an unmistakably divine aspiration after unlimited power; a power, that is, which shall be unlimited by any outward impediment, being limited only by his own interior taste or attraction. He will seek the gratification of this instinct by any means the constitution of society ordains; thus, by the utter destruction of every rival merchant, if society allows it.

So much for Mr. A. or B. regarded as in subjection to nature and society, or as still seeking a field for his personality. But this is not the final and divine Mr. A. or B. The final and divine Mr. A. or B. will have subjected both nature and society to himself, and will then exhibit, by virtue of that very force in him, which is now so destructively operative, a personality of unmixed benignity to every one. The voice of God, as declared in his present instincts after unlimited power, bids him, as it bade the Israelites of old, to spoil the oppressor, to cleave down every thing that stands in the way of his inheritance: suppose him once established in that good land which flows with milk and honey, and which God has surely promised him, and you will immediately find the same instinct manifested in measureless and universal benediction.

The Artist, then, is the Divine Man,—the only adequate image of God in nature,—because he alone acts of himself, or finds the object of his action always *within* his own subjectivity. He is that true creature and son of God, whom God pronounces very good, and endows with the lordship of the whole earth. It would not be difficult, in the writers's estimation, to show the reason why the evolution of this man has required the whole past physical and moral experience of the race, nor yet to show how perfectly he justifies all the historic features of Christianity, standing symbolized under every fact recorded in the four gospels concerning the Lord Jesus Christ. In some other place, or at least on some future occasion, the writer will undertake these tasks.

8

THE PERFECT LIFE

Having defined the divine or perfect man as the
"Artist," James went on in another lecture written
about the same time to define the perfect life as that of
"Art." Yet again "The Principle of Universality in Art,"
as James called it, was to be dissociated from all of its
distinct manifestations in this or that particular form
of expression. James was concerned instead with the
nature of art as such, his intention being to show that
art is man's most characteristic and natural activity.
By art, then, James did not mean some particular kind
of object but rather some particular kind of action,
one which was wholly spontaneous in expressing the
true being of the actor or maker. Art, he therefore
described in the formulas of the time, is the internal
made external, the ideal made actual, but with the
proviso that the personal element thus released is none
other than that which is common to the humanity of
all men. In other words, art was the mode of divine or
perfect life precisely because it served as a vehicle for
the expression of that principle of universality which
to James was "Life Itself."

The following selection is drawn from Lecture 3,
"The Principle of Universality in Art," in *Lectures
and Miscellanies* (New York, 1852), 101–8, 111–17,
118–34.

———•◦•———

I do not intend to discuss in this Lecture the principles of any specific
art, or the methods of excellence it offers to its votary, for this would be
a discussion to which I am wholly incompetent. I simply propose to consider the nature of Art universally, of all Art whatever be its specific manifestation, and to show what it is which makes it man's characteristic or
sovereign activity.

It is very evident that Art is a universal spirit, from the circumstance of
its having so many distinct manifestations. We sometimes call the painter
Artist, sometimes the musician, sometimes the poet, sometimes the actor,
and so forth *ad infinitum*. Now in speaking thus we virtually assign a universal empire to Art, and regard these several vocations as only so many of

its particular provinces. What I propose to do then just now, is, to state the principle of universality in Art, to state what it is which makes the poet, the musician, the sculptor, and so forth, an Artist, and so commends him to homage.

The sphere of Art properly so called, is the sphere of man's spontaneous productivity. I say his spontaneous productivity, in order to distinguish it on the one hand from his *natural* productivity, or that which is prompted by his physical necessities, and on the other by his moral productivity, or that which is prompted by his obligations to other men. Thus the sphere of Art embraces all those products of human genius, which do not confess the parentage either of necessity or duty. It covers whatsoever is produced without any external constraint, any constraint imposed by the exigencies either of our physical or social subsistence. We do not call the shoemaker an artist, because we know very well that he is animated in his vocation not by any inward attraction to it, not by any overmastering love of making shoes, but simply by the desire of making a living for himself and his family. What prompts him to work is not any spontaneous and irrepressible delight in it, any such delight as makes the work its own reward, but simply a feeling of obligation to himself and his family. He makes no shoe for the pure pleasure of making it, but because he would so put bread into the mouths of his family. Thus his productivity, being enforced both by necessity and duty, being enforced by the necessity of providing for himself and the duty of providing for those whom society makes dependent on him, is not spontaneous or free, does not in other words obey an internal attraction, and consequently falls utterly without the sphere of Art. The shoemaker is not an Artist. He is only an Artisan or Workman.

It is evident from this analysis then that Art does not simply imply production, but production of a certain order. It implies as I have already said, spontaneous production, or production which is energised from within the producer, and not by his physical or social necessities. And now that I may remove all manner of ambiguity or obscurity from the subject let me explain to you exactly what is meant by spontaneity in man, exactly what is meant by his spontaneous action.

All action is the product of two forces or elements, one internal which we call its end or object; the other external which we call its means or subject. No action is possible unless it enjoy this double parentage, unless it proceed from a certain generative or paternal end, through a certain formative or maternal means. Here for example is an action. I place my hat on my head. This action acknowledges the congress or conjoint parentage of two elements, one originating or begetting, the other mediating or serving: namely, 1. a desire in me to protect my head from the weather; 2. an obedient physical organization. Were it not for the first element here, which was my desire to protect my head from the weather, the second element which is my physical organization would have remained inert, and the action accordingly would not have taken place.

Now the first or propagative element of this action, is denominated its object; the second or instrumental element is denominated its subject.

Such is the invariable genesis of action, that its objective element or the object *for* which the action is done, bears the relation of father to it; and its subjective element, or the means *by* which it is done, bears the relation of mother.

You perfectly perceive then that all action properly so called embodies two elements, one internal and generative which we denominate its end or object, the other external and formative which we denominate its means or subject.

Now such being the nature of all action, it is the precise peculiarity of spontaneous action that it always makes the object fall *within* the subject, that it never allows the object to lie out of or beyond the subject's self. I call this the peculiarity or distinction of spontaneous action, because both natural and moral action exhibit an exactly contrary order. They both place the object of the action without the subject, make the object external to the subject. When I act spontaneously the object or motive of my action lies within myself who am the subject of it: when I act simply naturally, much more when I act merely morally, the object or motive of my action lies without myself: that is to say in the one case, the object is my external physical organization; in the other case, it is my fellow-man. Let me make all this plain by an example or two.

First, take an example of natural action. Let it be the most familiar of all natural actions, that of eating or drinking. The object of this action is the gratification of a natural appetite. I do not eat or drink to gratify my private taste, but simply to satisfy a physical necessity. Thus the object of the action in this case is made external to the subject, while the subject is made internal to the object. Nature imposes this activity on me the subject, under the penalty of acute suffering. I am not at liberty to neglect it. It is a necessity of my natural existence. Hence you perceive that the objective element in the natural action of cating or drinking, is made external, and the subjective element is made internal.

It is true that I may make this natural action of eating and drinking the basis of an exquisite Art, for art being universal disdains no field of minis-tration however humble, but avouches its redeeming virtue most in de-scending to what is lowly, and exalting that which is despised. It sheds a divine splendor over the meanest things, and glorifies the infinite riches of its resources in the exact ratio of the intrinsic poverty of its materials. But in this case, that is to say, when I exalt my eating and drinking into the realm of Art, the action of course ceases to be any longer merely *natural,* and so puts itself out of relation to our immediate inquiry.

Let us next take an example of moral action, and let it be the most familiar of all moral actions, that of paying a debt. Now the object of this action is the satisfaction of a social obligation. Society makes one of its members at present dependent upon another, the child upon the parent, the wife upon the husband, the poor man upon the rich one, and conse-quently imposes certain duties or debts upon the former towards the latter. These duties or debts must be paid under penalty of social reprobation.

The child must pay the debt imposed by its state of dependence upon the parent, the wife must pay the debt imposed by her state of dependence upon the husband, and the poor man the debt imposed by his state of dependence upon the rich man. Otherwise society will go into disorder. In the case supposed to illustrate the nature of moral action, I pay a pecuniary debt. I may do it very much against my will. That is to say, it may involve very serious embarrassment to me to part with the money. Or the creditor may have rendered himself so extremely obnoxious to me, as to destroy my good-will towards him. Nevertheless I pay him. Much as I may suffer from the payment in my domestic relations, or much as I may detest the person of my creditor, I yet feel so keenly the imperative nature of my social obligations, as promptly to discharge the debt. Thus my action becomes in the highest degree moral, or expressive of the sentiment of duty. Its object is not to gratify myself, but purely to satisfy the legal claim of another, to satisfy the claim which society gives another upon me. Thus you perceive in this case also that the object is made external, and the subject internal, which is exactly contrary to the order of spontaneous action.

It may indeed be asked whether a debt may not be paid spontaneously, whether in other words duty and taste, duty and beauty, may not be coincident? Decidedly so. In the absolute truth of things there is no variance between duty and pleasure. In the absolute truth of things, duty and taste, duty and inclination, or self-love and neighborly love are perfectly united. But man very slowly conforms to the absolute truth of things. Fully to conform to that constitutes his destiny. The whole of his social history is a gradual approximation to this conformity. For society, or the phenomenon of human fellowship, is bent upon solving no other problem but this, so to adjust the relations of man to man, as that no possible conflict may exist between our public and private interests, between the obligation I am under to myself, and that which I am under to my fellow-man. . . .

But this is a sad digression. In endeavoring to discriminate moral action from spontaneous action I have been tempted somewhat beyond the strict limits of my subject, to which I now return. My object was to shew you that moral and physical action, all that sort of action which is enforced by our finite circumstances, by physical and social penalties, differs from spontaneous action in this, that it makes one man's object external to him instead of internal, while spontaneous action exactly reverses this order. And I wished to bring this discrimination before you only in order that I might have your intelligent appreciation when I proceed to say that *invention* supplies all the requisites of spontaneous or aesthetic action, when I proceed to say for example that the man who *invents* shoes is an Artist, while the man who only makes shoes is not.

Invention fulfils all the conditions of aesthetic activity. A work of Art is that which is complete in itself, which involves its own end, or presents the perfect unity of object and subject. Thus in the case in question—the invention of shoes—the human feet are unclad. They need a protection against the elements, but such a protection as shall not impair the natural vigor and freedom of the foot. Now in performing this work, my object, or that which generates and governs my activity, is a certain idea or conception within my own mind. If the result perfectly express this idea or mental conception, the work will be complete in itself, will be a work of Art. The shoe may not fit any actual foot of man, yet this circumstance will not affect its aesthetic merit. My design was not to fit a shoe to a particular foot: that is the business of the shoemaker or artisan: but to give outward form or body to an inward idea. If I do this, then I have done a perfect work, a work of Art, whether the actual result be or be not available to a particular use.

Now what the artisan or shoemaker does, is merely to adapt my invention to a particular foot. He seizes the universal idea to which I have given embodiment, and applies it to a specific use. He does not invent a new form; he merely moulds an existing and universal form to a particular exigency. Thus his activity is imperfect, is not complete in itself. If his shoe does not fit the foot it is intended for, it is made in vain, since it was made not for its own sake like my shoe, but for the sake of that particular foot which after all it does not fit.

Let me not be misunderstood. I do not mean to deny the existence of every degree of skill in the workman. I only mean to deny that the highest skill constitutes what men call Art. The Artist is oftentimes extremely deficient in skill, or mere executive talent; in other words he is often unhappily a very poor artisan. Talent or skill belongs to the artisan. It may abound in one man, and be extremely defective in another, so that one shall properly be called a good workman and the other a poor one. But we do not talk of a good Artist, or a poor Artist. For Art is positive, claiming a substantive majesty, and beggaring all adjectives to set forth its praise. The Artist is not the man who paints a landscape or a portrait better than any other man. It is not the man who writes a better poem, or builds a more symmetric edifice than another. It is not the man of any specific mode of industry or productive action. It is simply the man who in all these modes works from an ideal, works to produce or bring forth in tangible form some conception of use or beauty with which not his memory but his inmost soul is aglow.

Thus in estimating a work of Art, you would seek to ascertain how far its genetic idea or mental conception had been fulfilled, how far in other words the sentiment of the piece impressed you. It may be that Salvator[1] paints trees more accurately than Poussin.[2] This proves not that Poussin was not a true disciple of Art, but only that Salvator was a better workman, a more faithful reproducer of nature. For all this Poussin may impress you with a much deeper feeling of Art than the other. His pictures may be much fuller of sentiment, may be a far ampler revelation of beauty to the soul. For Art does not lie in copying nature. Nature only furnishes the Artist with the material by means of which to express a beauty still unexpressed in nature. He beholds in nature more than nature herself holds or is conscious of. His informing eye it is which gives her that soul of beauty, that profoundly human meaning, which alone keeps her from being burdensome to the spirit. Nature *rules* only in the young and immature, only where the sensuous imagination still predominates. She is the menial of the Artist, or if that word seem too harsh, she is his nimble and airy servitor eager to do his royal bidding. She is simply the platform or theatre for the revelation of that infinite and divine beauty which dwells in the soul of man, and makes itself visible in all his spontaneous action. Hence nature should never predominate in the realm of Art, but only serve. And accordingly no one ever employs a painter to reproduce upon the walls of his chamber the actual landscape which smiles before its windows. For no one wishes to see nature merely imitated or reproduced. He wishes to see it imaging a nobler beauty, a subtler ideal charm, than his eyes have yet beheld. Therefore he imports a foreign sky to adorn his parlors, and finds in the sunny meads and terraced cliffs of other lands, a delight unexhausted by his past experience.

If the past train of observation be just, then we may not fear to accept the definition I have given of a work of Art. It is a work which involves its own end, or is complete in itself. Art is not a term designed to express any particular mode of external activity, but simply to characterize, *throughout the whole range of human production*, that performance which obeys a purely ideal end, or represents a conception of beauty in the performer's soul. Whatever work of man does not come under this definition, whether it be painting or poetry or sculpture, falls without the sphere of Art. It may be a work of surpassing cleverness, it may greatly excel the work of every other man in the same walk, but it is not a work of Art. It is at best an unsurpassed copy of Nature, and always remains inferior to the original. Zeuxis[3] may paint natural effects better than Apelles.[4] He may give you such miraculous distances, and so embathe his foliage with the tender freshness of the dawn, that you would swear he knew the very heart of nature, and could utter all her secrets at will. But all this only leaves Zeuxis a painter. It by no means makes him an Artist. For take away a certain effect from nature, and you leave him powerless. To be a first-rate painter one must be a faithful copyist of nature, as to be a first-rate poet one must be a faithful copyist of the human heart. But to be an Artist in either sphere is to do something more than copy. It is to make poetry and painting serve ideas, or express a beauty above nature and beyond the range of our private affections. Zeuxis accordingly has been a zealous student or copyist of nature. He has watched her more wistfully than the spider watches the fly. In the voluminous note-book of his memory, he has recorded all her shifting phantasmagoria, and is quite sure that he will one day seize her with a grasp which all men shall deem immortal.

But the Artist avoids all this fidget. He loves and enjoys nature, but with no sinister design. He enters the chambers of the morning for a present refreshment, and with no view to the scraps he may carry home in his wallet. He watches the lingering glance of the god of day, because it evokes a mystic rapture in his soul which no other natural symbol can, but he has not the remotest intention of reporting the transaction for the newspapers. He may of course be, as to his specific intellectual activity, a painter or a poet, and in either capacity will use these fruits of his observation with admirable advantage. All I wish to say is that so far as he is also Artist, the inspiration of his activity will come from within and not from without, will date exclusively from a supersensuous idea, and not from the most gorgeous landscape the sun ever lighted. . . .

These considerations explain why men so much dislike mere toil or compulsory work. It is servile and imitative. It is always enforced by some bodily necessity or social duty, by some exigency of one's natural or social position. Aesthetic activity, the activity of the Artist, on the other hand is free and original. It springs not from necessity or duty, but purely from taste or delight. It has an exclusively inward genesis. It proceeds from within to without. It is in every case the embodiment of an idea, and therefore complete in itself. Thus the Artist, the man who is striving to actualize an idea, inevitably feels a sense of human dignity or worth to which the mere paid laborer is a stranger.

This is the reason why merely mechanical or ritual labor is not loved. It is not that one may not have a genius or attraction for that sort of occupation, for such is not the case. Louis XVI[5] passed his sunniest hours this side the scaffold in his little workshop, fashioning locks of every pattern, and there is scarcely any of us but delights occasionally to enact the carpenter within his own cupboard, and even supersede the tailor in respect to a deficient button or so. It is only that these occupations are usually enforced by necessity. One's genius prompts a wholly free resort to them as to all other occupations, and when one is held to them therefore without any intermission by the necessities of his actual subsistence, he feels that his human instincts are violated.

Mechanical occupations are in themselves as respectable as any other. Mechanics themselves embody probably a larger measure of human worth than any other class of the community, both because they are the largest in point of numbers, and because they have not the same temptations to self-conceit, or an undue estimate of themselves, as the others. Indeed when I recur to my own memory for its best illustrations of solid manly worth, of true human sweetness, it refers me to individuals of this class. But our unintelligent society does not bear this in memory. It fixes its regard upon the fact that mechanical occupation is usually enforced by necessity, and hence refuses to bestow the honor upon the tailor or shoemaker which it bestows upon the painter or sculptor. Doubtless society acts herein with an instinct wiser than its wisdom, by way of stimulating the masses not to a disgust of their occupations which are in themselves full of honor, but to a *disgust of the actual servitude they are under to these occupations*, and an effort consequently to better their social position. In this point of view we may amply justify the temporary social inferiority of the mechanic to the clergyman and lawyer; but the fact of that inferiority is undeniable. What clergyman, what lawyer, invites his carpenter to dine with him and meet Lord Morpeth,⁶ who very possibly might more relish such a guest than such a host? No, society will allow none of her members to remain content with enforced or mercenary labor. She will goad him with incessant slights and sarcasms, until he compels her to lift him also above this accursed necessity of earning his bread by the sweat of his brow. So true is this, that if by chance a lucky investment in real estate makes his descendants rich and leaders of fashion, society is sure to visit them with a perpetual recurrence to the ancestral wax-end, or at least a very frequent prick of the paternal needle.

No, talk as we may on gala days, we all of us hate compulsory labor, labor which the body lays upon the soul, because it does not express the true order of human life, does not express that inward and divine force which is the proper glory of man, and which reveals itself only in free or spontaneous action, action that descends from the soul to the body. In his profoundest soul every man rebels against the servitude of his body, and the servitude of society. It takes whips and dungeons and gibbets and a ceaseless army of men affirming the terrors of a vindictive future, to keep him to it, or prevent his supplying his wants in a more summary way. And after all, as we see in the Old World, this expensive machinery does its work very ineffectually. For human individuality is the very citadel of God's omnipotence, and you can no more repress its blind and perverse manifestations by penal statutes, than you can tame the electric current by a vote of the common council, or an expression of the public indignation. This fluid has from the beginning been at bottom full of friendliness towards you, and it has toppled your steeples, and burned your barns, and devastated your sideboards, for no other purpose than to compel your attention, and force you to provide it a safe conduct to the hungry and exhausted earth. So the mightier force of human individuality has resorted to eccentric and explosive methods, only by way of compelling society to do it tardy justice, by furnishing it suitable *media* for the display of its inmost and essential innocence.

The position of the *technical* Artist in past history confirms the statement I have made in a very perfect manner. The votary of what we call the *fine* arts, those arts which have the service of ornament for their end, has had a much higher conventional rank than the votary of the useful arts. Painters, poets, sculptors, actors, story-tellers, have been the chosen companions of kings and nobles. All saloons have been open to them, and even the inflexible canons of morality have been freely suspended in their behalf. Such has been the lot of these men, not because of any personal superiority in them to other men, but simply because their special activity revealed a deeper glimpse of destiny than was commonly apprehended. As against the complete subjection to nature and society which the hard toil of the masses declared to be the lot of man, this artistic activity perpetually opened up the fountains of the ideal in him, and visited him with gleams and promises of an inward divinity so radiant and refreshing as to make the base outward itself comparatively tender and tolerable. For this service these men reaped a consideration to which on personal or moral grounds they could have no title. Personally they have very often proved downright social nuisances, full of affectation, full of self-conceit, full of selfishness, full of petty malignity toward rival aspirants.

Surely then it is not for his own sake that the technical Artist has been honored, but purely for his sacerdotal or representative function. He has been the priest, in his sphere, of a higher worship than mankind has yet realized, and therefore men have done him honor. In the sphere of labor, in the sphere of production, he has revealed a more humane law of action for man than utility or duty, even taste or attraction, and hence only it is that men have canonized him. It is never the actual worth of what he does in point of talent that men care about, for the painter, sculptor, poet and musician have not been remarkable for general ability. Still less is it the moral worth of his performance, or its relation to established public senti-ment, that wins the Artist esteem, for the poorest pictures in the eye of a connoisseur are precisely those which are fullest of didactic intention, those which daringly prostitute the universality of nature to purposes of sycophancy, to the service of established opinions, to the flattery of the powers that be. For if a man should embody the pictorial skill of every painter from Apelles to Turner,[7] and yet propose nothing more than the illustration of existing public sentiment, than the vindication of the cur-rent morality, he would instantly confess himself a mere *terræ filius* ["clod"] unvisited by one ray of the true Apollo. In fact whatever be his executive talent or craftsmanship, if he propose anything at all in his per-formances but the bare revelation of a humanitary idea or sentiment, a sentiment which knows no statute-books, and is unconfessed in any cate-chism, and is the appanage of no persons, but in truth pervades the uni-verse like a vital Deity deluging the soul with unexpected enchantments, he falsifies his mission, offers up strange fire which Art has not com-manded, and all the academies on earth cannot shield him from a plenary damnation.

The principle of universality then in Art, or that thing which gives it a universal empire within the field of production, I find to be invention, individuality, or the power of giving outward form to purely inward con-ception. Every work of Art embodies an idea, and so confesses its dis-tinctively human genesis. Art is nothing more than the shadow of hu-manity. To make the ideal actual in the sphere of production, in the sphere of work, is the function of the Artist. To make the ideal actual *in the sphere of life,* is the function of Man. Talent, a healthy organization, knowl-edge of history or of the past achievements of the race, and an intercourse with nature and society wide enough to educate him out of all local preju-dice, these no doubt are indispensable conditions of the Artist's worthy manifestation, but they no more create or give him being, than the ele-ments of nature give being to man.

What the Artist does for us is, not to repeat some laborious dogma learned of nature or society, but to show nature and society everywhere pregnant with human meaning, everywhere pervaded by a human soul. His business in a word is to glorify MAN in nature and in men. All our sensible experience proceeds upon the fact of a unitary and therefore omnipresent soul or life within us. Were this soul or life finite like my body, were it finited by other souls as my body is finited by other bodies: were it in short an intrinsically heterogeneous soul in my body to what it is in other bodies: then all sympathy between me and universal nature would be impossible. Not only would my fellowship with man in that case obviously cease, but my eyes could no longer discern the glories of the earth and sky, nor my nose inhale the fragrance of innumerable flowers, nor my ears drink in the myriad melodies which are the daily offering of earth to heaven. For the splendor of the morning and evening landscape, the fragrance of flowers, and the melody of birds, are not substantial things having their root in themselves: they are merely masks of a certain relation between me and universal nature, of a certain unity between my soul and the soul that animates all things. The landscape is not glorious to itself, nor the flower fragrant, nor the bird melodious; they are severally glorious, fragrant and melodious only to me. The fragrance of the rose, the splendor of the landscape, the melody of the bird, are only an overt sacrament or communion between my soul and their soul, between God in me and God in them. Because an infinite or unitary life animates all things, we never come into outward contact without our inward unity flashing forth in these delicious surprises.

Now the Artist is saturated with this sentiment of universal unity, this sentiment which binds all nature together in the unity of a man, and he ever strives to give it a perfect expression. Why does he not succeed in doing so? Why does no painter, no poet, no sculptor succeed in snatching the inmost secret of Art, and so making his name immortal?

It is because the inmost secret of Art does not lie within the sphere of Art, but belongs only to Life. Art or doing, as I have said before, is itself but a shadow of the eternal fact which is life, or action. To live or to act is more than to produce: hence the technical Artist has never succeeded and never will succeed in achieving the universal empire which belongs only to Man. The poet, painter or musician is not the perfect man, the man of destiny, the man of God, because the perfect man is so pronounced by his life or action rather than by his production. He is not constituted perfect by any work of his hands however meritorious, but simply by the relation of complete unity between his inward spirit and his outward body, or what is better, between his ideas and his actions.

The Artist has typified the perfect man, because in the sphere of work or production he has wrought only from ideas, or from within outwards. But he has not *been* the perfect man, because in the sphere of life he has exhibited precisely the same conflict between the ideal and the actual as other men exhibit. Sometimes he has been a morally good man, and won the commendation of society; at others he has been a morally **evil** man and

exposed himself to its reproach. But the perfect man is above both commendation and reproach. He is neither morally good nor morally evil. His
goodness is infinite, being a goodness in himself, and hence all his physical
and social relations must infallibly reflect it.

The two moral poles, the poles of good and evil are *alike* requisite to
humanity. Neither of them by itself defines humanity. The good man by
himself, or the evil man by himself no more defines humanity, than the
North pole by itself, or the South pole by itself defines the earth. As the
earth is defined by the north and south poles equally, so humanity is defined by the good and evil man equally. The body of humanity lies between
these two extremes, as the body of the earth lies between north and south.
Accordingly if we regard the matter with some attention, we shall find that
as the best fertility of the earth comprises a middle region equidistant from
either pole, so the true vigor of humanity has never lain in the direction
either of good simply, or of evil simply, but in a middle plane equidistant
from both.

For the true vigor of humanity hitherto it will be admitted, has been
displayed in a social direction, that is to say, in promoting and strengthen-
ing human society or fellowship. Now it is manifest to a glance, that society or fellowship among men could never have been promoted by the cultivation either of the good element, which is charity, to the destruction of
the evil element, which is self-love; or by the cultivation of the evil element
to the destruction of the good one. If charity to the exclusion of self-love,
had been the policy of society, every man would have so deferred to every
other, that even the comparative fellowship we now enjoy would have
been forever unattainable, would in fact have argued great corruption. And
if self-love to the exclusion of charity, had been the mode, every man
would have so bullied every other, that fellowship would have been equally
inconceivable in that way. In the one case, suicide would have been the
logical culmination of morality, would have constituted one's social apotheo-
sis: in the other case, murder.

Society means fellowship, and fellowship means equality. Whoso is the
fellow of another, is so far forth his equal. Human society, accordingly, is
a state of fellowship or equality among men. The reason why equality is
a legitimate state of man, is that he is one in origin, and therefore one
in destiny. Mankind have one source, God or infinite goodness. Hence a
perfect fellowship or equality among them is a prime law of their constitution. It is an actual necessity of their development. No man can be truly
himself so long as any inequality exists between him and his fellow. If
therefore society, as now organized, as determined by its existing institutions, decree the inequality of man with man, it of course confesses itself
imperfect, or hostile to the divine unity, and pleads therefore, in an irresistible manner, with all the rational and humane potencies of the universe,
to come and modify it. For man having an essential equality, an equality
in God, which means of course an equality (I do not say an identity) of
spiritual endowment, of genius, of active force, his very divinity forbids

him resting content with unequal social relations. He will incessantly agitate society, incessantly urge it onward, until at length it realizes its own ideal by the legislative destruction of all privilege, or by the extension of an equal subsistence and an equal education to all its offspring.

Thus, society having had from the beginning one sole end, which is the organization of human fellowship or equality—the equality which man has in God or his creative source,—its practical attitude or operation could not have been hostile towards either moral pole of humanity, towards either charity or self-love, but must have incessantly tended on the contrary to their effectual reconciliation. Accordingly if we look at the course of history, we find the progress of human life generating an incessant equilibrium of these moral elements. While the distinction of the two elements continues unabated, we nevertheless find human life assuming a shape which is properly neither good nor evil, but rather their equilibrium or indifference. While we find both the saint and the sinner still extant and emphatic in their several ways, we yet find the great mass of men very little occupied with moral action, strictly considered. We find comparatively few men concerned in devising good to others at their own expense, or in devising good to themselves at the expense of others. We find the bulk of mankind occupied simply in devising how to put bread into their own mouths and those of their offspring, consistently with their social obligations. The mass of mankind, that portion of the race which has constituted its real glory and vigor, has never devoted itself to the direct cultivation of the affections whether of self-love or benevolence, but purely to the prosecution of the arts of life, those arts or methods which enable man to subdue nature to himself and live in amity with all other men.

Thus the past operation of society has served to stimulate Art, or a mode of industry distinctively human. I call Art a distinctively human development, because it fully recognizes both elements of human nature, the good and the evil, the higher and lower one, or brotherly love and self-love. Art denies neither love, but accepts both and gratifies both, for every work of Art promotes both the advantage of the community and the honor or emolument of the Artist. Hence Art may be styled man's characteristic activity, as expressing the whole of his nature, or inviting the freest play of both its moral elements. It excludes from its field neither the saint nor the sinner, neither serpent nor dove, but perfectly authenticates the aspiration of both. In his private relations a man may obey either moral pole: he may be a man of acute or deficient sympathies with his kind: he may habitually consult his neighbor first and himself last, or conversely. But so far as he prosecutes any distinctively human function, in so far as he pursues any of the recognized arts of life, his attitude is neither good nor evil, neither animated by self-love purely nor purely by charity, but is rather the equilibrium or indifference of the two. The three learned professions fall under this rule; all the functions of civil and political administration, all the trades, all the pursuits of science and mechanical invention, all mimetic and histrionic achievements, all games and sportive enterprises of every kind, are only so many colanders or sieves for the distillation of this true human essence. The clergyman, the lawyer or the physician may be very clever, very devoted, and very successful in his profession, while as to the bent of his private affections he may be a good or bad man indifferently. The statesman may excel in judgment and zeal for his country's service: the tradesman, the *savant*, the mechanic, the poet, painter, actor, may exhibit an extreme brilliancy of achievement in their several spheres: and yet no one upon that evidence shall be able to give the private attitude of any of these men towards the ten commandments. Thus of all the chief names in civil and political history, in the history of the church, in the history of science and the arts, some have been saints and some sinners; some have habitually obeyed the inspirations of moral good, some have habitually neglected them. In their public aspect, that aspect in which their names and memories have become the property of humanity, they satisfied both these elements. That is to say, by the work they accomplished they both promoted the public good and advanced their own interests. Their merely personal private qualities accordingly are forgotten, or remembered only by industrious literary gossips.

Thus the aim of society from the beginning has been practically to shed both saint and sinner, practically to ignore the mere finite and differential man, and so prepare the way for that infinite and unitary man to whom the lordship of the earth is divinely due. Its incessant practical operation has been to disuse the man whose affections are at all disproportionate either by excess or defect to his active fellowship with others, to his cordial social activity, and so prepare the way for the perfect man, the man who shall have no affection unauthenticated by the demands of his immediate life, or all whose capital shall be invested in enterprises of present profit. In strict subserviency to this end it has opened up within the bounds of the moral universe the temple of Art, that great theatre of human industry which invites all aspirants indifferently, without respect to creed or complexion, and in which the good and evil man having severally laid aside their private badges at the entrance, meet on equal terms to prosecute a common destiny by common methods. It is to this sphere accordingly, the sphere of Art, that we are authorized to look for the truest emblems of the consummate man, for the clearest revelation and foretaste of that positive manhood which shall one day lift us above nature, and give us the plenary fellowship of God. . . .

NOTES

1. Salvator Rosa (1615–1673) was an Italian painter of the Neopolitan school known chiefly for his landscapes and battle scenes.—Editor's note.
2. Nicholas Poussin (1594–1665) was a French historical and landscape painter who was regarded as a master of the classical school.—Editor's note.
3. Zeuxis, an ancient painter whom Pliny dates around 397 B.C., was famous for having added the use of highlights to shading.—Editor's note.

4. Apelles, an ancient painter whom Pliny dates around 332 B.C., was known for his portraits of Philip, Alexander, and their circle.—Editor's note.

5. Louis XVI (1754–1793) was king of France during the period just prior to the French Revolution.—Editor's note.

6. Lord Morpeth (George Howard, 1773–1848) was a famous British statesman and Whig politician who first came to public notice by opposing George Fox's motion for the repeal of the Treason and Sedition Acts.—Editor's note.

7. Joseph Mallord William Turner (1775–1851) was a noted English landscape painter who helped inaugurate the Romantic movement in England.—Editor's note.

9

THE NATURE OF EVIL
AND THE PERVERSION
OF FREEDOM

If the perfect life was defined as a life of spontaneous
freedom of expression and the perfect man as one who
completely realizes that freedom in action, then how
was James to account for the existence of evil in life,
and what definition could he offer of it? This was the
chief question which he tried to address in his book on
The Nature of Evil, though he kept returning to the
problem and reformulating his answer to it throughout
the entire course of his career. James wrote *The Nature
of Evil* in the form of a lengthy "Letter to the Rev.
Edward Beecher, D.D., Author of 'The Conflict of
Ages,' " in an effort to challenge the latter's view that
the Christian doctrine of the Fall referred not to some
present or recurrent event in time but rather to some
preexistent fact which occurred, so Beecher claimed, as
a result of "a temporary limitation of divine power in
the early stages of his system." Beecher's reinterpreta-
tion was intended to soften the traditional Calvinist
understanding of the Fall by treating it almost as a
kind of accident or mistake on God's part for which
man himself bore very little responsibility. James,
however, found the whole idea repellent. If man was
not culpable for the Fall, then the very idea of it only
served to condemn God Himself as some kind of cruel
tyrant; and if the Fall itself, and man's discovery of
evil as a consequence, was not part of God's beneficent
plan for man's redemption, for his spiritual reunion
with his Creator, then Creation itself lacked any logic
and admitted of no sensible laws of operation.

In the selection which follows, James not only
explains the nature of evil and its relation to the Fall
but also indicates the function of Adam and Eve in
the economy of divine salvation.

This is a composite selection, the first part of which
is taken from *The Nature of Evil* (New York, 1855),
70–77, 128–34, and the second from *Christianity the
Logic of Creation* (New York, 1857), 249–56.

———•◆•———

Let me proceed at once to give as orderly an account as I can of those
laws of the Divine creation which permit the origination of evil in the
creature, without involving any disparagement to the Divine perfection.

When we speak of inquiring into the origin of evil, we do not mean
physical evil, or the evil which one SUFFERS: nor *moral* evil, or the evil
which one DOES: but *spiritual* evil, or the evil which one IS.

Physical and moral evil, like physical and moral good, are constitutional
facts with man. They originate in the necessities of our finite nature, or
inhere in our animal and rational organization. Physical evil is merely a
negative attestation of the limitation which the animal subject is under
to nature, or the external world. Moral evil is only a negative attestation
of the limitation and dependence which the rational subject is under to
society, or his fellow-man. They are completely normal facts, originating
in the necessities of our physical and social existence, and there is consequently no obscurity attaching to them. When a man suffers from hunger,
or the lack of any necessary of life, which are instances of physical evil,
I perceive that his suffering grows out of his animal organization, or the
dependence he is constitutionally under to his voluntary action for the
supply of the necessaries of life. Expose the vegetable to similar suffering,
and it will die, while the animal is only stimulated by it to his proper or
distinctive life. He suffers only because some outward impediment exists
to the ordinary supply of his wants, calling for some extraordinary exertion of activity on his part: and I cannot conceive of his being animally
organized at all without a liability to suffer under similar circumstances.
So also when the same man steals my purse or filches from me my good
name, which are instances of moral evil, I perceive that this evil grows out
of his rational organization, or the constitutional freedom he enjoys to act
in any given case according to his own conceptions of duty and interest.
Nor can I conceive of his being rationally constituted without such freedom. The intellect consequently has no quarrel with the existence of either
physical or moral evil. They are possibilities and potentialities inherent in
the very nature of man, or his finite constitution, and if accordingly any
one be disposed to quarrel, he must quarrel exclusively with this latter
fact. As long as he admits the fact of man's finite nature, or of his physical
and rational existence, he also admits by necessary implication the existence of evil as well as good, and it is only by denying the former fact that
he logically excludes the latter.

And if any one be disposed to urge this irrational denial, it suffices to
reply that there is no way of avoiding a finite constitution on our part
short of making ourselves Divine. We are finitely constituted, simply be-

cause our being is not infinite, simply because we are creatures of God in place of being God Himself. We must therefore consent either to be finite or to be nothing. If my being were underived or independent, if like God I possessed life in myself, then indeed I should be destitute of a finite nature or constitution. But as my being is wholly derivative and dependent upon the Divine perfection, so my existence or formal development must be purely relative or conditional. That is to say it must exhibit certain *boundaries*, or present the equilibrium of two opposing forces. Finite existence is bounded or limited existence, and the things which bound or limit it, are what *constitute* the existence, or give it development to its own intelligence. Thus the boundaries of animal life are pleasure and pain, health and disease, plenty and want. Destroy these boundaries, that is to say, make the animal insensible to pleasure and pain, and you destroy him as animal. They are laws of the animal constitution, so that to the extent in which you impair their force, or what is the same thing, impair his subjection to them, you at the same time impair his constitution, and destroy the animal life.

The boundaries of moral life are duty and interest, or brotherly love and self-love. There is no morality possible which is not contingent upon this bipolarity, or transacted within these limitations. It is the balance, or equal pressure, of these opposing forces upon man which constitutes him a moral subject, or makes him responsible for his own actions. Consequently if you destroy this bipolarity, if you do away with the antagonism of brotherly love and self-love, you destroy or do away with man's moral constitution. You deny him selfhood or moral consciousness. For inasmuch as he has no absolute selfhood or consciousness, because he has no life *in se*, he must necessarily have a conditional one; and if, therefore, you deny the conditions upon which such selfhood or consciousness proceeds, you deny *a fortiori* the latter phenomenon itself. His selfhood, whether animal or moral, posits itself simply as the middle, third, or neutral term of two opposing poles or forces: and this by the sheer necessity of the case, or because his being is derivative. When therefore you vacate these constitutional conditions or limits of the animal and moral selfhood or life, you necessarily vacate this selfhood or life also.

I repeat then that good and evil, and pleasure and pain, are facts which fall within the strictly constitutional plane of human life, and hence do not supply the conception of spiritual evil, or that which separates the soul from God. For example, there is no man living who is not constitutionally liable to falsehood, to theft, to adultery, to murder, and to covetousness. Some persons doubtless are *peculiarly* liable by nature to some of these evils, and other persons *peculiarly* liable to others. But no persons are absolutely exempt from such natural liability, on the presence of temptation, unless they are either physically or mentally diseased. So on the other hand there is no person of average physical and mental health, who is not constitutionally liable to gentleness, kindness, patience, generosity, magnanimity, on the presentation of adequate motives. Some persons are by nature doubtless peculiarly susceptible to these emotions, or to some of them, and others to others: but no person is absolutely void of such susceptibility, provided a sufficient motive be exhibited. Hence we are not inwardly or spiritually chargeable with this good and evil: they are common to the race of men, and we are consequently forbidden to make any individual appropriation of them. They are simply features of our physical and rational organization, not of our internal or spiritual creation, and we cannot identify ourselves with them consequently, or place our happiness in them, without damage and affront to the latter interest.

The sole curse of man, indeed, from the beginning, has consisted in his obstinately "eating of this tree of the knowledge of good and evil," or attributing to himself the good and the evil, which are in truth only the indispensable conditions of his spiritual manifestation, or self-consciousness. The conceit of one's finite endowments, or the attribution to one's self of the good and the evil, by whose antagonism that self is vivified or constituted, is original sin, is the origin of all the sin which afflicts humanity. This alone is spiritual evil, the only evil known to the spiritual universe, namely, self-sufficiency, and the consequent renunciation of God from the life. . . .

Thus morality discloses a life superior to nature in man, discloses a *super*natural life, or one which allies him with the Infinite. Hence in order to solve the problems your book[1] opens, it is necessary to give them an entirely new intellectual statement, abandoning promptly and totally the old and sterile hypothesis of an arbitrary and extrinsic derivation of evil to man. What is called the Fall of man consisted in no change of his intrinsic nature from good to evil. He never lapsed from a state of goodness-in-himself into one of evil-in-himself, for the simple reason that he never was and never could have been good-in-himself. All goodness possible to the creature is *ex vi termini* ["by virtue of its function"] a derivation from God to him. Hence man viewed in himself, or apart from God, is and ever was unchangeably evil, and his fall consisted therefore not by any means in his becoming evil *in se*, but in his lack of acquiescence in that fact, or his unwillingness to make such a judgment of himself. The Fall did not signalize the conversion of man from good *in se* to evil *in se*. It merely signalized his own dawning aversion to regard himself any longer in that light, or what is the same thing, the gradual access of self-love, and the consequent cessation of love to God and the neighbor. His fall was his elevation in his own conceit, and hence it was a pure mercy upon the part of God to endow him with conscience or the faculty of self-condemnation. It never was and never can be a legitimate opprobrium to man that he is destitute of life by nature, or *in se* and apart from God, since the very communication to him of the Divine life implies, or is conditioned upon such destitution. His sole just opprobrium is, that BEING THUS DESTITUTE *he gives himself airs of self-sufficiency,* airs of supreme goodness and wisdom, and like a fool unlearns his dependence.

Thus it is never the fact of our intrinsic or natural destitution which spiritually separates us from God, and renders His voice plaintive in our behalf: it is only the fact of our superinduced or accessory pride, which makes us ashamed of that destitution, and leads us to conceal or cover it up by the fig-leaves of natural good. Our intrinsic or natural destitution is the infallible badge of our creatureship, and is therefore what most surely unites us with God so long as we heartily acknowledge it. One would not shrink accordingly, from the imputation of all the natural and moral evil in the universe to him, provided he were kept free at the same time of the spirit of self-justification, or spiritual pride. The truth of our creatureship, the great truth that in the Lord alone we live and move and have our being, perfectly reconciles us to the fact of our essential and intrinsic destitution, by quieting every ambitious aspiration, or divorcing us from all desire to be any thing in ourselves. The lowliest shrubs send up the most grateful fragrance to heaven. And it is only when a spirit of unbelief in our creatureship actuates us, or when we aspire to be our own goodness and wisdom, and hence stifle the instinct of dependence, that we truly forfeit the Divine smile, and taste the bitterness of eternal death. Adam and Eve were as naked or free from all intrinsic righteousness, before the Fall as after, but their nakedness gave them no conscience of shame, or sense of separation from God. But when the serpent (or growth of the sensuous understanding) inflamed them with the pride of freedom, and the lust of becoming something in themselves, they immediately grew ashamed of this nakedness, and by that shame felt themselves separated from God. They were afraid of the Divine presence because *they knew* they were naked. They knew the fact quite as well before they had eaten of the tree as after, but then the knowldge was unimportant and gave them no shame, because it was unattended by spiritual pride or self-seeking. And the Lord said unto the man, *"who has told thee that thou wert naked? Hast thou eaten of the tree of knowledge of good and evil?"* You observe the Lord is not represented as inquiring, "what has *made* you naked?"–but only "how have you *become conscious* of your nakedness?" Thus the Fall is always a fall from previous peace and enjoyment in God, to a state of turmoil, labor and sorrow in ourselves. It does not imply any change in the Divine goodness towards us, for that goodness is unchangeable, but only such a change in our own intelligence as makes the all-sufficiency of the Divine goodness seem questionable, and throws us consequently on our own resources. Accordingly the death we partake in Adam, and from which we are delivered in Christ, is not natural death or the death of the body, for nothing can be sweeter than this or more orderly, but an adventitious and accessory death growing out of our spiritual aversion from God, and an insane effort to become our own centre of life.

Here then is the origin of spiritual evil, or the evil which equally besets you and me and all mankind, whatever moral or physical diversities relatively characterize us. It consists in looking upon the moral life or freedom which God gives us purely as a basis of our subsequent spiritual conjunction with Him, as an absolute gift, or as a final instead of a mediatorial possession. The moral consciousness I enjoy, that is to say, the freedom or power which I feel to do—or not to do—this, that, and the other thing, is a great and blessed reality, for it is incessantly communicated to me by God, in order that feeling as if my life were in myself, while yet reflectively attributing it to Him, I may incessantly and cordially aspire after a growing spiritual conjunction with Him. But the selfhood into which I interpret the freedom or power thus communicated, is a pure fallacy, growing out of the domination of the sensuous principle in me. There is no such thing in the universe (there is no such creation possible to the divine power) as a simple, absolute, or independent selfhood; and yet I habitually count upon this selfhood as if it were the most indisputable of realities, elated by its good and dejected by its evil, exactly as if it were the divinely indicated source of these things. Is morality then a cheat, an illusion? By no means. It is the grandest of facts, because it is designed to serve as the platform or basis of an otherwise impracticable conjunction between God and ourselves. It will always be good accordingly for a man to deal justly with his neighbor; it will always be evil for him to deal unjustly with his neighbor. But it is fatal to appropriate this good and evil, or what is the same thing, to be content with this merely moral existence without rendering it subservient to a higher. It is fatal, in other words, to grow conceited, or to believe that we are something in ourselves. For we instantly cease in that case to eat of the tree of life, and begin to eat of the tree of knowledge of good and evil, whose fruit is death. That is, we cease to live by God, and begin to live by ourselves. . . .

The creative and eternal Word to man runs thus: "Of every tree in the garden thou mayest *freely* eat, *but of the tree of knowledge of good and evil thou shalt not eat,* BECAUSE IN THE DAY THOU EATEST THEREOF THOU SHALT SURELY DIE." Philosophers have long sought to demonstrate the reality of human freedom as evinced in the phenomena of our moral consciousness, but they have only succeeded in demonstrating the unhappy muddle Philosophy herself amounts to, so long as she superciliously disdains the guiding light of revelation, and seeks to interpret nature by the servile light which nature herself supplies. Our moral freedom is in truth only a semblance, not a reality. We *seem* to act freely, or of ourselves, when we steal or refrain from stealing, when we commit adultery or refrain from it: and man's judgment accordingly, which is limited to appearances, asks no further warrant to render us in either case blame-or-praise-worthy. But, as Swedenborg proves on every page of his remarkable writings, we really never do act in freedom or of ourselves under these circumstances. He shews by the most luminous exposition of spiritual laws that we never steal or commit adultery, however free the act *seem* to our foolish selves, but by the overwhelming tyranny of hell; and that we never refrain from doing these things except by virtue of the Lord's power constraining us to do so in spite of our natural tendencies. We *feel* this power to be in ourselves, that is to be freely exerted, only because we do not sensibly discern the fields of spiritual existence from which alone it inflows, and our senses have hitherto ruled our reason in place of serving it. No man since the world has stood has ever had power to draw a physical or moral breath, independently of those celestial and infernal companies with which all his past ancestry interiorly but unconsciously associates him. Of course therefore the Divine Love is incapable of ascribing any one's physical and moral merit or demerit to the person himself, because it would be absurdly false to do so. On the contrary, it seeks with endless pains to prevent the man himself from doing this by the organization of conscience as an unfaltering ministry of death. Our most accredited theologies and philosophies have always alike misapprehended the scope of this relentless ministry. They suppose that conscience was originally intended as a ministry of life or righteousness, and that Adam accordingly enjoyed its favourable testimony in Paradise before he had eaten of the tree of knowledge, that is, before he had learned to appropriate good and evil to himself. But of what possible use could the approbation of conscience be to a being who was still ignorant of the difference between good and evil? The transparent contradiction involved in the assumption sufficiently demonstrates its absurdity to the reason; but the literal text of revelation demonstrates it also to the very senses, by shewing us that conscience first dawned in Adam after selfhood (Eve) had been developed in him, and he had been led by it to eat of the tree of knowledge, that is, to appropriate his influent good and evil to himself.

Adam symbolizes the immature condition of the mind, the merely seeming and constitutional side of man, the life of instinct which we derive from nature, and which through the decease operated in us by conscience, we ultimately lay aside in order to the assumption of our true and spontaneous life derived directly from God. Hence—what is perfectly consistent, if you regard the spiritual purport of the narrative, but perfectly absurd if you regard only its letter—the most pregnant service which Eve (representing the divinely endowed selfhood) renders Adam, is to throw him instantly out of Paradise, by unmuzzling within him the relentless jaws of conscience. Do you ask me what I mean by Eve, as the symbol of our divinely quickened selfhood? I will tell you. Adam, as we have seen, represents our finite or constitutional existence, that which flows from our connection with the race. It seems to be a most real existence, while in truth it is a purely reflected one, the subject being nothing but what he is made by the spiritual world, being in fact as destitute of real selfhood or freedom as if he were only dove or rabbit and not man. The dove or rabbit remains spiritually unquickened, devoid of true individuality, because it is a purely animal form, that is, a form in which the universal element dominates the individual one. It is, in other words, and ever remains, an unshrinking subject of its nature, and hence incapable of "eating of the tree of knowledge of good and evil," that is, of appropriating good and evil to itself. It has no consciousness of a selfhood underived from its nature, and is consequently utterly incapable both of moral experience, and of that lustrous life of conjunction with God in which such experience, when left unperverted, infallibly merges. But Adam, the beautiful symbol of our nascent humanity, of our still instinctual and *pre-moral* beginnings, is lifted above animality by his human form, that form being the only one in which the universal element *serves* the individual one, and which therefore fitly images God. Hence, though he is but a rudimental and seeming man, he is bound at once to vindicate his essential divinity, by exhibiting, in however rude and purely negative a form, the real and distinctive life which animates humanity. The distinction of man from all lower existences is, that he is in strictest truth the child of God, that Infinite Love and Wisdom constitute his veritable and exclusive parentage, and Infinite Love and Wisdom are utterly inconsistent with selfishness or with littleness of any description. Hence in Christ, who is the perfected and fully conscious Divine Man, we see his merely finite and *quasi* or constitutional life, his purely Adamic selfhood, incessantly deposed in order to his glorification, in order to his consummate union with God. In Adam consequently, who is but the prophetic or typical and unconscious divine man, we must expect to see death installed as the very *fons et principium vitæ*, as the very fountain and spring of human life; we must expect to see despair enthroned as the fertile and abounding womb of man's distinctive hope. In short, we must demand from Adam, as the symbol of our rudimental and initiatory manhood, a purely negative and mortuary experience; that is to say, we must expect to see him divorced from his merely seeming and dramatic existence, by falling under the dominion of conscience or the moral law.

By Eve, then, or our divinely vivified selfhood, is meant the power which is incessantly communicated to man of separating himself from his mere animal conditions, of elevating himself out of the realm of law into that of life, or of subjecting nature and society to the needs of his individuality. In short, Eve signifies the power in man of spiritually appropriating good and evil to himself, the faculty of spiritual consciousness. Let the animal do as he will, he is but the abject vassal of his nature, and therefore destitute of personality or character, destitute of spiritual consciousness. The animal is only naturally, never spiritually, good or evil. The dove is naturally good as contrasted with the vulture, the tiger is naturally evil as contrasted with the sheep, but you would never think of deeming the dove spiritually good or the tiger spiritually evil as contrasted with any other animal, especially as contrasted with any other dove or tiger. Why? Because spiritual good and evil is individual good and evil, that is, it implies in the subject a spiritual individuality uncontrolled by his nature. The animals have no such individuality, and hence are ignorant of moral distinctions, are unworthy of individual praise or blame. They have a purely natural individuality, and hence are incapable of eating of the tree of knowledge of good and evil, or of viewing themselves as spiritually responsible for their influent good and evil. Of man alone is it lawful to predicate moral distinctions, because he alone is capable of appropriating his influent good and evil to himself in place of charging it upon his nature. He alone is capable of an alternate individual expansion and collapse, which unless the Divine Mercy overruled them to his endless benefit, would breed only the most disastrous consequences. He is capable at one moment of a spiritual conceit and pride which plunges him gaily into hell, at the next of a spiritual despair which shuts him sorrowfully out of heaven. For example, if moral good prevail in my natural disposition, if I pass my life in visiting prisons, building hospitals, feeding the poor, scattering tracts, circulating the Bible, forwarding every conventionally righteous enterprize, while maintaining at the same time an irreproachable private and social deportment, I shall be infallibly certain —unless the Divine Love expose me to incessant secret or spiritual shipwreck, to the most withering internal humiliation and disaster—to appropriate this good to myself, and so turn out a monster of spiritual pride, a being too inflated even for hell to tolerate. Or if moral evil preponderate in my natural character, if on all occasions of temptation I succumb, and convict myself of lying, theft, adultery, and what not, I shall be sure in these circumstances—unless the Divine Love visit me with incessant outward success and prosperity—to shut myself up in a despair too obdurate even for the warmest love of heaven to penetrate it. These experiences, mournful as they seem when too narrowly viewed, nevertheless attest the grandeur of human nature. They are possible to us only because our distinctively human life dates from God, and is therefore a spontaneous life, a life whose principle of action falls exclusively within the subject, and renders him therefore eternally free. Of course this life presupposes the complete reconciliation of self-love with brotherly love, presupposes the scientific inauguration of human society, human fellowship, human equality, and these issues again presuppose a conflict of these two forces, suppose, that is, a previous stage of human experience in which self-love is at war with brotherly love, or hell antagonizes heaven in lieu of promoting it. Now so long as this infantile state of things endures, so long as self-love and brotherly love, or hell and heaven, are kept unreconciled by the immaturity of the scientific understanding in man, we each of us, by virtue of the solidarity that binds us to the race, feel this conflict in our own bosoms as if it originated there, or belonged to ourselves, instead of being a veritable influx from the entire spiritual world, or the universal mind of man. We have not the least suspicion that the conflict is not our own private affair, is not a legitimate feature of our divinely given individuality, and accordingly as one or the other principle prevails in our life, we contentedly write ourselves down good or evil in the Divine sight, turning out wretched Pharisées in the former case, and despised publicans and harlots in the latter. We have not the slightest conception of our true and spontaneous life, nor consequently of the miraculous exhibitions of Divine wealth and power with which it is fraught. We have no idea that that life is so divinely majestic and perfect as to involve in itself the complete reconciliation of hell and heaven, the intensest harmony of self-love and brotherly love, of the external and internal man. Not knowing this, we inevitably suppose that our spiritual experience belongs to our isolated private bosoms, qualifying us individually in the sight of God; and we therefore go on to eat of the tree of knowledge of good and evil with a stupid *gusto* that of necessity disallows the true consciousness of God in our souls, and turns His inward voice of love and mercy into one of implacable condemnation and death.[3]

NOTES

1. James is referring here to Beecher's *The Conflict of Ages* to which the whole of his own book, *The Nature of Evil,* is a reply.—Editor's note.
2. From *The Nature of Evil* (New York, 1855), p. 70–77, 128–34.
3. From *Christianity the Logic of Creation* (New York, 1857), p. 249–56.

10

MORALITY AND RELIGION
AS SUBSTANCE AND SHADOW

The various introductions and appendixes James
wrote for his books often afford some of the richest
summaries of his thought. This is particularly true of
the introduction to his book *Substance and Shadow*.
With these two words "substance" and "shadow," James
refers to the functions which morality and religion
serve, respectively, in relation to what he calls "the
Physics of Creation." His interest, in other words, is in
the role which morality and religion play in the divine
plan of redemption.

The following selection constitutes the Introduction
to *Substance and Shadow: or, Morality and Religion in
Their Relation to Life: An Essay on the Physics of
Creation* (Boston, 1863), 1–28.

————•◆•◆•————

THE leading words of my title-page call for a precise definition, in order
that the reader may clearly discern the aim of the discussion to which
I invite his attention.

By morality I mean that sentiment of selfhood or property which every
man not an idiot feels in his own body. It is a state of conscious freedom
or rationality, exempting him from the further control of parents or
guardians, and entitling him in his own estimation and that of his fellows, to the undivided ownership of his words and deeds. It is the basis of
conscience in man, or what enables him to appropriate good and evil
to himself, instead of ascribing the former as he may one day learn to
do exclusively to celestial, the latter exclusively to infernal influence. The
word is often viciously used as a synonyme of spiritual goodness, as when
we say, "A is a very moral man," meaning a just one; or, "B is a very
immoral man," meaning an unjust one. No man can be either good or
evil, either just or unjust, but by virtue of his morality; *i. e.* unless he
have selfhood or freedom entitling him to own his action. This is a *conditio
sine quâ non*. The action by which he becomes pronounced either the one
sort of man or the other could not be his action, and consequently could

never afford a basis for his spiritual development, unless he possessed this original moral force, or strict neutrality with respect to heaven and hell; but would on the contrary be an effect in every case of overpowering spiritual influence. We should be very careful, therefore, not to confound the condition of an event with the event itself, as we do when we call the good man moral, and deny morality to the evil man. For if the good man alone be moral, while the evil man is immoral, then morality ceases to be any longer the distinctive badge of human nature itself, which separates it from all lower natures (so furnishing a platform for God's spiritual descent into it), and becomes the mere arbitrary endowment of certain persons. The error in question originates in, at least is greatly promoted by, our habit of calling the decalogue "the moral law." As the law is instinct with an ineffable Divine sanctity, we get at last to think that the word which we so commonly couple with it partakes of right the same sanctity, and accordingly call only the man who obeys it moral, while he who disobeys it is immoral. In point of fact, however, morality means nothing more nor less than that state of natural neutrality or indifference to good and evil, to heaven and hell, which distinguishes man from all other existence, and endows him alone with selfhood or freedom. Thus the term properly designates our natural majority or manhood, what every man, as man, possesses in common with every other man.

By religion I mean—what is invariably meant by the term where the thing itself still exists—such a conscience on man's part of a forfeiture of the Divine favor, as perpetually urges him to make sacrifices of his ease, his convenience, his wealth, and if need be his life, in order to restore himself, if so it be possible, to that favor. This is religion in its literal form; natural religion; religion as it stands authenticated by the universal in- stincts of the race, before it has undergone a spiritual conversion into life, and while claiming still a purely ritual embodiment. It is however in this gross form the germ of all humane culture. Accordingly we sometimes use the term in an accommodated sense, *i. e.* to express the spiritual results with which religion is fraught rather than the mere carnal embodiment it first of all offers to such results. Thus the apostle James says: Pure and undefiled religion (*i. e.*, religion viewed no longer as a letter, but as a spirit), is to visit the fatherless and the widow, and keep oneself un- spotted from the world (*i. e.*, has exclusive reference to the life). We also say proverbially, handsome is that handsome does; not meaning of course to stretch the word handsome out of its literal dimensions, but only by an intelligible metonomy of body for soul, or what is natural for what is spiritual, to express in a compendious way the superiority of moral to physical beauty. My reader will always understand me, then, as using the word religion in its strictly literal signification, to indicate our ritual or ceremonious homage to the Divine name.

Now morality and religion, thus interpreted are regarded on my title- page as concurring to promote the evolution of man's spiritual destiny on earth.

Man's destiny on earth, as I am led to conceive it, consists in the realiza-

tion of a perfect society, fellowship, or brotherhood among men, proceeding upon such a complete Divine subjugation in the bosom of the race,
first of self-love to brotherly love, and then of both loves to universal love
or the love of God, as will amount to a regenerate nature in man, by converting first his merely natural consciousness, which is one of comparative isolation and impotence, into a social consciousness, which is one of
comparative omnipresence and omnipotence; and then and thereby exalting his moral freedom, which is a purely negative one, into an æsthetic
or positive form: so making spontaneity and not will, delight and no
longer obligation, the spring of his activity.

But morality and religion are further regarded on the title-page as
bearing, in the evolution of the spiritual destiny of man on earth, the
relation respectively of substance and shadow. It only remains that I ex-
plicate this point, in order to put in the reader's hands the clew to my
entire thought.

A shadow is a phenomenon of vision produced by some body intercepting the light. Thus the shadow of the tree upon the lawn is an effect of
the tree intercepting the sun's rays. My shadow on the wall is an effect
of my body intercepting the rays of the candle, and so forth. Evidently
then three things concur to constitute a shadow: 1. a light; 2. an opaque
body which drinks up or refuses to transmit its rays; 3. a background or
suitable plane of projection on which such refusal becomes stamped.
Thus the shadow which anything casts is strictly proportionate to its power
of absorbing the light, or appropriating it to itself: which is only saying, in
other words, that the shadow of a thing is the exact measure of its finiteness or imperfection, *i. e.* of its destitution of true being. And this remark
prepares us to ask what purpose the shadow serves, what intellectual use
it renders.

Obviously the use or purpose of shadows is to attest finite substance, or
separate between phenomenal and real existence. Real existence is that
which exists in itself, being vitalized from within. Phenomenal existence
is that which exists only by virtue of its implication in something not itself,
being vitalized wholly from without. In short real existence is spiritual;
phenomenal existence natural. So far as I am spiritual, that is, to all the
extent of my æsthetic or spontaneous life, I am a real existence, possessing life in myself. So far as I am simply natural, that is, to all the extent
of my instinctual and voluntary life, I am a phenomenal existence, deriv-
ing my life from without. My spiritual manhood consequently casts no
shadow. Whatsoever I do spontaneously; whatsoever I do in obedience to
the inspiration of Beauty; whatsoever I do, in short, from individual taste
or attraction in opposition to the common instinct of self-preservation; is
good and beautiful in itself, is positively or infinitely good, as being without any contrast or oppugnancy of evil. But my physical and moral existence never fails to project a shadow. Let me be as beautiful physically
as Venus or Apollo, still I am not really or positively, but only actually or
apparently, so; as by contrast with some opposite ugliness. Let me be

morally as good as all saints and angels, it is yet not a good which is positive or stands by itself, but one which stands in the opposition of evil. In short, my beauty in the one case, and my goodness in the other, is finite; and like all finite existence claims its attendant and attesting shadow.

Clearly, then, the purpose of shadows is to attest finite or imperfect existence, existence which does not involve its own substance. The shadow which the tree casts upon the lawn, and that which my body projects upon the wall behind me, are a mute confession on the part of body and tree that they are purely finite and phenomenal existences: that while they sensibly appear to be in themselves, their being is yet in something very superior to themselves. Seek this tree a few years hence, and you will find no vestige of it remaining. Ask for this body a few months hence, possibly, and it will be indistinguishable from the dust of the earth. This is what the shadow invariably says:—that the substance which projects it is a mere appearance to the senses, not a reality to the philosophic understanding; and that if we would penetrate the world of realities we must transcend the realm of sense, the finite realm, and enter that of mind or spirit.

We now fairly discern the constitution of the shadow, and what is its rational scope and significance; and are thus prepared to interpret the greatest of shadows which we call Religion, and which falls everywhere across the page of human history darkening the face of day, turning the fairest promise of nature to blight, undermining the most towering pride of morality by a subtle conscience of sin, and forbidding man to content himself with a righteousness, a peace and a power which shall be anything less than Divine.

The reader recalls the constitution of the shadow, namely, that it is always an effect of some opaque body intercepting the rays of light. Thus the shadow which the tree projects upon the lawn is an effect of the tree intercepting the sun's rays; and the shadow of my person on the wall an effect of my body intercepting the rays of the lamp. In like manner precisely this stupendous shadow designated by the name of Religion, is an effect produced by our moral consciousness intercepting the rays of the Divine Truth as they shine forth from man's social destiny. The three elements which determine its constitution as a shadow are thus distributed: History being the sole field of its projection; Morality the opaque substance which alone projects it; and the Social principle, the principle of a perfect society fellowship or brotherhood among men, being the great Divine light, of whose obscuration by morality religion has always been at once the shadow and the scourge.

So much definition seems due by way of preface in vindication of the title of my book, or in order to apprise my reader that I regard Religion and Morality as respectively shadow and substance in their relation to the social development of the race. Society—fellowship—equality—fraternity, whatever name you give it, is the central sun of human destiny, originating all its motion, and determining the pathway of its progress towards infinite Love and Wisdom. Morality and Religion together constitute the subject-earth of self-love which revolves about this centre, now in light now in shade; morality being the illuminated side of that love, religion its obscured side; the one constituting the splendor of its day, the other the darkness of its night. Morality is the summer lustihood and luxuriance of self-love, clothing its mineral ribs with vegetable grace, permeating its rigid trunk with sap, decorating its gnarled limbs with foliage, glorifying every reluctant virgin bud and every modest wifely blossom into rich ripe motherly fruit. Religion is the icy winter which blights this summer fertility, which arrests the ascent of its vivifying sap, and humbles its superb life to the ground, in the interests of a spring that shall be perennial, and of autumns bursting with imperishable fruit. In other words, religion has no substantive force. Her sole errand on earth has been to dog the footsteps of morality, to humble the pride of selfhood which man derives from nature, and so soften his interiors to the reception of Divine Truth, as that truth stands fulfilled in the organization of human equality or fellowship.

The backbone of mortality has long been providentially broken. The moral force men once had, the power of controlling natural appetite and passion, has abated, and in its place has come a sense of God's presence in Nature, and the aspiration to realize in life the infinite Beauty which she reveals. Almost no one is now strong by himself, strong against the floods of natural arrogance and cupidity which are sure to assail him, but only by association with others. Scarcely any one resists the temptation to which he is naturally prone on religious grounds, or from a sentiment of reverence to the Divine name, but only on social grounds or from a sentiment of what is due to good-fellowship. The failure to see this great change in human nature, and to organize it betimes in appropriate institutions, is what keeps us in this state of public and private demoralization, which has at last resulted in the downfall of our political edifice. See what thorough-paced unconscious scoundrels we have long had for politicians. Observe how apt our men in office are to lend themselves to atrocious jobbery; how incessantly public and private trusts are betrayed; how our clergy in such large numbers habitually emasculate and stultify the gospel, in order to adapt it to the dainty ears of the fierce worldlings who underpin their ecclesiastical consequence; how ostentation, unbridled luxury of every sort, and the shameless apery of foreign class-pretension, even down to the decorating our imported servants with imported liveries, are corrupting us from our original democratic simplicity; how rapidly immodesty, dissipation, insolence, and the most unblushing egotism are vulgarizing the manners, hardening the visages, and hopelessly blasting the hereditary remains of innocence of our rich young men and women;—and who can doubt that Jeff Davis, Joe Smith, filibuster Walker, secretary Floyd, James Buchanan,[1] and all the other dismal signs and portents of our current political and religious life, have been only so many providential scourges sent to devastate and consume a world long ripe for the Divine judgment?

The only possible explanation of the existing crisis in human affairs, everywhere indeed, compatible with the Divine sovereignty, is, that the moral force in man no longer subserves the great spiritual uses which once sanctified and sweetened it; that the mission which was once Divinely given it of nurturing men for the skies has been revoked and put in more competent hands. This to my judgment is as plain as anything can well be. The moral force was never anything but a scaffolding for God's spiritual house in the soul; it was never designed to give permanent substance but only temporary form to God's finished work in human nature; and when accordingly it ceases to look upon itself in this subordinate plight, and insists upon being treated not as the scaffolding but as the house, not as the mould but as the substance to be moulded, not as the matrix but as the gem, in short, not as an accessory but as a principal, it loses even this justification and becomes a positive nuisance. The social sentiment, the sense of a living organic unity among men, is accordingly fast absorbing it or taking it up into its own higher circulation, whence it will be reproduced in every regenerate æsthetic form. Art is the resurgent form of human activity. The artist or producer is the only regenerate image of God in nature, the only living revelation of the Lord on earth. Society itself will erelong release her every subject from that responsibility to his own material interests which has hitherto degraded human life to the ground, and by providing for his honest and orderly physical subsistence, leave his heart and mind and hand free to the only inspiration they spontaneously acknowledge,—that of infinite Goodness, Truth, and Beauty. This most profound and intimate life of God in our nature is groping its way to more and more vivid consciousness in us every day; and the consequence is that we see the proud old Pagan ideal of moral virtue, a virtue which inheres in the subject himself as finitely constituted or differenced from all other men, giving place to the humble and harmless Christian ideal of a purely spiritual virtue in man, a virtue which inheres in him only as he becomes infinitely constituted, or united with all other men, by the unlimited indwelling of God in his nature. The Pagan goodness proceeds upon self-denial, and hence implies merit. The Christian goodness proceeds upon the frankest and fullest possible self-assertion, and hence implies boundless humility or gratitude. "After those days, saith the Lord, I will put my law in their inward parts, and write it in their hearts."

As the shadow obeys the law of the substance, so religion is bound to undergo a proportionate modification with that of morality. This is why religion in the old virile sense of the word has disappeared from sight, and become replaced by a feeble Unitarian sentimentality. The old religion involved a conscience of the profoundest antagonism between God and the worshipper, which utterly refused to be placated by anything short of an unconditional pledge of the utmost Divine mercy. The ancient believer felt himself sheerly unable to love God, or do anything else towards his salvation, were it only the lifting of a finger. To un-love was his only true loving, to un-learn his only true learning, to un-do his only true doing. The modern religionist is at once amused and amazed at these curious archæological beginnings of his own history. He feels towards them as a *virtuoso* does towards what is decidedly *rococo* in fashion, and not seldom bestows a word of munificent Pharisaic patronage upon them, such as the opulent Mr. Ruskin[2] dispenses to uncouth specimens of early religious Art. He has not the slightest conception of himself as a spiritual form inwardly enlivened by all God's peace and innocence. On the contrary, he feels himself to be a strictly moral or self-possessed being, vivified exclusively by his own action, or the relations he voluntarily assumes with respect to human and Divine law. The modern believer aspires to be a saint; the ancient one abhorred to be anything but a sinner. The former looks back accordingly to some fancied era of what he calls conversion: *i. e.* when he passed from death to life. The latter was blissfully content to forget himself, and looked forward exclusively to his Lord's promised advent in all the forms of a redeemed nature. The one is an absolutely changed man, no longer to be confounded with the world, and meet for the Divine approbation. The other is a totally unchanged one, only more dependent than he ever was before upon the unmitigated Divine mercy. The one feels sure of going to heaven if the Lord observes the distinctions which his own grace ordains in human character. The other feels sure of going to hell unless the Lord is blessedly indifferent to those distinctions.

I might multiply these contrasts to any length, but my desire is only briefly to indicate how very near and intimate God's spiritual approximation to our nature must have become, in order to justify those hopes of the purely natural heart towards him. It is impossible to go to the —— Church in ——, and observe how skilfully and yet unconsciously the gifted minister of that parish appeals to all that is most selfish and most worldly in the bosoms of his hearers, in order to build them up a fragrant temple for the Divine indwelling, without feeling one's heart melt with adoration of the Infinite Love which is taking to itself at last the riches of the earth, and making the kingdoms of this world also forever its own. In short, both the world and the church from having been very dense are becoming almost transparent masks of God's ineffable designs of mercy to universal man, and are helping along in their blind delirious way the speedy advent of a scientific human society or brotherhood upon earth. If accordingly my reader discover as he conceives in the progress of my book any *animus* of hostility either to the polite or the religious world, he will do me the justice to believe that such appearance is only the negative or literal aspect of a love, which on its positive or spiritual side embraces universal man.

Let me indeed insist on this justice. It is evident enough throughout my book, of course, that I assail ritual or professional religion with undissembled good-will; yet it is quite equally evident, I hope, that I never for a moment do so in the interest of irreligion, but exclusively in the interest of its own imprisoned spirit. Daily I visit this sepulchre in which the Lord lay buried. I find the spiced linen garments in which he was embalmed reverently exhibited, and the napkin that was about his sacred head tenderly folded away and cherished; but no familiar feature of his vanished form remains; he is indeed no longer there but risen. All that was late so helpless in him has become glorified and triumphant; all that was late so human and finite has become Divine and infinite. I find, in other words, any amount of literal or personal homage addressed to Christ in the church; but never a glance that I can discern of spiritual recognition. And yet this alone is real and living; all the rest is dramatic and dead. Let us call him Lord! Lord! as much as we please, and lift up the devoutest possible eyes to some imaginary throne he is supposed to occupy in the super-celestial solitudes; we are utterly inexcusable for so doing, since if we believe his own most pointed and memorable counsels, (Matthew xxv. 31–46),) he is no longer to be found spiritually isolated from, but only most intimately associated with, the business and bosom of universal man: that is to say, only wherever there is hunger to be filled, thirst to be slaked, homeless want to be housed, nakedness to be clad, sickness to be relieved, prison-doors to be opened.

No doubt the church will answer that a man's soul is worth more to him than all the world beside; that God busies himself with the spiritual interests of humanity rather than its material interests. Unquestionably. But how if He cannot deal directly with its spiritual interests without impairing them? How if His only safe way of dealing with them, is to do so indirectly, that is, by means of its material interests? Of course no reasonable man can doubt that God's real and primary delight is to appease the spiritual wants, and assuage the spiritual woes of humanity, which are accurately symbolized under these images of mere material destitution and distress. But then we must recollect that He is utterly unable to effect these ends save by the mediation of his own truth, or in so far as our private individual commerce with him has been organized upon, and energized by, a previous recognition of his boundless presence and operation in human nature itself. God's private mercies to us, in other words, do not prejudice, but on the contrary irresistibly exact or presuppose, this grander public operation of His, this stupendous work of redemption which he has practised in our very nature itself, as the basis of their own vitality. Let me elucidate this proposition a little.

Whatever be the Lord's unmistakeable good-will towards the spiritual or immortal conjunction of every individual soul of man with himself, it is nevertheless evident that such a result to be permanent can never be forced, but must conciliate in every case the legitimate instincts of the soul, which are freedom and rationality. If God would have my love and have it eternally, he must exhibit his perfect worthiness to be loved in such a way as to take captive my heart and understanding. Now as naturally constituted, or when left to myself, I am a being of consummate selfishness and covetousness. I unconsciously exalt myself above all mankind, and would grasp, if that were possible, the riches of the universe. It were obvious and unmixed deviltry simply to condemn this natural make of mine, or turn it over to ruthless punishment. It is, on the other hand, unmixed divinity to condescend to these natural limitations, to come down to the level and breathe the atmosphere of these overpowering lusts, to live in the daily and hourly intimacy of their illusions, their insanities, their ferocities and impurities, until at length by patiently separating what is relatively good in them from what is relatively evil, and then subjecting the latter to the unlimited service of the former, the two warring elements become bound together in the unity of a new or regenerate natural personality, in which interest will spontaneously effect what principle has hitherto vainly enjoined; or self-love accomplish with ease what benevolence has only been able hitherto weakly to dream of accomplishing. If now we appeal to the word of God, which is Christian doctrine, this is precisely what God does; and if we appeal to his work, which is the history of Christendom, the response is equally full and clear. Revelation and History both alike proclaim with unmistakeable emphasis that God chooses the foolish things of the world to confound the wise, the weak things to confound the mighty, and base things and things which men despise, yea and things which are not, hath God chosen, to bring to nought established things, in order that no flesh should exalt itself in his presence.

This alone is why I love God, if indeed I do at all love Him. I hate Him with a cordial hatred—of this at least I am very sure—for his alleged incommunicable infinitude, for that cold and solitary grandeur which my natural reason ascribes to Him, and which entitles Him, according to the same authority, to exact the endless servile homage of us poor worms of the dust. For all this difference between God and me as affirmed by my natural deism—which is my reason unillumined by revelation,—my crushed and outraged affections writhe with unspeakable animosity towards him. It is only when I read the gospel of his utter condescension to my foul and festering nature, and discern the lucent lines of his providence in the world illustrating and authenticating every word and tone of that gospel,—it is only, in other words, when I see how sheerly impersonal and creative his love is, *i. e.*, how incapable of regarding itself and how irresistibly communicative of its own blessedness to whatsoever is not itself, to whatsoever is most hostile and repugnant to itself, that my soul catches her first glimpse of the uncreated holiness, and heart and head and hand conspire in helpless, speechless, motionless adoration.

In short, no one can love God simply by wishing to love Him, still less by feeling it a duty to love Him. At this rate one could never love his fellow-man even, but would come at last infallibly to hate him. In other words, love is never voluntary but always spontaneous. Its objective or unconscious element invariably controls its subjective or conscious one. I love my wife or child not by any force of my own, but by virtue altogether of a force which their innocence and sweetness lend me. It is their natural or cultivated grace which empowers me to love; abstract this, and I should be impotent as a clod. So also I can never love God by any force of my own. His absolute worth indeed makes it even more impossible for me to love Him, than my wife's or child's relative imperfection makes it impossible for me to love them: namely, by removing Him spiritually to such a distance from me as to make hatred rather than love towards Him, an instinctive dictate of my own self-respect. If then I can never hope to love God by my own force, He himself must enable me to love Him. How shall He do this without overpowering my conscious freedom or rationality? Why simply by taking upon Himself the conditions of my nature, or coming to know experimentally how irresistibly prone the finite mind is by the mere fact of its finiteness to lie, to steal, to commit adultery and murder, in order that, being thus tempted like as we are, yet without sin—being thus touched with a feeling of our infirmities, and yet rigidly self-debarred from the actual disorder in which they are sure to terminate with us—He may give them totally new and unexpected issues in harmony with His own universality of love and providence. In other words, let God reveal Himself to my intelligence as a natural man, as a sympathetic partaker of my own corrupt nature, not with any view as my natural reason alleges to condemn and denounce it, but only to purify and exalt it to the measure of His own infinitude, and I shall necessarily love Him, love Him with such a reality and intensity of love as reconciles me even to my past natural animosity, and fills me moreover with His own unspeakable tenderness towards the possible natural animosity of all mankind.

This briefly stated is all I mean by saying that our private or individual regeneration is wholly conditioned upon a great and sincere work of redemption accomplished by God in human nature; so that every really regenerate person, every one reconciled in heart to the Divine ways, feels himself an unlimited dependent upon the unbought Divine mercy, and scorns nothing so cordially as the pretence of a superior personal sanctity in the Divine regard, to that of the veriest reptile that shares and illustrates his nature.

And this will also explain to the reader why, in the progress of my book, I have felt myself called upon to deal so frankly with our ritual or professional religion. It is because religion as an institution no longer subserves the great human uses which once alone consecrated it, but has sunk into an impudent canonization of the vulgarest private and sectarian pretension. It has so completely renounced its ancient and purely typical sanctity, and challenges nowadays such an absolute prestige, or prestige in its own right, to men's regard, that the veracious public witness it once bore to the truth of all men's equal and utter personal alienation and remoteness from God, has become degraded into the lying testimony of some A, B, or C's individual regeneration and salvation. From a sincere record of our universal natural destitution and despair, it has sunk into a flattering witness of our private wealth, of our strictly individual assurance or presumption. The distinctively spiritual or human substance which alone sanctifies religious aspiration and saves it from blasphemy, is humility, is an unaffected contrition on the part of the worshipper for the pride and rapacity which he perceives underlying his finite consciousness, and forever separating him from the Divine. In short, a conscience of death is the sole legitimate flower of the religious experience; death to every cherished pretension the worshipper feels of ever being personally any purer better holier in the Divine sight than any criminal that ever was hung.

Scarcely a vestige of this most ancient truth survives in our modern profession; or if it does, survives in chronic not in acute form. To "experience religion," or "become converted," means now not what it once meant, to pass from the noon-tide radiance of natural force and self-confidence into the grimmest midnight of spiritual impotence and self-distrust, but all simply to jump from a grossly absurd fear of God's personal enmity to us grounded on our moral delinquencies, or perhaps our purely ritual uncleanness, into a more grossly absurd hope of His personal complacency towards us, based upon some inward mystical change which He himself has arbitrarily wrought in us. Thus viewed, religion no longer witnesses to the truth of God's immutable perfection, but only to the capricious operation of His spirit ordaining certain differences in human character, whereby one man becomes avouched in his proper person an heir of heaven, another stigmatized as a child of hell. Look at the social consequences of this most real but unrecognized spiritual buffoonery, how inevitably it depresses all that is sweet and modest and unexacting in manners, and forces into conspicuity whatsoever is forward, ungenerous, and despotic. Look at any of our ecclesiastical coteries, and observe how torpid grows the proper spiritual or human force of its members, while every shabbiest pattern of a formalist is radiant, twittering, and alert with preternatural activity. No doubt very many of the clergy are personally superior to their office, and feel their instinctual modesty outraged by the spirit of servility and adulation which it appears to have the faculty of eliciting on the part of their adherents. But how can they help themselves? Professional religion means the claim of a private sanctity, of a strictly personal and individual worth in God's sight, by which the subject is eternally differenced from other men; and the clergy are the protagonists or defenders each in his sect of this debased state of the public mind, so that to be personally flattered and cockered and excused and apologized for out of all reasonable shape of manhood, by precisely the style of people whose opinions they least value, seems above all things their just official Nemesis or retribution. In a spiritual point of view the clergy are most real martyrs to their perilous calling.

As to the attitude of the Divine mind towards the separatist or Pharisaic portion of the world, *i. e.* towards those who are identified with the outward profession of serving Him, the New Testament leaves no doubt on that subject, but ratifies every instinct of our proper humanity. The parables of the Prodigal Son and of the Publican and Pharisee praying, justify every prevision of common sense in the premises. Surely if I have a family of children the eldest of whom is alone legitimate, and therefore alone entitled to my name and estate, while all the younger children are bastards, and consequently destitute of all legal righteousness, I should be a worm and no man, if, while according to the former his fullest legal consideration, I did not bestow my tenderest and ripest affection and indulgence upon the latter. If my acknowledged heir, conceiving himself prejudiced by this action on my part, should grow angry and reproach me thereupon, saying, "Lo! these many years do I serve thee, neither have I ever transgressed thy commandments, and yet thou hast never given me the slightest expression of thy heart's delight, such as thou art now lavishing upon those others who have wasted thy substance with riotous living:" this strain of remonstrance would only prove how essentially incompatible legal or literal heirship is with spiritual heirship; how infinitely short the most faultless moral righteousness falls of inward or spiritual innocence; but it would never prove me unrighteous. Nothing could be easier for me than to show my dissatisfied and envious offspring that I had at all events done him no injustice. I should say, "My son, I leave it to yourself to estimate the claim which the service you boast of exerts upon my heart, now that your shameless inhumanity to your less fortunate brethren reveals even to your own eyes the spirit which has always animated that service; a spirit of unlimited self-seeking, of low prudence or worldly conformity, befitting indeed the elder son (or head), but totally alien to the temper of the younger son (or heart). The service you render I am sure of at all times [*son, thou art ever with me*], because it is an interested service, prompted by your self-love alone. It is the homage of the proud self-righteous rapacious head, and though I have no power and no desire to balk its legal expectations [*and all that I have is thine*], it yet awakens in my bosom no emotion of pleasure, begets no throb of gratified paternal affection. It is the homage of the heart exclusively, the prodigal, unrighteous, unexacting heart [*I will say unto him, Father, I have sinned against heaven and before thee, and am no more worthy to be called thy son: make me as one of thy hired servants*] which opens up the responsive fountains of my heart, which satisfies the hunger and thirst of my paternal bosom, and irresistibly compels therefore every answering outward demonstration of my inmost pride and joy, of my exquisite spiritual delight and blessedness. You shall have accordingly your legal deserts to the utmost, all that you have bargained for; all that I outwardly possess shall be yours, while I bestow myself, all that I inwardly am, upon your humbler brethren."

Thus much I feel called upon to say to the reader by way of forewarning, or in order that he may observe that I do not quarrel with the living spirit of religion, which glows in every breast of man where God's own spirit of humility, meekness, equality, fellowship, is cultivated and reproduced however feebly; but only with what the best men in history have always quarrelled with, namely, its dead and putrid body which still goes unburied and taints God's wholesome air with its baleful exhalations. Religion disdains any longer a literal or ritual establishment. It claims a purely living and spiritual embodiment, such as flows from God's sanctifying presence and animating power in every form of spontaneous human action. It has no longer anything to do accordingly with churches or with clergy, with sabbaths or with sacraments, with papacy or with prelacy, with Calvin or Socinus[3]; but only with a heart in its subject of unaffected love to all mankind, and unaffected fellowship consequently with every person and every thing however conventionally sacred or profane, that seeks to further that love by the earnest distaste, disuse, and undoing of whatsoever plainly withstands, perverts, or abuses it.

NOTES

1. Jefferson Davis (1808–1889) was of course the President of the Confederacy; Joseph Smith (1832–1914), son of the Joseph Smith (1805–1844) who founded the Mormon sect, was himself the founder of the Reorganized Church of Jesus Christ of Latter-Day Saints; William Walker (1824–1860) was an American adventurer and filibuster who became a revolutionary leader in Nicaragua; John Buchanan Floyd (1806–1863), the Secretary of War in the Buchanan administration at the time of the Fort Sumter incident, later to become a Confederate general during the Civil War, refused to send aid to the Federal troops garrisoned there; James Buchanan (1791–1868) was the fifteenth President of the United States.—Editor's note.

2. John Ruskin (1819–1900) was primarily a critic of the fine arts.—Editor's note.

3. James is referring here, first, to John Calvin (1509–1564), the Great Swiss Reformation theologian from Geneva and author of the *Institutes* and, second, either to Lelio Francesco Maria Sozini (1525–1562) or to his nephew, Fausto Paolo Sozzini (1530–1604), two Italian Reformed theologians whose family name bore the same latinized form and whose work became known in America. —Editor's note.

Philosophical and Religious Writings

11

THE OLD THEOLOGY
AND THE NEW

As one of James's earliest theological essays,
the lecture which follows presents an unusually
clear statement of the way he differentiated his own
perspective from the more traditional one which he had
inherited from the past. Careful students of theology,
however, will quickly discern that some of James's
distinctions, both here and elsewhere, have the effect
of caricaturing "the old theology" in order to place "the
new theology" in a more favorable light. Indeed, it is
sometimes difficult to know just what James means
by "the old theology," since he makes little or no effort
to specify any of its chief representatives. Nonetheless,
his lively formulations still possess a good deal of
merit, not only because they highlight important
characteristics of his own position, but also because
they serve to indicate certain assumptions which were
very much a part of that residual Calvinistic legacy
which still permeated the haunted air.

The following selection is taken from Lecture 4, "The
Old and New Theology: Part 1," *Lectures and
Miscellanies* (New York, 1852), 139–40, 146–66.

———•–•–•———

The summary form which the gospel took at the hands of Jesus and
his apostles, was that he the crucified and risen man was the true Christ
of God: and all they who believed this gospel were declared his people.

The old controversy is now past. No one any longer pretends to deny
that Jesus was the Christ. We all believe it traditionally. So true is this,
that the original formula has lost all meaning for us. We never think why
Jesus should be the Christ, nor dream of finding the gospel in that fact.
But there it lies, and there only. The truth that Jesus was the Christ, when
all the facts of his life are viewed in their bearing upon Jew and Gentile,
really represents to my understanding an infinite goodness and wisdom.
It involves no mystery. Spiritually viewed, it is indeed the complete anti-
dote to darkness on the whole field of human destiny, or of man's rela-

·173·

tions to God. For it spiritually imports that the divine power and glory shall be manifested in man, only when man shall have become emancipated from his natural and social thraldom, and made obedient exclusively to his inspirations. . . .

But let us take a closer view of the fundamental discrepancy between the Old and New Theology. By the Old theology let me premise that I mean that which under every form of superficial difference remains substantially the same in all the sects, from the old Romish down to the modern Swedenborgian. I say that the theology of all these sects is substantially the same under whatever varieties of doctrinal drapery, because in all alike it begets the conception of God as a person finited from man by space and time, and consequently makes ritual or dramatic religion permanent, makes it indeed the only possible religion.

The New theology, on the other hand, is not so easy to define, because it appeals exclusively to the rational understanding instead of the memory. It is not a new *credo* or formulary, but rather the spirit of all creeds and the substance of all formulas. It disavows every sect, because it authenticates all mankind in avouching God to be the inmost and inseparable life of every man great or small, wise or stupid, good or evil. This theology claims to be the spiritual or impersonal meaning of all the literal or personal facts of the four gospels: claims to shew how the birth, life, death and resurrection of Jesus Christ, symbolized that complete lordship of nature which universal man shall ere long achieve, by virtue of his essential or indwelling divine force. Doubtless this theology being spiritual constitutes its own evidence, and can neither be much advanced nor much retarded by ratiocination. By its very terms it excludes all outward or miraculous attestation, appealing only to the scientific intellect or the intellect devoid of prejudice. Not only its existence but the grounds of that existence in the nature of God and man, have long been set forth even to tedium in the humane and philosophic page of Swedenborg. But it derives no lustre even from his shining endowments.[1]

Having thus posited our combatants, let us next ascertain what is the precise bone of contention between them. This decidedly is no other than the religious problem itself. What the Old and New theology differ about is *the true significance of the religious instinct* in man. When we survey the history of the race, we find that the church has always claimed a *supernatural* basis, or shed contempt upon the merely natural life of man. Wherever ritual religion, or the sensuous worship of God, has existed most purely, that is to say least modified by social refinement, it has alleged a profound disjunction between God and the merely natural or carnal man. And the bearing of this fact upon human destiny accordingly, or in other words, the philosophic import of the religious instinct, has always aroused the liveliest activity of the human intellect.

Now, to make a long story short, the more you fix your attention upon this fact, the more inevitable one or other of the following conclusions will appear to you, namely: 1. That creation is a failure and the destiny of the creature consequently extremely dubious, if not decidedly wretched: or 2. That the natural life is not our essential life, but rather the form or mould by means of which that life becomes pronounced or defined.

The Old theology affirms the former of these conclusions. It declares that creation failed at its very inception, and that the destiny of the creature consequently is not normal, but medicated or remedial. Thus it abandons the field of nature utterly, and removes man's destiny to another world, where it exhibits him subject either to the hospitalities of heaven or the inclemencies of hell. He never regains his normal *status* in either of these conditions. Heaven is at the best always a hospital to him. Hell at the best is always a prison to him. In either state alike he bears the scars of his original fall, and drags the chain of an eternal servitude or dependence.

The New theology on the other hand, which also calls itself Christian, though in an exquisitely thorough and internal sense, affirms the latter of these conclusions. It denies that creation ever was or ever can be a failure, but declares that the natural life of man is intrinsically subordinate to his true or divine life, and that the office of religion hitherto in depressing the former, has been necessary simply as a means of introducing him to an acquaintance with the latter. The true life of man, which comes from God, which is God in him, and which is therefore an infinite life welling up from the fountains of his inmost spirit, cannot of course become manifested to man's consciousness so long as the outward or bodily life governs his activity. While the natural life controls his spirit, or governs his action, man cannot realize the life he has in God. He may believe in it as a tradition: he may believe that God originally created the fathers of his race: he may believe in God moreover as an outward and finite person living clear away in some celestial *limbo*, and that he shall receive at His hands after death the life promised to obedience, just as he might receive any other sensible gift. But he has no belief in God as a present life, because appearances do not warrant it. For the quality of our present life is undivine, is such as to make the divine benignity appear partial, which of course destroys its divinity. Infidelity is thus almost the best tribute which the superficial or uncultivated mind can now render to the divine perfection, because the marvels of its power still lie so far beneath the surface of things, and yield themselves up only to reflection. Go speak to your footman or the cook in your kitchen, both of whom are mastered by their mere bodily necessities, both of whom toil year in and year out all their days, for no other end than to keep the base breath of nature in their bodies: go ask these persons whether God is a very present life to them? Will not their instinctive loyalty to God or the perfect life, make them laugh in your face, or else put on that expression of stupid and idiotic assent, which has become almost the sole expression of the human countenance, when divine things are mentioned? There can be no doubt on this point, as every one's experience bears me witness. So long as the natural life controls man's spirit, he cannot realize the life he has in God. Religion consequently has always borne a protest against this life being considered our true life. It has always appealed to the instincts of infinitude within us, to depress or dishonor the natural life, in hope of one day achieving another which shall befit our illimitable aspirations.

Thus the New theology differs from the Old. While the latter makes self-denial an end, the former makes it a means to an end. While the one declares the natural life to be absolutely evil, and therefore to be cast out, the other declares it to be simply servile or ministerial, and therefore to be reduced to order or subjection. In short, the Old theology views the religious problem as significant of despair for man; the New as significant of hope and consolation. It is true that the old theology in words allows its disciples a hope of the divine clemency, provided they exhibit a certain differential attitude from other men towards a certain scheme of recovery provided by God: but the difference in question is so faintly shaded, and liable besides to so many intrinsic attenuations, as to afford no practical comfort to the modest and sober-minded, while it frequently heightens a previous self-conceit into fanaticism.

The different bearing of the two theologies upon the divine character, is especially deserving of note. The Old theology makes creation a *voluntary* procedure on God's part, or a distinct exhibition of *will*, and hence makes God imperfect or finite. For will has no other fountain than want, and to feel a want in any respect is to feel so far forth insufficient to oneself, and to be insufficient to oneself is the very citadel and armory of imperfection. The New theology, on the other hand, makes creation a purely *spontaneous* procedure on the part of God. That is to say, it declares God creative, not through any effort of will, but in Himself, thus without effort. God is *essentially* active, active *in se*, or in His very self, and not as we are through our natural passions or wants. And to be active in oneself, and not by pressure of one's nature, is obviously to be creative. Hence the New theology declares that God creates or gives being to the universe, not by his will, but by Himself. He alone it is, and not His will, as discriminated by the Old theology from Himself, which creates or gives being to things.

It is precisely here that the immense scientific advantage of the New theology appears, for in making God creative *in se*, or by dint of His essential perfection, *it necessarily makes the creature His image, and so binds science to the celebration of the divine infinitude*. The harmonies of creation are the theme of science, and if these harmonies, according to the New theology, only reflect those which are uncreated or absolute, it follows of course that science has at bottom no other task than the illustration of Deity. Thus the New theology links science to the altar of God, and endows her radiant priesthood with sole and plenary power to intercept cursing and bring down blessing from on high. The Old theology, with a fine instinct, subjects its priesthood to a perpetual baptism or purification, because it is merely a symbolic priesthood, ministering a *quasi* divine benediction to a *quasi* divine people. The New theology disallows every baptism, or denies the relevancy of purification, because her priesthood being exclusively a scientific one is final, ministering a true divine benediction to a truly divine people, that is to universal humanity, without respect to creed or complexion.

The Old theology moreover in affirming creation to be strictly voluntary on the part of God, leaves the creature in very insecure relation to Him. For it is notoriously the attribute of will to be fickle or inconstant. A fixed will, a will pertinaciously anchored upon any thing or event, to the intolerance of any other thing or event, is the definition of insanity. Surely then, unless our continuance be grounded in something else than the divine will, unless it be grounded in the essential and immutable perfection of God, we have a wretchedly insecure hold upon existence. The immaculate sanity of that will stamps our existence ephemeral. In fact, the old theology in denying any rational *principle* to creation, denies it also any rational prognostic. In excluding an exact *diagnosis* from its field of vision, it of course excludes an exact *prognosis*, and consequently confutes its own pretension as a true *rationale* of creation. For an event contingent upon pure will confesses itself irrational, or immethodical, and consequently permits no account of itself. And this is virtually the aspect of creation as represented by the old theology. It affirms substantially though not in words, that God created us in sport, or merely for the display of His arbitrary will, a will irresponsible even to His own essential perfection: that having given us faculties of the most admirable temper, and an apprehension of perfection so vivacious and profound as to beget the most burning aspirations towards it, He has after all left these aspirations unbacked by any proportionate power, and so made both the mode and the duration of our existence simply lawless, or what is the same thing dependent upon His own will.

The New theology, on the other hand, asserts a very secure relation between creator and creature. It denies that creation is an exhibition of the divine will, strictly so called, and affirms it to be an operation rather of the essential perfection of God, an outgrowth of His very selfhood, so to speak, in which case of course it is the very image of reason, the very model of order. It claims that the whole being of God, not His power merely but His love and wisdom, in short His total selfhood, is implicated in creation, and consequently that the creature's welfare is as assured as God's own perfection.

Now both these theologies, that which is rapidly setting and that which is as rapidly rising, claim the name of Christian, though the latter in a much more eminent sense than the other. In order therefore to compass an intelligent judgment of their quarrel, let us ascertain the precise point of view in which they severally regard the Christ.

Every person knows that it is possible to contemplate Jesus in two aspects, either a literal or fixed one, which was that cherished by his immediate disciples up to the period of his death, because it related him to their sensuous and superstitious conceptions of Deity: or a spiritual and expansive one, capable of growing with the growth of the human mind, and relating him therefore to the most advanced and scientific conceptions of Deity. This latter aspect was apparently the more congenial one to his own spirit, and was plainly provided for by the entire tenor of his parabolic or mystical instruction. Thus with the early disciple we may still regard the Christ after the flesh or carnally, and look upon his word as purely literal, as having an import only to the ear. Or we may with Paul cease to know him after the flesh, viewing his words only as spirit and life, or as addressing the spiritual understanding of the hearer instead of his omnivorous memory. In short we may view him simply on his finite personal side, or as to all those limitations which made him a Jew, and brought him into collision with that desperate people: or we may view him on his infinite and spiritual side, that is as to that temper of mind which lifted him out of all private or partial affinities, and gave him unity with universal man. In the former case we leave him a mere finite person, although greater in degree than other persons. In the latter case we exalt his finite personality into a type of universal truth.

Now the Old theology contemplates the Christ exclusively in the former or limitary aspect. It makes his worth to us a purely outside and arbitrary thing, attributing to him the power of literally influencing the divine will, and so preventing any person that pleases him suffering an otherwise inevitable damnation. It takes every fact of his life and death at its *prima facie* or obvious value, and affirms in the roundest of terms that unless we yield him a certain voluntary submission, unless we make a certain personal surrender of ourselves to him, we shall suffer inconceivable sorrows. Thus it makes the noble battle which Jesus fought with the ignorance and superstition of his people, a battle in behalf of his own personal glory, not in behalf of universal man. He seemed a man of the purest benevolence, and cherished sympathies so universal as to provoke the keenest disgust from his bigotted kindred. But all this was subordinate to an ulterior selfish aim. He indulged these sympathies not for their own sake simply, or as a finality, but as a means to an end, or by way of winning a title to universal dominion. Hence consistently the old theology forever crowds us Gentiles, us Christians, back to that narrow Judean platform, and makes us simulate first every tedious feature of the Jewish or personal opposition to Jesus, and then every tedious feature of Jewish or personal submission to him, before it allows us any hope of his favor. For once in the history of humanity, for once in all time and space, it allows the Deity to break the sullen monotony of His displeasure, and take delight in a man. But once only. The snow-flake upon the river which is a moment white, then gone forever, is a miracle of perpetuity compared with the transitory clemency it ascribes to Deity. It denies that Jesus came merely to reveal a grandeur of perfection in Deity to which mankind were strangers by ignorance and unbelief, a perfection which is never more and never less whether men believe it or not. No, his gospel is not a revelation of the uncreated and unchangeable divine perfection; it is rather the affirmation of a certain change induced upon the divine mind by Jesus; the product of a certain softening operation which he effected upon the hitherto unmalleable properties of Deity. He came not to show God magnanimous, but to make him so. He enabled God to be merciful and just. He actually empowered God to be Godlike. Consequently it is only in so far as he is concerned that God is great and generous. It is only as shut up to his *physique* that the universal Father appears arrayed in any human or attractive qualities. Hence whoso does not catch the divine favor as let down through the chink of his personality—a personality whose historic reality moreover is necessarily unknown to the vast bulk of the race—must need pocket the loss eternally.

It is easy enough to see that this old theology so affronts the common sense of men, so outrages our conceptions of the divine perfection, that it necessitates its own decease.[2] It discharges Deity of every amiable and dignified attribute, and therein discharges man of all homage towards Him save that of abject fear. It represents Him as forever gloomily devising vengeance towards men for an infirmity induced upon them by the very nature which He himself gives them, and then as stayed in His sanguinary purposes not by any merciful relentings, not by any touch of sweet human pity, but only by the superior allurements of another victim, whose superhuman nature enables him to assuage a superhuman thirst of blood. I am perfectly familiar with the special pleading by which the apologists of the old theology seek to palliate the naked deformity of its dogmas in this direction. One indeed gladly acquits them of a personal complicity with dogmas of which they are ashamed: but they cannot alter the logical import of the dogmas themselves. On the showing of the Old theology it is undeniable, that the sufferings of man for an offence involved in his very nature, and therefore inevitable to him, are actually *bought off* from the framer of that nature by the sufferings of a being above man. Accordingly the relation between God and man induced by this transaction is not one jot more genial and human than it was before. It is simply the relation of indifference which the vulture is under to the dove, which the tiger is under to the lamb, when once its hunger has been effectually appeased.

Of course in taking this view of Christianity the Old theology does but carry out its fundamental view of creation. It holds creation itself to be a product of will exclusively, or to have originally proceeded from the mere arbitrary *fiat* of Deity, and consequently absolves its subsequent history from all responsibility to the laws of order or reason. For if you concede an irrational beginning to a phenomenon—a beginning that is which bears no *ratio* to the human understanding—you may postulate any disorderly development or termination for it you please. Your premises exempt you from accountability.

The New theology in taking a profounder view of creation, takes also a less superficial view of Christianity. For in making creation to start from the essential perfection of God, or His most intimate selfhood, it of course makes the whole tenor of its developments strictly orderly, or consonant with the highest reason. Thus in affirming God himself as the sole source of life to the universe, it denies any absolute superiority among His creatures, denies that any one person possesses any *absolute* claim to the supremacy of other persons. For from the fact of the precisely equal creatureship of all, whatever superiority one may exhibit to another must attach not to himself but to the Creator, must be not a passive but an active superiority, the superiority of genius, of power, of function. Hence the New theology pronounces the current literal view of Christianity absurd and superstitious, save as the basis or continent of a spiritual view. It regards the Christ not from person, which is to finite him, but from spirit, which is to give him infinitude. It views the recorded incidents of his life, death and resurrection, not as possessing a merely historic and superficial value, but much more a philosophic value as symbols or exponents of universal truth. The person of Christ it says belonged of course only to the Jews. His spirit belongs in a most eminent manner to entire humanity. The Gentiles had no personal relations to him, nor any personal knowledge of him. He was dead and buried before they had heard the authentic mention of his name. He was heralded to them only as a spiritual redeemer. The quarrel which the Jews had with him as the desecrator of their law, as the blasphemer of their national God, as the contemner of their most honored priests and rulers, was all unknown to the Gentiles; or if known could not be appreciated by them, because they knew nothing of the fanatical sanctity the Jew arrogated to himself. It was therefore only by his humanitary doctrines and deeds, only as the vindicator of universal man from spiritual tyranny and oppression, that the Christ could have appealed to Gentile sympathy. They cherished his memory, not because they supposed him to entertain any personal regard for them over his own brethren, but simply because he avouched a Deity higher than their thought had yet conceived, a Deity great enough to bless all his children alike, and extremely prone therefore to despise every laborious claim to distinction which the technical saint preferred to the technical sinner.

Thus while the New theology concedes the unprecedented personal virtue of the Christ, and his legitimate historic influence, it at the same time interdicts him any *personal* claim upon our *spiritual* allegiance. Without going into the philosophic ground of this interdict, which imports *that the spiritual idea of man is without the idea of person*, let it suffice to say here that the New theology in making it is exactly consistent with its own fundamental axiom, which is that God gives being to the universe by Himself alone, and hence that every man is what he is solely by the indwelling of God, or to the exclusion of all desert in himself. Accordingly whatsoever grandeur of endowment may have hitherto befallen any person, the lesson conveyed by it accrues to the benefit of universal man, and not to that of the person himself. For inasmuch as God is one and his creature one, no person is great on his own independent account, but only by virtue of his identification with the most enlarged humanity, only in so far as he represents universal man. Hence the great Providential men who have diversified the page of history and turned its level march into a glittering pageantry, claim no passive or personal but only a functional superiority to other men, a superiority which grows out of their humanitary obedience, which is imposed upon them in fact by the necessities of human destiny, and thus subjects them equally with all other persons to the issues of that destiny. The sacredness of Deity does not—except to the sensuous or brute understanding, still dominated by the mere shows of time and space—arise from any antagonism he presents to us, because where as in this case one party is all, and the other nothing, antagonism is simply impossible: but only from His boundless furtherance and beneficence towards us. He is great and adorable not by His invincible distance from us, but by His intimate nearness, by stooping as it were to our native littleness and lifting us to the dimensions of His majesty. Did He measure His strength by our weakness—did He aggrandize Himself by our dimunition—He would be detestable, not adorable. Rather it is impossible to say what emotion he would excite, because the creature of such a power being of course proportionate to its creator, could have no sentiment in common with God's creature.

Hence the prime ministers of Deity, they who speak the most directly from His inspiration, commend themselves to our recognition chiefly by a humanitary temper. The sole personal distinction they claim over others is that of a spotless humility. The measure of their veracity as stewards of divine mysteries, is the sense they entertain of their personal insignificance, of their precise personal equality with other men. Thus the New theology estimates heroic or exceptional men not at their obvious and finite value, but at their humanitary, prophetic, and infinite worth. It glorifies them by resolving whatsoever is personal and superficial about them, into what is universal and substantial. Preeminently therefore is it bound to observe this method with Jesus, for every incident of his life owns such an inseparable humanitary flavor, all his words and deeds—when viewed according to the spirit which animated them—are so grandly human and impersonal, as to force upon us the conception of their typicality, and make a literal interpretation in fact derogatory.[3]

In thus discriminating between the Old and New theology, I beg that you will acquit me of any intention to reflect upon the persons of those who make up the existing sectarianism. Surely no suspicion of the kind should attach to me, while I expressly disclaim all personal aims or interests for the New theology. This theology so far as I apprehend its meaning, knows no persons, confers no personal consequence, receives honor from no man. Having a purely scientific basis, setting forth only what is eternally and infinitely good and true, it of course drops from view whatsoever is peculiar to any *cultus* under the sun, whatsoever is merely finite and differential in every worship, and preserves that which is unitary and essential in all, namely, the spirit of the worshipper. It is a doctrine of universal man in relation with God, not of persons. It declares that no name known on earth is known in heaven, because as I have already said the spiritual idea of man is destitute of the idea of person. Person or name to the spiritual understanding means quality. Hence you perceive that the New theology is bound to shed every ritual, Pagan and Christian alike. It makes baptisms superstitious and sacraments profane, whenever either claims a literal sanctity. It anoints man, and consequently supersedes the priest.[4]

NOTES

1. It is by the way much to be regretted that an ecclesiastical sect should have seen fit to nucleate itself upon this long-suffering old philosopher; because from the nature of the case a sect has necessities which no writings are adequate to meet save in so far as they are destitute of humanitary interest, or confess themselves unworthy of general attention. But Swedenborg's writings palpably exclude all sectarian ambitions, affording matter only of universal or scientific interest. Hence the sectarian attitude of his *soi-disant* disciple should no more be allowed to prejudice him in public regard, by suggesting a low estimate of his scientific value, than the climbing parasite is allowed to prejudice the hearty and unconscious oak, whose robust age shall live down a thousand of its deciduous generations.

2. I am aware that a certain diligent transmutation of orthodoxy is going on in New England, by which it is eviscerated of its immemorial contents, and yet avouched to be the same gospel. But somehow, in spite of the extreme zeal and good faith embarked in this enterprise, no dispassionate observer of the process can help feeling that the solid nutmeg aroma of the old orthodoxy is rapidly dissipating into a thin flavor of brasswood.

3. Probably the highest tribute ever paid to the personality of Jesus, was that recently enacted by a distinguished German scholar, in attempting, very unsuccessfully however, to resolve the entire record of his personal history into a humanitary myth. This good man finds the evangelic facts so full of sheer *manliness*, so full of the widest human meaning and promise, that he resolves henceforth to deny them actuality, and regard them simply as a rhythmic dance of the human intellect celebrating the oncoming splendors of the race.

4. I have indeed heard as I have intimated in a previous note, of attempts made both in England and this country to dramatize the new theology, and give it a decorous Sunday outfit and institution, as though it were only some new edition in larger type of the old ecclesiasticism. But these attempts are so incongruous with every rational perception of its drift, and they logically involve, whether they have actually begotten or not, so many and such tiresome controversies, as to whether for example the new ministry be an institution of trine or of simple dimension—whether the minister's tie to the flock be strictly conjugal or not—as to how the new ministry and the new ordinances become more efficacious than the old—and how far the spheres of new Jerusalem children may be prejudiced by those of the old Jerusalem—that the whole pretension tumbles off into mere ecclesiastical wantonness.

12

THE OLD PHILOSOPHY
AND THE NEW

One of James's most affecting traits of character was
his willingness to plunge in where angels fear to tread.
Here he takes on no less a figure than Immanuel Kant
and argues that the Copernican revolution which Kant
was supposed to have effected in philosophy was, in
fact, the very opposite: if Copernicus could be said
to have moved man from the center of the universe out
to its circumference, then Kant's new epistemological
discoveries succeeded only in making man once again
the center of all intellectual movement with everything
else relegated to the periphery. Whatever its merits
as a convincing philosophical argument, this essay
does much to clarify James's own epistemological
assumptions, and also demonstrates the lively way
in which he refused to be cowed by authority.
This selection constitutes chapter 17 of *Substance
and Shadow* (Boston, 1863), 286–98.

——————•◦•◦•——————

The important addition which Kant made to Philosophy consists in a
new analysis of knowledge, which gives its subjective element as he conceives it, the decided primacy of what he calls its objective element. The
old Philosophy erred in his estimation by allowing the matter of knowledge
as constituted by the various things we are said to know, to preponderate
over its form as constituted by our sensibility and intelligence. And by
exactly reversing this order he thought he had succeeded in rectifying
metaphysics, and earning the name of a philosophic Copernicus. The
name is singularly ill-adjusted however, since Kant's rectification of the
old metaphysics consists in making us the centre of intellectual movement
and all other things circumferential to us; while the rectification which
Copernicus operated in the popular astronomy altogether consisted in placing us in the circumference of physical motion, and removing its focus to
the greatest possible distance from us. This is Kant's initial blunder, his
unpardonable sin to Philosophy, that like a geographer who confounds the
mouth of a river with its source he makes our knowledge take its rise in

us as well as issue from us, and hence denies it any absolute validity. Ever since his time accordingly Philosophy has been playing such fantastic tricks before high heaven, here deifying all things, there denying any Deity, as to degrade herself to the level of a common brawler, unfit any longer to occupy attention.

But let us look more closely at the matter in hand.

"All knowledge is a product of two factors, a knowing subject, and an external world. Of these two factors the latter furnishes our knowledge with experience as the matter, and the former with the conceptions of the understanding as the form, through which a connected knowledge—or synthesis of our perceptions in a whole of experience—first becomes possible. If there were no external world, then there would be no phenomena; if there were no understanding, then these phenomena which are infinitely manifold would never be brought into the unity of a notion, and then no experience were possible. Thus while intuitions without conceptions are blind, and conceptions without intuitions are empty, knowledge is a union of the two, since it requires that the form of the conception should be filled with the matter of experience, and that the matter of experience should be apprehended in the net of the understanding's conceptions."[1]

We have not yet got the entire *corpus delicti* under our view, but let us pause here to establish a few preliminary considerations, which go to prove this elaborate pedantry a pure superfluity, so far as the fact of knowledge is concerned.

Doubtless the foregoing analysis does convey a sort of general predicament of the great fact of knowledge; such a predicament as you put a coat in, logically, when you mention a tailor and a piece of cloth. Every coat of course logically pre-dicates a tailor and a piece of cloth, but you convey a very inadequate notion of the actual garment by enumerating these purely constitutional elements of it. I utterly refuse to conceive the coat upon such niggardly terms. I am free to admit that the tailor and the cloth are necessary *data* of the coat, are logically implied in its constitution: but this sort of knowledge is purely scientific as interesting only the tailor and manufacturer, and not philosophic as interesting all mankind. As a philosopher I am not concerned to ask what gives the garment phenomenality, but only what gives it being. In other words I do not ask what makes the garment, *i. e.* what elements enter into its material constitution; but only what creates it or gives it absolute existence. The coat itself or spiritually, *i. e.* in the use or power it exerts, is something very different and superior to the material elements which go to constitute it: it indeed involves (or presupposes) these elements, and can therefore never be involved in them. The coat when truly conceived, when conceived as a finished garment, causes both the tailor and the piece of cloth to disappear in the bosom of its own unity or individuality, whence they never reappear till the coat itself disappears or falls to pieces. The tailor and the cloth furnish an unexceptionable material parentage to the coat; they combine to give it visible existence or embodiment, so that no coat could ever appear without the sartorial art on the one side to give it soul or paternity, and a tegumentary tissue on the other to give it body or maternity. But obviously the coat is not merely a visible existence, it possesses also an invisible or spiritual BEING in that distinctive use or power which it exerts over other existence, and which accordingly constitutes its true individuality, its distinctive personality or discrimination from all other things.

Now the philosopher I repeat is concerned only with this invisible spiritual substance of the coat, this absolute individuality of it, which alone ordains its visible constitution, and makes it comprehend within itself both tailor and clothier. The coat itself is neither the tailor who makes it, nor the cloth out of which it is made; though both of these things are prerequisites of its phenomenal apparition: neither is it any conceivable combination of the two which yet leaves them reciprocally discernible; since every coat in proportion to its desert of its name, makes you forget both tailor and cloth, and never recalls them to mind until it ceases to be itself, i. e. until its merely constitutional side comes uppermost again by the garment itself falling into decrepitude and decay. The invisible substance of the coat which is its use, is what alone gives it unity or individuality; is what alone creates it, i. e. gives it true being, or causes it to exist not only to our perception or relatively, but also in itself or absolutely. The constitutional elements of the coat, which are the tailor and the piece of cloth, are equally implicated in a thousand other existences, and do not therefore contribute to the coat that element of individuality, without which it would not be a coat, but might be a pair of trousers or anything else having like constitutional identity. This element is purely spiritual, consisting in the distinctive use the coat fulfils, the characteristic service it renders to other existence, a use or service which never meets the eye, but certainly is not therefore the less but all the more spiritually discernible. It is thus the use of the coat exclusively which gives it invisible being, or spiritually creates it; and hence infallibly prescribes that material constitution by which it exists visibly to us.

This spiritual side of existence then, this absolute or creative aspect of it, which includes in itself and accounts for the entire lower world of its relative or phenomenal existence, is what alone interests Philosophy: and this unhappily is what Kant and especially Sir William Hamilton[2] are treacherous to. Philosophy is not a search into the material constitution of things, into what is purely phenomenal and relative in existence. This is the exclusive domain of science. Philosophy seeks to know only what is essential to things, demands to know what is that living or substantial reality which invariably determines their material constitution, and forbids it to be different from what it actually is. It takes the existing constitution of things as determined by science for granted; and then demands what it is which alone confers this fixed constitution upon things, which makes them precisely what they are, and forbids them ever to be otherwise. That is to say, it asks what is the creative substance under all this conflict of appearances, what its most intimate verity, what its fundamental *raison d'être.* Kant on the contrary degrades Philosophy to the level of Science by identifying the spiritual essence of things with their sensuous constitution, so turning Philosophy from an inquiry into the absolute being of things, to an investigation of their phenomenal existence. He makes it an analysis primarily of the constitution of existence; and as he finds there no trace of being, no evidence of creation, no sign of life or infinitude, he at once declares that Philosophy is an incompetent witness to these truths, and devolves its burden upon the moral instinct.

Every fact of life or consciousness doubtless, like every fact of experience, involves a constitutional side which gives it identity with all other existence, and adapts it to our capacity of sensuous recognition. But you give a monstrously false notion of the living fact, if you attempt to run it into these sensuous conditions. Knowledge does indeed always pre-suppose on its constitutional side, does always predicate in other words to the understanding of a looker-on, a thing knowing and a thing known. But the precise miracle of the living fact—the very life of the conscious experience—is, that it utterly obliterates the discrimination which sense alleges between these elements, and blends or fuses them in its own unitary and absolute individuality. Life or consciousness always unites what mere existence or sense disunites; so that to attempt reproducing the living experience called knowledge, by alleging its purely constitutional elements or simples, would be like attempting to convey an image of a trunk by enumerating its contents, or to give an idea of marriage by evoking the lineaments of a mourning bride and a bereaved husband. As marriage is nothing if it be not indissoluble, as it confesses itself instantly falsified by whatsoever impedes the essential unity of the parties to it, so every fact of life or consciousness supposes a complete fusion of man and nature, supposes a marriage between them so real and vital as to make any subsequent divorce, such as Kant alleges in his discrimination of subject and object, of the me and the not-me, utterly futile and impracticable. Yet the whole current Philosophy of Perception is built upon this shallow fallacy of observation, upon this profoundly vicious and incompetent estimate of the fact in hand; and no rectification of it is possible therefore unless we clearly understand ourselves here.

What we have already seen is, that science is a research into the physical constitution of things, into whatsoever gives them visible body or existence, and so relates them to our intelligence; while Philosophy is a research exclusively into the spiritual essence of things, into whatsoever gives them invisible being, or stamps their existence absolute and independent of our intelligence. Science guards the natural pedigree of existence; Philosophy takes all that labor for granted, and cares only to assert the spiritual essence of the existence thus generated. Now what we are about to scrutinize is, the endless imbecility which Kant has fathered upon Philosophy by confounding these utterly distinct fields of research; that is to say, by sinking the Infinite in the finite, dissolving life in mere existence, and running the philosopher into the logician. The whole subsequent evolution of Philosophy in Germany, starting from this initial blunder, has tended towards such a deadly objectifying of the me to its own consciousness, that Hegel[3] or somebody else in his place was bound to put a climax to the speculative dotage and delirium of his race, by gravely proclaiming the identity of being and thought, or what is the same thing, making God to be vivified by us rather than us by Him. But let us begin at the beginning.

Our intelligence is conversant with two orders of facts: 1. facts of Life, which are known only from within, or by Consciousness; 2. facts of Existence, which are known only from without, or by Sense. The rose, the horse, the mountain, the lake, the stars, the man, are facts of existence simply, which are given in my sensible organization, and are consequently known only *ab extra*. But the emotion of delight I experience when I view the lake spreading its smiling bosom before my window, bounded by the verdurous slopes of the opposite mountain, and reflecting now the busy industry of man, now the repose of the tranquil heavens, is exclusively a fact of life, shut up to my proper consciousness, or known only from within, and quite above the power of sense to produce or even adequately to report. The senses involve in their varied realm all the scattered particulars, or merely material constituents, of the landscape; but the joy I experience in seeing these disunited details, these *disjecta membra*, melt into living unison, is a purely spiritual fact, denoting a sensibility greatly interior and superior to that of my body. No doubt the animal sees—so far as the mere organic fact of sight is concerned—every material feature of the landscape just as we see it, perhaps better. But that which gives these things all their charm and meaning to us, and which is their fitness to reflect a certain interior sentiment we profoundly feel of the spiritual unity that constitutes Life, and binds all existence together, this is entirely lacking to the animal, however superior he may be to us in sensible organization, and can never by any possibility be communicated to him.

Try the experiment. Suppose for example that you lead your horse, some starry night, to an eminence whence an unobstructed view of the heavens may be commanded. He will doubtless sees the stars, see those which fall under the horizon of his vision, quite as accurately as you see them. But will he also look at them? Will his gaze be attracted and riveted to them as yours is? Will he feel the emotions of grandeur you feel, those intimations of a life higher than the stars, which makes their hoariest orbs seem indeed but of yesterday, and turns the overpowering galaxy itself into glittering tinsel? Assuredly not. He will snuff and nibble the obscure herbage at his feet by way of pastime, and will remind you by an expostulatory snort, that good straw is awaiting him in the warm stable whence you have so superfluously dislodged him. But as for any sympathy with you, that is absurd. The horse sees the spectacle, it is only you who regard and admire it. What then is the inference? It is, manifestly, that his proper life is all contained and exhausted in his natural organization, and the experience which that enfolds; while your proper life on the other hand, the distinctively human life, which is spiritual, being garnered away in the

Divine depths of consciousness, only ultimates itself in Nature, and feels itself at best but dimly imagined, but feebly reflected, in her most vital experiences. It is in fact always and only the infinite and ineffable Divine beauty which struggles to make itself known in these emphatic natural experiences; which lets itself down so to speak in these transcendent moments to our rapt intelligence: and in the surprise of the rich discovery, in the bewilderment of such unsuspected wealth, we often very generously accredit Nature itself, which is but the stupendous mirror of the transaction, with a glory not its own.

Thus life clearly pre-supposes existence, or consciousness presupposes sense, just as a finished house presupposes bricks and mortar: but as he would be a monstrous dolt who should be content to define a house by analyzing it into these base materials, so he who confounds life with existence, consciousness with sense, proves himself incompetent to deal with questions of this magnitude. As in resolving a house into the material elements involved in its construction, you utterly leave out its characteristic soul or individuality which is its form, and which is no material existence whatever but a wholly spiritual one, being a pure derivation of the architectonic art, demanding all these material conditions for its own manifestation: so à fortiori when you relegate life into those facts of mere existence which relate it to our intelligence, you utterly evaporate its creative spirit, or reduce it to instant unconsciousness by destroying its individuality. No one looking at a house and estimating its distinctive character or individuality, regards or even sees the bricks and mortar implied in its structure. These things unless the architect has been a noodle, are forever covered up from sight, only to reveal themselves again when the edifice shall have tumbled into dilapidation. Every house accordingly that deserves the name stands forth to the beholder a pure form of heavenly Art, beckoning onward and upward the soul.

In like manner precisely in estimating a distinctive fact of life, you have nothing whatever to do with those purely constitutional conditions which ally it with all other facts; your business lies exclusively with that thing which separates it from all other facts and causes it to be itself, or gives it absoluteness. You may analyze existence to its last gasp and you will never lay your hand upon a fact of life; simply because life is in all cases a spiritual fact, being known only by consciousness or from within, never by sense or from without. It is true that before the horse can realize his proper life, i. e. before he can consciously enjoy his oats, and fling up his heels in the abundance of his pasturage, he must have a basis for it in an organized natural existence. But you may ransack this organized natural existence to its primitive germ, without ever catching a whisper of the life the horse enjoys, without discerning a gleam of the horse himself, in other words. In fact the deeper your analysis goes the further you get away from the living animal, from the realm of life or consciousness: for life is built only upon the intensest synthesis or unity of existence, and shrinks aghast therefore from its analysis or dissolution. So too all the facts of our proper life or consciousness presuppose our physical organization, involving as its contents the universe of nature. But you may traverse this organization to its core, without detecting a solitary ray of Life. Life presupposes organization, that is to say, it begins only where organization ends or is perfected; and to look for it therefore among the mere contents of organization, or in any analysis however subtle of existence, would be like looking into the works of a watch to ascertain the time of day. Undoubtedly the works of a watch are all presupposed in the creative spirit of the watch, which is its distinctive use; just as our physical organization involving in itself the universe of sense, is presupposed in our conscious life or selfhood. But what would you think of a droll, who, when you asked him the time of day, should insist upon consulting the bowels of his watch rather than its dial-plate?

NOTES

1. I quote from Schwegler's excellent manual of *The History of Philosophy,* translated by Julius H. Seelye, pp. 230, 231.

2. Sir William Hamilton (1788–1865), to whom James is referring, was a Scottish metaphysician of comparatively modest intellectual distinction whose chief philosophical contribution was to recognize the importance of German philosophy, and in particular Kant. He is best known for his essay on the "Philosophy of the Unconditioned" in which he argues that the finite human mind can have no knowledge of the infinite.—Editor's note.

3. Here James refers to Georg Wilhelm Friedrich Hegel (1770–1831), the greatest of the German Idealists and one of the seminal minds in the history of modern European philosophy.—Editor's note.

13

RELIGION, SCIENCE, AND PHILOSOPHY

It may come as a surprise to some readers that
James thought of these various modes of access to
truth in the above order. Religion and science could
only take one part of the way toward the secret of
creation, since neither was competent to perform
philosophy's office of determining the relation between
the infinite and the finite, the absolute and the relative.
It was just here that James differed with Kant and the
whole thrust of critical philosophy. To a mind like
his own, which perceived the complete unity between
God and man or the ideal and the actual, it seemed
that Kant was merely reducing philosophy to a form of
science by acknowledging as real little more than that
which is admitted to sense, and thus turning his back
upon the marvel of creation which for James was an
undisputed fact of consciousness. "You ask Kant a
question of creative substance or spirit," James
suggested at one point, "and he answers you by an
analysis of constitutive surface or body. You ask him
what creates things, or gives them absolute being
irrespective of our intelligence; he replies by telling
you what produces them to sense, or gives them
phenomenal existence. You ask him to explain to you
the great supernal mystery of selfhood or Life, and he
hastens to plunge his foolish head in the purely
subterranean fact of existence. In short you expect him
to marshal you into the drawing-room, and he
incontinently locks you up in the kitchen."

James wanted to restore philosophy to its ancient
Platonic vocation as a study of the relation between
essence and existence. To do this required the
adumbration of a new metaphysics of experience which
he began to flesh out in this selection and those
that follow.

This selection constitutes chapter 20 of *Substance
and Shadow* (Boston, 1863), 347–70.

I have said that Philosophy is most strictly a research of the Infinite in the finite, of the Absolute in the relative. It is either this, or it is demonstrably nothing at all; because we know only the finite and relative, and consequently (unless we make knowledge contradict itself, which is absurd) we can never know the Infinite and absolute save in so far as they become disclosed or revealed in the finite and relative. The Infinite and Absolute are what we are naturally ignorant of, because, being by nature finite or relative existences, our knowledge must of course reflect that imperfection, and confess itself unable to ascend to the Perfect. Unless the Perfect therefore condescend to our disability by revealing Himself in what we already know, *i. e.* in the imperfect, we must remain forever excluded from His knowledge. I repeat then that Philosophy is a demonstration of the Infinite and Absolute, not apart from the finite and relative, but exclusively by means of them. She rejects every other definition than this as manifestly incommensurate with her interests; whereas this position being once made good to her she is put upon an inexpugnable basis forever. Her sole business in life is to vindicate the eternal mystery of godliness, which is God manifest in the flesh; or what is the same thing, the perfect marriage-fusion of the Divine and human natures in a new or regenerate manhood: a business to which the purely religious and the purely scientific intellect are both alike profoundly incompetent; the former from its inveterate superstition, the latter from its equally inveterate scepticism: the one being sure if unimpeded by the other to originate an incessant practical Pantheism; the other an incessant practical Atheism.

Now the fundamental incompetency of the Critical Philosophy avouches itself just here, in that it totally misapprehends this tie of reciprocal amity and unity between God and Man, infinite and finite, absolute and relative, and converts it into one of reciprocal distrust and aversion. It construes the infinite not as the friend but as the impassioned enemy of the finite; and postulates not merely a logical but an essential contrariety between the absolute and the relative in knowledge. Kant shows correctly enough that all our vital experience involves or presupposes a close relationship between our organization and the external world; but he instantly forgets that this is a fact strictly of involution, and not of evolution—of presupposition and no longer of supposition—and proceeds consequently to dogmatize upon the experience as if it were exhausted in that relationship.

The idea is simply absurd. The experience does not begin until the relationship in question is fully consummated. The relationship invariably precedes the experience, is rigidly presupposed by it in every case; and hence has simply no power whatever to determine the experience, but only to serve or promote it: no power rationally to explain or elucidate it, but only to afford it a material platform of evolution. It was a dim instinct of the truth here which alarmed Kant: a ghastly dread lest—if the living experience ITSELF should be seen in every case to involve an absolute quantity—Philosophy might suddenly and superbly authenticate both science and religion: that made him hurry the experience itself breathlessly out of sight, by seeking to dissolve the substantial unity it implies to consciousness in the purely superficial and structural diversity it yields to sense. It is as if being asked to define a house to your imagination, he should reply: so much bricks and mortar on the one hand, so much architect on the other: or being asked to describe a child he should content himself with introducing you to its father and mother. Surely, you say, the house itself is neither the materials nor the scientific skill which were necessary to generate it, being wholly contained in the active USE it promotes to its occupants; and the child himself, or spiritually, is utterly incapable of being resolved into the loins of his parents, however truly he may be demonstrated to have come from them in all corporeal and even psychical regards. Spiritually he never came from them, but claims on the contrary an instantly Divine origin. Kant's replies might pass, if your questions had turned upon the mere material genesis of either product: but as this knowledge was rigidly presupposed in your inquiry, nothing being supposed unknown but the quality of the house itself considered as a finished structure, and of the child himself considered as a living person, they are simply puerile and irrelevant.

Let me be perfectly understood. I repeat that the reason why Kant was thus persistently driven to blink the solar splendor of Life, and immerse his intelligence in the comparative night of mere Existence: the reason why it was necessary for him to render our living experience thus preposterously exanimate by exorcising from it its total individuality as ascertained by consciousness, before he would consent to account for it: is because Philosophy in his degenerate hands had renounced all memory of her true mission. A true Philosophy whenever confronted with this grand fact of selfhood, this supreme fact of life or consciousness, cannot help feeling herself on hallowed ground; cannot help feeling herself in the presence, veiled it is true but still most vital, of the Infinite and Absolute: and it is a rare philosopher as philosophers have hitherto been estimated, who is not utterly disconcerted by the apparition. Kant at all events was not that philosopher. He was in fact less a philosopher than a man of science, his intellect being far more eminently analytic than synthetic. He lent himself with extreme good will to the scientific demolition of religion as a doctrine; but he had no foresight whatever of its philosophic reconstruction as a life. He had no objection to exalt the purely negative scientific research of cause into a positive utterance of Philosophy; but when as here he found it bringing him face to face with the infinitely more august because truly philosophic problem of creation, he felt an instant instinct of disaster to all those cherished interests of scepticism by which his intellectual vision was bounded, and without more ado accordingly he gathered up his coat-tails and fled ignominiously to the uttermost parts of the earth.

I am persuaded that it was nothing but this mortal dread of Philosophy as the sole authoritative voucher and exponent of the Divine creation, which, unconsciously to Kant himself, aroused his scientific scepticism and drove him to interpret all our experience as a compromise between our subjectivity on the one hand and the truth of things on the other. Surely if I am willing to look upon phenomenal existence as created: if I am willing to perceive in it the evidence of a power superior to itself as alone accounting for it: I shall never feel tempted to postulate for it an existence more real than appears. If the phenomenon be a created existence, its phenomenal selfhood is plainly its only real selfhood, the only one which does not manifestly belie the truth of the case. Accordingly it is only when I put the truth of its creation in doubt, or claim for it an underived existence, that I feel myself tempted to separate between its apparent and its real selfhood, or posit for it a mode of existence which is as truly repudiated by its own consciousness as by my intelligence. Thus had Kant been willing to accept the vulgar hypothesis of a supernatural creation, he would have seen with half a glance that of no created thing could it be asserted with truth that it was its own substance as well as its own form; and hence he would never have organized that monstrous basis of disagreement between Philosophy and the common sense of mankind, which was afterwards in the writings of his German and Scotch disciples to avouch their reciprocal deadly hostility, by turning Philosophy, whether it be regarded with the former as a positive doctrine, or with the latter as a purely negative one, into the most flagrant outrage upon common sense ever planned, at all events ever practised, by human wit and human learning.

The common sense of mankind affirms with no misgiving that every thing we see is created by God, that absolutely everything which exists does in some infallible way confess His exclusive power. No doubt the common sense of the race begets very crude very superstitious very unworthy conceptions of this great theme, and as a general thing degrades the creative process from a purely spiritual to a purely physical and even mechanical one. For this reason the philosopher has been from time immemorial very shy of the vulgar conclusions upon the subject: but Philosophy herself has never demanded that these conclusions should be ignored, but only that the popular conceptions should be chastened and elevated. Least of all has she ever been willing to sink the idea of spiritual creation in the purely scientific and preparatory notion of material constitution. She equally disavows the ancient philosopher who sought to run creation into a scheme of physical order; and the modern philosopher who seeks to run it into one of logical order: because they both alike deny creation in any intelligible sense of the word, and so vacate Philosophy as a substantive vocation by attempting both alike to account for existing things on scientific principles, or without the allegation of spiritual substance. The modern philosopher especially has drunk of the new wine of science till he has become foolishly inebriated and lost the remembrance of higher worlds; till he is no longer ashamed in fact to maintain that what we popularly term creation and conceive of as the exhibition of strictly supernatural power, is in truth but the carnal interpretation of a profound logical verity, which is eventually sure to come into general recognition by the normal progress of science, and without the misleading light of Revelation. It is this contented and inveterate myopy of Philosophy which turns her into the toothless ineffectual crone she confesses herself to be in the pages of Kant and Sir William Hamilton; fit only to sit in the chimney-corner and doze over the golden memories of her prime, while the great problems of Creation Redemption and Providence are not only left unsolved but are authoritatively pronounced insoluble. Kant indeed allows these questions a *quasi* philosophic interest in reducing them to so many unrecognized anticipations of natural order. But Sir William Hamilton frankly disowns them altogether as being completely foreign to the jurisdiction of Philosophy, so consigning us to the tender mercies of an irresponsible priesthood on the one hand, and of an unlimited scepticism on the other.

But let us endeavor to be more precise. Kant's philosophic delinquency grew as I have already shown out of a defective scientific observation, which led him to exteriorate the objective to the subjective element in experience, or give the latter systematic priority and control of the former. The fundamental antithesis which all thought and all action exhibit, of subject and object, of me and not-me, properly falls, not between man and nature, *i. e.* finite and finite, but between man and God, *i. e.* finite and infinite. The senses do indeed authorize and validly assert this discrimination between man and nature: but then we must remember that sense regards man as a natural phenomenon or product exclusively, having no capacity to discern him in his spiritual nature and attributes. So far the testimony of sense is irrefutable. To all the extent of my physical manhood I am properly subject to nature. I breathe her atmospheres, I eat of her corn and her oil, I drink of her wine and her milk; her light organizes my eye, her sounds animate my ear, her odors quicken my smell, her savors vivify my palate, her forms enliven my touch: in a word her various forces constitute the sole and total field of my bodily sensibility and intelligence, so that to all the extent of my finite organization I am literally built up of her substance, and propose to myself no higher end or object of action because I recognize no surer spring nor ampler provision of life. But Philosophy rejects these natural *data* as furnishing an every way base and meagre estimate of true manhood, and proceeds at once to assign it worthier dimensions. Philosophy makes the characteristic sphere of human life to be spiritual, and is manifestly therefore in no danger of yielding to sense in regarding man as primarily a subject of nature. But science also ought to be above any such temptation, inasmuch as she herself makes morality the true characteristic of human nature, so endowing man with an individuality unknown to all earth's tribes, and insuring him the unlimited dominion of nature. She thus most distinctly reverses the order which sense establishes between man and nature. For man as a moral force renounces his obligation to nature, compelling her fiercest appetites and passions into his individual subserviency: so that throughout the moral realm nature invariably posits herself as properly subject to man, or defers to him as her own legitimate and adequate sovereign. What else explains our rational growth? How else is it that we alone reject the light of sense as competent for our guidance, and substitute for it the more subtle and penetrating flame of reason in all our conclusions?

Clearly then Kant was as treacherous to science as he was to Philosophy, as disloyal to reason as he was to Revelation, in making the objective sphere of human life fall outside of man's subjectivity or below it, rather than within or above it. He systematically identified the realm of the not-me with nature instead of God: or if he allowed it any pertinency to the latter designation, it could only be by divesting God meanwhile of every spiritual attribute, and postulating Him as a purely natural existence separated from man by the totality of space and time, or the integrality of nature. It is as instructive as it is melancholy to observe how the whole current of subsequent philosophic, or rather logical, speculation in Germany reflected the unhappy scientific bias Kant had thus impressed upon it, by hastening to precipitate itself into the fatal embraces of Pantheism. For of course if, not negligently but on principle, you exteriorate object to subject, being to seeming, substance to form, you necessarily exalt the minor element of thought to the unchallenged primacy of its major element, and consequently end by identifying man with Deity. Fichte[1] accordingly in accepting without examination the Kantian analysis of knowledge, found himself logically driven to interpret Philosophy as a scheme of absolute subjective Idealism, in declaring the me the sole and universal reality. Pantheism was only impossible on this meagre stoical basis, because God himself according to Fichte is but a creature of the me. It was not that the system fell short of God, but exceeded Him, or absorbed Him in its own ampler contents. Pantheism, according to this stupendous tom-foolery, supplies an imperfect theory of the universe, only because God Himself falls short of the universality of the me: *i. e.* cannot pretend, in vulgar parlance, to be near so great a swell. Schelling[2] transformed Fichte's subjective scheme into one of objective idealism, without in the least degree arraigning, or even suspecting, the egregious scientific blunder or fallacy of observation on which it was based. In fact Schelling merely affirmed in contradiction to Fichte the coreality of subject and object, or man and nature: the affirmation being just as barren of philosophic consequences strictly speaking as its predecessor had been; since its author had no sooner vindicated the joint and equal scientific validity of subject and object or of man and nature, than he at once proceeded to demonstrate their joint and equal philosophic invalidity, by resolving them both into an inconceivable transcendental identity or indifference, which, instead of vivifying them both, simply obliterates or neutralizes them both; and which he thereupon calls The Absolute; in fact the head of that distinguished family of Absolutes of whom Sheridan's Sir Anthony[3] was a diminished specimen. Thus it was however that Schelling laboriously cleared the way for that unscrupulous juggle of "the identity of contradictories"—*i. e.* the identity of yes and no, white and black, true and false, good and evil, right and wrong—which was soon in the hands of a hardier thaumaturgist to arrest the intellectual progress, and even undo the intellectual existence, of the race; not merely by confounding God with the universe and proving creation in any sincere sense of the term an abject swindle: for all this had been already gleefully accomplished by Schelling: but by converting our very faculty of knowledge itself upon which we fondly relied to give us eternal conjunction with God, into a faculty of unlimited self-deception merely: *i. e.* into a guarantee of our eternal and most righteous incorporation in the devil.

But we have by no means done with Kant.

What I want to bring my reader clearly to see in the end, is, that Kant's analysis of knowledge vitiates the integrity of the mind or destroys its unity, simply by making consciousness reproduce—instead of annul—the fallacious separation which sense organizes between man and nature. To Kant's senses he himself existed within the visible limits of his own body; nature existed without those limits; and God existed (if indeed any such existence were) still without the limits of nature. This is all very harmless and inevitable. The foundations of the mind are laid in sense, and he who quarrels with them because they are directly fallacious and only inversely true, forgets that the foundation of every edifice physical or mental would be plainly inadequate to its function, unless what was ceiling to itself became floor to the superstructure; or what was heaven to the one became earth to the other. So far then Kant is blameless.

But Kant instantly ceases to be blameless when he proceeds to reproduce this necessity of the foundation in the freedom of the superstructure itself, by reorganizing sense in the outraged lineaments of consciousness. Sense divides where consciousness unites; and to represent the one therefore as simply reflecting the verdict of the other, is virtually to stop the growth of the mind and fix it in infancy. Physically, or to my own senses and those of other men, I exist in one place and nature in another. But mentally or to my own rational consciousness I am consubstantiate and coextensive with nature in all time and all space, having no life but what she imparts. She supplies every sensation every emotion every perception I experience; in short my sensibility and intelligence are completely filled out and vivified with her substance, so that a conscious unity reigns where sense records only a lifeless duality. Descartes[4] made thought the argument of existence. *Cogito, ergo sum* ["I think, therefore I am."]. Yes, but this reasoning avails to nature quite as much as to myself; since thought is always concrete never abstract, *i. e.* presents me and nature in indissoluble unity. Thought is always composite never simple; a product of marriage not of concubinage; in short a fact of most orderly relation and therefore of unity between two sensibly divided existences, never of mere disorderly finiteness and disunion. " I THINK," says Descartes. "But *what* do you think?" I reply. "You cannot think nothing. If you think, you are bound to think something: which something is furnished you either 1, by nature directly; or 2, by God as imagined by you under natural attributes; or else 3, by yourself as similarly imagined: so that nature may be said to furnish directly or indirectly the whole substance or body of your thought, while you yourself give it mere visible surface or cuticle. Thus you may think things which are directly presented in sense, such as stones or trees or horses or houses or lands or waters: or you may think things which are only indirectly presented there, *i. e.* re-presented; namely rational things, such as goodness and truth, evil and falsity, simplicity and deceit, magnanimity and meanness, pride and humility, chastity and uncleanness: but whether you think one or the other, the process of your thought is invariably concrete not discrete, and forbids you accordingly to allege within its own living or conscious limits the distribution of object and subject, or the duality of nature and man."

Now Kant, practically at least, ignored this all-important truth, in persistently separating between the subject and object of knowledge, or in representing knowledge not as evidencing a mental unity in the midst of a physical diversity, but as organizing a most real and substantial diversity where sense ordains only a seeming and formal one. I have no doubt for my own part that he also theoretically ignored the truth of the case; for although he in terms acknowledges nature as contributing the matter of knowledge while we contribute only its form, he yet organizes such a controversy between these livingly united elements, as plainly proves that he for his part conceives that puny and pedantic reflex of the truth upon his understanding, to be the vital truth itself: thus reducing knowledge from a purely synthetic to a purely analytic function, or swamping consciousness, which affirms both infinite and finite, both absolute and relative, in sense, which affirms only the finite and relative. In short Kant regarded the mind as strictly an individual possession, and never suspected its universal scientific unity. He looked upon his own mind as shut up spatially to his corporeal limits, so that he as a mental subject not less than a physical one might be said to exist in time and space, or claim to be only here and now while nature was everywhere and always. He had not the remotest idea that nature reflects the united and entire mental personality of the race, and that he himself consequently had no mind apart from nature: on the contrary he maintained that we by the forms of our sensibility and understanding furnished the entire personality of nature, and consequently viewed himself as absolutely, or within the spatial dimensions of his body, a seeing, hearing, smelling, tasting, and touching, in short, knowing, subject; and then as simply applying these absolute faculties to natural things.

Perhaps we may illustrate Kant's philosophic insolvency more succinctly to the reader's apprehension by saying, that he conceived the finite and relative to be one and the same existence, or at all events looked upon the latter as bearing a direct and not an inverse ratio to the former. His habitual though no doubt inconsiderate identification of science whose testimony is wholly of the relative, with sense whose witness is wholly of the finite, warrants us perfectly to say that such practically at least was his error. And no error can be more disastrous to Philosophy, since it vacates the only basis to which Philosophy may lay claim, namely, the distinctively scientific evolution of the human mind. Existence or the finite is given in sense, and in sense alone. Life or the relative is given in consciousness, and consciousness alone. Existence is presupposed in life, the finite is presupposed in the relative, just as sense is presupposed in consciousness: and for that very reason there can be no direct but only an inverse accord between them, precisely like that which exists between a house and its foundation, or between substance and shadow. Science accordingly, as concerned only with the higher phenomenon of life or the relative, takes existence or the finite for granted; using the materials which sense supplies without the least distrust of their absoluteness. But let sense beware how she presumes upon this good-natured attitude of science! Let her take good heed lest she desert her own humble province, which is that of attesting the finite exclusively, and assume on that experience to attest the relative as well! For science in that case must instantly pronounce her a false witness. Sense is perfectly competent to attest facts of simple or disunited existence, facts of body in other words: and within all this range consequently her testimony is absolute over all but metaphysicians and madmen. But the moment she attempts to suggest a fact of life or soul, which is a composite fact, a fact of relation and therefore of order, she makes herself simply ridiculous. She reveals to us sun moon and stars existing each in visible contrast or oppugnancy to the others; but if she goes on to allege the scientific order which nevertheless binds these discordant bodies in the unity of a pervasive soul or life, she is sure to turn the truth literally and exactly upside down.

Now Kant was practically indifferent to this all-important mental hierarchy. He thought that the relative as well as the finite—facts of logical ratio or order as well as facts of palpable existence or body—were given in sense; thus that the analogy of one to the other was always direct never inversive: and he consequently plunged—drawing the unsuspecting and even jubilant Sir William after him—into a tipsy scientific imbroglio only to be rivalled by the folly of an architect, who, fancying a house to be a mere extension of its foundation, a direct and not an inverse projection of its base, should insist upon building it downwards instead of upwards; or by that of a pedant, who, looking upon his coat and trousers as a direct and not inverted form of his body, as a continuation and not a correspondence of his person, should insist upon wearing those astonished garments inside out. It was in fact the inveterate because unsuspected error of both of these distinguished men, as it is of all men whose attention has never been given to the subject, to confound the rational or composite in experience with the finite or simple, thus to dissolve life in mere existence, or swamp the spiritual and generative element in consciousness in its strictly material and passive constitutional conditions. They both of them saw very clearly that every fact of mere existence or physics as given in sense, involves a dual or divided parentage; that is to say, exhibits

its objective element falling apparently without never within its subjective element. But they neither of them ever saw—what however is of much nearer concern to Philosophy—that every fact of life or metaphysics as given in consciousness, presents an inextinguishable fusion or unity of these previously divided elements—how? simply by operating the thorough interioration of the objective one to the subjective. Let me explain.

I perceive the rose. Here is a verbal proposition reciting a strictly unitary fact of perception, i. e. of life, existing only in consciousness, in language borrowed from sense. It recites a pure fact of marriage, and therefore exclusively of relation, in terms belonging to simple unwedded existence; analyzing it back from the unity it presents in consciousness to the disjunction it exhibits in sense. Sense puts me here and the rose there: that is, it exteriorates object to subject or postpones substance to form. To my senses I exist in hopeless disunion with nature, the rose being invariably in one place and I in another; so that no possibility offers of any sensible coalition between us. And reason of course so long as it is in abeyance to the mere light of Nature, repeats the servile lesson and fills science with the echo of an eternal discord. But spiritually the truth is exactly opposite. To my living consciousness, (of course not to my memory or merely reflective one, with which Kant and Sir William Hamilton commonly confound it) I am indissolubly one with nature; the mental or metaphysical experience called sight or smell or hearing or taste or touch, being nothing but the literal consummation of a spiritual marriage between us so intimate and vital that only the absolute decease of the parties can dissolve it. Life annuls within its own limits the sensible distinction between me and nature, by bringing nature within my subjectivity or making it vivify my intelligence. I should be literally uninformed with mind or soul, which is life, unless the patent disunion enacted between me and nature by sense, gave way to the higher latent unity revealed in consciousness. Consciousness, the living consciousness, always posits me mentally or psychically, as made up and constituted of my natural sensibilities and susceptibilities, so that in dissolving the unity between me and nature, you literally discharge me of soul or life. Every fact of mental experience accordingly blends me and nature in indissoluble unity, whatever previous disunion mere sense ordains between us; and Kant only proves his own thorough misconception of the truth, when he interprets the experience into a fact of divorce instead of marriage. The truth is that Kant merely dissects the dead body of an experience after its living or unitary soul has fled; and finding naturally enough no evidence there of the marriage which life alone constitutes, he makes the tie between man and nature to have been one of dry and hopeless celibacy on both sides; or if he permits it to be spiritually prolific in any case it is only *par amours* [literally, "by illicit love"] and never by any inwardly authenticated nuptials. In this poor pedantic way, fumbling within the disorganized carcass of an experience to catch the perished odor of its life, Kant and Sir William Hamilton succeeded at last to their perfect satisfaction in reducing the man of science to a coroner, and the philosopher to an undertaker. The insufferable airs of all-sufficiency which Sir William especially puts on as he now flourishes the scalpel of the former, now wields the pickaxe and spade of the latter, while they dispel all doubt that his notions of Philosophy owed much less to his soft warm broad human heart, than to his hard cold narrow Scotch head, would be purely ludicrous if they had not the power which all false pretension has in proportion to its audacity, to impose upon the servile imagination of scholars.

What can be more clear than that the living perception in question (my perception of the rose) does not reproduce, but on the contrary completely annuls within its own precincts the duality or distance which sense alleges between me and nature, by converting it into an inextinguishable mental unity? Life to be sure does not war with existence, consciousness with sense. The former merely unites what the latter divides. Such is the perpetual miracle of life reflected in consciousness. Existence as given in sense makes nature fall without my subjectivity, so impoverishing me by all her wealth. Life on the other hand as given in consciousness reverses this ungenerous decree, or presents nature so intimately fused and blent with myself that it is no longer possible for me consciously to discriminate between us, both of us in fact becoming indissolubly married in what is called my mind or intelligence, i. e. my mental personality. Life and mind are convertible terms. Science brings all nature within the realm of mind, or stamps it with the unity of a man. What we call the laws of Nature are in truth projections of our own mind exclusively, claiming an objective validity to us individually only because the mental unity they express is that of the race and not of the individual. When the man of science attributes certain facts of nature to what he calls the influence of gravitation, he has or should have no intention to intimate that there is any such thing in nature, any such substance or entity, as gravitation. The word marks a mere mental generalization on our part of certain widely diffused and various facts of experience, the generalization itself being only an instinctive effort of the common or associate mind of the race to indue itself, by the instrumentality of the individual mind, with that perfect scientific form or order which shall constitute its own eventual and permanent self-consciousness. All these generalizations of our natural experience are only so many approximations, on the part of the common mind of the race, to the recognition of its own universality and unity. Nature is but the spiritual man turned inside out, or the contents of his otherwise unknown and unimaginable spiritual personality revealed to his senses. It is not a substance, but the shadow of a substance whose reality is altogether spiritual. Yet when you see the energy with which our so-called philosophers pursue cause to its last fastness, and seek to waylay heat and take light captive in the web of their cunning devices, or bleat forth idle prayers to know what after all is electricity and what magnetism, you must inevitably infer that the living and unitary substance they seek under all these shifting forms, the absolute personality they demand under all these Protean disguises, is altogether physical and not mental. Never was a grosser hallu-cination. The unity which underlies and animates all the so-called forces of nature, is exclusively human and not physical, belonging to the sphere of consciousness not of sense, being nothing more nor less than the unity of the universal human mind itself. These things are only so many flash-ings-forth through the chinks of sense and reason, of a great spiritual fact too subtle ever to be otherwise apprehended, namely, the unity or person-ality of the great race itself. They are none of them things which exist in nature: they are all of them only so many revelations or inverted images of itself which the human mind projects upon the mirror of natural fact, and by means of which it will ultimately come to a true self-consciousness; or what is the same thing, to the recognition of life as exclusively spiritual in substance, while material only in form or appearance out of deference to the needs of our nascent intelligence. Science is only a blind instinctive groping under the flickering guidance of reason after this most human unity which subtends all the disjointed facts of existence and gives them life.[5] From the lowest or most diffused and therefore most inhuman type of life exhibited in nature which is gravitation, up to its highest or most concentrated and therefore most human type, which is spontaneity, sci-ence sees not nature but man, and consequently demands of Philosophy a metaphysics which shall no longer exclude physics, but reverently accept its slightest admonition.

NOTES

1. Johann Gottlieb Fichte (1762–1814) came under the influence of Im-manuel Kant comparatively early in life but then moved considerably beyond him by turning the entire world of experience into no more than a construction of the self.—Editor's note.

2. Friedrich Wilhelm Joseph von Schelling (1775–1854) started from Fichte's later Idealist position and then tried to rescue it from the charge of subjectivism by giving it a new objective basis.—Editor's note.

3. Here James refers to a character in Richard Brinsley Sheridan's *The Rivals* who is a parody of self-righteous dogmatism.—Editor's note.

4. René Descartes (1596–1650) first advanced the ideas which James alludes to here in his epoch-making *Discourse on Method* (1637).—Editor's note.

5. The well-meant efforts of Mr. Grove, Mr. Faraday and a thousand similar conscientious men of science, to lay this ghost of a unitary or presiding natural force by which they are incessantly haunted, must prove simply abortive, so long as they look upon Nature as involving her own substance, or confessing any unity out of the human mind.

14

CHRISTIANITY
AND THE LOGIC OF
CREATION

In the minds of most conventional Christians of
James's day, the word *creation* typically referred to
some event which took place in the dim, inaccessible
recesses of the past, to an historical incident which,
however difficult to conceptualize, actually occurred in
time and space. With his more spiritual view of the
creative process, James was bent upon reversing this
idea by arguing that history, in fact, was a mere
incident in creation and that nature, as Jonathan
Edwards would have agreed, is no more than an image
or shadow of divine things. The logic of creation was
determined by God's gradual revelation of Himself to
His creatures, His communication of being to life,
in which history constituted "the evolution of that
distinctive human form which belongs to us as
veritable creatures of God" and nature demonstrated
how this process of evolution confirms the identity of
substance and form, of reality and appearance.
The following selection is chapter 19 of *Christianity
the Logic of Creation* (New York, 1857), 168–96.

———·•·———

Paris, Jan. 20th, 1857.

My dear W.,[1]
You complain of my last Letter as insufficient. It could not very well be
otherwise, seeing that I had not bargained to send you a volume of well-
digested metaphysics, but only a friendly and suggestive Letter. Let me
endeavour now to resume the same theme in a form somewhat more
expansive.

You know that ninety-nine persons out of a hundred (and this is speaking with exemplary moderation) envisage creation as a question of time
and space—as, at most, a series of sensible facts or incidents, like the
American Revolution—and as essentially involving therefore no considera-

tions beyond the ordinary collation and discrimination of evidence. The mass of people believe that creation took place "once upon a time," somewhere in Asia probably, and was complete on the instant by an exertion of physical energy on the part of the Creator. They suppose that some six thousand years ago, more or less, man was effectively created, and that his entire subsequent history consequently has been little better than a vigorous and unaccountable kicking up of his heels in his Creator's face. The abject childishness of this conception fails to strike them, only because the application of reason to sacred subjects has been so effectually discouraged by the clergy, that our popular intellectual stomach has grown indurated and ostrich-like,—stowing away all manner of innutritious corkscrews, jack-knives, and rusty nails, which may be presented to it by its lawful purveyors, as if they were so much reasonable and delectable Christian diet. Indeed, if you commit yourself to the orthodox conception of the Divine name, you have no right to denounce such a diet as unreasonable. A faith full of revolting difficulties is a logical necessity of the orthodox conscience. It prefers such a faith to one from which all rational contradiction has been studiously eliminated. For, having no strictly *human* conception of God, having only the *personal* conception which allows Him to be (at least in all *practical* regards) a supremely wilful arbitrary and disorderly being, intent upon forcing all things into his allegiance and crushing what cannot be so forced, the orthodox worshipper can of course conceive no homage half so propitiatory toward this terrible power, can contrive no flattery half so subtle, as that which lies in pain and anguish of body and mind voluntarily incurred for its sake.

Regarded from any such point of view, creation incontinently tumbles into a rational absurdity or contradiction, driving us to infidelity and atheism as to a plain intellectual obligation, as to the only bed capable of refreshing the weary harassed soul. For, as Swedenborg declares, so long as we regard creation as a mere physical event, or as a phenomenon of space and time, we fail to discern it altogether: and what we altogether fail to discern by the understanding, we certainly cannot admit to be true. The truth is indeed exactly opposite. Creation is never a mere physical performance on the part of God, or an event in time and space, else hounds and hares, cats and rats, spiders and flies were as authentic creatures of God as man himself. On the contrary, it is a purely spiritual process, falling wholly within the sphere of consciousness, that is within the realm of affection and thought; or what is the same thing, depending for its truth upon the evolution of the human form, which is the sole spiritual form known to the universe. It is not possible for God to create, or give being to, hounds and hares, cats and rats, spiders and flies, because these things are utterly devoid of spiritual consciousness. They are strictly animal forms, in which the feminine or individual element is completely controlled by the masculine or universal one; and God cannot possibly dwell in, or give being to, forms so remote from His own image, so incapable of free or spontaneous action. To suppose Him inhabiting such forms would be, analogically, to deny His strict objectivity to the universal consciousness, and affirm in lieu thereof His strict subjectivity: would be, in plain English, equivalent to denying that all things were subject to God, by making God subject to all things. He creates only man, who is above all things a spiritual form, a form of spontaneity or freedom exactly proportionate as we have seen to the Divine form, because in him the individual or feminine element is internal and superior, while the universal or masculine one is external and inferior. Only in such a form may God "dwell," to use Swedenborg's phrase, "as in Himself." He truly vivifies only the virgin selfhood, the selfhood which has been released from the bondage of the finite, or from all physical and social compression, and obeys the sole voice of attraction, the inspiration of what we call ideas, meaning thereby infinite or supersensuous good. When my individuality transcends its wonted physical and moral anchorage, when it soars away from the servile earth of necessity and duty into the clear majestic heavens of spontaneity or freedom, it then obeys its essential spirituality, it then becomes feelingly immortal, I then feel the interior and inseparable Divinity of my source, and for the first time taste the rapture of deathless conjunction with infinite goodness, truth and power. What does the hare know of this experience? or the cat, or the spider? Simply nothing: because they are all alike spiritually incompetent, being all alike void of spiritual consciousness, all alike incapable of transcending the natural plane, and allying themselves with infinitude. I am capable as man of postponing appearances to realities, or of preferring an infinite good to a finite one. I am capable of hating father and mother, brother and sister, wife and child, lover and friend, home and country, in pursuit of an interior ideal object, or whenever these base actualities claim to separate me from that infinite Divine reality which is the inmost life of my life, the inextinguishable bliss of all my being. But the hound will never know a superior inspiration to that which his nature devolves upon him, as it devolved equally upon all his forefathers; nor the spider ever conceive any bliss comparable with that of fly-catching, which has descended to it from a lineage so bloodstained and immemorial, as to make your ruddiest English pedigrees look pale and cheap and modern in the comparison.[2]

So far then from looking at creation as a Divine improvisation, as at best a mere initiatory incident of history, we are bound to turn the tables and look upon history itself as a mere initiatory incident of creation. If you posit creation as a physical event, as an event of time and space; if you reduce it in short to the dimensions of nature; it is still most incomplete, and all our past history with its lively disputes of Atheist and Deist, of believer and sceptic, is but the flagrant witness of this incompleteness. Who can imagine scepticism existing in the presence of a really Divine creation? In view of a creature visibly vivified by infinite Love, who can conceive of belief as driven to suspend itself upon a laborious balance of probabilities? Our historic experience in fact is nothing but our gradual approximation to human consciousness, and to the consequent consciousness of ourselves as Divinely created. It marks nothing but the endless interval which separates the highest animal form from the lowest human one. We have indeed no business to look upon human history as an accident, as a something *supervening* upon our creation, as a direction impressed upon us by some power extraneous to our nature. On the contrary it is a most strict incident of our creation, being nothing more nor less than the ceaseless effort of our essential Divinity to give itself adequate formal utterance or embodiment. God is essential man, and human history is but the gradual adaptation of this superb spiritual truth to the natural imagination of the race. All its sacredest incidents accordingly, far from denoting any outside interference with our nature, are the strict outgrowth and efflorescence of august interior powers. Thus what we call a Divine revelation, what we call religion, or the Church, is never an arbitrary external imposition upon the human mind, but on the contrary is always a normal though fruitless effort of our interior Divinity worthily to assert itself in the plane of the senses, or to attain to scientific recognition. It is in every case the Divine or spontaneous life of man seeking to secure itself a representative or figurative projection, so long as it is denied a living or conscious one. In short, history, strictly speaking, is our process of FORMATION. It is the untiring effort which the creative Love makes to bring us up to the human form, to develop in us spontaneous life, to endow us with a selfhood adequate to image its own perfection, and therefore adequate to its own indwelling: and all its successive stages mark only so many successful crises of that effort.

Let us then boldly reverse our point of view. Let us cease to regard creation as an historical incident, as an event in time and space, by learning to regard history itself, or all the events of time and space, as mere incidents of creation. History, I repeat, means nothing else than the evolution of that distinctive human form which belongs to us as veritable creatures of God, as beings vivified by a really infinite breath, by a really perfect power. It is the gradual vindication of a Divine NATURAL humanity. It is in a word our needful natural formation in the Divine image. The fundamental import of Christianity, the fundamental import of all authentic Divine revelation, is, that we need to undergo a natural formation in the Divine image in order to our spiritual creation; that our spiritual or individual creation by God really exacts for its own permanent basis our natural regeneration. The religious idea, separated from the caricatures of superstition, implies, that it is incumbent upon the Divine bounty to give us natural selfhood quite as much as spiritual selfhood; that unless we first bear a common or associated likeness to the Divine, we shall be destitute of a private or individual likeness. The ground of this exaction lies no doubt in the great law so often cited already, that God creates only subjective or spiritual existence: but you will not be prepared to do justice to this law, or accurately to comprehend its bearings, so long as you cherish vague and obscure conceptions of what is meant by creating. Let us manfully free ourselves of the stifling traditional nonsense on this subject, and then we shall perfectly understand why we require to be naturally as well as spiritually fashioned in the Divine image, or what is the same thing, why a Divinely-given natural form is an indispensable preliminary basis to our Divinely-given spiritual being. And, understanding this, we shall have an infallible clue to the religious history of the race, which is the veritable history of the human mind, and be able clearly to conceive why that history intimately involves the doctrine of a Divine revelation or incarnation.

Let me beg of you then distinctly to remember that I use the word *create* with strict scientific accuracy, as always meaning *giving being*. To create a thing means to give it inward or substantial being; he who creates a thing *himself constitutes the substance* of that thing: so that the relation between Creator and creature is invariably the relation of object and subject, of internal and external. Creating or giving being is an exactly inverse process to that of making or giving form. When I say that God creates me, I suppose myself already formed or existing; I take my existence for granted, or as inseparably implied in my proposition. Existence is an absolute and indisputable fact, and unless we had this preliminary basis of sensible experience, we should be utterly void of supersensuous experience of every sort, whether belief, or hope, or aspiration. Accordingly in alleging my creation by God I do not refer to any mere fact of existence, to any sensible operation of God, but wholly to a spiritual and invisible operation; one which utterly transcends the realm of time and space, because it falls altogether within that of affection and thought. In other words, in alleging my creation, I do not project myself back in imagination to some period more or less remote, when an exertion of voluntary energy on God's part resulted in my physical genesis or formation—resulted in giving me existence. Far from it. I take my physical formation or existence *pro confesso*, as an indispensable platform of the creation which I allege. For I say that God creates *me*, and obviously by *me* I mean my human form, my phenomenal existence, my conscious personality. It would be absurd of course to allege any abstract creative energy on God's part, to say for example that He creates what has no existence, or what is unconscious and invisible: because, as we have already seen, that would be only saying in a round about way that He creates nothing, or that He is no creator. We can never conceive of creation except as proceeding on the basis of some existing selfhood, as involving some subsidiary sphere of formation, as predictable in short of certain conscious or visible existences. By saying that they are created existences, we do not mean to allege any physical fact whatever concerning them, but on the contrary a purely metaphysical fact, which is, that their being is not identical with their visible form or existence, or, what is the same thing, that they as subjects involve a far profounder objectivity than that of nature. And by saying that God creates them, we mean that He who is infinite Love and wisdom constitutes their spiritual and invisible being: that He stands to them in the eternal relation of inward genetic source or object, and they to Him in the eternal relation of outward derivative stream or subject.

You may doubtless ejaculate a ready *Amen* to all this, by way of inducing me to resume my initial proposition, which is: that God creates only spiritual forms, gives being only to subjective existence: but I feel so cordially disposed to disabuse your excellent understanding of certain sensuous fallacies and prejudices engendered by the Old Theology, that I cannot forbear to solicit your indulgent attention a few moments longer. I want you perfectly to comprehend both what is included in, and what is excluded from, the rational or scientific conception of creation.

Let me distinctly say then, that the technical infidel is completely justified in denying creation, so long as you represent it as implying an outward exertion of the Divine power, as meaning a physical operation of God. The letter of revelation no doubt represents creation in this guise, that is, as a simple projection in time and space, as a strictly *impromptu* proceeding on God's part, involving nothing more than a new determination of His will, and the consequent utterance of an authoritative *fiat*. But all this is a purely symbolic or pictorial statement of the truth, without the slightest value as history. If indeed you view it as literal history, it becomes at once downright puerility and nonsense, since it represents God as creating mere natural existence, or as being simply what is termed "the author of nature," which is totally to degrade His name, and render it the inevitable butt of the flimsiest sentimental devotion, the tattered target of the mildest Unitarian archery. Natural existence is absolute existence, being that in which substance and form are identical. Nature means the identity of substance and form, of being and seeming. The stone for example, the tree, the horse, *is* exactly what it *seems* to your eye. Its being is a pure seeming, is wholly phenomenal, as the philosophers say. There is no spiritual stone, nor horse, nor tree, lying back of and animating the apparent one. The sensible form before you perfectly embodies its own being or substance, so that every stone, tree, and horse of the specific family in question will repeat the same monotonous story over again till time and space shall be no more. You can't imagine a stone or tree, or horse, out of relation to time and space, that is as having any purely subjective or spiritual existence by virtue of its inward commerce with infinite goodness and truth. You can only conceive of them as natural existences, thus as essentially finite and perishable. Observe then that natural existence is purely phenomenal existence, being destitute of internal or individual being and hence out of all immediate relation to God. Yet this is the prevalent conception of creation, the only conception tolerated by the carnal or superstitious mind. And what is very melancholy, the clergy as a body do their best to confirm and aggravate our natural hallucinations on this and every subject. They are wont, as a general thing, to attribute to God the dreariest and most tedious existence imaginable, by diffusing His infinitude over the wilderness of space, and trickling His eternity through the endless succession of minutes which make up time; and then they represent Him as suddenly resolving to variegate this barren infinitude—to diversify this monotonous eternity—by summoning into life certain absolute or physical forms, which shall henceforth be and exist by virtue of that momentary *fiat*. In short the ecclesiastical intellect all the world over has the inveterate habit of confounding being with form, creating with making, reality with semblance. It supposes that every thing really *is* which *appears* to be: or that things have *being* by virtue of their *form*. If for instance you should consult the Pope of Rome or the Archbishop of Canterbury, they would never betray the slightest distrust of their official existence being a Divine reality. They have not the least suspicion that the higher powers are blessedly ignorant of all the conventional dignities of the earth; they have never imagined that all those distinctions, official and personal, which make up so often our best knowledge, and give many an empty head among us the reputation of wisdom, are sheer vacancy to the celestial mind, raying out darkness, not light; and if you should hint your own suspicion of the truth, they would cordially unite in proclaiming you an infidel, and bid you begone as a tiresome revolutionary bore.[3]

But there is no need of troubling Pope or Archbishop with these inquiries, especially as they have already trouble enough on their hands, I dare say. Suppose the question put to you, John Doe, and to me, Richard Roe: "if the visible selfhood we are each of us born to, be indeed the vital reality which it seems to us to be:" we should unhesitatingly answer, Yes. You have an undisturbed conviction that you are *personally* known to God, that your luxuriant locks, your dark eyes, your tint embrowned by sun and air, are perfectly familiar to the Divine eye. And I for my part have never questioned that the Divine mind was as cognizant of my visible limitations (short stature, obese figure, fair complexion, flaxen wig, and so forth) as I myself am. Yet this is a sheer mistake. Swendenborg, who had a great eye for realities as discriminated from mere appearances, could never find a vestige "of the old familiar faces" beyond the grave. The phenomenal selfhood was fatally transfixed and dissipated by the first contact of trans-sepulchral light. He knew many persons of a very conspicuous conventional make, heroes and saints, statesmen and clergymen, abounding in learning and piety; but when he saw them illumined by celestial light, he frequently found them full of rapacity cruelty and excess of all sorts, and degraded to the most menial positions. And so, on the other hand, he not unfrequently found persons, who on earth and to their own consciousness were destitute of every claim to sanctity, who lived in affluence and luxury, who frequented theatres, who loved jocose conversation, who had in short no properly *ascetic* fibre in their composition—mere unbaptized Turks and Pagans very often in fact—enjoying an intimate commerce with the angels, and heartily allied with all Divine perfection.

All this (and very much more) is true, I say, simply because the phenomenal is never the real, because what *appears* never *is*. The sensible world is purely formal, not essential: it is, and ever will be, the realm of shadow, not of substance; of seeming, not of being. It is not the theatre of the Divine creation, but of the Divine formation exclusively, being, to use Swedenborg's phrase, a sphere of effects not of ends. In short, Nature is a purely *experimental* world, and experience is a first-rate mother, but a most incompetent father. Experience incarnates our wisdom, or gives it outward body: it does not vitalize it or give it inward and rational soul as well. In all procreative action the father is generative, the mother simply prolific or productive: the former gives life or soul, the latter existence or body: the one is creative, the other formative. And this diversity of function is but an image of the universal spiritual truth, that experience (or our natural memory) serves only as a ground or matrix, only as a warm mother-earth, in which to inseminate certain formal traditions, which are the mere husks of truth, inherited from the past, while God alone (or Infinite Love *within* the soul) constitutes the stainless overarching heavens by whose genial beams these rude and lifeless husks become quickened into every form of living wisdom. We know that every seed must die in order to bring forth fruit. All food must be dissolved before it can be assimilated, before it can make flesh. Now these natural facts are but the shadows of spiritual things. All the literal dogmas we receive into the memory, which is the mental stomach, are of no more promise in a spiritual point of view, than so many stones taken into the natural stomach would be in a hygienic point of view. They give us hope of spiritual increase only in so far as they undergo intellectual levigation or maceration, only in so far as they become converted into that rich rational chyme and chyle whose white depths nourish and embosom the immortal pillars of the soul.[4] Understand then that Nature is the realm, not of wisdom, but of that experience which is the indispensable soil of wisdom. It is the sphere not of soul, but of that needful preliminary bodily organization without which the soul itself would never come to consciousness. God cannot directly create natural things therefore, because these things, being fixed or absolute, forbid that interior expansion, that perfect individual freedom, which is the inseparable heritage of His creatures, and which alone conjoins them with Him. The horse, the lily, and the diamond, are beautiful natural existences, but how impossible to fancy them in any relation to God, simply because though they have each a marked natural individuality, they are yet all alike destitute of spiritual or real individuality: in other words, because, though they are all subjects of a beautiful existence, they are none of them subjects of life.

This explanation ended, I am now ready to resume my initial proposition, which was, that God creates only subjective or spiritual forms. This follows, almost obviously, from the definition of creating; for as creating always means, when properly used, the *giving being* to things, so consequently God can only create or give being to things which are in themselves destitute of being, having at best but a subjective semblance or appearance thereof. He cannot possibly give being to what already has being, since this would be contradictory, but only to what appears, only to what seems to be, that is, to subjective or spiritual existences. I repeat, then, that by the strict necessity of the case, God creates only subjective spiritual forms, in which He resides as in Himself, so and not otherwise communicating life.

Now the condition of subjective or spiritual existence is, that it be vitalized from *within,* or what is the same thing, that the object it obeys, the ideal it serves, reside strictly within the limits of its own nature. Natural existence is the opposite of this. What the philosophers term "objective" existence, meaning by that word whatsoever sensibly exists, as mineral, vegetable, and animal, is always vitalized from without, that is to say, its objective element is strictly exterior to its subjective one. The mineral exists for the vegetable, the vegetable for the animal, and the animal for man. In short, natural existence is servile existence, finding its proper object or ideal out of the bounds of its own nature. Of course this peculiarity puts the merely natural form of life out of all immediate contiguity to the Divine, by leaving it destitute of internality, of private or spiritual individuality. The horse, for example, who obeys an ideal essentially aloof from his own nature, whose deity in a word is man, is by that fact denuded of spiritual consciousness, of what we call selfhood or character, and hence remains essentially unprogressive or incommensurate with God. He has abundance of physical life, of selfhood or character derived from his natural progenitors, but he has no Divinely-vivified individuality athirst for the fountains of a better life. No sweet radiant Eve grows up in the unconscious depths of *his* bosom, becoming evermore bone of his bone and flesh of his flesh, and leading him to eat of the tree of knowledge of good and evil, that through the disease and death thus revealed he may rise to the experience of immortal peace and joy. He knows, no doubt, the natural love of the sex, or recognizes the partner his nature provides him : but he has no glimpse of the ravishing amplitude of bliss which is spiritually locked up in the conjugal symbol, and which makes the *wife* as contradistinguished from the woman, an exquisite shadow of all that is most intimate, ennobling, and enduring in the ineffable commerce of the Divine and human natures. This experience, I repeat, is denied the animal, because the animal form is vitalized from without, because its objective element is strictly exterior to its subjective element, or in other words, because the ideal it promotes, the object it serves, the deity it obeys, is human and not animal, that is to say, does not fall within the grasp of its own nature.

But the exact reverse obtains with regard to man. The human form is vitalized from within exclusively. The objective element in all human activity will be seen on a fair analysis to lie strictly *within* the subjective one. The ideal which I propose to myself as man, the object I seek to promote in every form of action, in short, the Deity I worship, is always of an intensely human quality, invariably puts on the lineaments of my own nature, and hence my life of necessity becomes evermore beautiful and free, abhorring nothing so much as servility. In a word, man's existence is purely subjective or spiritual, compelling even the infinite Divine perfection into his own natural dimensions before it can win his honest and hearty acknowledgment. What is the inmost meaning and confession of all evil but this? To the inner or instructed sense evil is only the running away of the fish with the line which binds him to his captor, and is but a surer argument of the skill which is bound eventually to bring him to land. Lying, fraud, adultery, murder, covetousness, are only so many temporary diffractions of the pure and stedfast Divine ray operated by our intellectual opacity and indocility; are only so many incessant and stupid crucifixions, wrought by our infatuated carnality and self-conceit upon that Divine and long-suffering Love which underlies and animates our nature. The horse is destitute of morality because, being a purely outward or natural existence, he must for ever remain incapacitated for that spiritual or subjective freedom of which morality is but the shadow. Morality implies a relation of independence, in so far forth as it is predictable, on the part of the subject towards his nature. But the horse is the abject slave of his nature. Every existence indeed below the human exhibits the complete identity of being and seeming, of substance and form, of soul and body. You, on the contrary, as man heartily repugn such identity. You feel so sure of nothing as that your being will always transcend your richest experience of it, or what is the same thing, that your amplest actual must ever fall hopelessly short of your feeblest possible. The real horse is always the visible horse, and no lily has being but that which actually blows in the garden, and fills the worshipping air with its dazzling sheen. But the opulence of man is such, the opulence of God's true creature, that what is visible of him always confesses itself nothing, however glorious, while what is relatively invisible claims to be the only reality. Thus the visible man is never the real one. The man that veritably *is* never shews himself except by proxy. The true friend must ever despair of disclosing the passionate depths of his friendship, and the genuine lover strives always in vain to interpret himself worthily to his mistress' sense. Though he heap Pelion upon Ossa[5] in the fond effort to storm the flaming heavens of his love, and compress them into appreciable measures, they for ever mock his aching embrace, for ever falling back into the impalpable abysses of the infinite. Such, I say, is the normal state of man. This is his state, when, being emancipated from physical and social thraldom, he stands erect in true human proportions. He is then a purely spiritual or subjective form, made conscious of himself no doubt by the background or basis of his physical and social organization, but utterly incapable of identifying himself with that organization. He instinctively feels himself to be superior to his circumstances, to be dearer to the heart of God than all that calls itself nature and society put together, and in the robust confidence of that intimacy seeks evermore to bring both nature and society into his own unlimited subjection. And manifestly all this is true of our human instinct and experience, only because the human form alone is divinely vivified, only because God does literally create us or give us inward being, while He does not do so to cabbages and horses. He gives them *outward* being, which is natural existence, and which leaves them destitute of all private individuality, of all spiritual lift above the dead level of sense. But He gives us *inward* being, which is spiritual existence, and which fills us with a private individuality so pronounced and expansive as eventually to precipitate Nature, much as we drop our garments from about us at night, or rather to transmute her from an all-enveloping and absorbing egg into the very texture and substance of the new consciousness, into the very pith and marrow of the new and diviner manhood.

Of course then the Divine creation rightly viewed, stamps Nature with a deeper significance than she herself is at all aware of. While to her own consciousness she seems absolute and final, she is nevertheless but the seminary or seed-place of the soul, the mere husk and tally, so to speak, of those august interior forces which are for ever shaping the spiritual universe (or the mind of man) into harmony with all Divine perfection. Nature is in short but the perishable body of the imperishable mind of the race, and we fail to see her in this intrinsically subordinate plight, only because we habitually estimate her by the light which she herself supplies, or what is the same thing, because our reason, in place of being *served* by sense, is actually *controlled* by it. Revelation itself is bound of course to conform its utterances to this natural necessity; is bound to respect the limits of the sensuous understanding in man, under penalty of forfeiting its true character and becoming degraded into mere information. That is to say, the Divine and eternal truth can never reveal itself to sense except in a *symbolic* manner, because if it should attempt to assert itself as a fixed or absolute quantity, the human mind would have no chance to grow, being thus authoritatively robbed of its freedom. In other words, the letter of a Divine revelation avouches its authenticity only in so far as it embodies spiritual or universal truth. The general vague impression on this subject no doubt is very different. It is popularly conceived that revelation is not a symbolic unveiling of truth, addressed only to the spiritual understanding of man, but a literal unveiling of it, addressed to his senses. It is sensuously supposed to be a direct and unaccommodated communication on the part of the creator to the creature, leaving the latter no option but to obey. Thus all the gospel facts, so far from being viewed as the normal natural outgrowth and expression of certain Divine operations within the universal soul of man, are supposed to have a purely absolute genesis which discharges them of all strictly human or scientific validity. But this is the mere dotage and delirium of sense. The eternal splendour of the Christian facts lies on the contrary just here, that what seems personal and limitary about them is precisely what adapts them to mask universal truth, or to symbolize the relations of all mankind to God. They have in truth nothing arbitrary about them, but are one with the highest reason, being the outgrowth not of private causes but of universal ones, of causes which are as wide as the universe of being. I hold (perhaps more strenuously than you can at present imagine) that Christ was conceived of the holy Ghost, that he was born of a virgin, that he lived a life of helpless humiliation and infamy in the eyes of the most reputable persons of his age and nation, while at the same time he became inwardly united with the Divine spirit to such a degree as at length to grow exanimate on his finite or maternal side, and find his literal flesh and blood becoming vivified by the infinite Love. But then I cannot conceive of these things being literally true save on one condition, which is, that nature be not the absolute and independent existence she seems; that she be in fact *the mere shadow or image of profounder realities*, projected upon the field of the sensuous understanding. For if nature be a direct creation of God, if she be an existence fixed by the actual creative *fiat*, then the pretensions of the Christian revelation are to the last degree absurd: because the Divine creation once actually posited, must ever after prove incapable of amendment, or find itself beyond the need of any officious tinkering. This needs no argument. But if nature be nothing more than the common or ultimate bond and covering of the spiritual world, which is the universal mind of man, just as the skin is the common or ultimate bond and covering of all the diversified kingdoms of the body: why then of course we may regard all natural phenomena only as so many graduated effects from interior spiritual causes, precisely as we regard a blush upon the skin, or a sudden pallor, as an evidence of heightened or depressed vital action. And so doubtless day and night, the succession of the seasons, birth and death, growth and decay, the subordination of mineral to vegetable, of vegetable to animal, and of all to man, *are* so many natural types, are so many ultimate symbols, of a vast and beneficent spiritual order which is inwardly shaping the universal soul of man, and which will eventually bring about the perfect reciprocal fusion or unity of each with all and all with each. But how to divine this recondite knowledge! Nature has as little consciousness of man, as the waters have of the sun and stars which irradiate their darkened and tumultuous bosom. Nature herself therefore is incapable of blabbing the secret with which she is fraught, or of proving a revelation of Divine mysteries to the soul, because she is utterly unconscious and incredulous of Divinity. She has no more comprehension of the being she images, than the looking glass has of the human substance whose various phenomenality it reflects. She is a pure surface whose depth or soul is man. No doubt she will faithfully lend herself to the reflection and illustration of his intimate worth, in so far as his own intelligence learns to demand that service of her. But she has no independent power of origination or suggestion. She feels no forewarning of the lustrous use she fulfils, until his advancing self-knowledge imposes it on her. She has no clearly articulate speech which she does not catch up from his commanding accents. In short she knows herself truly only as the echo of his majestic personality, and shrinks from nothing so much as the pretension to lisp even a syllable of original Divine revelation. Revelation descends exclusively from the human consciousness, or from the soul of man to his senses, because man alone being the true creature of God is alone competent to reveal Him. In short the true theatre of revelation is not our mere natural or animal consciousness, but our historic or veritably human consciousness. It demands for its proper platform not merely that humble field of relations which man is under to his own body, and which constitutes what we call his *existence*, being all comprehended in the fixed quantity denominated Nature: but also and above all that superb field of relations which he is under to his own soul, or to God, and which constitutes what we properly term his *life*, being all comprehended in that great unfixed quantity which we denominate History. . . .

NOTES

1. This letter, like all the others which make up *Christianity the Logic of Creation*, was most probably addressed to J. J. Garth Wilkinson with whom James carried on a lifelong correspondence.—Editor's note.

2. No English nobleman can possibly be as thoroughbred as the rat which burrows in his own ancestral walls; because, let him do what he will traditionally to paralyze the human or spiritual force in him, his bare natural form perpetually prevents his lapsing into animality, by itself allying him with God, so forbidding him to remain the mere child of his father. The nobleman of to-day, whatever be his private vices, is vastly nearer the human type than the nobleman of five centuries ago, simply because his very nature itself is progressive, while the animal nature is not. For man's natural form being itself spiritual, is incessantly created, vivified, quickened, inhabited by the Divine, and hence is essentially progressive. On the other hand the rat of to-day exhibits not a whit of natural advance upon his antediluvian progenitor, nor ever will, simply because he *is* a rat, and therefore divinely uninhabited or uncreated and consequently unprogressive. Spiritually or interiorly viewed, the whole pretension of an hereditary aristocracy is to animalize the human soul, or dissociate man from his divine original, by making him a creature of *bloods:* than which there can be no profounder blasphemy. This is the secret of those apparently dying throes with which all Christendom is now politically agape and aghast. We are at a crisis in the life of humanity, one of those periods in which man is providentially summoned to shed his old skin, and put on a new one, more pliant to the behests of his inward and essential freedom.

3. I feel no *positive* admiration for the revolutionary forces which are now enthroned in France, and only waiting to be effectually enthroned over the rest of the European continent; because I see that they are mere Providential tools employed to work out far diviner ends than they themselves dream of. But when one reflects upon the crowned imbecilities which actually rule over men, sacerdotally and secularly: when one considers the fearful distance which separates the conventionally upper classes from the lower; their utter aloofness from the common loves, the common wants, the common hopes of man; their luxurious self-indulgence; their unrighteous social privileges, and the inevitable pride and arrogance engendered by such privileges; their stolid opposition to popular elevation; their hardened indifference to the voice of God's great minister, science; their flippant contempt of every force but brute force, and their inveterate estimate of humanity as an essentially brute existence, never to be regulated from within, or Divinely, but only from without, or diabolically: then Louis Napoleon, Mazzini, and all the rest, become irresistibly precious and sweet to my heart, even as terriers and weasels are precious to the agriculturist long vexed by predatory and fugacious vermin, even as the advent of death's angel is sweet to the soul long imprisoned in a diseased and suffering body. In fact one respects the Revolution very much as one respects Death. It is not in itself

a Divine presence any more than the rotten and odious régime which it has displaced; but it constitutes the only door which our double-dyed stupidity and unbelief will ever leave open to the entrance of the Divine kingdom on earth.

4. This is what makes mere *professional* religionists so tiresome. For having not merely the ordinary human but also a distinctly private or personal end in the maintenance of our traditional creeds, they sedulously guard them from all intellectual fecundation, from all rational trituration and fermentation, and hence perpetually suggest to the imagination the painful similitude of people in a colic. They present the same contrast to our ordinary unconscious and placid acquaintance, that the shop of a seedsman and florist presents to a blooming and beautiful garden. In the professional religionist, the memory is sure to grow plethoric at the expense of the reason, just as we often see a man cultivating a portentous abdomen to the serious neglect and discredit of his brain: and intercourse is never at its just human pitch, until it is above all things rational. When our intercourse is one of cant, being vitalized only by the memory; when, in other words, my friend and I meet only to parade and compare our mutual wealth in current orthodox coin, the image we project upon the spiritual sense is that of two foolish persons diligently rubbing their stomachs together, or belching in each other's face, in order to inflame a reciprocal good understanding.

5. In Greek mythology the giants were supposed to have piled Mt. Pelion on top of Mt. Ossa in order to scale Olympus, the abode of the gods.—Editor's note.

15

WHY CREATION
INVOLVES A DIVINE
INCARNATION

It is no accident that James appended the above phrase to the top of more than a third of the pages in his *Christianity the Logic of Creation.* The issue it raises was absolutely central to his whole system. Interestingly enough, James refused to give the anticipated answer to his own question. Creation involved a Divine Incarnation not because men would recognize the truth in no other way, clothed in the incarnate form of their own humanity, but rather because, in taking upon Himself in the person of Jesus Christ the abject human form that He did, God reversed all of man's expectations about the incarnate form in which the Divine Life would make Itself fully manifest.

The following selection is taken from chapter 20 of *Christianity the Logic of Creation* (New York, 1857), 197–98, 199–200, 200–218.

———•••———

Paris, Feb. 1st, 1857.
My dear W.,

I do not know how it strikes your intelligence, but it appears to me that I have to some extent indicated in my last Letter the true ground of the difficulty men have in rationally conceiving of the Divine Incarnation. Let us recall for a few moments what has gone before, in order that we may the more clearly take the final step.

We have seen that Christianity abolishes the Pagan conception of Deity, which represents God as an essentially arbitrary, insane, or inhuman, force,—capable at will of any amount of deviltry and destruction,—by revealing Him henceforth as a glorified natural man, as a rightful and permanent denizen of human nature. In other words, the service which Christ rendered humanity—a service to which there has been, and, in the nature of things, can be, nothing similar or second—consists in this: that

He furnished by His life of unparalleled self-denial a perfect natural embodiment to the Divine Love: that He shut up the infinite and hitherto
inconceivable Divine within the dimensions of the humblest of human
bosoms; constraining it thenceforth to know no other activity but that
which is supplied by the intelligible forms of human nature, that is to say,
compelling it to run henceforth eternally in the familiar mould of our
natural passions and appetites. Let there be no obscurity upon any meaning. I say that what Jesus Christ did to entitle Him to our eternal and
spontaneous homage, was that He, by His unflinching denial, even unto
death, of the popular religion of His nation (a religion which, as to its
fond, was fed by every infernal influence, and as to its form, by every
celestial one), He, for the first time brought the infinite creative love into
perfect harmony with the individual bosom of man—into complete and
unobstructed *rapport* with the finite human form—so that Deity might once
for all experimentally know how it felt to be husband and father, lover
and friend, ruler and teacher, patriot and citizen, under that base natural
inspiration merely; and so knowing, for ever vivify and redeem those
finite ties, by the communication of His own infinite substance. . . .

The whole problem of creation may be summarily formulated thus: the
natural man (or man in a state of nature simply, without historic experience) is a form of supreme self-love, and thus presents an exactly opposite
aspect to the Divine Love which is incapable of selfish regards: of course
then creation must remain an eternal impossibility unless some middle
term can be projected capable of reconciling or fusing these inveterate
opposites. . . . But in the bosom of Jesus, exposed through the letter of His
national hope to the boundless influx of every selfish lust, and yet persistently subjugating such lust to the inspirations of universal love, the
requisite basis of union was at last found, and infinite Wisdom compassed
at length a direct and adequate access to the most finite of intelligences. In
Christ unfalteringly renouncing His own sacred writings, in so far as they
were literal, personal, and Jewish, and accepting them only in their spiritual, universal, or humanitary scope: in His cheerfully submitting to
life-long obloquy for this unprecedented manliness; to the scorn envenomed by disappointment of all that was most decent, devout, and respectable in His nation; to the daily derision of that large class in every community, who, not being devout themselves, yet hope to commend their
sneaking souls to heaven's favour by blindly doing the dirty work of the
devout, and hastening brutally to finish what these are sometimes fearful
even to begin; to the contempt of His own brethren and neighbours; to the
constant misconception and unbelief of His own avowed, and forward, and
foolish disciples; finally, to death itself—a death from which no element
of ferocious cruelty was absent, which, on the contrary, all hell found a
truly religious joy in promoting: in this sublime and steadfast soul, I say,
the marriage of the Divine and Human was at last perfectly consummated,
so that thenceforth the infinite and eternal expansion of our nature became, not merely possible, but most strictly inevitable. Accordingly, ever
since that period, husband and father, lover and friend, patriot and citizen,

priest and king, have been gradually assuming more human dimensions, have been gradually putting on glorified lineaments; or what is the same thing, the universal heart of man has been learning to despise and disown all *absolute* sanctities: not merely our threadbare human sanctities, sacerdotal and regal, conjugal and paternal, but also every the most renowned Divine sanctity itself, whose bosom is not the abode of the widest, tenderest, most patient and unswerving human love.

Now what I shewed in my last Letter was, that we deny, or misapprehend this Christian revelation, only because we have the folly to regard space and time as substantial things, as veritably Divine ideas, and to look upon nature consequently rather as the primary than as the intensely ultimate and subordinate field of the Divine operation. Nature is in truth but the basement or culinary story of the Divine edifice; and when we make her primary, or allow her to dominate the house, we of course degrade the drawing and bed-room floors, filling them with sounds and odours fatal to every cultivated sense. Theology and philosophy have done little hitherto but fill the world with this odious din and stench of cookery. Obstinately regarding nature as the final rather than the mediate sphere of the Divine operation, as the real or substantial world instead of the purely formal and phenomenal one, they incessantly drown our rational intelligence in the mire of sense, whence we have now actually no more lively theologic tendency extant than Unitarianism, nor any more lively philosophic one than Pantheism; from both of which the scientific intellect, heedful of its own sanity, is bound to heartily to recoil, even if the alternative should be downright scepticism and atheism.[1] The new theology and philosophy reverse the spell. They teach us that creation is primarily spiritual and only derivatively natural, thus that the science of nature is rightly comprehended in the higher science of man. "Yes," they say, "cookery is a strict necessity of things, and claims its proper acknowledgment: but it should never be exalted into an end of life. Its sole end is to nourish and prepare the body for the uses of the soul. So also what we call spiritual regeneration is an actual necessity of things, but it is a necessity which belongs wholly to the natural plane of experience. The soul, coerced by the appearances of things, demands it: instructed by realities, disavows it." As long as I am instructed in spiritual things only by sense or appearances, I deem myself an absolute person in God's sight, and look upon all His dealings towards me as having a most special intention, which is an absolute conversion of me from evil to good. But the reality of the case is, that God never acts upon us individually, save by acting at the same time universally, and consequently that what I regard as a change of nature in me, is in reality a separation of spiritual spheres taking place in the universe of the human mind, by which its external principle (self-love, or *hell*) becomes precipitated, and its internal principle (which is brotherly-love, or *heaven*) elevated, that so the mind of man in nature may be at length effectually harmonized with all Divine perfection.[2] I feel in myself, for example, a great horror on account of some sin, real or imaginary,

which I have committed; I humble myself before God by whatsoever penitential methods my traditional conscience prescribes, having no shadow
of suspicion all the while that God is not literally feeling very angry with
me, and even extremely dubious whether or not He will pardon me. Such
are the crude and abject *data* of my natural experience. But hereupon
come the theologian and philosopher, not to give me intellectual elevation
out of this superstitious lore, but actually to confirm all its teaching, telling
me that my experience is an exact measure of the real and eternal intercourse between God and the soul. They affirm that He is in truth very
much offended with me, just as my still grovelling intelligence proclaims
Him to be; that I have in fact committed a grievous sin against Him, and
that I only follow the obvious dictates of prudence in aiming to propitiate
Him by every customary usage of self-abasement. Such is the help they
give my reason, utterly immersing it in sense. It is as if my cook, in a
moment of revolutionary frenzy, should transport his *batterie de cuisine*
into my drawing-room, and insist upon henceforth preparing my dinner
under my proper nose. For it is really most untrue that God has ever felt,
or ever can feel, an emotion of personal approbation or personal disappro-
bation towards any human being. All this is the mere abject gossip of the
kitchen, the mere idle *bavardise* ["babble"] of cooks and scullions theoriz-
ing in their dim subterranean way upon the great solar mystery of life.
It is, I say, untrue, because the only conceivable basis of such an emotion
to the creative mind would be the creature's independence, and this basis
is utterly wanting, being swallowed up in his sheer and ceaseless dependence. Thus, in order that man really do anything either praiseworthy or
blameworthy in the Divine sight—in order, in other words, that God Himself should charge us with any of the good or evil which we with obdurate
stupidity are for ever charging upon ourselves—it would be necessary for
Him first to forget His creative relation to us, and begin to look upon us
as essentially underived and independent existences; which is absurd. I
perfectly admit that the truth, as reflected in fact, *seems* directly otherwise. It actually does, and must, seem to the sensuous understanding—the
intelligence controlled by sense—that man is an absolute selfhood, that is
to say, that his affections and thoughts, far from being an influx from
spiritual association, originate in himself exclusively, and hence leave him
properly chargeable with all the good and evil issuing from such affections
and thoughts. The senses confined to the *seeming*, cannot help bedevilling
in this way our nascent scientific intellect. They recognize only what
appears to them, having no glimpse, however faint, of internal realities;
and hence they cannot but teach to every one who seeks instruction at
their hands, that the actual is the only real, that the spiritual sphere, if
any such sphere exist, is only another natural, governed by the same laws,
and reproducing the same phenomena. Thus they insinuate that our physical finiteness—our visible insularity in time and space—is a real and eternal
truth. They teach me that I am in all real or spiritual respects precisely
what I am in natural or seeming ones, that is to say, an utterly discon-

nected being, regarded by God not as inseparably interwoven and united with my kind, but as distinctly disunited with all other existence, and governed by Him on strictly private and special methods.

Hence it falls out that the dull and sombre walls of our ecclesiastical Zion, and the less sombre but flippant courts of our received philosophy, enclose a far more organized hostility to spiritual Christianity than you will find in conventionally disreputable quarters. The scientific mind, like Pilate, "finds no evil" in the new Divine spirit which is quickening the nations like life from the dead: on the contrary, it dimly feels that the new spirit is full of blessing for itself, and stands ready to ask of it, "What is truth?" But the *soi-disant* "regenerate" mind, we who think we see—we who are not, like the vulgar herd, "accursed, because they know not the law," but are in fact sanctified by such knowledge, and actually rule the world by its *prestige*—we feel our unrighteous sway menaced by this tender and loving spirit, and do, as the Jew did of old, everything we can to ensure its endless triumph, by stupidly trying to stifle and crush it. What the Jew did to Christ in the flesh, was only a type, inexpressibly faint, of what we Christians are daily doing to him in the spirit. The Jew had never any power to harm Jesus but by patronizing him. Had he done this, had he espoused the Christian teaching and temper, Christ would have been bound indefinitely to remain the mere Jew He was born, and there is no saying accordingly how long Judaism might have perpetuated itself, no longer indeed as a hurtful, but now as a beneficent, yoke upon the nations, nor consequently how long the Gentile mind might have failed to attain to the scientific sentiment of human equality, which yet is the exclusive basis of the Divine creation. So now, the only hindrance which our existing authorities in Church and State could offer to the new ideas, would be to patronize them, to lend them the furtherance of their adoption: for then the common mind of Christendom, which is very docile to good influences, would be so full of admiration and gratitude towards these old established and now undeniable stewards of God, that a new and worse idolatry, a new and more benumbing servitude of the human mind, would be sure to ensue, and a third advent of the Christ behoove to take place, in order to strike off the fetters forged by the preceding one. The new wine of Protestantism and Democracy—the spirit of an ever-advancing humanity— would seek in that case to confine itself evermore within the old established bottles of Church and State, within the purely symbolic dimensions of priest and king, and by dint of so seeking would be infallibly sure to turn vapid and lifeless, to tumble finally, in fact, into the condition of mere disreputable swipes, only fit to be poured out upon the ground, a scorn and avoidance to men and animals.

This, in literal verity, is the fatal sign about European Christendom, that it has inherited in Christianity a soul altogether disproportionate to its meagre and inexpansive body. Protestantism is the actual limit of the Church's elasticity,—one strain more, and it snaps into Mormonism or other downright deviltry, which reasonable people will some day be forced to sweep bodily from the earth: and the State can go no further than Democracy without going into visible extinction. In fact, all astute priests and politicians have perceived for years past that Protestantism and Democracy are not so much expansions of the old symbolic institutions of Church and State, as actual disorganizations of them. They mark the old age of those institutions, their decline into the vale of years, preparatory to their final exit from the historic scene. Hence that prevalent movement of unbelief and despair among our upper classes in Church and State, which christens itself *Conservatism,* and which consists in seeking refuge from the onward Providence that governs the world, by flinging oneself into the arms of the stolidest civil and ecclesiastical despotisms, or in calling upon the mountains and rocks to crush one, by way of shielding one's eyes from the entrance of unwelcome light. How utterly absurd then to suppose our existing Christendom formally competent to embody the Divine spirit in humanity! This spirit seeks the infinite expansion of human nature, seeks to lift the beggar from the dunghill and to set him among princes, simply because he is man, simply because he is a living form or image of God, and hence capable of an immortal conjunction with God. God is blessedly indifferent to the interests of every priesthood and every government under the sun, because He stands in an infinitely nearer attitude to man than these priesthoods and governments can any way conceive of as possible. They have not the slightest conception of God as the Lord, or of a Divine *natural* humanity, but on the contrary, maintain, under Christian names, the most inveterately Pagan conceptions of the Divine character. Take, for example, any reigning Pope or Emperor, and chase the Divine image through all the windings of his official heart down to its fundamental quality, and you will find it turn out some sheer personal will, some strenuous physical existence, reeling with the possession of mere wanton power, and odious from the exercise of every jealous revengeful and malignant disposition. It is high time that all the world confess themselves atheists with respect to this orthodox deity. It is high time that every disciple of Christ seize this obscene and skulking god of the nations by the beard with one hand, and with the other smite him between the eyes till he fall down and die. The famous M. Proudhon,[3] who snaps his whip louder than any contemporary Frenchman, very much shocked his hypocritical generation a little while since by crying *haro* upon this Gentile conception of God, or exclaiming against Deity thus viewed as the true curse of human existence. Proudhon's critics, who themselves are fond of snapping their whips in the loudest possible way, seem to have been disheartened by the tremendous *eclât* of his performance, and are accordingly doing what they can ever since to diminish it, by representing it as a mere insincerity on Proudhon's part—as a mere *annonce* to the travelling public that here at last was a postillion capable of taking them the shortest possible route to kingdom-come, provided they would only commit themselves to his audacious guidance. I do not personally enjoy the pleasure of M. Proudhon's acquaintance, but I cannot help feeling very serious misgivings as to the truth of this criticism. His judgment strikes

me as on the whole a very Christian one. I suppose that Proudhon would
be as much disconcerted to be called a Christian as those modest people
of whom we read in the Lord's similitude of the kingdom of heaven, as
replying to his beaming smile of recognition for services rendered, "But
when saw we thee hungry, and fed thee; or thirsty, and gave thee drink?"
Nevertheless I regard Proudhon as at bottom, if not a-top—in heart, if not
in head—an excellent Christian. His intellect has doubtless been sophisticated to some extent by the dense and blinding obscurity which has traditionally settled down upon the moral problem; but he is obviously a man
of the manliest make in heart, and I do not see how any clear-sighted
reader of the four gospels, which turn all subsequent revolutionary literature into child's play, can feel justified in denouncing him. Of course I
mean the unadulterate gospels, not that bleached and emasculate substitute which, under the name of "evangelical religion," does its weekly best
to defame and deface God's image in our souls, through the length and
breadth of established Church and State. Evangelical religion as it is
called . . . is such a religion as is fitly piped by the east wind—a religion
which cuts across the nerves of the soul like a knife, which chills all the
best sympathies of the heart, and ends by freezing its followers stiff in the
shallows of their own selfishness. It is of course not of this conventional
gospel that I speak, but of the unperverted gospel of Christ, when I say
that every intelligent reader will be slow to condemn Proudhon, because
throughout his unskilful books he will yet not fail to discern an unmistakeable flavour of that ancient and incomparable vintage. Clearly, if Christianity makes any distinct pretension, it is to have utterly exhausted natural
religion; and natural religion is the only thing with which the scientific
intellect of man has any quarrel. Science revolts at the idea of there being
any essential limitation of the human faculties, which nevertheless would
be inevitable if their vital source could be proved to lay outside of human
nature, or inhered as natural religion affirms it to inhere, in a being gener-
ically distinct from humanity, and *spatially* separable from all its individual forms. Science utterly revolts from the conception of a physical or
material Deity—a Deity cognizable to sense—and triumphantly careers
through the universe of space, to chase from the human mind every vestige of so baleful and disheartening a conception. But it is solely to Christianity that science owes this emancipation. Christianity eternally explodes
the naturalistic conception of Deity as a being essentially disproportionate
to man, and therefore inaccessible to human intelligence, by identifying
Him with conventionally the meanest and humblest of men, with a man
who was so genuinely humble and insignificant as actually to feel no personality apart from the interests of universal truth and justice, who had
not spirit enough to be angry at the grossest of personal insults, or to
resent the cruellest of personal wrongs; but, on the contrary, habitually
and patiently endured degradations which any rustic English pedagogue
at the present day would be parochially disowned for submitting to for a
moment, and which would drive the most sonorous of your English

bishops to doubt the Divine existence, if he were even so much as threatened with them. Yet He, adorable man of men, bore unflinchingly on, nor
ever ceased to eat the bitter bread of humiliation, until He had made his
despised and suffering form the adequate and ample temple of God, and
so for ever wedded the infinite Divine perfection to the most familiar
motions and appetites of our ordinary human nature. Jesus vindicated his
prophetic designation as above all men *"a man of sorrows,"* because in
the historic position to which he found himself born, he was exposed on
the one side to the unmeasured influx of the Divine Love, and on the other
to the equally unmeasured influx of every loathsome and hellish lust of
personal aggrandizement. The literal form of Christ's pretension was profoundly diabolic. View his personal pretension as literally true and just, as
having an absolute basis, and you can imagine no more flagrant dishonour
to the Divine name. To suppose that the universal Father of mankind
cared for the Jew one jot more than for the Gentile, and that He cared for
one Jew also more than for another, actually intending to give both the
former and the latter an endless earthly dominion, was manifestly to
blacken the Divine character, and pervert it to the inflammation of every
diabolic ambition. And yet this was that literal form of the Jewish hope
to which Christ was born. The innocent babe opened his eyes upon mother
and father, brother and sister, neighbour and friend, ruler and priest,
stupidly agape at the marvels which heralded his birth, and no doubt as
his intelligence dawned he lent a naturally complacent ear to the promises
of personal advancement and glory they showered upon him. He sucked
in the subtlest spiritual poison with every swallow of his mother's milk,
and his very religion bound him, so far as human probabilities went, to
become an unmitigated devil. I find no trace of any man in history being
subject to the temptations that beset this truest of men. I find no trace of
any other man who felt himself called upon by the tenderest human love
to loathe and disavow the proud and yearning bosom that bore him. I find
no other man in history whose profound reverence for infinite goodness
and truth drove him to renounce the religion of his fathers, simply because
that religion contemplated as its issue his own supreme aggrandizement;
and whose profound love to man drove him to renounce every obligation
of patriotism, simply because these obligations were plainly coincident
with the supremest and subtlest inspirations of his own self-love. No doubt
many a man has renounced his traditional creed because it associated him
with the obloquy and contempt of his nation, or stood in the way of his
personal ambition; and so no doubt many a man has abjured his country,
because it disclaimed his title and ability to rule. In short, a thousand men
can be found every day who do both of these things from the instinct of
self-love. But the eternal peculiarity of the Christian fact is, that Christ
did them utterly without the aid of that tremendous lever, actually while it
was undermining his force, and subjecting him to ceaseless death. He
discredited his paternal gods simply because they were bent upon doing
him unlimited honour; and shrank from kindred and countrymen, only

because they were intent upon rendering him unparalleled gratitude and benediction. What a mere obscenity every great name in history confesses itself beside this spotless Judean youth, who in the thickest night of time,— unhelped by priest or ruler, by friend or neighbour, by father or mother, by brother or sister, helped, in fact, if we may so consider it, only by the dim expectant sympathy of that hungry rabble of harlots and outcasts who furnished His inglorious retinue, and still further drew upon Him the ferocious scorn of all that was devout, and honourable and powerful in His nation,—yet let in eternal daylight upon the soul, by steadfastly expanding in his private spirit to the dimensions of universal humanity, so bringing, for the first time in history, the finite human bosom into perfect experimental accord with the infinite Divine Love. For my part I am free to declare that I find the conception of any Divinity superior to this radiant human form, inexpressibly treasonable to my own manhood. In fact, I do not hesitate to say that I find the orthodox and popular conception of Deity to be in the comparison a mere odious stench in the nostrils, against which I here indite my exuberant and eternal protest. I shall always cherish the most hearty and cheerful atheism towards every deity but him who has illustrated my own nature with such resplendent power, as to make me feel that man henceforth is the only name of honour, and that any God out of the strictest human proportions, any God with essentially disproportionate aims and ends to man, is an unmixed superfluity and nuisance. In short, I worship the LORD alone, the God-MAN, that peerless and perfect soul whose unswerving innocence and sweetness gathered up the infinite forces of Deity as wheat is gathered up in a sheaf, and for ever linked them with the natural life of man, with every commonest lineament of human nature, so that we are not only authorized henceforth to view the human spirit as inwardly refined from all grossness, which is pride or selfishness, and instinct with universal love and humility, but also to regard the human body itself as the only visible shrine of God, as the destined temple of all lustrous health and beauty, the native home of every chaste, and generous, and magnanimous affection. I take it that every man of sense and feeling will infallibly join in this ennobling worship. I take it that all atheism and scepticism are inwardly fragrant with this devout incense, that to the loving and knowing heart of God they have never been anything else than a negative but most sincere form of the vital worship I here avow. It is, indeed, obvious that Proudhon's manly revolt contemplates only that old Pagan conception of the Godhead which Christianity exhausts, but which nominally Christian priests and kings, for their own private unloving ends, still continue diligently to *exploit*. Against this lurid power—half-pedagogue, half-policeman, but wholly imbecile in both aspects—I, too, raise my gleeful fist, I lift my scornful foot, I invoke the self-respect of my children, I arouse their generous indignation, I instruct their nascent philanthropy, because I know that he spiritually departed this life long centuries ago, and that it is only his grim unburied corpse which still poisons the popular air. . . .

NOTES

1. Confiding in the fallacious dogmatism of sense (that *old serpent* whose speech is far too subtle and insinuating to be suspected prior to experience), our theologians and philosophers regard being and seeming, truth and fact, reason and experience, as identical, and hence vainly rummage the phenomenal world for an original glimpse of those lustrous Divine footsteps which fall wholly within the soul of man, and of which nature herself is at best but the distant reverberation. Nature is but the echo of the soul, and images nothing therefore of the Divine creation and providence which is not primarily impressed by the soul. Your delicious English landscape, for example, palpitating with its rich subserviency to every human need, reflects a far more evangelical lesson in these respects than the hideous jungles of Asia, or our own unsubdued forests and indolent savannas; because the humanized English *man* has first taught it so to do. Abstract this comfortable Christian English soul, who believes in nothing more soundly than a deity favourable to good cheer, prolific of everlasting cakes and ale, and your peaceful English landscape would have been by this time as ruthless and unchristian as that of Switzerland, which for the most part suggests no thoughts of Divinity but as of some huge, frowning, thunderous, overshadowing, overbearing power, eternally allied with pride and self-will, and essentially untouched by all those blissful human sympathies and charities whose inseparable root is humility.

2. Of course it is only when self-love claims the primacy of neighbourly love or charity, that it is contrary to Divine order. When it spontaneously defers to the latter, as it does in the scientific sentiment of human society or fellowship, nothing can be half so orderly and beneficent, and we cannot have too much of it.

3. The reference is to Pierre Joseph Proudhon (1809–1865), a French moralist and advocate of social reform.—Editor's note.

16

SUMMING UP:
SOCIETY AS THE REDEEMED
FORM OF MAN

All of James's work converged upon an explication
of the latter phrase above. The notion of "society as the
redeemed form of man" represented the quintessential
assumption upon which his philosophy was built and
towards the realization of which it was entirely
directed. The aspiration from which it first took root
lay well back in the obscure origins of the Transcendental movement, but the visionary state of being
which it was intended to announce still lies far beyond
the horizon of the future. In this selection from the
concluding chapter of his last completed book, James
seeks to show how all of nature, life, and history
conspire to vindicate the divine natural humanity by
incarnating it in social form. To James this entire
process was a revelation of God's infinite creative love
for the human race, a love so limitless and profound
in its extent that it contents itself with nothing short
of recreating individual men and women in the form
of its own perfect sociality.

The following selection constitutes chapter 28 of
Society the Redeemed Form of Man (Boston, 1879),
444–80.

———·•◆•·———

My dear friend:—

In my last letter I answered, or tried to answer, two questions each of
sovereign import to the speculative welfare of philosophy. The first question was about human nature itself, its origin and quality. The second led
us to consider its method of actual development to the consciousness of
its carnal votary, as *conscience,* or *the negative law of human freedom.*
If you will allow me now briefly to resume or recapitulate the answers I
gave to these questions, bearing as they do so profoundly on the speculative interests of religion and philosophy, we shall both of us be better able

to do justice to a third question which we are more particularly bound to consider in the present letter, and which is of transcendent practical importance to the interests, not of any special science perhaps, but certainly to the general science of human life.

We saw then in our last letter that human nature is a strictly metaphysic existence, postulating the entire realm of physics beneath it or under it precisely as the pedestal is postulated in the statue, or the body in the soul: in order adequately to base it, that is, to finite it, or give it on its objective side permanent fixity or isolation. Human nature originates spiritually in God who is real or essential man, and it merely expresses on its inward or spiritual side the ceaseless effort of His providence to manifest itself creatively, that is, to attain to adequate actual or existential form in His creature. The creature of course *ex vi termini* ["by virtue of its function"] is in himself, or *quâ* creature, utterly "without form, and void" of distinctive quality, and any form or quality he may exhibit therefore is not attributable to himself but to the creator in him: unless indeed it be a purely evil and fallacious form or quality, in which case it exists only to consciousness, and has no fibre of reality outside of it.

But although God is in truth most real or essential man it will not do to infer that He is, *ipso facto* merely, formal or existential man as well. Of course He who alone is real or essential man is *ipso facto* also *virtually* formal or existential man, since there can be no such thing as an absolute divorce between substance and form: but only virtually, or in potency, not actually. His becoming actually what He is potentially, or outwardly what He is inwardly, depends entirely upon His being creative and thus having a sphere of actual or outward manifestation put within His grasp. For the creator who is real or inward and essential man becomes actual or outward and existential man only through His creature, or by virtue of His first giving spiritual or inward being to the creature. The creature no doubt, unapprised as yet save by revelation of his being spiritually created, or of his having any *inward* potency of life, *seems* to himself to be a most veridical actual man. But this is all a seeming. For he being created is of necessity in himself a mere finite form or image of humanity; and even as such form or image can only reproduce the human type in so far as he is freely united to his brethren: which he can never be, which in fact he selfishly loathes to be, until his proper interest tardily constrains him to that mercenary policy. Besides, as I have already intimated, it is illogical and stupid to suppose that any one can be actual or formal man but He who is first real or substantial man. For if substance and form differed in themselves, and not simply in relation to a finite intelligence, creation would be at a *nonplus*. In truth then God alone is both real, or inward and essential man, and actual, or outward and existential man. In short, He alone is man in substance, and man in form.

Be it understood then between us that we ourselves, however truly we may be said to symbolize actual human nature, or typify formal manhood, have yet no shadow of a claim to constitute such manhood, any more than we have a shadow of claim to constitute Divinity, or real and essential manhood. For we are only at our best finite phenomenal men, and neither singly nor in mass therefore can we ever hope to be that actual and unitary *form* of man, which as being correlative to its real or essential Divine substance, must be every way proportionate to such substance, and therefore itself Divine and infinite. But though we have no shadow of justification in so doing, we do nevertheless all the while betray our spiritual ignorance in assuming *bona fide* to constitute *the whole of the formal and actual humanity which exists on earth*, and which in theory reflects the inward and essential humanity of God: thus and thereby baffling or indefinitely retarding the Divine purpose (and indeed the Divine ability) eventually to show us the spiritual truth of the case. For God is too wise and good a being (since He is real or essential man) practically to contemn or over-ride His creature's natural prejudices, and very much prefers to make His creature also, like Himself, wise and good by gradually illumining those natural prejudices, and bending them to the truth.

Allow me then to repeat to you a truth which we have as yet barely glanced at, but which is calculated yet to shed an infinite amount of light upon the philosophy of human nature and human history. That truth is as follows, and I conjure you to ponder it well if you would ever hope to master the true secret of the spiritual creation: Although God our creator is real or spiritual and inward man, and *by that fact stands pledged eventually to show Himself sole actual or natural and outward man also*, nevertheless His entire ability to do this is in strict abeyance to His creature's good pleasure in the premises, or depends upon the human race giving Him a chance to accomplish the task. For He is the absolute creator of men, and by that very fact bound in such intimate solidarity with them, that He cannot bestow any of His own potencies and felicities upon them without their own free consent and concurrence. Much less therefore can He bestow upon them that knowledge of Himself as the only true subject of their nature which is immortal life, so long as they each stupidly persist in maintaining that they themselves are its sole true subjects, and He himself consequently its sole undeniable object. We cannot hope then to see God avouching himself both inwardly and outwardly, both really and actually, both spiritually and naturally, true man, and alone fit to bear the untarnished name of Man, until the human race becomes so fused *within itself*—that is, so constituted in felt or conscious unity with itself—as to form a perfect society, brotherhood, or fellowship of its particular and universal elements, each of its members spontaneously devoting himself to the welfare of all, and all the members in their turn freely espousing the welfare of each.

Then doubtless, and not before, the creator of men will have become formal, existential, or natural man as well as substantial, essential, or spiritual man, and you and I will never again be such arrant idiots spiritually as to deem ourselves God's true creatures in our own private right, or out of social solidarity with all other men. For the great phenomenon of human society—*of men made social out of, and* so to speak *by virtue of, their extreme and inveterate selfishness*—will then strike every eye as the consummate miracle of God's spiritual perfection in our nature, and the eternally sufficing manifestation of His matchless adorable name. But until the human race attains to plenary social form we may be very sure that as the end of God's spiritual creation in human nature meanwhile must be perfectly obscured or overlaid by men's prevalent ignorance and superstition, so, much more, the origin of that nature in God's infinite love and wisdom will be completely misapprehended, as we see in point of fact it has been. For men have always been wont to attribute any thing but a Divine genesis to their nature, assigning a purely *à posteriori* origin to it in place of an *à priori* one. That is to say, they make it originate in a gradual evolution of humanity from precedent mineral, vegetable, and animal forms: thus in effect or figuratively making the head of creation take the place of its heels, or subjecting soul to body, statue to pedestal, oyster to shell, ship to sails, church to steeple, house to foundation, man to clothing.

Now let me say that it is nothing but this helplessly *carnal* habit of mind in us—this instinctive and inveterate tendency on our part to envisage creation, not as a spiritual Divine life or truth in man, but only as a dead material fact or thing—which forever condemns us *in ourselves* to a purely natural or metaphysic and phenomenal existence; that is to say, to an existence which is as remote in itself from spiritual truth as it is from material fact, being equidistant from, and inaccessible to, the inward life of the angel on the one hand, and the purely outward or sensuous life of the devil on the other. And the obvious reason of this state of things: that is to say, the reason why nature exhibits this strictly neutral or equatorial quality—making the divided hemispheres of good and evil, heaven and hell, spirit and flesh, eternally spherical in itself, that is, making them one and equal as the two opposing abutments of a bridge are made one and equal in the bridge—is that the problem of creation to the Divine mind, being how eternally to reconcile two factors, creator and creature, which are totally irreconcilable in themselves, one being all fulness, the other all want, one all spirit or life, the other all flesh or death, inexorably demands therefore for its solution a third or middle term which shall be neutral or indifferent to either factor, infinite or finite, by avouching itself a rigidly indefinite or universal quantity as the unity of each and all. Accordingly this requisite and accommodating middle term which actually solves the creative problem is supplied by human nature. Human nature impartially solves the creative problem, because while it is absolutely neutral or rather altogether negative with respect to either interest, creative or created, *in se*, it is therefore most positive or affirmative with respect to both as they become conjoined in living unity. The method of this conjunction, from which the spiritual creation results, arises from the gradual experimental conversion of the principle of self in man, the evil principle, which represents the finite man, into the principle of society or fellowship, the good principle, which represents the infinite humanity, so making God and man naturally, as they always have been spiritually, one.

This then is an explicit statement of what I implicitly said about nature in the last letter; but after all it is an account of nature on its theoretic rather than its practical side, or as it exists to the mind of its author only and not as it appears to a finite dependent intelligence. Practically then, or to the finite mind, nature, as I went on to say in that letter, reveals itself not, to be sure, in its own perfect or consummate spiritual way, as an undefined or universal form, being the unity of the whole and its parts, but in the specific form of *conscience,* or the law upon which man's natural freedom is negatively conditioned, the purpose of conscience being to redeem him out of the bondage he is under by birth to his physical organization, and so qualify him for social or distinctively human form, which is the only form commensurate with the spiritual Divine perfection or infinitude. In other words creation in its finite natural aspect, its aspect towards the carnal creature, necessarily wears the appearance of an emancipating, spiritualizing, or redemptive operation, divorcing the creature from the organic bondage to which he is born subject, and investing him instead with moral and rational freedom.

But here I must beg you to note with most minute attention one thing, which is: that *morality and rationality, although they separate man from animal, and thereby qualify him to take the name of man, yet they do this only provisionally.* They do not invest him with absolute, but only with phenomenal, manhood, making his real participation of human nature altogether contingent upon his personal humanity, or the degree in which he freely admits the neighbor to a first place in his habitual regard, and limits himself to the second place. Freedom and rationality by no means give any of us a title to the Divine potencies and felicities which inhere in human nature; they only make him, or inscribe him as, a candidate for such title. In short they give man a *quasi* or mere negative and seeming natural consciousness, by no means a real or positive one, and hence they do not guarantee him the spiritual Divine being of which human nature is the sole possible vehicle whether to man or angel.

For example. My moral manhood, which stands in my felt freedom of will to choose between good and evil, is not absolute but contingent or conditional: being rigidly conditioned *upon my actually choosing good.* If, as some persons not very clear-sighted are wont to pretend, my will cannot feel itself free to do one thing unless it feel itself also free at the same time to do the exact contrary thing, I would not call this latter faculty by the sacred name of freedom, but by that of bondage, since it can be exercised only at the expense of renouncing one's manhood. *My moral manhood depends,* and depends absolutely, *upon my felt freedom always to take the side of good in preference to evil whenever and wherever I find them conflicting, and never the side of evil in preference to good.* Thus if in case of conflict I actually choose evil, or prefer it to good, my moral or provisional manhood not only turns out an actual sham, but *by the foreclosure of the condition on which its entire possibility was based,* sinks below animality even, and becomes frankly evil or diabolic. It is true, I may not in so doing recognize that I am incurring a forfeiture of all human possibilities, and probably shall not, going on indeed to prate of my superb and lustrous manhood even after I have shut myself up in hell. But this will be simply because manhood is an inward not an outward form or quality, and therefore only to be inwardly discerned, whereas I in the circumstances supposed am really or inwardly knavish not human, and recognize manhood therefore only as accomplished knavery.

In like manner precisely my rational manhood, which stands in the freedom of my understanding to discriminate the true from the false, proves itself no manhood at all, but the veriest monkeyhood and mockery of humanity, if I forbear to exert it, or devoutly exercise myself in it, *by actually loving the true and rejecting the false.* To be sure, as some of our egregious logic-choppers counsel me to do, I may interpret my moral and rational manhood into a state of utter serene indifference with respect to the rival claims of good and evil upon my heart, and the rival claims of truth and falsity upon my understanding. But in that event my vaunted moral and rational manhood turns out a mere faculty to prefer good *or* evil, truth *or* falsity, at my own ungodly pleasure. In which case my moral manhood is my right to do just as I please, without regard to any holier or higher law. In other words it expresses my actual independence both of God and man. But this is a manhood which can never come from God, for there is no fibre of foundation for it in the whole range of His perfection. He himself has no independence of action, and He could never impart to His creature therefore what He did not Himself possess. His inmost life is dependent upon His actually equalizing His creature with Himself, or making Himself over to the latter in all the plentitude of His resources. And all His action is constrained by this unselfish end, and addressed unfalteringly to its promotion. Any freedom or manhood therefore which looks towards independence, or makes the moral and rational subject his own law, should be indignantly spurned by him as a base infernal counterfeit of the true Divine manhood. That a man in loving good should feel himself free to love its opposite can only be possible on one of two conditions: Either good and evil must be at bottom identical, and differ only in name; which is an hypothesis too obviously stupid to invite consideration: or else the man does not honestly love good but for some temporary motive is willing to make a pretence of loving it: and this hypothesis thoroughly vitiates the problem, or reduces it to actual insignificance, by changing its terms. I do not deny of course that a man may actually or outwardly *take* tea, when he really or inwardly *prefers* coffee. But that while he prefers coffee he should also feel himself free to prefer tea, is plainly a phenomenon referring itself to that grotesque world imagined by the late hard-headed but warm-hearted Mr. Mill,[1] which no sun enlightens, but where a mild moonshine reigns supreme, and even the virtuous multiplication table grows wanton and indulgent, permitting all its tender mathematical nurslings to say twice two are five, and if five, why not fifty?

At any rate there is no such freedom as that here combated in God, and there can be no appearance of it in man His creature save as a diabolic illusion.[2] Whatever his silly creature may do in the premisses, or rather boast himself of doing, God at least has no privilege of arbitrary or capricious action, because He has not the slightest power to do as *He* pleases, or make Himself into His own end of action. For God, as I have often enough said already, is *essentially* creative, creative by the whole force of His being; and His action therefore is inexorably under law to the welfare of His creature. He is not creative from any inspiration of the head merely, that is, morally or voluntarily creative, as either from a sense of duty to His creatures, or from a sense of what is expedient with a view to enliven His own solitude, or better His own condition in any way; for His creatures have their being wholly in Him, and consequently can impose no outward obligation upon Him, and He himself consequently has no existence save in His creatures, and can therefore feel no obligation to act with a view to the improvement of His own independent circumstances. Neither is He æsthetically creative, like the artist, that is, creative from the hand, through taste or overpowering attraction: for His taste would utterly revolt from producing such loathsome vermin as His creatures are bound to be in their finite *selves*, if like the artist's creations those finite selves were unhappily to know no natural renewing. He is creative therefore only from the heart, that is, freely or spontaneously creative, creative in Himself, or with His whole vital energy: which insures in the first place that His inmost life lies in communicating His own deathless being to the creature, that is, His own infinite and eternal potencies, felicities, and beatitudes, and then that all His innocent wisdom will go to supplant or render superfluous the wretched *self*-righteousness of the creature, in endowing him first of all with a righteous nature, or stable constitutional basis of existence, whence he in his turn may every way freely or spontaneously react to the interior creative impulsion.

We see then that the creator does not, and absolutely cannot, spiritually exist save in His creature. *A fortiori* therefore He has no power to make His own pleasure the law of His action, unless the blessedness of his creature be always subsumed in that pleasure as its total substance and root. Thus He is absolutely inhibited by His *essential* infinitude or freedom from making self the end of His action, or ever doing under any circumstances as *He* pleases, without reference indeed to everybody else's welfare. He cheerfully allows us a monopoly of that saddest and most vulgar delight. For he who is essentially free or infinite as being creative, abjures all empirical, or felt conscious and phenomenal, freedom, because He is absolutely without selfhood, and has no contact with the unclean thing save in His creatures. All His infinitude or freedom is mortgaged to the necessity of bringing His creature to ripe natural or spontaneous manhood, and only when that burden is accomplished and that most Divine pleasure realized will He enjoy His first faint chance of seeing *Himself* reflected—*in the happiness of His creature.*

Very well then: our moral and rational manhood is not our natural manhood, but only a distorted and diffracted image of that unitary substance as seen in the mirror of our divided and discordant personalities. It is a similitude of our natural manhood, a sort of photographic negative of it, by whose constant schooling the Divine Artist prepares and leads us eventually to descry and detect the positive truth upon the subject. It is a similitude or semblance which we indeed are long content to mistake for the reality, but this comes of our never having yet known the reality by living contact, but only by hearsay. It is true that the reality once made itself known to men in a general prophetic way through a very remarkable historic person, miraculously born at a great crisis of the church's history, when the church itself was putting off her ritual or ceremonial dress, and taking on actual flesh-and-blood substance. But the great and merciful truth at that time clothed itself in such weak, dejected, dying literal form, that though its perfect humanity was seen, men have always been afraid to argue from that to its equally perfect divinity, and have been content instead simply to cherish the ecclesiastical tradition on that subject.[3] On his Jewish side of course, which related him to a purely typical or figurative economy, Christ was bound to be accursed both of God and man; for his personal pretension as the Jewish Messiah, sent to deliver his brethren according to the flesh from bondage, and exalt *them* to the supremacy of the nations, was as full of inward blasphemy towards the Divine name, as it was full of outward contempt towards the human race. It was only in his *crucified* aspect accordingly that he vindicates the spiritual truth of his mission, or allows any trace of his divinity to appear; for here he is seen, in open contempt of every most sacred national tradition, sternly rejecting from himself a Jewish humanity, and putting on a universal one, that is, one which should be neither Jewish nor Gentile, but broadly unitary or universal, to the effacing of all literal discriminations whatever among men.

But I have not taken so much pains to prove to you: that our moral and rational manhood is not a real manhood, but a *quasi* one, intended only as a preparation for our real or natural manhood when it comes: altogether for its own sake, but with a view also to get some needed light upon the answer to our third question, which it is high time we were considering. Our actual manhood as we have seen is an altogether provisional one intended to serve as a mere scaffolding to our natural manhood, as a mere foil or set-off to it when it is ready to appear on its own infinite Divine lustre; and I have thought that by first familiarizing your imagination somewhat with this mighty truth I might assist you to a fuller comprehension of the answer I am about to give to the question now before us. That question may be formulated thus: *What precise machinery does human nature require in order historically to avouch itself, or authenticate itself to the public conscience of men,* AS THE WORLD'S SOLE LIFE: so at long last harmonizing the finite, phenomenal, or merely conscious man with God's spiritual infinitude or freedom?

The machinery of human nature by which it ultimates its proper life, turning all history into its obedient vehicle, and filling the entire public consciousness of men with its renown, is solely made up of what we call *the church* and *the world*. These terms, however, remember, express no objective but a purely subjective reality in man; or what is the same thing they neither of them indicate a physical or material, but on the contrary a purely metaphysical or immaterial, substance in humanity. And a purely metaphysical or immaterial substance in humanity can only be A MIND. This accordingly is what *the church* and *the world* mean, *a purely mental or subjective reality in man;* the former term being employed to designate in those to whom it is applied affections turned heavenward; the latter, affections turned earthward: "the church," in other words, characterizing the sphere of man's progressive mental development, "the world" the sphere of his arrested mental development. The whole of humanity is comprised in these two forms of man's mental subjectivity. A man must necessarily have his affections turned towards heaven, or confined to earth, and according as either is the case with him, he is a least or minia-ture form either of the church, or the world. The church of course tends to issue spiritually in a heaven made up of inwardly *re*generate men, and the world in its turn to issue in a coequal hell made up of inwardly *de*generate men, so that unless the Divine power had effectually ultimated itself in human nature, and thereby broken up this fatal spiritual equilibrium, heaven and hell must have practically forever divided the spiritual world between them, and forever have given the lie consequently to the sover-eign truth of God's creative infinitude.

Nothing, I venture to say, can be imagined more revolting to our hu-manitary instincts of such infinitude than the perfectly veracious or un-exaggerated pictures which Swedenborg's phlegmatic genius gives us of what he witnessed among our *post-mortem* friends and cronies. If the friend or crony in question had been on earth a reverential person, and now consequently had his lot among the angels, Swedenborg invariably found that the man's natural imbecility, or insufficiency to himself, had undergone no change through the event of death, the man being all the while spiritually restrained from *the frankest profligacy solely by the providence of God exerted towards him through angelic association.* And if, on the other hand, our deceased acquaintance had been on earth an habitual votary of self and the world, and therefore inwardly a mocker of God and the neighbor, so that he now found himself to his great delight enrolled among the lowest of the low, Swedenborg nevertheless invariably discovers that the fellow's braggart selfhood is at bottom a pure hallucina-tion or sham, dependent every moment for its illusory existence upon hellish influx and association, and tolerated only for some transient inci-dental use promoted by it to other existence.

Could any thing then well be more hideous and implacable to human pity than such a picture of men's celestial or infernal possibilities, if the picture were intended to represent an eternal reality? The picture to be sure was not intended to represent an eternal reality, but we see from it excellently well what the eternal reality must have been (only much worse), if the true sphere of the creative infinitude had not been realized in our nature. Now the evolution of man's natural destiny, and with it consequently his participation of immortal life, has been strictly identical with the growth of the civilized State, that is, with the growth of our earthly life out of absolute bondage to the material elements of nature into a condition of free citizenship: so that we may say with entire truth that the advent of this (prospectively) free State of man on earth under which we have the happiness to live, has been the fruit of a gradually fiercer attrition between the church and the world, and of that exclusively.

The two universally recognized elements then of our Christian civilization, which are *the church* and *the world,* make up between them that requisite machinery of human nature by whose conflicting yet concurrent play it finally avouches itself the supreme law of man's activity. I do not say, mind you, that the church and the world are in the least identical with human nature, or that they have any claim to a particle of her Divine prestige and dignity. God forbid! All I say is that they constitute the mere *machinery* of human nature by which it gradually works itself out to the light of day. They are *the simple machinery of its evolution* by which it eventually succeeds in bringing itself to men's recognition as the *conditio sine quá non* of their Divine and immortal life. Their sole historic or Providential purpose has been to serve as a platform to the development of men's *real* or *natural* consciousness, as utterly distinct from and inveterately hostile to their phenomenal or personal consciousness; and when this use has been accomplished they are bound, both of them, to tumble off into "the condition of weeds and worn-out faces." Thus the church and the world bear to each other the relation of base and superstructure, or negative and positive conditions of one and the same metaphysic result, that result being the evolution of humanity, or of men's natural consciousness in orderly social form. The incessant attrition to which these base mechanical factors of human nature are doomed by their fierce mutual antagonism, is practically obviated in great part by their engendering between them what we term the civilized State of man, as a temporary compromise between creature and creator, or a richly provisional outcome of human destiny while the social form of our nature is still unachieved, or its grand consummate celestial flower is still in abeyance to the coarse earthly necessities of leaf, and stem, and roots. And they both appear at last so approximately humanized, or weaned of their inveterate animosity, in their child the State, but especially in their grandchild, which is the *free* State or republic, that although they have neither of them the least intrinsic fitness to guide or control human destiny, they have yet somehow had the art or address to perpetuate their bad empire over the human mind down to this very day.

This in fact is to-day the world-wide tragedy of human life. Human life, even now when its social ideal is so imperfectly realized even in thought, would be a tolerably clean and reputable thing, were not its honest interests so foully complicated with those of the self-righteous church and the selfish, servile world. This metaphysic machinery of human nature, instead of any longer unconsciously promoting its evolution, has consciously undertaken to stifle it by compressing its nascent activity. That is to say, the church and the world, in the persons of their more astute adepts, have begun dimly to feel that their joint offspring, the civilized State of man, was never intended by God's providence to be a finality in human history. I don't mean to say that worldly and ecclesiastical minds, however astute they may be, have the least intellectual insight of God's truth upon this subject. I haven't the slightest idea, myself, that they have any intellectual discernment of the entirely provisional or providential character of our existing civilization, in that it was intended to base a *Divine-natural* evolution of human life, and disappear bag and baggage when that end is accomplished. But these secular and ecclesiastical minds are at least in sensible contact with the actual facts and leading providential tendencies of the time, and their own inordinate self-love and love of rule insure that none shall feel so keenly as they the gathering clouds that are rolling up *from within* over the technical State, erelong to descend in floods of devouring rain, hail, and tempest upon the devoted heads of those whose hope in God is limited to it. Hence their present persistent efforts to perpetuate and extend their empire, by appealing no longer to the political or civic conscience of men for support, but to the hopes and fears of the private or personal consciousness.

This however is a gross usurpation. Neither church nor world has a shadow of claim upon men's individual respect and attention, save in so far as men first of all have a purely superstitious regard for the State as a finality of God's earthly providence. Nothing can be more preposterous than this baleful superstition. The State has no permanent or absolute rights over the human conscience. It was never intended, as I have already shown, for any thing else than a mere *locum tenens,* a simple herald or lieutenant, to Society, while Society itself was as yet wholly unrecognized, and indeed undreamt of, as the sole intellectual truth of man's Divine-natural destiny. And the church meanwhile as the *genitor* of this temporary civilized State of man, has no other office in the name of the celestial or paternal providence that presides over it, than prophetically to promise every man a *mens sana,* that is, a sound mind. Neither has the world, as the *genitrix* of the State, any other office derived from the earthly or maternal providence involved in the State, than prophetically to promise every man a *corpus sanum,* that is, a sound body, wherein his *mens sana* may house itself with comfort, and exercise its power unimpeded. But no one has ever been such an abject noodle as to maintain that this Divine prophecy and promise in behalf of universal man kept up by the church and the world, were ever intended to be fulfilled by the merely instituted State of man, that is, by a regimen of mere citizenship, in which the conscience of men should be persistently held submissive to tutors and governors. At all events, the actual facts of the case must soon disenchant him. For no fact is more notorious than that there is actually no man within the precincts of civilization possessing an absolutely healthy mind, or an absolutely healthy body. In truth the church and the world, in gencrating civilization, have had a purely prophetic relation to the human mind, and no pretension can be more utterly absurd on their part than to claim any relevancy to man's living or spiritual consciousness. They have never had the slightest claim to human respect in themselves, but only in producing their joint offspring, the State. They rightfully end or merge in her formation, and have no logical pretension to survive it a single instant. Above all and at this day they have no particle of right to arrogate the least control over the mind of any man who does not conscientiously identify his manhood with the State, or limit it to good citizenship, so forever rejecting the invitations of infinite goodness and truth.

For this empirical State of man, whereby he is providentially led into accurate self-knowledge, and so prepared for an immortal destiny, is with us—as our constitutional polity as a community announces—*functus officio* ["performed officially"], or thoroughly exanimate as to the beneficent spiritual uses which once consecrated it to men's respect. Our constitutional polity as a community makes no provision for priest or king, which seem essential to the State in its merely political form, and we may not unreasonably infer accordingly that the State under these skies is casting its old political skin, and putting on one which is more decidedly flexible, and congruous with the perfected or social form of our nature. In other words: the common life of man in this hemisphere is undergoing a marked formal or providential change, in ceasing any longer to acknowledge outward sanctions, and learning more and more to acknowledge only inward ones. Of course this improvement in the common lot involves a corresponding demoralization in the private or personal sphere, save where men's personal life distinctly reflects the common life, or acknowledges no law so sacred as that of the public welfare. For there are it must be admitted too many fierce and avaricious natures among us to whom the State no longer exists as the symbol or representative of an outward order in human life, and at the same time does not begin to reveal itself as the symbol or representative of a much more constraining inward order, and all these necessarily look upon their fellow-men as delivered over to their use to be fleeced *ad libitum*. But notwithstanding these deplorable limitations I insist that the distinctively common unconscious life of these spiritual latitudes—that is to say, the heart and mind of the American people, uncontaminated by European and especially sacerdotal pauperism —is one of great elevation. And there is no way to account for the fact but by acknowledging that the American State is really become the vehicle of an enlarged human spirit. I have myself no doubt of the constant operation of this cause.[4] Living as I for many years have done among plain New England people, I am continually struck with the singular natural or interior refinement I encounter in persons who have obviously been all their lives without any exceptional outward advantages. They spread many of them such a humane or impersonal savor around them that they seem "native born" to the skies, and if their culture were only equal to their nature, or their manners as good as their morals, heaven would begin to be realized on earth. But we cannot have everything at once, and they give us the essential at least.

The sum of all I have been alleging is that we as a community are fully launched at length upon that metaphysic sea of being whose mystic waters float the sapphire walls of the New Jerusalem, metropolis of earth and heaven. It is not a city built of stone nor of any material rubbish, since it has no need of sun or moon to enlighten it; but its foundations are laid in the eternal wants or passions of the human heart sympathetic with God's infinitude, and its walls are the laws of man's deathless intelligence sub-jecting all things to his allegiance. Neither is it a city into which shall ever enter any thing that defileth, nor any thing that is contrary to nature, nor yet any thing that produceth a lie; for it is the city of God coming down to men out of the stainless heavens, and therefore full of pure un-mixed blessing to human life, and there shall be no more curse. These things are hard to be believed as falling within the compass of our dis-honored and bedraggled life. But this is only because our feeble-minded and narrow-hearted clergy have been so utterly incompetent as a general thing to divine God's infinitude, or enlighten the public sense in His adorable ways. For do not they themselves regard our beggarly citizenship as the final achievement of God's omnipotence in our nature? Do they not perpetually sacrifice the patient bleeding truth of human brotherhood or society to it? Do they not consequently cling to their squalid and ven-omous little ecclesiasticisms as the last hope of humanity? These very ecclesiasticisms it is which are the foulest stain upon humanity, and do more as Christ alleged than all the world to make men willing children of hell. At the bottom of every human heart, not ecclesiastically perverted, there is, we may be sure, a latent belief in God's spiritual omnipotence or infinitude, and a hope of seeing it eventually realized in our natural form. But what chance have this benign belief and hope of surviving the torrent of falsity and unbelief which now descends from the Christian pulpit, or-thodox and unitarian alike? Christ's own name in the church has become a synonyme for the most signal dishonor shown to God's spiritual perfec-tion, and he who was put to his death of shame only by the righteous men of his day and generation, now finds himself in ours resuscitated to one infinitely more infamous and helpless, in being made the shibboleth of the frankest and most unconscious spiritual hypocrisy ever revealed under heaven.

The best life of the world is growing more than suspicious of the sanc-tity which attaches to facts or events, and insists accordingly upon finding the Christian facts and events interesting or memorable only in so far as they consent to *represent* a truth very much more universal than they lit-erally, or on their face, constitute. And this accounts for that alleged "decease of faith," which has become among our dishonest churchmen the fashionable religious cant of our day. Men of a spiritual or humanitary culture are becoming very contemptuous of any Divine credentials that are not first of all exquisitely and intensely human. They unaffectedly resent the old dogmatic traditions of God's outward or physical activity in creation as dreams of the race's pagan infancy. They are ashamed any longer to acknowledge God as a clever charlatan or conjurer, seeking by an incongruous display of magical power and majesty to propitiate men's inward and rational reverence. And in confirmation of this statement I appeal to your own testimony whether, when any noisy "evangelist" so-called, like the late collapsed Mr. Moody,[5] or the present distended Mr. Cook,[6] comes along to insult this tender, ineffable Divine-natural *renaissance* in us, and menace it with the blight of the lower regions, you have not yourself always observed that the energumenous mountebank never succeeds in doing anything beyond inflaming his fellow-quidnuncs of the conventicle but convert himself into an object of quiet public contempt and derision? This indeed is one of the most heavenly omens of our day, when we consider the hopeless inertness of the mass of men to the solicitations of spiritual truth, that some untidy zealot or other should ever and anon feel himself prompted by his irritable lusts to come forth from his subterranean lair, and vituperate the sunshiny upper world—this sunshiny, respectable, commonplace world—until by his grotesque antics he forces it in spite of itself to recognize the spiritual arrogance and blasphemy which are the veritable soul and substance of our professional religion. I don't, to be sure, very much love this respectable, commonplace world myself, and am very apt to feel my respiration impeded under its decent bondage; but I easily condone all its shortcomings, were they twenty times greater than they are, whenever I am thus made to see how steadfast a providential breakwater it makes to every recurrent wave of men's fanatical self-righteousness, or tyrannous love of dominion.

But it is time to bring this letter, and the whole series of which it is a part, to an end, for though many an interesting point remains to be touched upon, I have substantially finished the task I contemplated when I set out, and my bodily health is no longer good enough to make work for its own sake attractive to me. Now that my task is done, I wish I could have accomplished it more skilfully; though to have accomplished it at all, with the impoverished nerves left me, is matter of no little thanksgiving. I have had no help in writing but that of the Holy Ghost, which nowadays is no private possession, but is the common property of all spiritually upright men, being the identical spirit of their nature. And accordingly my only dread all along has been lest my inevitably private and particular accents should somehow overlay and obscure its public or universal ones. What I thought by its inspiration to say to you at the beginning was a very simple thing. I intended to show the exact harmony between the literal personal facts of Christ's life, and the spiritual or creative truth of which those facts have been our only adequate harbinger and revelation. Christ's suffering and glorified person was but a normal outcome and expression of the infinite creative love towards the human race; a love which contents itself with nothing short of the rescue of the created nature from the hands of the actual or phenomenal creature, and its exaltation to supreme dominion: and if we honor the historic type of this great transaction, much more ought we to honor the infinite and eternal spiritual substance which alone inwardly shaped it, and made it the only symbol of thoroughly perfect or Divine manhood the world has ever known, or ever will know. And having done this I thought to sing a pæan over our despised and dishonored nature, which is at last enthroned in omnipotent majesty above the spiritual world, so that the once divided but now united realms of heaven and hell fall beneath it, and equally attest its will: or if not equally, who knows whether in the miraculous providence of God, what is last in rank may not as heretofore avouch itself first in use?

This I repeat was all in effect I intended to say, and so do justice to the peaceful spiritual meaning of the Christian facts as they are reported in the gospels. But I found my pathway so beset with gainsaying not only on the part of our professional religionists, but on that also of our sectarian scientific zealots, that I was obliged to pay my respects to these several opponents as I went along, so that in spite of myself my voice grew full of tumult even in setting forth the pacific gospel truth. The sectarian religionist cleaves to the Christian facts, *but denies their subserviency to a higher order of truth.* The sectarian "scientist," as he is called, denies the authenticity of the Christian facts *in submission to a lower order of facts.* I hold the Christian facts to be authentic, because I see them to be needful ultimates or exponents of otherwise undiscoverable and inconceivable spiritual truth. Indeed I hold the life, death, and ascension of Jesus Christ to be the only facts of human history which are not in themselves illusory or fallacious, because they alone base a new creation in man to which every fibre of his nature—starved and revolted by the actual creation—eagerly responds. But viewing the facts absolutely: that is, regarding them apart from the light they reflect upon the creative infinitude and the destiny of man the creature of that infinitude, and consequently as designed merely to set off the person of Christ to the everlasting homage of mankind: they seem to me utterly flat, vapid, and contemptible. I by no means desire to apologize then for the contentious strain of my letter, but prefer to end by rehearsing a lovely bit of Swedenborg's experience.

"Once upon a time a numerous crowd of spirits was about me which I heard as a flux of something disorderly. The spirits complained, apprehending that a total destruction was at hand, for in the crowd there was no sign of association, and this made them fear destruction, which they supposed also would be total as is the case when such things [namely, the absence of mutual association] happen. But in the midst of this disorderly flux of spirits I apperceived A SOFT SOUND ANGELICALLY SWEET in which was nothing but harmony. The angelic choirs were *within,* and the crowd of spirits to whom the discord belonged was *without*. This flowing angelic strain continued a long while, and it was said that hereby was represented how the Lord rules things confused and disorderly which are without or on the surface, namely: by virtue of A CENTRAL PEACE, whereby the inharmonic things in the circumference are reduced into order, each being restored from the error of its nature."

If then you discern the central peace which is in my little book, I do not think its superficial polemics will seem out of place. And so, farewell.

NOTES

1. The reference is to John Stuart Mill, one of James's favorite philosophers. —Editor's note.

2. Swedenborg accordingly traces the existence of the hells to the strength of this illusion in men, and this undeniably is a sufficient foundation for them. That is to say, the hells simply mean—nothing more and nothing less—the enforced or obligatory companionship of all those among men who feel no inward *liaison*, or Divine-human bond of cohesion, drawing them to unity, and hence depend for their highest happiness upon the activity of the prudential instinct in them, or a life involving the perpetual balance of hope and fear. And if men really persuade themselves that their Divinely given manhood or freedom involves the power of being good or evil at their own pleasure, I cannot for my part see that the hells are not the logical spontaneous outcome of such a persuasion. In fact their existence at once ceases to be a mystery, and becomes an open exigency of human welfare, an obvious inevitable necessity of man's natural development. For human nature, or the human race, is absolutely conditioned for its development upon man's power to love God (that is, infinite goodness and truth) *apparently*, but not really, of himself; or as Swedenborg writing in Latin prefers to say, *as* of himself, but not *of* himself. For if man spontaneously loved goodness, loved it of his own natural force, he would be God, and no longer a creature of God; and yet, so long as he does not love God or goodness of himself, if he did not at the same time love Him *apparently* of himself, or *as* of himself, he would not even have a negative approximation to his creative source, much less furnish a background or basis to the Divine being for the development of human nature. And failing both a positive and negative relation to God, of course the man can have no reality in him, spiritual or natural, and must remain the subject of a mere illusory or fantastic existence: and to be such a subject is to be a hell in least or miniature form.

3. This tradition does not appear to have profited men much intellectually, but doubtless it has kept their memory, which is the porch of the mind, open to the admission of the spiritual truth on the subject. I remember a good many years ago conversing on this topic with a highly valued friend, who was besides a very distinguished name in literature. And he said in reply to an account I had been giving him of Swedenborg's intellectual position with respect to the Christian revelation: *The fatal criticism upon Christ's pretension to Divinity will always be the fact of his having ignominiously succumbed to his persecutors, when if his personal pretension were well founded he ought to have annihilated them. If Christ had ever authentically revealed Deity, he would have flashed home the conviction of his truth to every man that saw him, in sheer despite too of the man's strongest rational prepossessions to the contrary.* I ventured to rejoin, that

my friend's own notion upon the subject seemed to reduce poor deity to what the French would call an *impasse* within his own creation, or what our own rustics would call "a very hard fix," inasmuch as it neither allows him to become known in himself, nor yet permits him to reveal himself to men's knowledge in the nature of his creature, without effectually blighting at the same time all that makes that nature respectable, namely, the creature's freedom and rationality. This freedom and rationality, which alone give the creature a consciousness of manhood, are however what actually prevent his ever truly knowing God, for he both instinctively and deliberately claims these superb attributes as proper to himself or *his own* absolutely, and not exclusively as *God's attributes in his common nature.* A revelation from God accordingly which should involve the least practical dishonor to these attributes in man, is not to be thought of as possible. In fact the only revelation at all possible or thinkable from God to man, is one which conciliates every man's private freedom and rationality to it, by showing that God himself is the sole and infinite substance of these attributes, only in natural or personal, that is, universal and unitary, human form.

4. It ought not to be forgotten in this connection that the form of our polity bears on its very face, that is, in its name, an intimation of the spiritual change it represents. It is not America, but the UNITED STATES *of America,* "one out of many," as its motto reads, to which the expiring states of Europe bow, or do deepest homage, in sending over to these shores their starving populations to be nourished and clothed and otherwise nursed into citizenship, which is a condition preliminary to their being socialized.

5. The reference is to Dwight Lyman Moody (1837–1899), the foremost American evangelist in the last quarter of the nineteenth century, who became particularly well known for conducting mass religious crusades in large cities throughout the United States and Great Britain.—Editor's note.

6. Thomas Cook (1808–1892), founder of the famous English travel service, later became an evangelical missionary for the Baptist Association and an advocate of temperance.—Editor's note.

Representative Men and Ideas

17

MR. EMERSON

This essay on Emerson from an uncompleted manuscript entitled "Spiritual Creation" is actually a revision of an earlier and more deferential essay on Emerson which James had written a dozen years before. The earlier essay also had remained in manuscript until William James placed it with the *Atlantic* a year after the Emerson centenary in 1903. The later version, reproduced here, which the elder James had reworked in order to contrast his own insistence upon the necessity of a sense of sin with Emerson's utter lack of one, is by all odds the more discerning and acute. However, the earlier version possesses interest if only because of the introductory note which William produced for it, defining therein from his own point of view the chief religious differences between Emerson and his father:

> My father was a theologian of the "twice-born" type, an out-and-out Lutheran, who believed that the moral law existed solely to fill us with loathing for the idea of our own merits, and to make us turn to God's grace as our only opportunity. But God's grace, in Mr. James' system, was not for the individual in isolation: the sphere of redemption was *Society*. In a Society organized divinely our *natures* will not be altered, but our spontaneities, because they will then work harmoniously, will all work innocently, and the Kingdom of heaven will have come. With these ideas, Mr. James was both fascinated and baffled by his friend Emerson. The personal graces of the man seemed to prefigure the coming millennium, but the resolute individualism of his thought, and the way in which his imagination rested on superior personages, and on heroic anecdotes about them, as if these were creation's ultimates, set my father's philosophy at defiance. For him no man

was superior to another in the final plan.
Emerson would listen, I fancy, as if charmed, to
James' talk of the "divine natural Humanity," but
he would never *subscribe;* and this, from one
whose native gifts were so suggestive of that same
Humanity, was disappointing. Emerson, in short,
was a "once-born" man; he lived in moral
distinctions, and recognized no need of a
redemptive process.

The following selection entitled "Mr. Emerson"
constitutes chapter 10 of *Spiritual Creation* and is
reprinted from *The Literary Remains of the Late Henry
James,* edited, with an introduction by William James
(Boston, 1884), 293–302.

———•◦•———

At all events, if we are still to go on cherishing any such luxury as a
private conscience towards God, I greatly prefer for my own part that it
should be an evil conscience. Conscience was always intended as a rebuke
and never as an exhilaration to the private citizen; and so let it flourish
till the end of our wearisome civilization. There are many signs, however,
that this end is near. My recently deceased friend Mr. Emerson, for example, was all his days an arch traitor to our existing civilized regimen, inasmuch as he unconsciously managed to set aside its fundamental principle
in doing without conscience, which was the entire secret of his very exceptional interest to men's speculation. He betrayed it to be sure without
being at all aware of what he was doing; but this was really all that he
distinctively did to my observation. His nature had always been so innocent, so unaffectedly innocent, that when in later life he began to cultivate
a club consciousness, and to sip a glass of wine or smoke a cigar, I felt
very much outraged by it. I felt very much as if some renowned Boston
belle had suddenly collapsed and undertaken to sell newspapers at a street
corner. "Why, Emerson, is this *you* doing such things?" I exclaimed.
"What profanation! Do throw the unclean things behind your back!" But,
no; he was actually proud of his accomplishments! This came from his
never knowing (intellectually) what he stood for in the evolution of New
England life. He was lineally descended to begin with, from a half-score
of comatose New England clergymen, in whose behalf probably the religious instinct had been used up. Or, what to their experience had been
religion, became in that of their descendant *life.* The actual truth, at any
rate, was that he never felt a movement of the life of conscience from the
day of his birth till that of his death. I could never see any signs of such
a life in him. I remember, to be sure, that he had a great gift of friendship,
and that he was very plucky in behalf of his friends whenever they felt
themselves assailed—as plucky as a woman. For instance, whenever

Wendell Phillips[1] ventilated his not untimely wit at the expense of our club-house politicians, Emerson, hearing his friends among these latter complain, grew indignant, and for several days you would hear nothing from his lips but excessive eulogies of Mr. Garrison,[2] which sounded like nothing else in the world but revilings of Mr. Phillips. But, bless your heart! there was not a bit of conscience in a bushel of such experiences, but only wounded friendship, which is a totally different and much lower thing.

The infallible mark of conscience is that it is always a subjective judgment couched in some such language as this: "God be merciful to *me* a sinner!" and never an objective judgment such as this: *God damn Wendell Phillips, or some other of my friends!* This latter judgment is always an outbreak of ungovernable temper on our part, and was never known to reach the ear of God save in this guise: *God* BLESS W. P. *or any other friend implicated!* Now Emerson was seriously incapable of a subjective judgment upon himself; he did not know the inward difference between good and evil, so far as he was himself concerned. No doubt he perfectly comprehended the outward or moral difference between these things; but I insist upon it that he never so much as dreamed of any inward or spiritual difference between them. For this difference is vitally seen only when oneself seems unchangeably evil to his own sight, and one's neighbor unchangeably good in the comparison. How could Emerson ever have known this difference? I am satisfied that he never in his life had felt a temptation *to bear false-witness* against his neighbor, *to steal, to commit adultery,* or *to murder;* how then should he have ever experienced what is technically called a conviction of sin?—that is, a conviction of himself as *evil* before God, and all other men as *good.* One gets a conviction of the evil that attaches to the natural selfhood in man in no other way than—as I can myself attest—by this growing acquaintance with his own moral infirmity, and the consequent gradual decline of his self-respect. For I myself had known all these temptations—in forms of course more or less modified— by the time I was fourteen or fifteen years old; so that by the time I had got to be twenty-five or thirty (which was the date of my first acquaintance with Emerson) I was saturated with a sense of spiritual evil—no man ever more so possibly, since I felt thoroughly *self*-condemned before God. Good heavens! how soothed and comforted I was by the innocent lovely look of my new acquaintance, by his tender courtesy, his generous laudatory appreciation of my crude literary ventures! and how I used to lock myself up with him in his bed-room, swearing that before the door was opened I would arrive at the secret of his immense superiority to the common herd of literary men! I might just as well have locked myself up with a handful of diamonds, so far as any capacity of self-cognizance existed in him. I found in fact, before I had been with him a week, that the immense superiority I ascribed to him was altogether personal or practical—by no means intellectual; that it came to him by birth or genius like a woman's beauty or charm of manners; that no other account was to be given of it in truth than that Emerson himself was an unsexed woman, a veritable fruit of almighty power in the sphere of our *nature*.

This after a while grew to be a great discovery to me; but I was always more or less provoked to think that Emerson himself should take no intellectual stock in it. On the whole I may say that at first I was greatly disappointed in him, because his intellect never kept the promise which his lovely face and manners held out to me. He was to my senses a literal divine presence in the house with me; and we cannot recognize literal divine presences in our houses without feeling sure that they will be able to say something of critical importance to one's intellect. It turned out that any average old dame in a horse-car would have satisfied my intellectual rapacity just as well as Emerson. My standing intellectual embarrassment for years had been to get at the bottom of the difference between law and gospel in humanity—between the head and the heart of things—between the great God almighty, in short, and the intensely wooden and ridiculous gods of the nations. Emerson, I discovered immediately, had never been the least of an expert in this sort of knowledge; and though his immense personal fascination always kept up, he at once lost all intellectual prestige to my regard. I even thought that I had never seen a man more profoundly devoid of spiritual understanding. This prejudice grew, of course, out of my having inherited an altogether narrow ecclesiastical notion of what spiritual understanding was. I supposed it consisted unmistakably in some doctrinal lore concerning man's regeneration, to which, however, my new friend was plainly and signally incompetent. Emerson, in fact, derided this doctrine, smiling benignly whenever it was mentioned. I could make neither head nor tail of him according to men's ordinary standards—the only thing that I was sure of being that he, like Christ, was somehow divinely begotten. He seemed to me unmistakably virgin-born whenever I looked at him, and reminded me of nothing so much as of those persons dear to Christ's heart who should come after him professing no allegiance to him—having never heard his name pronounced, and yet perfectly fulfilling his will. He never seemed for a moment to antagonize the church of his own consent, but only out of condescension to his interlocutor's weakness. In fact he was to all appearance entirely ignorant of the church's existence until you recalled it to his imagination; and even then I never knew anything so implacably and uniformly mild as his judgments of it were. He had apparently lived all his life in a world where it was only subterraneously known; and, try as you would, you could never persuade him that any the least living power attached to it. The same profound incredulity characterized him in regard to the State; and it was only in his enfeebled later years that he ever lent himself to the idea of society as its destined divine form. I am not sure indeed that the lending was ever very serious. But he was always greedy, with all a Yankee's greediness, after facts, and would at least appear to listen to you with earnest respect and sympathy whenever you plead for society as the redeemed form of our nature.

In short he was, as I have said before, fundamentally treacherous to civilization, without being at all aware himself of the fact. He himself, I venture to say, was peculiarly unaware of the fact. He appeared to me utterly unconscious of himself as either good or evil. He had no conscience, in fact, and lived by perception, which is an altogether lower or less spiritual faculty. The more universalized a man is by genius or natural birth, the less is he spiritually individualized, making up in breadth of endowment what he lacks in depth. This was remarkably the case with Emerson. In his books or public capacity he was constantly electrifying you by sayings full of divine inspiration. In his talk or private capacity he was one of the least remunerative men I have ever encountered. No man could look at him speaking (or when he was silent either, for that matter) without having a vision of the divinest beauty. But when you went to him to hold discourse about the wondrous phenomenon, you found him absolutely destitute of reflective power. He had apparently no private personality; and if any visitor thought he discerned traces of such a thing, you may take for granted that the visitor himself was a man of large imaginative resources. He was nothing else than a show-figure of almighty power in our nature; and that he was destitute of all the apparatus of humbuggery that goes to eke out more or less the private pretension in humanity, only completed and confirmed the extraordinary fascination that belonged to him. He was full of living inspiration to me whenever I saw him; and yet I could find in him no trivial sign of the selfhood which I found in other men. He was like a vestal virgin, indeed, always in ministry upon the altar; but the vestal virgin had doubtless a prosaic side also, which related her to commonplace people. Now Emerson was so far *unlike* the virgin: he had no prosaic side relating him to ordinary people. Judge Hoar[3] and Mr. John Forbes[4] constituted his spontaneous political conscience; and his domestic one (equally spontaneous) was supplied by loving members of his own family—so that he only connected with the race at secondhand, and found all the material business of life such as voting and the payment of taxes transacted for *him* with marvellous lack of friction.

Incontestably the main thing about him, however, as I have already said, was that he unconsciously brought you face to face with the infinite in humanity. When I looked upon myself, or upon the ordinary rabble of ecclesiastics and politicians, everything in us seemed ridiculously undivine. When I looked upon Emerson, these same undivine things were what gave *him* his manifest divine charm. The reason was that in him everything seemed innocent by the transparent absence of selfhood, and in us everything seemed foul and false by its preternatural activity. The difference between us was made by innocence altogether. I never thought it was a real or spiritual difference, but only a natural or apparent one. But such as it was, it gave me my first living impression of the great God almighty who alone is at work in human affairs, avouching his awful and adorable spiritual infinitude only through the death and hell wrapped up in our finite experience. This was Emerson's incontestable virtue to every one who appreciated him, that he recognized no God outside of himself and his interlocutor, and recognized him there only as the *liason* between the two, taking care that all their intercourse should be holy with a holiness undreamed of before by man or angel. For it is not a holiness taught by books or the example of tiresome, diseased, self-conscious saints, but simply by one's own redeemed flesh and blood. In short, the only holiness which Emerson recognized, and for which he consistently lived, was innocence. And innocence—glory be to God's spiritual incarnation in our nature!—has no other root in us than our unconscious flesh and bones. That is to say, it attaches only to what is definitively universal or natural in our experience, and hence appropriates itself to individuals only in so far as they learn to denude themselves of personality or self-consciousness; which reminds one of Christ's mystical saying: *He that findeth his life (in himself) shall lose it, and he that loseth his life for my sake shall find it.*

NOTES

1. James here was referring to Wendell Phillips (1811–1884), a prominent Boston abolitionist who was active in behalf of this and other causes on the lyceum circuit.—Editor's note.

2. William Lloyd Garrison (1805–1879) was the spearhead of the New England abolitionist movement which he helped direct partially through his editorship of *The Liberator*.—Editor's note.

3. Ebenezer Rockwood Hoar (1816–1895), a prominent American jurist known for his moral rectitude, led the antislavery wing of the Whig Party; John Murray Forbes (1813–1898) was a businessman and statesman whose eminent good sense, personal integrity, and self-modesty commended him to Emerson.—Editor's note.

18

SOME PERSONAL
RECOLLECTIONS OF
CARLYLE

Apart from what they tell us about Carlyle–which
is a great deal–these "personal recollections" are also
important for what they tell us about James himself.
What they exhibit chiefly is James's ability as a
critic not only of ideas but also of persons. If James is
best known for his tendency to see the Man in men,
he still possessed an acute sense of individual
differences and was capable of making the subtlest
kinds of moral discriminations on the basis of things
as concrete but complex as manners, style, and tone.
His capacities as a critic were greatly enhanced, of
course, by virtue of his having an opinion on almost
everything, and, further, because of his willingness to
express these opinions no matter who was involved.
"Truth," James once said, is "essentially combative,"
and he loved a good fight. But, in the selection which
follows, the critic as combatant or censor plays a far
less prominent role than the critic as sympathetic
interpreter and analyst. Judgements are made, but they
carry authority only because James has been able to
evoke, on the basis of little more than remembered
conversations, so vivid an impression of the man
himself, even down, as F. O. Matthiessen once
remarked, to "the very cadences and accents of
Carlyle's voice."
  The following selection first appeared in *The Atlantic
Monthly* in 1881. It is here reprinted from *The Literary
Remains of the Late Henry James,* edited, with an
introduction, by William James (Boston, 1884),
421–33, 439–46, 449–68.

———•◆•———

Thomas Carlyle is incontestably dead at last, by the acknowledgment of
all newspapers. I had, however, the pleasure of an intimate intercourse

with him when he was an infinitely deader man than he is now, or ever will be again, I am persuaded, in the remotest *seculum seculorum* ["infinity"]. I undoubtedly felt myself at the time every whit as dead (spiritually) as he was; and, to tell the truth, I never found him averse to admit my right of insight in regard to myself. But I could never bring him, much as he continually inspired me so to do, to face the philosophic possibility of this proposition in regard to himself. On the contrary, he invariably snorted at the bare presentation of the theme, and fled away from it, with his free, resentful heels high in air, like a spirited horse alarmed at the apparition of a wheelbarrow.

However, in spite of our fundamental difference about this burly life which now is,—one insisting upon death as the properer name for it, the other bent upon maintaining every popular illusion concerning it,—we had for long years what always appeared to me a very friendly intercourse; and I can never show myself sufficiently grateful to his kindly, hospitable *manes* for the many hours of unalloyed entertainment his ungrudging fireside afforded me. I should like to reproduce from my notebook some of the recollections and observations with which those sunny hours impressed me and so amuse, if I can, the readers of "The Atlantic." These reminiscences were written many years ago, when the occurrences to which they relate were fresh in my memory; and they are exact, I need not say, almost to the letter. They will tend, I hope and am sure, to enhance the great personal prestige Carlyle enjoyed during life; for I cherish the most affectionate esteem for his memory, and could freely say or do nothing to wound that sentiment in any honest human breast. At the same time, I cannot doubt that the proper effect of much that I have to say will be to lower the estimation many persons have formed of Carlyle as a man of ideas. And this I should not be sorry for. Ideas are too divinely important to derive any consequence from the persons who maintain them; they are images or revelations, in intellectual form, of divine or infinite good, and therefore reflect upon men all the sanctity they possess, without receiving a particle from them. This estimate of Carlyle, *as a man of ideas*, always struck me as unfounded in point of fact. I think his admirers, at least his distant admirers, generally mistook the claim he made upon attention. They were apt to regard him as eminently a man of thought; whereas his intellect, as it seemed to me, except where his prejudices were involved, had not got beyond the stage of instinct. They insisted upon finding him a philosopher; but he was only and consummately a man of genius. They had the fatuity to deem him a great teacher; but he never avouched himself to be anything else than a great critic.

I intend no disparagement of Carlyle's moral qualities, in saying that he was almost sure finally to disappoint one's admiration. I merely mean to say that he was without that breadth of humanitary sympathy which one likes to find in distinguished men; that he was deficient in spiritual as opposed to moral force. He was a man of great simplicity and sincerity in his personal manners and habits, and exhibited even an engaging sensi-

bility to the claims of one's physical fellowship. But he was wholly impene-
trable to the solicitations both of your heart and your understanding. I
think he felt a helpless dread and distrust of you instantly that he found
you had any positive hope in God or practical love to man. His own intellectual life consisted so much in bemoaning the vices of his race, or drew
such inspiration from despair, that he could not help regarding a man
with contempt the instant he found him reconciled to the course of history.
Pity is the highest style of intercourse he allowed himself with his kind.
He compassionated all his friends in the measure of his affection for them.
"Poor John Sterling," he used always to say; "poor John Mill, poor Frederic
Maurice, poor Neuberg, poor Arthur Helps, poor little Browning, poor
little Lewes,"[1] and so on; as if the temple of his friendship were a hospital,
and all its inmates scrofulous or paralytic. You wondered how any mere
mortal got legitimately endowed with a commiseration so divine for the
inferior race of man; and the explanation that forced itself upon you was
that he enjoyed an inward power and beatitude so redundant as naturally
to seek relief in these copious outward showers of compassionate benediction. Especially did Carlyle conceive that no one could be actively interested in the progress of the species without being intellectually off his
balance, and in need of tenderness from all his friends. His own sympathy went out freely to cases of individual suffering, and he believed that
there was an immense amount of *specific* divine mercy practicable to us.
That is to say, he felt keenly whatever appealed to his senses, and willingly
patronized a fitful, because that is a picturesque, Providence in the earth.
He sympathized with the starving Spitalfield weaver; and would have
resented the inhumanity of the slave's condition as sharply as any one,
if he had had visual contact with it, and were not incited, by the subtle
freemasonry that unites aristocratic pretension in literature with the same
pretension in politics, to falsify his human instincts. I remember the
pleasure he took in the promise that Indian corn might be found able to
supplant the diseased potato in Ireland; and he would doubtless have
admitted ether and chloroform to be exquisitely ordained ministers of the
Divine love. But as to any sympathy with human nature itself and its
inexorable wants, or any belief in a breadth of the Divine mercy commensurate with those wants, I could never discern a flavor of either in him. He
scoffed with hearty scorn at the contented imbecility of Church and State
with respect to social problems, but his own indifference to these things,
save in so far as they were available to picturesque palaver, was infinitely
more indolent and contented. He would have been the last man formally
to deny the Divine existence and providence; but that these truths had
any human virtue, any living efficacy to redeem us out of material and
spiritual penury, I do not think he ever dreamt of such a thing. That our
knowledge of God was essentially expansive; that revelation contemplated
its own spiritual enlargement and fulfilment in the current facts of human history, in the growth and enlargement of the human mind itself,—
so that Thomas Carlyle, if only he had not been quite so stubborn and

conceited, might have proved himself far better and not far worse posted in the principles of the Divine administration than even Plato was, and so have freed himself from the dismal necessity he was all his life under to ransack the graves of the dead, in order to find some spangle, still untarnished, of God's reputed presence in our nature,—all this he took every opportunity to assure you was the saddest bosh. "Poor John Mill," he exclaimed one night,—"poor John Mill is writing away there in the Edinburgh Review about what he calls the Philosophy of History! As if any man could ever know the road he is going, when once he gets astride of such a distracted steed as that!"

But to my note-book.

"I happened to be in Carlyle's library, the other day, when a parcel was handed in which contained two books, a present from some American admirer. One of the books proved to be a work of singular intellectual interest, as I afterwards discovered, entitled 'Lectures on the Natural History of Man,' by Alexander Kinmont, of Cincinnati; the other a book of Poems. Carlyle read Mr. Kinmont's titlepage, and exclaimed: 'The natural history of man, forsooth! And from Cincinnati too, of all places on this earth! We had a right, perhaps, to expect some light from that quarter in regard to the natural history of the hog; and I can't but think that if the well-disposed Mr. Kinmont would set himself to study that unperverted mystery he would employ his powers far more profitably to the world. I am sure he would employ them far less wearisomely to me. There!' he continued, handing me the book, 'I freely make over to you all my right of insight into the natural history of man as that history dwells in the portentous brain of Mr. Alexander Kinmont, of Cincinnati, being more than content to wait myself till he condescend to the more intelligible animal.' And then opening to the blank leaf of the volume of Poems, and without more ado, he said, 'Permit me to write my friend Mrs. So-and-So's name here, who perhaps may get some refreshment from the poems of her countryman; for, decidedly, I shall not.' When I suggested to him that he himself did nothing all his days but philosophize in his own way,—that is, from the artist point of view, or ground of mere feeling,—and that his prose habitually decked itself out in the most sensuous garniture of poetry, he affected the air of M. Jourdain, in Molière, and protested, half fun, half earnest, that he was incapable of a philosophic purpose or poetic emotion."

Carlyle had very much of the narrowness, intellectual and moral, which one might expect to find in a descendant of the old Covenanting stock, bred to believe in God as essentially inhuman, and in man, accordingly, as exposed to a great deal of divine treachery and vindictiveness, which were liable to come rattling about his devoted ears the moment his back was turned. I have no idea, of course, that this grim ancestral faith dwelt in Carlyle in any acute, but only in chronic, form. He did not actively acknowledge it; but it was latent in all his intellectual and moral personality, and made itself felt in that cynical, mocking humor and those bursts of tragic pathos which set off all his abstract views of life and destiny. But a genuine pity for man as sinner and sufferer underlay all his concrete judgments; and no thought of unkindness ever entered his bosom except for people who believed in God's undiminished presence and power in human affairs, and were therefore full of hope in our social future. A moral reformer like Louis Blanc or Robert Dale Owen, a political reformer like Mr. Cobden or Mr. Bright, or a dietetic reformer like the late Mr. Greaves or our own Mr. Alcott,[2] was sure to provoke his most acrid intellectual antipathy.

Moral force was the deity of Carlyle's unscrupulous worship,—the force of unprincipled, irresponsible will; and he was ready to glorify every historic vagabond, such as Danton or Mirabeau,[3] in whom that quality reigned supreme. He hated Robespierre[4] because he was inferior in moral or personal force to his rivals, being himself a victim to ideas,—or, as Carlyle phrased it, to formulas. Picturesqueness in man and Nature was the one key to his intellectual favor; and it made little difference to his artist eye whether the man were spiritually angel or demon. Besides, one never practically surmounts his own idea of the Divine name; and Carlyle, inheriting and cherishing for its picturesque capabilities this rude Covenanting conception, which makes God a being of the most aggravated moral dimensions, of a wholly superhuman egotism or sensibility to his own consequence, of course found Mahomet, William the Conqueror, John Knox, Frederic the Second of Prussia, Goethe, men after God's own heart, and coolly told you that no man in history was ever unsuccessful who deserved to be otherwise.

Too much cannot be said of Carlyle in personal respects. He was a man of even a genial practical morality, an unexceptionable good neighbor, friend, and citizen. But in all larger or human regards he was a literalist of the most unqualified pattern, incapable of uttering an inspiring or even a soothing word in behalf of any struggling manifestation of human hope. It is true, he abused every recognized guide of the political world with such hearty good-will that many persons claimed him at once as an intelligent herald of the new or spiritual divine advent in human nature. But the claim was absurdly unfounded. He was an amateur prophet exclusively,— a prophet "on his own hook," or in the interest of his own irritable cuticle,— without a glimmer of sympathy with the distinctively public want, or a gleam of insight into its approaching divine relief; a harlequin in the guise of Jeremiah, who fed you with laughter in place of tears, and put the old prophetic sincerity out of countenance by his broad, persistent winks at the by-standers over the foot-lights.

My note-book has this record:—

"I heard Carlyle, last night, maintain his habitual thesis against Mr. Tennyson,[5] in the presence of Mr. Moxon[6] and one or two other persons. Carlyle rode a very high horse indeed, being inspired to mount and lavishly ply the spur by Mr. Tennyson, for whom he has the liveliest regard; and it was not long before William the Conqueror and Oliver Cromwell were trotted out of their mouldy cerements, to affront Sir Robert Peel[7] and the Irish viceroy, whose name escapes me. 'Nothing,' Carlyle over and over again said and sung,–'nothing will ever pry England out of the slough she is in, but to stop looking at Manchester as heaven's gate, and free-trade as the everlasting God's law man is bound to keep holy. The human stomach, I admit, is a memorable necessity, which will not allow itself, moreover, to be long neglected; and political economy no doubt has its own right to be heard among all our multifarious jargons. But I tell you the stomach is not the supreme necessity our potato-evangelists make it, nor is political economy any tolerable substitute for the eternal veracities. To think of our head men believin' the stomach to be the man, and legislatin' for the stomach, and compellin' this old England into the downright vassalage of the stomach! Such men as these, forsooth, to rule England,–the England once ruled by Oliver Cromwell! No wonder the impudent knave O'Connell[8] takes them by the beard, shakes his big fist in their faces, does his own dirty will, in fact, with England, altogether! *Oh, for a day of Duke William again!'*

"In vain his fellow Arcadian protested that England was no longer the England of Duke William, nor even of Oliver Cromwell, but a totally new England, with self-consciousness all new and unlike theirs; Carlyle only chanted or canted the more lustily his inevitable ding-dong, 'Oh, for a day of Duke William again!'

"Tired out at last, the long-suffering poet cried, 'I suppose you *would* like your Duke William back, to cut off some twelve hundred Cambridge-shire gentlemen's legs, and leave their owners squat upon the ground, that they mightn't be able any longer to bear arms against him!' 'Ah!' shrieked out the remorseless bagpipes, in a perfect colic of delight to find its su-preme blast thus unwarily invoked,–'ah! that *was* no doubt a very sad thing for the duke to do; but somehow he conceived he had a right to do it,–and upon the whole he had!' 'Let me tell your returning hero one thing, then,' replied his practical-minded friend, 'and that is that he had better steer clear of my precincts, or he will feel my knife in his guts very soon.' "

It was in fact this indignant and unaffected prose of the distinguished poet which alone embalmed the insincere colloquy to my remembrance, or set its colors, so to speak.

Carlyle was, in truth, a hardened declaimer. He talked in a way vastly to tickle his auditors, and his enjoyment of their amusement was lively enough to sap his own intellectual integrity. Artist like, he precipitated himself upon the picturesque in character and manners wherever he found it, and he did not care a jot what incidental interest his precipitancy lacer-ated. He was used to harp so successfully on one string,–the importance to men of *doing*,–and the mere artistic effects he produced so infatuated him, that the whole thing tumbled off at last into a sheer insincerity, and he no longer saw any difference between *doing* well and *doing* ill. He who best denounced a canting age became himself its most signal illustration, since even his denunciation of the vice succumbed to the prevalent usage, and announced itself at length a shameless cant.

Of course I have no intention to represent this state of things as a conscious one on Carlyle's part. On the contrary, it was a wholly unconscious one, betokening such a complete absorption of his faculties in the talking function as to render him unaffectedly indifferent to the practical action which such talk, when sincere, ought always to contemplate. . . .

He was not constitutionally arrogant; he was a man of real modesty; he was even, I think, constitutionally diffident. He was a man, in short, whom you could summer and winter with, without ever having your self-respect wantonly affronted as it habitually is by mere conventional men and women. He was, to be sure, a very sturdy son of earth, and capable at times of exhibiting the most helpless natural infirmity. But he would never ignore nor slight your human fellowship because your life or opinions exposed you to the reproach of the vain, the frivolous, the self-seeking. He would of course curse your gods ever and anon in a manful way, and scoff without mercy at your tenderest intellectual hopes and aspirations; but upon yourself personally, all the while,—especially if you should drink strong tea and pass sleepless nights, or suffer from tobacco, or be menaced with insanity, or have a gnawing cancer under your jacket,—he would have bestowed the finest of his wheat. He might not easily have forgiven you if you used a vegetable diet, especially if you did so on principle; and he would surely have gnashed his teeth upon you if you should have claimed any scientific knowledge or philosophic insight into the social problem,—the problem of man's coming destiny upon the earth. But within these limits you would have felt how truly human was the tie that bound you to this roaring, riotous, most benighted, yet not unbenignant brother. Leave England, above all, alone; let her stumble on from one slough of despond to another, so that he might have the endless serene delight of walloping her chief "niggers,"—Peel, Palmerston, Russell, Brougham,[9] and the rest,—and he would dwell forever in friendly content with you. But only hint your belief that these imbecile statesmen were the true statesmen for the time, the only men capable, *in virtue of that very imbecility,* of truly coworking with the Providence that governs the world, and is guiding it full surely to a haven of final peace and blessedness, and he would fairly deluge you with the vitriol of his wrath. No; all that can be said for Carlyle on this score is, that, having an immense eye for color, an immense genius for scenic effect, he seized with avidity upon every crazy, time-stained, dishonored rag of personality that still fluttered in the breeze of history, and lent itself to his magical tissues; and he did not like that any one should attempt to dispute his finery with him. The habit was tyrannous, no doubt, but no harm, and only amusement, could have come of it; least of all would it have pushed him to his melancholy "latter-day" drivel, had it not been for the heartless people who hang, for their own private ends, upon the skirts of every pronounced man of genius, and do their best, by stimulating his vanity, to make him feel himself a god.

I again have recourse to my note-book.

"I happened to be at Mr. Carlyle's a Sunday or two since, when a large company was present, and the talk fell upon repudiation, which Jefferson Davis and Mississippi legislation are bringing into note. Among others a New Yorker was present, to whom his friends give the title of General, for no other reason that I can discover but to signify that he is nothing in particular,—an agreeable-mannered man, however, with something of that new-born innocence of belief and expectation in his demeanor and coun- tenance which Englishmen find it so hard to do justice to in Americans; and he was apparently defending, when I went in, our general repute for honesty from the newspaper odium which is beginning to menace it. Mr. Henry Woodman,—I will call him,—from Massachusetts, was also present; an amiable, excellent man, full of knowledge and belief in a certain way, who in former times was a Unitarian clergyman in good standing, but having made what seemed to him a notable discovery, namely, that there is no personal devil,—none, at least, who is over six feet in height, and who therefore is not essentially amenable to police discipline,—he forthwith snaps his fingers at the faded terror, drops his profession, and betakes him- self to agriculture, for which he has a passion. He overflows with good feeling, and is so tickled with the discovery he has made of old Nick's long imposture, that he never makes an acquaintance without instantly telling him of it, nor ever keeps one without instantly, in season and out of sea- son, reminding him of it. He had saturated Carlyle's outward ear with the intelligence, but to no inward profit. For Carlyle's working conception of the Deity involves so much of diabolism that the decease and sepulture of a thousand legitimate old bogies, authentically chronicled in 'The Times,' would hardly enliven his sombre imagination; and he entertains a friendly contempt and compassion, accordingly, for the emancipated Mr. Woodman, which are always touching to me to witness. The evening in question my attention was suddenly arrested by Carlyle saying somewhat loudly to General——that we were all on our way to the devil in America, and that unless we turned a short corner we should infallibly bring up in that perilous company. Mr. Woodman was talking, at the moment, with his hostess, of whom he is deserved favorite, at the other extremity of the room; but he would have heard the name of his vanished adversary had it been pronounced in a whisper. The grateful sound no sooner reached his ear, accordingly, than he averted himself from his companion, and cried out, delighted, 'What devil do you speak of, Mr. Carlyle?' 'What devil, do you ask?' Carlyle fairly roared back in reply. 'What devil, do you ask, Mr. Woodman? The devil, Mr. Woodman, that has been known in these parts from the beginning, and is not likely soon to become unknown,—the father of *all liars, swindlers, and repudiators,* Mr. Woodman! The devil that in this Old World boasts a very numerous though unconscious progeny, and in your New World, Mr. Woodman, seems, from all accounts, to be pro- ducing a still more numerous and still more unconscious one! That is just the devil I mean, Mr. Woodman; and woe be to you and yours the day you vote *him* lifeless!'

"Mr. Woodman was discouraged, and at once reverted to his quiet col-

loquy with his softer companion, while the rest of us profited by the ex-
hilarating breeze he had so suddenly conjured up. 'Speaking of the evil
one,' General——hastened to say, 'I have been visiting to-day subterranean
London, its sewers, and so forth,'—and the conversation soon fell into its
ordinary undulations. But earnest as Carlyle's reply to his friend undoubtedly sounded, any listener would have very much mistaken the truth
of the case if he had supposed that it meant anything more than his hopeless, helpless, and consequently irritable way of contemplating social facts
and tendencies. Carlyle does not believe, of course, in the literal personality of the devil near so much as Mr. Woodman does; that is, he believes
in it so little as to disdain the trouble of denying it. But he has a profound
faith that there is at the head of affairs some very peremptory person or
other, who will infallibly have his own will in the end, or override all other
wills; and he is able, consequently, to variegate his conversation and writing with lurid lights that seem most orthodox and pious to innocent imaginations, and would make the ghost of John Knox roll up the whites of his
eyes in grateful astonishment. Whatever be Carlyle's interest in any question of life or destiny, he talks so well and writes so well that it can hardly
escape being swallowed up in talk or writing; and he would regard you as
a bore of the largest calibre if, talking in the same sense with him, you
yet did not confine yourself to talk, but went on to organize your ideas in
some appropriate action."

You would say, remembering certain passages in Carlyle's books,—nota-
bly his "Past and Present" and his pamphlet on Chartism,—that he had a
very lively sympathy with reform and a profound sentiment of human
fellowship. He did, indeed, dally with the divine ideas long enough to suck
them dry of their rhetorical juices, but then dropped them, to lavish contempt on them ever after when anybody else should chance to pick them
up and cherish them, not for their rhetorical uses, but their absolute truth.
He had no belief in society as a living, organizing force in history, but only
as an empirical necessity of the race. He had no conception of human
brotherhood or equality as the profoundest truth of science, disclosing a
hell in the bosom wherever it is not allowed to reveal a heaven, but only
as an emotional or sentimental experience of happily endowed natures.
On the contrary, he used to laugh and fling out his scornful heels at the
bare suggestion of such a thing, much as a tropical savage would laugh
and fling out his heels at the suggestion of frozen rivers. He looked at
the good and evil in our nature as final or absolute quantities, and saw no
way, consequently, of ever utilizing the evil element. He saw no possible
way of dealing with weak races but by reducing them to slavery; no way
of dealing successfully with evil men but by applying lynch law to them,
and crushing them out of existence. In short he had not the least conception of history as a *divine drama, designed to educate man into a self-
knowledge and the knowledge of God;* and consequently could never meet
you on any ground of objective truth, but only on that of your subjective
whim or caprice. It was this intellectual incapacity he was under to esteem

truth for its own sake, or value it except for the personal prestige it confers, that made him so impotent to help a struggling brother on to daylight, and fixed him in so intense and irritable a literary *self*-consciousness. . . .

Carlyle used to strike me as a man of genius or consummate executive faculty, and not primarily of sympathy or understanding. Every one is familiar with this discrimination. We all know some one or other who is a genius in his way, or has a power of doing certain things as no one else can do them, and as arrests our great admiration. And yet, as likely as not, this person so marvelously endowed, is a somewhat uncomfortable person apart from his particular line of action. Very possibly, and even probably, he is domineering and irritable to the pitch of insanity in his personal intercourse with others, and his judgments are apt to be purely whimsical, or reflect his own imperious will. We admire the genius in his own sphere of work or production, and feel a divine force in him that moves the world. But at the same time we are persuaded that there is something in us, not half so resplendent as genius, which is yet a vast deal better; and that is spiritual character, or a cultivated deference to the humblest forms of goodness and truth. At best, genius is only a spiritual temperament in man, and therefore, though it serves as an excellent basis for spiritual character, should yet never be confounded with it. The genius is God's spoiled child upon earth; woe be unto him, if he look upon that indulgence as consecrating him for the skies as well! Character, or spiritual manhood, is not created, but only communicated. It is not our birthright, but is only brought about with our own zealous privity, or solicitous concurrence in some sort. It is honestly wrought out of the most literal conformity to the principles of universal justice. It puts up with no histrionic piety, tramples under foot the cheap humility of the prayer-book and the pew, and insists upon the just thing at the just moment, under pain of eternal damnation,—which means, *an abandonment to the endless illusions of self-love*. Hence it is, that, while the genius cuts such a lustrous figure in the eyes of men, and wins oftentimes so loud a renown, we yet know many a nameless person whom we value more than a raft of genii, because we confide without stint in their living truth, their infinite rectitude of heart and understanding. We like the genius, or whatsoever makes life glorious, powerful, divine, on Sundays or holidays; but we prefer the ordinary, unconscious, unostentatious stuff which alone keeps it sweet and human on all other days.

It always appeared to me that Carlyle valued truth and good as a painter does his pigments,—not for what they are in themselves, but for the effects they lend themselves to in the sphere of production. Indeed, he always exhibited a contempt, so characteristic as to be comical, for every one whose zeal for truth or good led him to question existing institutions with a view to any practical reform. He himself was wont to question established institutions and dogmas with the utmost license of scepticism, but he obviously meant nothing beyond the production of a certain literary surprise, or the enjoyment of his own æsthetic power. Nothing maddened him so much as to be mistaken for a reformer, really intent upon the interests of God's righteousness upon the earth, which are the interests of universal justice. This is what made him hate Americans, and call us a nation of bores,—that we took him at his word, and reckoned upon him as a sincere well-wisher to his species. He hated us, because a secret instinct told him that our exuberant faith in him would never be justified by closer knowledge; for no one loves the man who forces him upon a premature recognition of himself. I recall the uproarious mirth with which he and Mrs. Carlyle used to recount the incidents of a visit they had received from a young New England woman, and describe the earnest, devout homage her credulous soul had rendered him. It was her first visit abroad, and she supposed—poor thing!—that these famous European writers and talkers, who so dominated her fancy at a distance, really meant all they said, were as innocent and lovely in their lives as in their books; and she no sooner crossed Carlyle's threshold, accordingly, than her heart offered its fragrance to him as liberally as the flower opens to the sun. And Carlyle, the inveterate comedian, instead of being humbled to the dust by the revelation which such simplicity suddenly flashed upon his own eyes of his essentially dramatic genius and exploits, was irritated, vexed, and outraged by it as by a covert insult. His own undevout soul had never risen to the contemplation of himself as the priest of a really infinite sanctity; and when this clear-eyed barbarian, looking past him to the substance which informed him, made him feel himself for the moment the transparent mask or unconscious actor he was, his self-consciousness took the alarm. She sat, the breathless, silly little maid, between him and Mrs. Carlyle, holding a hand of each, and feeling the while her anticipations of Paradise on earth so met in this foolish encounter that she could not speak, but barely looked the pious rapture which filled her soul.

One more extract from my note-book, and I shall have done with it, for it is getting to be time to close my paper. I mentioned a while since the name of O'Connell, and *apropos* of this name I should like to cite a reminiscence which sets Carlyle in a touchingly amiable spiritual light.

"Sunday before last I found myself seated at Carlyle's with Mr. Woodman and an aid-de-camp of Lord Castlereagh,[10] who had just returned from India, and was entertaining Mrs. Carlyle with any amount of anecdotes about the picturesque people he left behind him. To us enter Dr. John Carlyle[11] and a certain Mr.——, a great burly Englishman, who has the faculty (according to an *aside* of Mrs. Carlyle, dexterously slipped in for my information) of always exciting Carlyle to frenzy by talk about O'Connell, of whom he is a thick-and-thin admirer. The weather topic and the health inquiry on both sides were soon quietly disposed of; but immediately after, Mrs. Carlyle nudged my elbow, and whispered in a tone of dread, 'Now for the deluge!' For she had heard the nasty din of politics commencing, and too well anticipated the fierce and merciless *mêlée* that was about to ensue. It speedily announced itself, hot and heavy; and for an hour poor breathless Mr. Woodman and myself, together with the awe-struck aid-de-camp, taking refuge under the skirts of outraged Mrs. Carlyle, assisted at a *lit de justice* [literally, "bed of justice"] such as we had none of us ever before imagined. At last tea was served, to our very great relief. But, no! the conflict was quite unexhausted, apparently, and went on with ever new alacrity, under the inspiration of the grateful souchong. Mrs. Carlyle had placed me at her left hand, with belligerent or bellowing Mr. Bull next to me; and as her tea-table chanced to be inadequate to the number of her guests we were all constrained to sit in very close proximity. Soon after our amiable and estimable hostess had officiated at the tea-tray, I felt her foot crossing mine to reach the feet of my infuriated neighbor and implore peace! She successfully reached them, and succeeded fully, also, in bringing about her end, without any thanks to him, however. For the ruffian had no sooner felt the gentle, appealing pressure of her foot, than he turned from Carlyle to meet her tender appeal with undisguised savagery. 'Why don't you,' he fiercely screamed,—'why don't you, Mrs. Carlyle, touch your husband's toe? I am sure he is greatly more to blame than I am!' The whole company immediately broke forth in a burst of uncontrollable glee at this extraordinary specimen of manners, Carlyle himself taking the lead; and his amiable *convive*, seeing, I suppose, the mortifying spectacle he had made of himself, was content to 'sing small' for the remainder of the evening.

"Anyhow, I heard nothing distressing while I remained. But happening to have made an appointment with Mrs. Carlyle for the next day, I went down to Chelsea in the morning, and found my friend seated with her stocking-basket beside her, diligently mending the *gudeman's* hose. I asked her if any dead had been left on the battlefield the night before, and she replied, 'Yes; I never saw Carlyle more near to death than he is this dismal Monday morning! I must first tell you that he has been a long time in the habit of going to Mr.——'s in——Street, for a Sunday dinner, protesting that, though his friends have no acquaintance with books or literary people, he never pays them a Sunday visit without feeling himself renovated against all the soil of the week, and never comes away without being baptized anew in unconsciousness. Now, yesterday he had gone to this friend's to dine, and when he returned, about three or four o'clock, he said to me, "Jane, I am henceforth a regenerate man, and eschew evil from this hour as the snake does its skin!" This he said with conviction and earnest purpose, as if that lovely family had inoculated him with the blessed life! What a scathing sense of weakness, then, besets the poor man this morning! Such a contrast between the placid noon of yesterday and the horrid, hideous night!'

"To my inquiry whether anything had further occurred of disagreeable after I had left, Mrs. Carlyle replied, 'Everything went on swimmingly till about eleven o'clock, when it pleased your unfortunate countryman, Mr. Woodman, to renew the war-whoop by saying, "Let us return a moment to O'Connell." If the talk was frightful before you left, what did it now become? Altogether unbearable; and when about twelve o'clock John

Carlyle got up to go, taking his friend along with him, Carlyle, lighting his candle to see the company to the door, stretched out his hand to his late antagonist, with the frank remark, "Let bygones be bygones!" The latter scorned to take it saying, "Never again shall I set foot in this house!" I knew how cruelly Carlyle would feel this rebuff, and scarcely dared to glance at him as he came upstairs after lighting his guests out; but when I did look, there he stood at the door of the room, holding the candle above his head, and laughing with bitter, remorseful laughter, as he repeated the words of the morning: Jane, I am henceforth a regenerate man, and eschew evil from this hour as the snake does its skin!"

Alas, poor Yorick!

The main intellectual disqualification, then, of Carlyle, in my opinion, was the absoluteness with which he asserted the moral principle in the human bosom, or the finality which his grim imagination lent to the conflict of good and evil in men's experience. He never had the least idea, that I could discover, of the true or intellectually educative nature of this conflict, as being purely ministerial to a new and final evolution of *human nature itself* into permanent harmony with God's spiritual perfection. He never expressed a suspicion, in intercourse with me,—on the contrary, he always denounced my fervent conviction on the subject as so much fervent nonsense,—that out of this conflict would one day emerge a positive or faultless life of man, which would otherwise have been impracticable; just as out of the conflict of alkali and acid emerges a neutral salt which would overwise be invisible. On the contrary, he always expressed himself to the effect that the conflict was absolutely *valid in itself;* that it constituted its own end, having no other result than to insure to good men the final dominion of evil men, and so array heaven and hell in mere chronic or fossil antagonism. The truth is, he had no idea but of a carnal or literal rectitude in human nature,—a rectitude secured by an unflinching inward submission to some commanding *outward* or *personal* authority. The law, not the gospel, was for him the true bond of intercourse between God and man, and between man and man as well. That is to say, he believed in our moral instincts, not as constituting the mere carnal body or rude husk of our spiritual manhood, but its inmost kernel or soul; and hence he habitually browsed upon "the tree of the knowledge of good and evil," as if it had been divinely commended to us for that purpose, or been always regarded as the undisputed tree of life, not of death. He was mother Eve's own darling cantankerous Thomas, in short, the child of her dreariest, most melancholy old age; and he used to bury his worn, dejected face in her penurious lap, in a way so determined as forever to shut out all sight of God's new and better creation.

Of course this is only saying in other words that Carlyle was without any sense of a *universal* providence in human affairs. He supposed that God Almighty literally saw with our eyes, and had therefore the same sympathy for strong men that we ourselves have, and the same disregard for feeble men. And he conceived that the world was governed upon the obvious plan of giving strong men sway, and hustling weak men out of sight. In the teeth of all the prophets who have ever prophesied, he held that the race *is* always to the swift, the battle always to the strong. Long before Mr. Darwin had thought of applying the principle of natural selection to the animal kingdom, Carlyle, not in words but in fact, had applied it to the spiritual kingdom, proclaiming as fundamental axioms of the divine administration, "Might makes right, and devil take the hindmost." He thought the divine activity in the world exceptional, not normal, occasional, not constant; that God worked one day out of seven, and rested the remaining six; thus, that he had a much nearer relation to holiday persons like Plato or Shakespeare or Goethe than he has to everyday people like the negro, the prison convict, the street-walker. In this shallow way the great mystery of godliness, which the angels desire to look into, became to his eyes as flat as any pancake; Deity himself being an incomparable athlete, or having an enormous weight of selfhood, so that all his legitimate children are born to rule. Ruler of men, this was Carlyle's most rustical ideal of human greatness. Rule on the one hand, obedience on the other, this was his most provincial ideal of human society or fellowship, and he never dreamt of any profounder key to the interpretation of our earthly destiny. The strong man to grow ever more strong, the feeble man to grow ever more feeble, until he is finally extinguished,—that was his very pedantic and puerile conception of the rest that remains to the people of God. The glorification of force, ability, genius, "that is the one condition," he always said, "in my poor opinion, of any much-talked-of millennial felicity for this poor planet,—the only thing which will ever rescue it from being the devil's churchyard and miserable donkey pasture it now for the most part turns out to be."

The divine hieroglyphics of human nature are never going to be deciphered in his sensuous, childish way. The divine gait is not lopsided. As his special glory is to bring good *out of evil*, one can easily see that he has never had a thought of exalting one style of man outwardly or personally above another style, but only of reducing both styles to a just humility. "The tree of knowledge of good and evil" is a tree which belongs exclusively to the garden of *our* immature, sensuous, or scientific intelligence, and it will not bear transplantation to a subtler spiritual soil. Our moral experience has always been, in purpose, intellectually educative. It is adapted, in literal or outward form, to our rude and crude or nascent scientific intelligence, and as intended to afford us, in the absence of any positive conceptions of infinitude, at least a negative spiritual conception, that so we might learn betimes a modest or humble conceit of ourselves. Now, Carlyle's precise intellectual weakness was that he never had a glimpse of any distinctively divine ends in human *nature*, but only in the more or less conflicting *persons* of that nature; and hence he was even childishly unable to justify the advance of the *social* sentiment in humanity,—the sanest, deepest, most reconciling sentiment ever known to man's bosom. To escape Carlyle's fatuity, then, and avoid the just reproach which he is fated to incur in the future, we must give up our hero-worship, or sentimental reverence for great men, and put ourselves in the frankest practical harmony with the Providence that governs the world. Nor is this half so difficult a task as our leading lazy-bones in Church and State would have us believe. Our leaders should be called our misleaders, in fact, so often do they betray us as to the principles of Divine administration. The world is not administered, as Carlyle and Louis Napoleon would have us fancy, upon the principle of making everything bend to the will of the strongest. On the contrary, the true will of the Strongest is, and always has been, to efface himself before every the meanest creature he has made, and his profoundest joy, not to have His own way, but to give way to every such creature, provided, first of all, there be nothing in that way injurious to the common weal. In fact, the one principle of Divine administration in human affairs, as we learn from Christianity, is to disregard high things, and mind only low things; to contemn whatsoever is highly esteemed among men, and exalt or utilize whatsoever they despise and reject. Harry Carey[12] has been long and vainly showing us that a proper economy of the world's waste is all we need to inaugurate in the material sphere the long-promised millennium. And Liebig[13] published, not many years ago, what he calls a legacy to his fellows, in which he proves, first, that European agriculture is fast becoming so fruitless by the exhaustion of soils, that, unless some remedy be provided, Europe must soon go into hopeless physical decrepitude; and, secondly, that men have the amplest remedy against this contingency in their own hands, by simply economizing the sewage of large towns, and restoring to the land the mineral wealth their food robs it of. Only think of this! Europe actually depends for her material salvation upon a divine redemption mercifully stored up for her in substances which her most pious churchmen and wisest statesmen have always disdained as an unmitigated nuisance! If any one thing be more abhorrent than another to our dainty sensual pride; if one thing more than another has been permitted to fill our selfish, stupid life with disgust and disease,—it is this waste material of the world, which we, in our insanity, would gladly hurry into the abyss of oblivion! And yet in God's munificent wisdom this self-same odious waste teems with incomparably greater renovation to human society than all the gold, silver, and precious stones ever dug from earth to madden human lust and enslave human weakness!

Now, what is the philosophic lesson of this surprising scientific gospel? When science thus teaches us, beyond all possibility of cavil, that the abject waste and offscouring of the planet, which we ourselves are too fastidious even to name, is fuller of God's redeeming virtue, of his intimate presence, than all its pomp of living loveliness, than all its vivid garniture of mineral, vegetable, and animal beauty, what philosophic bearing does the lesson exert? It is the very gospel of Christ, mind you, reduced to the level of sense, or turned into a scientific verity. What, then, is its urgent message to men's spiritual understanding? Evidently this, and nothing else; namely, that human life is now so full of want, so full of sorrow, so full of vice,–that human intercourse is now so full of fraud, rapacity, and violence, only because the truth of human society, human fellowship, human equality, which alone reveals the infinitude of God's love, enjoys as yet so stinted a recognition, while race continues to war with race, and sect with sect. Society has as yet achieved only a typical or provisional existence, by no means a real or final one. Every clergyman is the professional fellow or equal of every other; every lawyer or physician enjoys the equal countenance of his professional brethren, but no man is yet sacred to his brother man by virtue of his manhood simply, but only by virtue of some conventional or accidental advantage. The vast majority of our Christian population are supposed to be properly excluded from an equal public consideration with their more fortunate compeers, by the fact of their poverty or enforced subjection to natural want, and the personal limitations which such want imposes; while outside of Christendom the entire mass of mankind is shut out of our respect and sympathy, if not exposed to the incursions of our ravenous cupidity, because they do not profess the exact faith we profess, nor practise the literal maxims we practise. Thus, the righteousness of the letter prevails everywhere over that of the spirit, everywhere betrays and condemns our divinest natural manhood to dishonor and death; the inevitable consequence being, that God's living energy in our nature, disdaining as it does anything but a universal operation, is shut up to the narrowest, most personal and penurious dimensions,–is assocated, in fact, with the meanest, most meagre bosoms of the race; while the great mass of men, in whose hearts and brains its infinite splendors lie seething and tumultuous for an outlet, are cast out of our Christian fellowship, are dishonored and reviled, as so much worthless rubbish or noisome excrement.

It is quite time then, in my opinion, that we should cease minding Carlyle's rococo airs and affectations; his antiquated strut and heroics, reminding us now of John Knox and now of Don Quixote; his owlish, obscene hootings at the endless divine day which is breaking over all the earth of our regenerate nature. We have no need that he or any other literary desperado should enlighten us as to the principles of God's administration, for we have a more sure word of prophecy in our own hearts,–a ray of the light which illumines every man who comes into the world, and is ample, if we follow it, to scatter every cloud that rests upon the course of history. We are all of us parents, potentially or actually, and although we represent the infinite paternity most imperfectly, we do nevertheless represent it. And how do we administer our families? Do we bestow our chief solicitude upon those of our children who need it least, or upon those who need it most; upon those who are most up to the world's remorseless demands upon them, or those who fall short of those demands? I need not wait for an answer. All our base, egotistic pride may go to the former, but we reserve all our care and tenderness for those whom an unkind nature, as we say, consigns to comparative indigence and ignominy. Now, God has absolutely no pride and no egotism, being infinitely inferior to us in both those respects. But then, for that very reason, he is infinitely our superior in point of love or tenderness. I do not believe that the tenderness we bestow upon our prodigals is worthy to be named in the same day with that which he bestows upon his. I do not believe, for my part, that he ever lifts a finger, or casts a glance, to bless those of his offspring who resemble him, or are in sympathy with his perfection,—for such persons need no blessing, are themselves already their own best blessing,—but reserves all his care and tenderness for the unblessed and disorderly, for the unthankful and the evil, for those who are disaffected to his righteousness, and make a mock of his peace. I doubt not, if a celestial visitor should come to us to-morrow in the flesh, we should engage the best rooms for him at the Parker House; supply his table with the fat of the land; place a coach-and-four at his beck, whisk him off to the State House; introduce him to all the notabilities, ecclesiastic, political, scholastic, financial; give him a public dinner, a box at the opera, the most conspicuous pew in church; in short, do everything our stupidity could invent to persuade *him*, at all events, that we regarded him as an arrival from the most uncelestial corner of the universe. Well, we have in truth at this time, and all the time, no celestial visitant in the flesh among us, but a divine resident in the spirit, whom the heaven of heavens is all unmeet to contain, and who yet dwells—awaiting there his eventual glorious resurrection—a patient, despised, discredited, spiritual form in every fibre of that starved and maddened and polluted flesh and blood which feeds our prisons and fattens our hospitals, and which we have yet the sagacity to regard as the indispensable base of our unclean and inhuman civilization. And it is my fixed conviction, that unless we speedily consent to recognize his humiliated form in that loathsome sepulchre, and give emancipation to it there, first of all, by bringing this waste life, this corrupt and outcast force of Christendom, into complete social recognition, or clothing it with the equal garments of praise and salvation that hide our own spiritual nakedness, we shall utterly miss our historic justification, and baffle the majestic Providence which is striving through us to inaugurate a free, unforced, and permanent order of human life.

NOTES

1. John Sterling (1806–1844) was a minor English poet and friend of Carlyle's; Frederic Denison Maurice (1805–1872), an Anglican theologian and leader of the Christian Socialist movement; Joseph Neuberg (1806–1867), a successful manufacturer in Nottingham who retired to become Carlyle's "volunteer secretary" and was of great assistance in helping Carlyle write *The History of Frederick the Great;* Sir Arthur Helps (1813–1875), an English historian who became clerk of the privy council and a confidante of Queen Victoria; Robert Browning (1812–1889), the eminent Victorian poet and author of *The Ring and the Book;* George Henry Lewes (1817–1878), an English philosopher and man of letters who was greatly influenced by the ideas of August Comte.—Editor's note.

2. Louis Blanc (1811–1882) was a French political leader and historian whose ideas helped shape the development of socialism; Richard Cobden (1804–1865), an English political economist and apostle of free trade in Victorian England who fought ardently for repeal of the Corn Laws; John Bright (1811–1889), a radical British statesman who was associated with his friend Richard Cobden in the fight against the Corn Laws; James Pierrepont Greaves (1777–1842), a mystic and follower of Jacob Boehme; Amos Bronson Alcott (1799–1888), one of the lesser lights of the American Transcendental movement who was nonetheless an educational reformer of considerable originality. —Editor's note.

3. George Jacques Danton (1759–1794) was one of the leaders of the French Revolution; Honoré Gabriel Riquetic, Comte De Mirabeau (1749–1791), a great orator and statesman during the French Revolution who tried in vain to reconcile the monarchy with the Revolution.—Editor's note.

4. Maximilien François Marie Isidore de Robespierre (1758–1794) was a French revolutionary whose name is particularly associated with the Period of Terror of 1793–94.—Editor's note.

5. Alfred, Lord Tennyson (1809–1892) is the great Victorian poet.—Editor's note.

6. Edward Moxon (1801–1858) was an English publisher and minor poet who is best known as the friend and publisher of many of his more eminent Victorian contemporaries.—Editor's note.

7. Sir Robert Peel (1788–1850), British home secretary and later prime minister who was a great advocate of free trade reform and the repeal of the Corn Laws.—Editor's note.

8. James is here referring most probably to Daniel O'Connell (1775–1847), an Irish nationalist sometimes known as "The Liberator."—Editor's note.

9. John Henry Temple Palmerston (1784–1865) was British foreign secretary for sixteen years and prime minister for nine; John Russell Russell (1792–1878), a champion of liberalism and parliamentary reform whose name is often associated with the Reform Bill of 1832; Henry Peter Brougham (1778–1868), a prominent figure in British political life for nearly thirty years who played an important role in movements of educational, legal and social reform.—Editor's note.

10. Robert Stewart Londonberry or Lord Castlereagh (1769–1822) was a British statesman and diplomat who was chiefly responsible for British policy in the peace settlement at the close of the Napoleonic wars.—Editor's note.

11. James is referring to Dr. John Carlyle (1801–1879), a Scottish physician and younger brother of Thomas Carlyle.—Editor's note.

12. Henry Charles Carey (1793–1879) was an American economist and sociologist who is often called the founder of the U.S. school of economics.—Editor's note.

13. Here the reference is to Baron Justus von Liebig (1863–1873), a German chemist who made important contributions to the fields of organic chemistry, biochemistry and agricultural chemistry.—Editor's note.

19

SELECTED LETTERS

James was an inveterate writer of letters in an age which still sought to raise that activity to the level of an art. Of all the forms of art, letter-writing appealed to James because it was at once the most personal and the most social. The author was committed—or at least invited—to speak in his own voice rather than through a mask or persona, and yet this highly personal form of utterance was designed for the express purpose of communicating with someone else and thus of furthering a human relationship. Beyond this, however, James simply loved to talk, not primarily because he enjoyed the sound of his own voice, but rather because the inherently social character of conversation provided a form of release and realization for those deepest instincts which in his more formal writing he constantly associated with our race nature. Conversation was for James one of the chief ways of being human, and in the selected letters which follow, his own humanity shines through in all its marvelously social radiance.

The following letters were first printed in full in Ralph Barton Perry's *The Thought and Character of William James* (2 vols., Boston, 1935), and are here reprinted with the kind permission of Mr. Alexander R. James.

———•◦•———

To Ralph Waldo Emerson

New York City, Thursday Evening [March 3, 1842?]

My dear Sir,—

I listened to your address this evening, and as my bosom glowed with many a true word that fell from your lips I felt erelong fully assured that before me I beheld a man who in very truth was seeking the realities of things. I said to myself, I will try when I go home how far this man follows reality—how far he loves truth and goodness. For I will write to him that

I, too, in my small degree am coveting to understand the truth which surrounds me and embraces me, am seeking worthily to apprehend, or to be more worthily apprehended of, the love which underlies and vivifies all the seeming barrenness of our most unloving world; but that yet for every step I have taken I find myself severed from friends and kindred, so that at last, and just when I am become more consciously worthy of love than I ever was, in so far as being more consciously and universally loving may argue me so, I find my free manifestations compressed into the sphere of my own fireside. I will further tell him that to talk familiarly with one who earnestly follows truth through whatever frowning ways she beckons him on, and loves her with so true a love as never to have been baffled from her pursuit by all the wearisome forms of error he may have encountered in the way, has never been my lot for one half-hour even; and that he, therefore, if he be now the generous lover of truth and of her friends which he seems to be, may give me this untasted pleasure, and let me once feel the cordial grasp of a fellow pilgrim, and remember for long days the cheering Godspeed and the ringing laugh with which he bounded on from my sight at parting. I will not insult his reverence for truth equally with my own by saying that I desire his guidance in any way, but I will tell him that when once my voice is known, I may now and then call him back to interpret some of the hieroglyphics which here and there line our way, and which my own skill in tongues may be unequal to,—which slight services he cannot well deny. I will tell him that I do not value his substantive discoveries, whatever they may be, perhaps half so highly as he values them, but that I chiefly value that erect attitude of mind about him which in God's universe undauntedly seeks the worthiest tidings of God, and calmly defies every mumbling phantom which would herein challenge its freedom. And finally, not to try his patience also, I will tell him that should his zeal for realities and his contempt of vulgar shows abide the ordeal I had thus contrived for them, I should gladly await his visit to me whenever he should be pleased to appoint it.

This in substance is what I said to myself. Now that I have told it to you also, you have become a sort of confidant between me and myself, and so in a manner bound to promote harmony there. If you shrink from the confidence thus thrust upon you, I shall certainly be blamed by *myself*, for making so indiscreet a communication to you; but if you abide it, I shall with equal certainty be highly felicitated by *myself* for achieving a result so undeniably auspicious to both. In every event, I remain, your true well-wisher,

H. JAMES

To Ralph Waldo Emerson

New York City [1842?]

To the Invisible Emerson, the Emerson that thinks and feels and lives, this letter is addressed; and not to the Emerson that talks and bewitches one out of his serious thought when one talks to him, by the beautiful serenity of his behaviour. This latter Emerson I shall begin to hate soon for keeping my stupid eyes so continually away from the profounder Emerson who alone can do one any good. But I will now have the true man's ear alone. I came home tonight from my lecture a little disposed to think from the smart reduction of my audience that I had about as well not prepared my lectures, especially that I get no tidings of having interested one of the sort (the religious) for whom they were wholly designed. And now I say to myself "the first step in your outgoing to the world having thus failed you, no second step of course offers itself, but you must come back to your perch, and look round the horizon for some other flight." No sooner said than done—my eyes are already open to look, and shall continue patiently open always. When I next see you I want a half-hour's help from you in this matter. And the purpose of this letter is to secure it. Whenever I am with you I get no help from you—that is, of the sort which you can give me, I feel sure—and this letter is to let you know what it is I want before I come next. Usually the temper you shew, of perfect repose, of perfect candour, so perfectly free from all sickening partizanship, so full of magnanimous tenderness towards all creatures, makes me forget my wants in your lavish plenty. But I know you have the same wants as I have, deep down in your bosom hidden from my sight, and it is by these I want somewhat to know you. Henceforth I commit the visible man to my wife for her reproof—and mine in leisure hours.

I am led, quite without any conscious wilfulness either, to seek the *laws* of these appearances that swim round us in God's great museum—to get hold of some central *facts* which may make all other facts properly circumferential, and *orderly* so—and you continually dishearten me by your apparent indifference to such law and central facts: by the dishonour you seem to cast upon our intelligence, as if it stood much in our way. Now my conviction at present is that my intelligence is the necessary digestive apparatus for my life. . . . Is it not so in truth with you? Is not your life continually fed by knowledge, and could you have any life but brute life without it? Do you not feel the necessity of reaching after these laws all the while,—some inner fact which shall link together mighty masses of now conflicting facts; and suddenly by getting hold of such fact, are you not sensibly lifted up to far vaster freedom of life? . . . But I cannot say what I want to say,—what aches to say itself in me—and so I'll hold up till I see you, and try once more to get some better furtherance by my own effort.

Here am I thirty-one years in life, ignorant in all outward science, but having patient habits of meditation which never know disgust or weariness, and feeling a force of impulsive love toward all humanity which will not let me rest wholly mute—a force which grows against all resistance that I can master against it. What shall I do? Shall I get me a little nook in the country and communicate with my *living* kind, not my talking kind —by life only—a word, may be, of *that* communication, a fit word, once a year? Or shall I follow some commoner method, learn science and bring myself first into men's respect, that thus I may the better speak to them? I confess this last theory seems rank with earthliness—to belong to days forever past. Can the invisible Emerson then put up from his depths some heart-secret-law which shall find itself reproduced in mine and so further me, or at least *stay* me? Let him try, and above all let him forgive *more suo* ["in his own fashion"] all my botherings.

H. JAMES

To Ralph Waldo Emerson

New York, May 11, 1843

My dear Emerson,—

Your letter was well-come, I assure you, every way, even in that of flesh and blood, as it bade begone a spell of the blues which two days prevalence of east winds and dyspepsia had conjured over me. . . . Something or other disturbs the deep serene of my rejoicing in you. . . . All that I can at present say is that, being better satisfied with you than any man I ever met, I am worst satisfied: which being interpreted means, that while your *life* is of that sort which, so far as I can detect it, lays hold of my profoundest love, ever and anon some provokingly perverse way of speech breaks forth which does not seem to me to come from the life, and incontinently knocks me into downright *pi* again. It all comes of some lurking narrowness in me, which shall be discovered if so it be—but which nevertheless shall be legitimately discovered, that is, through the experience of growing life. . . . So by and bye, when I come into greener and freer pastures, I will wonder at the straitness of my present paddock, which I am so blindly bent on deeming ample for your accommodation. Till then bear with me.

I shall right gladly welcome Mr. Thoreau for all our sakes to my fireside, or any preferable summer seat the house affords—and will so advise him at once. Of Tappan[1] I have seen nothing—but have hopes, so long as he continues to hold Montaigne,[2] and reverences honesty. Channing[3] I have not seen either of late—indeed, since you left. He is very busy with his church matters, and I with my matters; and although I should well like to lay hands upon him often, I have never ventured to his house, knowing not his habits nor surroundings. I observed by Greeley's[4] paper that he and Brisbane[5] have enlisted Channing in the service of the attractive phalanxes. An Albany paper had an account of a meeting which they severally addressed here. However, I presume Channing would not be carried so off by this matter as to look upon it in the way Brisbane and the rest do—as a perfect social vermifuge. . . .

I am cheered by the coming of Carlyle's new book,[6] which Greeley announces, and shall hasten off, as soon as I have leisure, for it. The title is provokingly enigmatical. Thought enough will be there, no doubt, whatever it may be named. Thought heaped up to topheaviness and inevitable lopsidedness, but more interesting thought to me than comes from any other quarter of Europe. Interesting for the man's sake whom it shews. According to my notion Carlyle is the very best interpreter of spiritual philosophy which could be devised *for this age,* the age of transition and conflict. And what renders him so is his natural birth- and education-place. Just to think of a *Scotchman* with a heart widened to German spiritualities! To have overcome his educational bigotries far enough to listen to the new ideas, this was wonderful. But then to give all his native shrewdness and humour to the service of making them *tell* to the minds of his people—what more fortunate thing for the time could there be than this? You don't look upon Calvinism as a fact at all, wherein you are to my mind philosophically infirm, and impaired as to your universality. I can see in Carlyle's writing the advantage his familiarity with this fact gives him over you with a general audience. What is highest in Carlyle is built upon that lowest. At least so I read. I believe Jonathan Edwards *redivivus* in true blue would, after an honest study of the philosophy that has grown up since his day, make the best possible reconciler and critic of philosophy—far better than Schelling *redivivus.*

Surely my heart goes forth to your invitation to Concord! We shall see. I am anxious to hear about the *Dial* from Mr. Thoreau. I did not like Mr. Lane's paper wholly.[7] Why should we put our trust in princes? You and I shall value Mr. Alcott to the full measure of his worth or of our capacity, and never cease to repeat to ourselves how worthy he is—but what divine sanction have we to go forth to the great race and proclaim *him a prophet*? Of what interest is that fact to any human being? Let him prove himself a prophet in silence, and he will be found out soon enough. Let his words prove him so—which is the convincing way—that will quite extinguish our demonstrations. That long extract from Alcott, how painful it was to me with all its eloquence. Why spend so much pains to *demonstrate* the poet —the prophet? Does he ever need it? Now I presume such is by no means the truth, yet the impression left by that friendly paper on my mind was that Alcott was musing considerably—or rather say, *acutely felt his claims upon his generation*—and this impression could not attract me to his books. I will expect to see a Jeremiah betaking himself to copious tears over the blindness of his generation to that truth which is their life—but utterly forgetting his own prophetic self in that sincere sorrow, at the same time. The truth must reach them at some time, by some truer Jeremiah— why should he send his attendants forth when his voice has failed to arrest the people, to sound the praises of that voice? Of course this is all nonsense except with that precise view of Mr. Lane's article.

But I must stop, ere I be stopped. My wife is grateful for your remembrance, and thinks nothing would so help me as a little intercourse with Concord. Another fine little boy now lying in her lap preaches to me that I must become settled somewhere at home.[8] I have left out just all, nearly, that I want to say, and may soon, if the want continues, write you again. I will speak to Godwin about Thoreau. I am, dear Emerson, ever truly yours,

H. JAMES

To Ralph Waldo Emerson

New York, Aug. 31, 1849

My dear Emerson,—

I wrote yesterday to Mr. Alcott accepting the invitation of the T. and C. Club for November, and enclosing five dollars for my subscription. I am horrified at the prospect of speaking before so urbane an assemblage as I am likely to meet, and nothing but the protection of your magnanimous countenance reconciles me. There is nothing I dread so much as literary men, especially *our* literary men. Catch them out of the range of mere personal gossip about authors and books, and ask them for honest sympathy with your sentiment or an honest repugnancy of it, and you will find the company of stage-drivers sweeter and more comforting to your soul. In truth the questions which are beginning to fill the best books and will fill the best for a long time to come, are not related to what men have called literature, and are as well—I think better—judged by those whom books have at all events not belittled. It seems to me the authorial vocation will not be so reputable in the future as in the past. If, as we are promised by all signs, the life which has hitherto glistened only in the intellect of men shall come down to their senses and put on every palpable form, I suspect the library will fall into disuse, and men will begin to believe that the only way for each to help the other is to live one's own life.

Your own books suggest this conviction incessantly. I never read you as an author at all. Your books are not literature but life, and criticism always strikes me, therefore, as infinitely laughable when applied to you. The opposite of this in literary men is what makes me hate them. You come to them with some grand secret that opens heaven to the lowest and most excluded hut, that lifts your own life out of bottomless and stifling mud, where living is abject toil, and expect some involuntary token of human sympathy, even of natural curiosity,—but no, a supercilious smile decks every visage, and the only notice taken of you is a muttered invocation of this, that and the other accepted name. These men do not live, and if books turn men into this parrot existence, I hope the Astor Library will meet the same fate as the Alexandrian. When a man lives he can scarcely write. He cannot read, I apprehend, at all. All his writing will be alge-braized—put in the form of sonnets and proverbs, and the community will feel itself insulted to be offered a great book, as though it were stupid and wanted tedious drilling like a child.

But I have lost sight of what I wanted to say. I am totally unfit to appear before your people except upon the subjects which usually engage my most earnest thought. I should greatly like to consider socialism from the highest point of view, but the name is a stench in the nostrils of all the devout and honourable, and I would not willingly outrage your kindness in introducing me by *obtruding* the topic upon my audience. Do you then think that any chance exists for my getting heard without long offense upon that subject? I cannot conceal my whole thought about it, if I speak at all, and therefore I await your dictum before I set to work. In case you think I had better leave this topic, I should like to read a paper on sin. It seems to me that a very beautiful philosophy underlies all our experiences in that line, and I should greatly like to say all I feel upon the subject. But on second thoughts, this would be very shocking, too, to prejudiced people, and besides would involve a practical social bearing; so it is perhaps rather worse than the other. The fact is, I am in a very bad way I am afraid, for I cannot heartily engage in any topic in which I shall appear to advantage. However, I will do what I can, and take on with me certificates of good citizenship from my wife and family and neighbours, in case the worst comes to the worst.

My wife and I are obliged—so numerous has waxed our family—to enlarge our house in town, and get a country house for the summer. These things look expensive and temporary to us, besides being an additional care; and so, looking upon our four stout boys, who have no play-room within doors, and import shocking bad manners from the street, with much pity, we gravely ponder whether it would not be better to go abroad for a few years with them, allowing them to absorb French and German and get a better sensuous education than they are likely to get here. To be sure, this is but a glimpse of our ground of proceeding—but perhaps you know some decisive word which shall dispense us from any further consideration of the subject. When my paper to the Town and Country Club shall be read I shall be functionless, and may study as well, and, better perhaps, abroad as here. Anyhow, and everywhere, I am, yours faithfully,

H. JAMES

To Ralph Waldo Emerson

New York, Oct. 30 [1851]

My dear Emerson,—

Your note finds me on the eve of starting for Albany, whence I leave for Boston next Tuesday, meaning to lecture there Wednesday evening (Nov. 5) at the Masonic Temple. The second lecture takes place Saturday evening. The third (I believe) on Tuesday, but I have fogotten the arrangement. . . . I should be greatly—appalled in some respects, but still—charmed to have you for an auditor, seeing thus an hundred empty seats obliterated; but I beg of you don't let any engagement suffer by such kindness to me.

Looking over the lectures again they horrify me with their loud-mouthed imbecility. But I hope they may fall upon less hardened ears in some cases. I am sure that the thought which is in them, or rather seems to me to struggle to be in them, is worthy of all men's rapturous homage, and I will trust that a glimpse of it may somehow befall my patient auditory. The fact is that a vital truth can never be transferred from one mind to another, because life alone appreciates it. The most one can do for another is to plant some rude formula of such truth in his memory, leaving his own spiritual chemistry to set free the germ whenever the demands of his life exact it. The reason why the Gods seem to powerless to the sensuous understanding, and suffer themselves to be so long defamed by our crazy theologies, is that they are life, and can consequently be revealed only to life. But life is simply the passage of idea into action. And our crazy theologies forbid ideas to come into action any further than our existing institutions warrant. Hence man leads a mere limping life, and the poor Gods who are dependent upon his manliness for their true revelation, for their real knowledge, are doomed to remain forever unknown. . . . However I shall try to convert *myself*, at least, into an army of Goths and Huns, to overrun and destroy our existing sanctities, that the supernal splendours may at length become credible and even visible. What do you think of Carlyle *vs*. Sterling?[9] It seems to me, from the little I know of Sterling, a very impudent performance. But the incidental matter is often very good. Good-bye till we meet in Boston, then, and cultivate your good nature according to my extensive needs. Yours ever faithfully,

H. JAMES

To Edmund Tweedy

New York, Feb. 24 [1852]

My beloved old Tweedius,—

Hang such weather! weather that overwhelms you with an hourly enchantment, and seduces you from the sacredest duties. How many letters have I written to you lately under its inspiration, to be sure not with mere vulgar pens and ink, but with the pen of my brain dipped into the inkstand of my heart! Ah! could you only get some of these letters! they would disqualify you for reading any of the present sort, as they do me for writing them. For my memory preserves only what is best and humanest of both of you, and I make you both sharers in imagination of all that is noblest and divinest in the life of my thought. . . .

Channing has done himself great credit, I am told, by his account of Margaret Fuller's last years. I have only read Emerson's narrative of her, which is first-rate and worthy of his youth. Ripley[10] has been scanning the whole record with a very curious eye, in order to gather some light which the biographers did not possess, or perhaps withhold. He does *not* mean to report the result in the *Tribune*. The impression the book[11] makes upon me so far, is that while Margaret was a person of fine intellect and aspiration, she was also a most uncomfortable neighbour, from the circumstance of her inordinate self-esteem. She thought herself somebody, and a somebody so large as to attract the gaze of the world, and perhaps bias human destiny. Omnibus drivers, and my splendid friend Derby the tailor, are sweet in comparison with that sort of pretension. . . .

Emerson is here lecturing—or rather he has suspended his lectures for a fortnight, in order to resume them when the public attention is less absorbed by other entertainments. I see a good deal of him. He expresses himself much interested in my ideas, only he thinks I am too far ahead.

He read the proof of one of my lectures the other day, now printing, and said many pleasant and apparently sincere things of it, only he would have it that I was (comparatively) "a modern gentleman in the Saurian era." This is because he has no faith in man, at least in progress. He does not imagine the possibility of "hurrying up the cakes" on a large scale. Indeed he denies that any cakes are baking upon any larger scale than that of the family griddle. He is much interested in the question of immortality, and pumps one dry thereon.—Curtis is getting better, having been shut up all winter with inflammation of the bronchia. He is first-rate in power. . . . Kate and the children are as well as usual. Kate is a partizan, and of course, a thorough one, of Kossuth,[12] who on the whole will gain nothing by his motion in this country but private sympathy. Nothing will move us but the invasion of England by the powers of (Continental) darkness. Then I think we should fill all our ships. But I beg pardon for introducing political topics to a mere *virtuoso* and worldling like you. . . . Give Mary my deepest love, and believe me, with a royal hug for the baby, my dear good old Tweedius, ever faithfully, your

H. J.

To Ralph Waldo Emerson

London [1856]

My dear Emerson,—

I suppose if you hadn't bestowed upon me so generous and noble a valedictory, I should have brought myself to your remembrance half a dozen of times at least. But your letter proved such a quickener of emotion, and so penetrated us all with a sense of the sweetness we had left behind, the sweetness that distils from the divine depths of the human bosom, that we were in some danger of precipitately retracing our steps, and I for my own part felt an actual depressing homesickness every time I thought of you. For really I find every want supplied here but that to which you minister, a want which grows, I hope, out of my American manhood, and which demands in one's cronies an openness of soul answering to one's own. This is certainly you, a soul full of doors and windows, a well-ventilated soul, open to every breeze that blows, and without any dark closets receptive of ancestral, political and ecclesiastical trumpery. I could sometimes wish indeed to find those gracious doors and windows a little more retentive of what comes in, or a little more humanly jealous of what goes too speedily out; I could wish, indeed, that those stately chambers should afford the hospitality of a frequent and spacious *bed,* in which the weary guest might lie down and sleep till the next breakfast time; but perhaps this is only my sensuality, and sure I am meanwhile that you are a matchless summer house, green with clambering vines, and girt with cool piazzas fit to entertain the democratic host as it marches from the old worn-out past to the beckoning and blossoming future.

But this is the lack of the men here, of all I know, at least. They are all of them depressed or embittered by the public embarrassments that beset them; deflected, distorted, or somehow despoiled of their rich individual manliness, by the necessity of providing for these imbecile old inheritances of church and state. Carlyle is the same old sausage, fizzing and sputtering in his own grease, only infinitely more unreconciled to the blessed Providence which guides human affairs. He names God frequently, and alludes to the highest things as if they were realities; but it almost looks as if he did it only for a picturesque effect, so completely does he seem to regard them as habitually circumvented and set at naught by the politicians. I took our friend McKay[13] to see him, and he came away greatly distressed and *désillusionné*, Carlyle having taken the utmost pains to deny and decry and deride the idea of his having done the least good to anybody, and to profess, indeed, the utmost contempt for everybody who thought he had; and McKay, being intent upon giving him a plenary assurance of this fact in his own case. It strikes me that the Scotch nature does not easily lend itself to the highest conventional culture, and Carlyle would have fared better in personal respects to have remained a Cameronian preacher, if only government persecution had still left a bounty on that career, than to have descended into the circle of London amenities. . . .

Wilkinson disappoints me, he is so eaten up with the spirits and all that. His imagination is so vast as to dwarf all the higher faculties, and his sympathy is as narrow as Dr. Cheever's or Brownson's.[14] No reasonable man, it is true, likes the clergy or the philosophers, but Wilkinson's dislike of them seems to be as envenomed as that between rival tradesmen or rival beauties. One can't endure the nonsense they talk, to be sure, but when one considers the dear human meaning and effort that are struggling at the bottom of all that nonsense, you can't feel any personal separation from the men. Wilkinson's sarcasm is awful, and on the whole he seems to be sowing his intellectual wild oats at present, and will grow more genial in good time. This is it: I think he is now finding his youth. That which we on our side of the water find so early and exhaust so prodigally, Wilkinson is finding later, namely, emancipation from the shackles of custom; and the kicking up of his heels consequently is proportionate to his greater maturity of muscle. Mrs. Wilkinson is a dear little goose of a thing, that fancies the Divine Providence in closer league with herself than most people, giving her intimations of events about to happen, and endowing her with peculiar perspicacity in the intuition of remedies for disease, etc.; and Wilkinson, the great brawny fellow, sits by and says never a word in abatement of the enormous domestic inflation, though every visitor feels himself crowded by it into the most inconsiderable of corners. A sweet, loving, innocent woman like Mrs. Wilkinson ought not to grow egotistical in the company of a truly wise man; and this, accordingly, is another quarrel I have with W. In short, I believe I am getting to the time of life when one values his friends for what they *are* more than for what they *do*. I am just as much impressed as ever by Wilkinson's enormous power, but the goodness out of which it is born, and the wisdom by which it is nurtured and bred, these things I do not exactly see. To be is better than to perform, or rather all performance is in order to being, and this preliminary stage of development is apt to prove very unhandsome. But the peaceful evening will come for Wilkinson too, tremendous as he now is, when every fierce wind of controversy shall hum itself asleep, and every dusky cloud that hangs about the horizon shall blush and glow with the promise of a royal and endless tomorrow.

Don't let Caleb Cushing elbow us into the war.[15] Hang him rather. The people are dreadfully shocked at the menace of such a thing, and I have no doubt it would indeed prove the ruin of England, outright. It would send a famine through Lancashire and Staffordshire, and famine would send revolution before it, and revolution in England would be an unspeakably indecorous thing, I fear, the lower classes seem of such a brutal make. But who knows what lies before us! All that seems certain is that these depraved old nationalities are bound to be destroyed to make way for the humaner fellowship of men. The time may be now. But farewell, my dear Emerson, and believe me, ever devotedly, yours,

H. JAMES

To Edmund Tweedy

Paris, Sept. 14, 1856

My dear Tweedius,—

Many thanks for Emerson![16] It came in most apropos to a great desire which I felt after it, and which had led me to go down to the Palais Royal bookseller the day before to look after it, but in vain. I am somewhat disappointed now that I have read it; the appreciation is so overdone. The study has been too conscientious. The manners—the life—he was investigating, haven't the depth either for good or evil he attributes to them. His own stand-point is too high to do justice to the English. They are an intensely vulgar race, high and low; and their qualities, good or evil, date not from any divine or diabolic *depths* whatever, but from most obvious and superficial causes. They are the abject slaves of routine, and no afflatus from above or below ever comes, apparently, to ruffle the surface of their self-complacent quietude. They are not worth studying. The prejudices one has about them, even when they are unjust, are scarcely worth correcting. There is nothing better supplied by the actual truth of the case, to put in the place of them. They belong, all their good and their evil, to the past humanity, to the infantile development of the mind, and they don't deserve, more than any other European nation, the least reverence from a denizen of the new world. They are a solider, manlier race than the French, according to the old ideas of manhood: that is, they do not lie, cheat, commit adultery and murder with half so much good-will: but of the spiritual causes out of which these evil things proceed, pride and self-love and the love of domineering, they have their full share, and perhaps more than most other people. They lack heart. Their love is clannish. They love all that wear their own livery, but they don't even *see* anyone outside of that boundary.

Mrs. Cranch[17] wondered the other day, upon some new experiences of French perfidy, "what the Lord *would* do with these French people." I wonder what He will do with any European people. Or rather I don't wonder: for I see that they are all destined to be recast and remoulded into the form of a new and *de-nationalized* humanity, a universal form which, being animated by God's own infinite spirit, the spirit of human fellowship, will quickly shed all the soils it has contracted in the past. Thackeray[18] was in here yesterday, and told Mary that he had just heard of an atrocious thing that happened to two American friends of his, by the name of Duncan, two very handsome women he said, or at least one was so: they had been invited to dine the day before with some English grandee living in Paris, and when they entered the drawing-room they were introduced to nobody, nor was any person requested by host or hostess to see them to the table, in consequence of which they were left, when the company were summoned to dinner, swinging their feet upon a sofa, until two good-natured fellows, looking back at them, and pitying their desolate state, returned and escorted them to the table. They ought to have left the house instead, for no milder hint will penetrate either Mr. Bull's or Mrs. Cow's hide, and bad manners will consequently maintain the ascendant. American disorder is sweet beside European order: it is so full of promise. But that reminds me that I sent last week a letter to the London *Leader*, headed "The Order in American Disorder"; and yesterday's *Leader* has just come to hand with the letter shockingly mutilated. . . .

Good-bye, my dear old Tweedius, and believe me ever faithfully yours,

H. J.

To Ralph Waldo Emerson

Boston, Sunday night [1861]

My dear Emerson,—

I am going to Concord in the morning but shall have barely time to see you, if I do as much as that: yet I can't forbear to say a word I want to say about Hawthorne and Ellery Channing. Hawthorne isn't a handsome man nor an engaging one anyway, personally: he had the look all the time, to one who didn't know him, of a rogue who suddenly finds himself in a company of detectives. But in spite of his rusticity I felt a sympathy for him amounting to anguish and couldn't take my eyes off him all the dinner, nor my rapt attention; as that indecisive little Dr. Hedge[19] found, I am afraid to his cost, for I hardly heard a word of what he kept on saying to me, and felt at one time very much like sending down to Mr. Parker to have him removed from the room as maliciously putting his artificial little person between me and a profitable object of study.

Yet I feel now no ill-will to Hedge and could recommend any one (but myself) to go and hear him preach. Hawthorne, however, seemed to me to possess human substance and not to have dissipated it all away as that debauched Charles Norton, and the good, inoffensive, comforting Longfellow. He seemed much nearer the human being than any one at that end of the table, much nearer. John Forbes[20] and yourself kept up the balance at the other end: but that end was a desert with him for its only oasis. It was so pathetic to see him, contented, sprawling Concord owl that he was and always has been, brought blindfold into that brilliant daylight, and expected to wink and be lively like any little dapper Tommy Titmouse, or Jenny Wren. How he buried his eyes in his plate, and ate with such a voracity that no person should dare to ask him a question!

My heart broke for him as that attenuated Charles Norton kept putting forth his long antennæ towards him, stroking his face, and trying whether his eyes were shut. The idea I got was, and it was very powerfullly impressed upon me, that we are all of us monstrously corrupt, hopelessly bereft of human consciousness, and that it is the intention of the Divine Providence to overrun us and obliterate us in a new Gothic and Vandalic invasion of which this Concord specimen is a first fruits. It was heavenly to see him persist in ignoring Charles Norton, and shutting his eyes against his spectral smiles: eating his dinner and doing absolutely nothing but that, and then going home to his Concord den to fall upon his knees, and ask his heavenly Father why it was that an owl couldn't remain an owl, and not be forced into the dimensions of a canary. I have no doubt that all the tenderest angels saw to his care that night, and poured oil into his wounds more soothing than gentlemen ever know.

William Ellery Channing, too, seemed so human and good, sweet as summer, and fragrant as pine woods. He is more sophisticated than the other of course, but still he was kin; and I felt the world richer by two *men*, who had not yet lost themselves in mere members of society. This is what I suspect; that we are fast getting so fearful to another, we "members of society," that we shall ere long begin to kill one another in self-defense, and give place in that way at last to a more veracious state of things. The old world is breaking up on all hands: the glimpse of the everlasting granite I caught in Hawthorne and William Ellery, shows me that there is stock enough left for fifty better. Let the old imposter go, bag and baggage, for a very real and substantial one is aching to come in, in which the churl shall not be exalted to a place of dignity, in which innocence shall never be tarnished nor trafficked in, in which every man's freedom shall be respected down to its feeblest filament as the radiant altar of God. To the angels, says Swedenborg, death means resurrection to life; by that necessary rule of inversion which keeps them separate from us and us from them, and so prevents our being mutual nuisances.

Let us then accept political and all other destruction that chooses to come: because what is disorder and wrath and contention on the surface is sure to be the deepest peace at the centre, working its way thus to a surface that shall *never* be disorderly. Yours,

H. J.

P.S. . . . What a world! What a world! But once we get rid of slavery and the new heavens and new earth will swim into reality.

To Ralph Waldo Emerson

Newport, March 26 [1861]

My dear Emerson,—

Only one word about Edward,[21] the good boy who smiles like opening violets, but who is not near so robust as he ought to be, because he is allowed to study too hard, in order that he may enter college one year rather than another. I hated to see the beautiful boy so imprisoned by these baneful books: but of course I did not broach any heresy in his hearing. Our true learning is to unlearn always, and our best doing to undo: but this experience belongs to manhood alone, and even transcends it in many cases. But anyhow it is a sin and shame to starve the physical life out of any deference to the intellectual. I am sure you are as clear about this as any one: but I thought nevertheless I would take the liberty of this one word about Eddy. Swedenborg has a good illustration, by the way, of the evil in our education, though he speaks at the moment of moral education. He was talking one day with some angels about the singular cruelty of much of the moral discipline children are subjected to on earth, in the snubbing of their innocent natural delights, which of course at that age are delights of sense; and while they were talking, the inward horror and aversion of the angelic mind was outwardly represented by the view of a woman combing the hair of a child (hair corresponding to the sensual life) and every time she drew the comb through its hair, *blood followed the comb.*

Remember me affectionately to all your heavenly household and believe me ever faithfully yours,

H. J.

P.S. I read a lecture here Thursday next which I call a "Philosophic View of the Crisis." I have waited for you and other superior voices to make themselves heard, but I am tired, and shall propound my own squeak incontinently.

To Ralph Waldo Emerson

Newport, Dec. 22 [1861]

My dear Emerson,—

I didn't need Ellen's letter to teach me what angels you all are there in Concord, for few days pass without some memory or other coming up to suggest the knowledge; but I did need it, apparently, to convince me of my own comparative infernality. For I had no sooner heard the letter than I gave the palpitating Alice *carte blanche* to go at any expense of health, and got her expectations so exalted, that her more affectionate and truly long-suffering Mama found it one of the trials of her life to reduce her to the ordinary domestic routine. All I know is I am hopelessly wicked, and cheerfully postpone myself to the world-after-next for amendment. I tell Alice, by way of make-up, of the delights of heaven, and say that the Emerson house is only a foretaste of that festivity, the Emerson girls being what they are only by an interior, most unconscious and un-suspected contact with benignities and generosities and sincerities that she shall there see one day, poor child, in beautiful human form. I think, however, the tears still trickle in solitude.

I am busy writing out my book for the printer. I call it "Substance and Shadow" or "Morality and Religion in their Relation to Life,"—"An Essay on the Metaphysics of History." I believe I shall dedicate it to you, unless you call upon the police, somewhat in this fashion:

"My dear E.

"I dedicate this book to you not in attestation of our old intimacy, but in hope of a superior future one. It can't help horrifying you at first sight, because it is so undisguised an attempt to prove that irreligion is now the truest tribute, the tenderest homage, a mind of any spirituality can render to God. For you being so blessedly 'irreligious' by nature, can afford to be extremely generous to 'religion' by culture, and will feel disposed to resent therefore my rude criticism. But when you reflect etc."

The idea didn't occur till this moment, but it runs off so easily that I believe I shall cleave to it. Give my cordial love to all your household and believe me, ever faithfully,

HENRY JAMES

To William James

Cambridge, March 18 [1868]

My dear Willy,—

Everything goes on from week to week without shock or agreeable surprise to tell you of, so that one's letters become mere love messages. You get plenty of love from us all here, and your friends everywhere abound in your praises. Emerson wants me to take all your letters down to him that touch upon the Grimms to be read there in conclave, and I go next Saturday for that purpose. I happened to read one of your first letters there from Dresden about German women and the language, etc., and Ellen Emerson was near going into fits over the reading. I hope she will escape a catastrophe on Saturday.

Emerson's unreality to me grows evermore. You have got to deal with him as with a child, making all manner of allowances for his ignorance of everything above the senses, and putting such a restraint upon your intellect as tires you to death. I can't find anything but a pedantic inten-tion in him. He has no sympathy with nature, but is a sort of a police-spy upon it, chasing it into its hiding-places, and noting its subtlest fea-tures, for the purpose of reporting them to the public; that's all. He is an uncommonly sharp detective, but a detective he is and nothing more.

He never for a moment drops his office, loses sight of himself, and becomes drowned in the beautiful illusion, but is sure always to appear as a fisherman with his fish upon the hook. The proof of all this is that he breeds no love of nature in his intellectual offspring, but only the love of imitating him and saying similar 'cute things about nature and man. I love the man very much, he is such a born natural; but his books are to me wholly destitute of spiritual flavour, being at most carbonic acid gas and *water*. . . .

Harry and Aunt Kate went to some private theatricals last night in Lyceum Hall, to see Alice Parkman[22] perform. They liked her, but the others were very bad. I suppose the reason private companies don't do better is that they act acting only. Alice is better on the whole, and we all—especially she—long for you consumedly. But stay on as long as you can. We hope for a letter today or tomorrow. Ever your loving Daddy

To Ivan Turgenev

Cambridge, June 19, 1874

My dear Sir,—

It seems a pity that you should be ignorant of the immense appreciation your books have in this region, and the unfeigned delight they give to so many good persons. I am not myself a representative reader, but I have some leisure at least, which all your readers have not got, and I may therefore without presumption perhaps, constitute myself your informant on their behalf. My son (Henry James, Jr., now in Europe) lately published a critical sketch of your writings in the *North American Review*, which I think he sent you a copy of. But this was only an individual token, and what I want to say to you is, that my son's high appreciation of your genius is shared by multitudes of very intelligent people here. . . . Your books came out here some five or six years ago in German and French translations, and became known at once to a few appreciative readers, and in a very brief while made their way to the acquaintance of all the reading world. They have indeed made themselves so widely honoured, that whatever you write is now immediately translated for our periodicals, or for independent publication, and the only matter left for the public to differ about is the pronunciation of your name. And some recent events lead me to hope that even this controversy, though still lively, will not be as protracted, nor as envenomed as that over Homer's birthplace.

I think the verdict of the large circle of admirers you have in this place is, that the novel owns a new power in your hands, a deeper fascination than it ever before exerted. . . . Men and women of great and surprising genius have made romance an instrument second only to the drama, as an educative power over the emotions. But it must be said of the greatest of these, that the most they do is, either like Scott to give us stirring pictures of human will *aux prises* ["coming to grips"] with outward circumstance, and finally victorious over it; or else, like George Sånd, Thackeray and George Eliot, to give us an idea of the enervating and palsying effect of social convention upon the conscience, in rendering men sceptical, self-indulgent and immoral. But you as a general thing strike a far deeper chord in the consciousness of your reader. You sink your shaft sheer through the world of outward circumstance, and of social convention, and shew us ourselves in the fixed grasp of fate, so to speak, or struggling vainly to break the bonds of temperament. Superficial critics revolt at this tragic spectacle, and pronounce you cynical. They mistake the profound spirituality of your method, and do not see that what touches the earnest heart of man, and fills it with divinest love and pity for its fellow-man, is infinitely more educative than anything addressed to his frivolous and self-righteous head.

Such, in a measure, is the tribute we pay your sympathetic genius, when we talk of you here in the evening on the piazza of the house, facing the setting sun. One of the young ladies present wonders whether an eye so at one with nature as yours, will ever do for American landscape what you have done for Russia; and her companion, whom I sometimes fancy is worthy to take her place beside some of your own heroines, wonders whether our humanity will ever be so defined as to justify an observer like you coming over to look at us. I can only emphasize their wonder by adding my own. But should you ever cross the ocean, you must not fail to come to Cambridge, and sit with us on the piazza in the evening, while you tell us between the fumes of your pipe what the most exercised and penetrating genius of the old world discerns, either of promise or menace for humanity in the civilization of the new.

Please look kindly on my intrusion, and believe me, my dear Sir, with the greatest esteem and admiration, yours,

HENRY JAMES

To Henry James, Jr.

Boston, May 9 [1882]

My darling Harry,—

I went out early after breakfast to see William yesterday, and he came down from his bedroom *dancing* to greet me. He was apparently ever so much better. . . . Dear Alice looked so burdened to sight by her new maternity, and her anxiety about Willy, and her solicitude in behalf of Harry, that all my compassion was drawn to her, and I expressed it very tenderly, I assure you. Harry [23] was incomparably sweet. I had met him in company with his Aunt Margaret Sunday afternoon in a Park Square horse-car, and he had been so preoccupied with the people in the car that he scarcely noticed his granddaddy. And I, in reproaching him with this remembrance before the family, got no satisfaction but what lay in these exact words: "Yes, I thought almost I wouldn't even speak to Grandpa." This *even* was too expressive. . . .

And now, my darling boy, I must bid you farewell. How loving a farewell it is, I can't say, but only that it is most loving. All my children have been very good and sweet from their infancy, and I have been very proud of you and Willy. But I can't help feeling that you are the one that has cost us the least trouble, and given us always the most delight. Especially do I mind mother's perfect joy in you the last few months of her life, and your perfect sweetness to her. I think in fact it is this which endears you so much to me now. No doubt the other boys in the same circumstances would have betrayed the same tender and playful love to her, only they were not called upon to do so. I am no way unjust to them, therefore, but I feel that I have fallen heir to all dear mother's fondness for you, as well as my proper own, and bid you accordingly a distinctly widowed farewell. That blessed mother, what a link her memory is to us all henceforth! I think none of us who remember her natural unaffected ways of goodness, and especially her sleepless sense of justice, will ever again feel tempted to do a dishonest or unhandsome thing. She was not to me a "liberal education," intellectually speaking, as some one has said of his wife, but she really did arouse my heart, early in our married life, from its selfish torpor, and so enabled me to become a man. And this she did altogether unconsciously, without the most cursory thought of doing so, but solely by the presentation of her womanly sweetness and purity, which she herself had no recognition of. The sum of it all is, that I would sooner rejoin her in her modesty, and find my eternal lot in association with her, than have the gift of a noisy delirious world!

Good-bye then again, my precious Harry! . . . We shall each rejoice in you in our several way as you plough the ocean and attain to your old rooms, where it will be charming to think of you as once more settled and at work. I wish England itself offered a less troubled residence to you than it does. A lingering good-bye, then, dearest Harry, from all of us! and above all from your loving father,

H. J.

NOTES

1. James here could be referring to any one of three Tappan brothers—Benjamin (1773–1857), an American jurist and legislator; Arthur (1786–1865), an American merchant and philanthropist; or Lewis (1788–1873), an American merchant, philanthropist, and founder of the American Missionary Society—all of whom were active in the antislavery movement.—Editor's note.

2. Michel de Montaigne (1533–1592) was, of course, the great French moralist and author of the *Essays.*—Editor's note.

3. James is here referring to William Henry Channing (1810–1884), nephew of the elder William Ellery Channing, who was a member of the Transcendental Club and eventually became a convert to Fourierism.—Editor's note.

4. Horace Greeley (1811–18⁻?), f⁰ᵘⁿder and for thirty years editor of the *New-York Tribune,* was a·crusading li⸺⸺ ᵥₙo attacked monopolies and slavery and advocated such things as labor organization, a protective tariff, temperance,

and, because of his attraction to Fourierism, the founding of the North American Phalanx.—Editor's note.

5. Albert Brisbane (1809–1890), an early disciple and proseletizer of Fourierism who joined William Henry Channing and others in the establishment of Boston's Religious Union of Associationists.—Editor's note.

6. The work referred to is Carlyle's *Past and Present.*—Editor's note.

7. James is referring to Charles Lane, an English admirer of Bronson Alcott's. —Editor's note.

8. The "fine little boy" alluded to here was the junior Henry James.—Editor's note.

9. James is here referring to Carlyle's *Life of John Sterling* which appeared in 1851.—Editor's note.

10. George Ripley (1802–1880), a prominent American Transcendentalist who helped found *The Dial* and organize Brook Farm before becoming much later (1849–1880) the book reviewer for the *New-York Tribune.*—Editor's note.

11. James is referring to the *Memoirs* of Margaret Fuller, by Emerson, William Henry Channing, and James Freeman Clarke.—Editor's note.

12. Lajos Kossuth (1802–1894), the Hungarian patriot and leader of the Revolution of 1848–1849, became to many in Europe and America a symbol of advanced radicalism and extreme nationalism.—Editor's note.

13. Col. James Morrison McKay, an artist, abolitionist, and man of affairs. —Editor's note.

14. James is referring to Orestes A. Brownson, one of Emerson's fellow Transcendentalists, who later converted to Roman Catholicism, and to the Rev. George B. Cheever, a Congregational and Presbyterian minister, who was also a temperance reformer, editor, and journalist.—Editor's note.

15. Caleb Cushing was at this time serving as Attorney-General in the cabinet of President Pierce.—Editor's note.

16. James is referring to Emerson's *English Traits,* a copy of which Tweedy had apparently just sent him.—Editor's note.

17. The wife of Christopher P. Cranch, the American poet and preacher who had now turned to painting and was living in Paris.—Editor's note.

18. James is referring to William Makepeace Thackeray (1811–1863), the English novelist.—Editor's note.

19. Frederic Henry Hedge, a Unitarian clergyman and later professor at Harvard Divinity School, who is credited with helping acquaint Emerson and other Transcendentalists with a knowledge of German idealistic philosophy.— Editor's note.

20. Sir John Forbes (1787–1861), a British physician and medical writer.— Editor's note.

21. James is referring to Emerson's son, Edward Waldo, who was a companion of Henry, Junior's, and spent several spring vacations with the James family in Newport.—Editor's note.

22. Alice Parkman's father, the Rev. John Parkman of Boston, was a cousin of the eminent historian Francis Parkman.—Editor's note.

23. The reference is to William James's eldest son, Henry, who was then a small child.—Editor's note.

"Father's Ideas": Filial Impressions

20

WILLIAM JAMES

In bringing out a posthumous collection of some of
his father's unpublished essays under the title *The
Literary Remains of the Late Henry James*, William
James regarded it as a filial as well as a philosophic
duty to introduce the volume with an essay of his own
which would offer, as he put it, "some such account of
their author's ideas as might awaken, in readers
hitherto strangers to his writings, the desire to become
acquainted with them." William's modesty about his
own aims is undeserved. His introduction to *The
Literary Remains . . .* , running in all to more than one
hundred pages, constitutes the best summary of his
father's thought that has ever been written and
possesses the added interest of reflecting his own
mature response to a kind of mind which, however
formative upon his own development, was decidely
different from his own. Much of the value of the son's
introduction derives from the generous but judicious
use he makes of his father's words, interlacing his own
commentary with extensive quotations which illustrate
the consistency of tone and unity of conception in his
father's system. Because so many of the passages which
William quotes are drawn from material included in the
selections comprising this work, I have here excerpted
only those portions of the introduction in which William
James reformulates in his own words his father's ideas.

The material which follows is drawn from William
James's introduction to *The Literary Remains of the Late
Henry James* (Boston, 1885), 8–27, 113–19.

————•◆•————

It has seemed to me not only a filial but a philosophic duty, in giving
these posthumous pages to the world, to prefix to them some such account
of their author's ideas as might awaken, in readers hitherto strangers to

his writings, the desire to become acquainted with them. I wish a less unworthy hand than mine were there to do the work. As it is, I must screen my own inadequacy under the language of the original, and let my father speak, as far as possible, for himself. It would indeed be foolish to seek to paraphrase anything once directly said by him. The matter would be sure to suffer; for, from the very outset of his literary career, we find him in the effortless possession of that style with which the reader will soon become acquainted, and which, to its great dignity of cadence and full and homely vocabulary, united a sort of inward palpitating human quality, gracious and tender, precise, fierce, scornful, humorous by turns, recalling the rich vascular temperament of the old English masters, rather than that of an American of to-day.

With all the richness of style, the ideas are singularly unvaried and few. Probably few authors have so devoted their entire lives to the monotonous elaboration of one single bundle of truths. Whenever the eye falls upon one of Mr. James's pages,—whether it be a letter to a newspaper or to a friend, whether it be his earliest or his latest book,—we seem to find him saying again and again the same thing; telling us what the true relation is between mankind and its Creator. What he had to say on this point was the burden of his whole life, and its only burden. When he had said it once, he was disgusted with the insufficiency of the formulation (he always hated the sight of his old books), and set himself to work to say it again. But he never analyzed his terms or his data beyond a certain point, and made very few fundamentally new discriminations; so the result of all these successive re-editings was repetition and amplification and enrichment, rather than reconstruction. The student of any one of his works knows consequently, all that is *essential* in the rest. I must say, however, that the later formulations are philosophically, if not always rhetorically, the best. In "Society the Redeemed Form of Man," which was composed while the lingering effects of an apoplectic stroke had not passed away, there are passages unsurpassed in any former writing. And in the work herewith published, although most of it was written when my father's *general* mental powers were visibly altered by a decay of strength that ended with his death, I doubt if his earlier readers will discover any signs of intellectual decrepitude. His truths were his life; they were the companions of his deathbed; and when all else had ebbed away, his grasp of them was still vigorous and sure.

As aforesaid, they were truths theological. This is anything but a theological age, as we all know; and so far as it permits itself to be theological at all, it is growing more and more to distrust all systems that aim at abstract metaphysics in dogma, or pretend to rigor in their terms. The conventional and traditional acquiescence we find in the older dogmatic formularies is confined to those who are intellectually hardly vitalized enough either to apprehend or discuss a novel and rival creed; whilst those of us who have intellectual vitality are either apt to be full of bias against theism in any form, or if we are theistic at all, it is in such a tentative and supplicating sort of way that the sight of a robust and dogmatizing theologian sends a shiver through our bones. A man like my father, lighting on such a time, is wholly out of his element and atmosphere, and is soon left stranded high and dry. His effectiveness as a missionary is null; and it is wonderful if his voice, crying in the wilderness and getting no echo, do not soon die away for sheer discouragement. That my father should not have been discouraged, but should have remained serene and active to the last, is a proof both of the stoutness of his heart and of the consolations of his creed. How many unknown persons may have received help and suggestion from his writings it is impossible to say. Of out-and-out disciples he had very few who ever named themselves. Few as they were, his correspondence with them was perhaps his principal solace and recreation.

I have often tried to imagine what sort of a figure my father might have made, had he been born in a genuinely theological age, with the best minds about him fermenting with the mystery of the Divinity, and the air full of definitions and theories and counter-theories, and strenuous reasonings and contentions, about God's relations to mankind. Floated on such a congenial tide, furthered by sympathetic comrades, and opposed no longer by blank silence but by passionate and definite resistance, he would infallibly have developed his resources in many ways which, as it was, he never tried; and he would have played a prominent, perhaps a momentous and critical, part in the struggles of his time, for he was a religious prophet and genius, if ever prophet and genius there were. He published an intensely positive, radical, and fresh conception of God, and an intensely vital view of our connection with him. And nothing shows better the altogether lifeless and unintellectual character of the professional theism of our time, than the fact that this view, this conception, so vigorously thrown down, should not have stirred the faintest tremulation on its stagnant pool.

The centre of his whole view of things is this intense conception of God as a creator. Grant it, accept it without criticism, and the rest follows. He nowhere attempts by metaphysical or empirical arguments to make the existence of God plausible; he simply assumes it as something that must be confessed. As has been well said in a recent little work,[1] "Mr. James looks at creation instinctively from the creative side; and this has a tendency to put him at a remove from his readers. The usual problem is,—given the creation, to find the creator. To Mr. James it is—given the creator, to find the creation. God is; of His being there is no doubt; but who and what are *we*?"

To sceptics of theism in any possible form, this fundamental postulate may naturally prove a barrier. But it is difficult to see why it should be an obstacle to professedly Christian students. They also confess God's existence; and the way in which Mr. James took it *au grand sérieux* ["with utter seriousness"], and the issues he read in it, ought, one would suppose, to speak to them with some accent of reality. Like any early Jewish prophet, like the Luther described in a recent work of genius,[2] he went back so far and so deep as to find the religious sentiment in its purest and most unsophisticated form. He lived and breathed as one who knew he had not made himself, but was the work of a power that let him live from one moment to the next, and could do with him what it pleased. His intellect reacted on his sense of the presence of this power, so as to form a *system* of the most radical and self-consistent, as well as of the most simple, kind. I will essay to give the reader a preliminary notion of what its main elements and outlines were, and then try to build up a more adequate representation of it by means of quotations from the author's own pen.

It had many and diverse affinities. It was optimistic in one sense, pessimistic in another. Pantheistic, idealistic, hegelian, are epithets that very naturally arise on the reader's lips to describe it; and yet some part there is of the connotation of each of these epithets that made my father violently refuse to submit to their imposition. The ordinary empirical ethics of evolutionary naturalism can find a perfect *permis de séjour* ["permission to reside"] under the system's wings; and yet close alongside is an insistence on the need of the death of the natural man and of a supernatural redemption, more thorough-going than what we find in the most evangelical protestantism. Dualism, yet monism; antinomianism, yet restraint; atheism (as we might almost name it,—that is, the swallowing up of God in Humanity) as the last result of God's achievement,—such are some of the first aspects of this at bottom very simple and harmonious view of the world.

It all flowed from two perceptions, insights, convictions, whatever one pleases to call them, in its author's mind. In the first place, he felt that the individual man, as such, is nothing, but owes all he is and has to the race nature he inherits, and to the society into which he is born. And, secondly, he scorned to admit, even as a possibility, that the great and loving Creator, who has all the being and the power, and has brought us as far as *this,* should not bring us *through,* and *out,* into the most triumphant harmony.

I beseech the reader from now onwards to listen to my stammering exposition in a very uncritical mood of mind. Do not *squeeze* the terms or the logic too hard! And if you are a positivist, do not be too prompt to throw the book down with an ejaculation of disgust at Alexandrian theosophizing, and of wonder that such brain-spinning should find a printer at the present day. My father's own disgust at any abstract statement of his system could hardly be excelled by that of the most positivistic reader. I will not say that the logical relations of its terms were with him a mere afterthought; they were more organic than that. But the core and centre of the thing in him was always instinct and attitude, something realized at a stroke, and felt like a fire in his breast; and all attempts at articulate verbal formulations of it were makeshifts of a more or less desperately impotent kind. This is why he despised every formulation he made as soon as it was uttered, and set himself to the Sisyphus-labor of producing a new one that should be less irrelevant. I remember hearing him groan, when struggling in this way, "Oh, that I might thunder it out in a single interjection that would tell the *whole* of it, and never speak a word again!" But he paid his tribute to necessity; and few writers in the end were more prolix than he.

To begin then,—trying to think the matter in as simple, childlike, and empirical a fashion as possible,—the negativity and dearth of the creature (which is surely a part of the truth we livingly feel every day of our lives)[3] is an elementary and primitive factor in the creative problem. It plays an active and dynamic part through Mr. James's pages, and is the feature which made me say, a moment back, that "hegelian" would be a very natural epithet to use in describing the doctrine they set forth. Hegel sometimes speaks of the Divinity making an illusion first, in order to remove it; setting up his own antithesis in order to the subsequent neutralization thereof. And this will also very well describe the creative drama as pictured by Mr. James, provided one bear in mind that the preliminary production of an illusory stage of being is *forced* upon the Creator by the character of that *positively yawning emptiness* which is the opposite of himself, and with which he has to deal.

The ordinary orthodox view of creation is that Jehovah explodes the universe absolutely out of what was previously pure blank; his *fiat* whacks it down upon the *tabula rasa* ["clean slate"] of time and space, and there it remains. Such simple, direct, and "magical" creation is always derided by Mr. James as a childish idea. The *real* nothingness cannot become thus promptly the seat of real being; it must taint with its own "abysmal destitution" whatever first comes to fill it, and reduce it to the status of a sham, or unreal magic-lantern picture projected on the dark inane.

This first result of the intercourse of the creative energy with the void may *become* however, by decaying unto itself, a surface of rebound for *another* movement, of which the result is real. Creation is thus made up of two stages, the first of which is mere scaffolding to the second, which is the final work. Mr. James's terminology is a little vacillating with regard to these two stages. On the whole, "formation" is the word he oftenest applies to the first stage, and "redemption" to the second. His view of the matter is obviously entirely different from the simple, direct process taught by natural theology and by the Jewish Scripture; and it as obviously agrees in point of form with the composite movement of the Christian scheme.

All this is verbally simple enough; but what are the facts it covers? To speak very oracularly, *Nature* is for Mr. James the movement of formation, the first quickening of the void itself; and *Society* is the movement of redemption, or the finished spiritual work of God.

Now, both "Nature" and "Society" are words of peculiar and complex meaning in Mr. James's writings, so that much explanation is needed of the assertions just laid down.

"Nature" and "Society," if I understand our author correctly, do not differ from each other at all in substance or material. Their substance is the Creator himself, for he is the sole positive substance in the universe, all else being nothingness.[4] But they differ in form; for while Nature is the Creator immersed and lost in a nothingness self-affirming and obstructive, Society is the same Creator, with the nothingness saved, determined to transparency and self-confession, and traversed from pole to pole by his life-giving rays.

The *matter* covered by both these words is Humanity and the totality of its conditions, nothing short of the entire world of phenomenal experience,—mineral, vegetable, animal, and human,—"Nature" culminating in, whilst "Society" starts from, the moral and religious consciousness of man. This is why I said the system could hospitably house anything that naturalistic evolutionism might ever have to say about man; for, according to both doctrines, man's morality and religion, his consciousness of self and his moral conscience, are natural products like everything else we see. Now, for Mr. James, the consciousness of self and the conscience are the hinges on which the process of creation turns, as it slowly revolves from its formative and natural to its redeemed and spiritual position of equilibrium. What I say will still be dark and unreal enough to those who know nothing of the original; but the exercise of a little patience will erelong make things clear.

What is self-consciousness or morality? and what is conscience or religion?—for our author uses synonymously the terms within each pair. The terminology is at first bewildering, and the metaphysical results confounding; for whilst the *stuff* of both morality and religion is, so to speak, the very energy, the very being, of God himself, yet in morality that being takes wholly, and in religion it takes partly, the form of a lie. Let us consider the matter *naïvely* and mythically, so as to understand. Remember, that for Mr. James a mere resistless "bang" is no creative process at all, and that a *real* creation means nothing short of a real *bringing to life* of the essential nothingness, which is the eternal antithesis to God—a *work*, therefore, upon that nothingness actually performed. Well, then, God must work upon the void; but how can the trackless void be wrought upon? It must first be vivified and quickened into some kind of substantiality of its own, and made existential and phenomenal instead of merely logical and essential that it was, before any further fashioning of it can take place. God then must, *in the first instance*, make a being that has the void for its other parent, and *involves* nothingness in itself. To make a long story short, then, God's first product is a Nature *subject to self-consciousness or selfhood*,—that is, a Nature essentially good, as being divine, but the several members whereof *appropriate* the goodness, and egoistically and atheistically[5] seek to identify it with their private selves. This selfishness of the several members is the trail of the serpent over creation, the coming to life of the ancestral void. It negates, because it entirely inverts, God's own energy, which is undiluted altruistic love; it intercepts the truth of his impartial flowing tides; it is an utter lie, and yet a lie under the dense and unsuspecting mask of which alone "the

great and sincere Creator of men" is able gradually to conciliate our instincts, and win us over to the truth.

This happens whenever we are weaned from the lie; for the abandoning
of the lie in this instance coalesces in the same conscious act with the
confessing of the truth. "I am nothing as substantive,—I am everything as
recipient;" this is a thought in which both I and the Creator figure, but
in which we figure in perfectly harmonious and truthful guise. It is
accordingly the threshold of spiritual life; and instead of obstructing and
striving to intercept, it welcomes and furthers all that the divine Love may
have in store for every member of the created family.

The agents of the *weaning* are conscience and religion. In the philosophy before us, these faculties are considered to have no other function
than that of being ministers of death to the fallacious selfhood. They have
no positive worth or character, and are mere clearers of the way. They
bring no new content upon the scene; they simply permit the pre-existing
content to settle into a new and truer form. The facts of our nature with
every man in it blinded with pride and jealousy, and stiffened in ex-
clusiveness and self-seeking, are one thing,—that thing whose destinies
Church and State are invoked to control, and whose tragic and discordant
history we partly know. Those very same facts, after conscience and religion have played their part, and undermined the illusion of the self, so
that men acknowledge their life to come from God, and love each other
as God loves, having no exclusive private cares, will form the kingdom of
heaven on earth, the regenerate social order which none of us yet know.
In a word, God will be fully incarnated at last in a form that no longer
contradicts his character, in what Mr. James calls, with Swedenborg, the
Divine-Natural Humanity. God's real creature is this aggregate Humanity.
He cannot be partial to one fractional unit of us more than to another.
And the only difference between the unredeemed and the regenerate social
form lies in the simple fact, that in the former the units *will* not fall into
relations accordant with this truth, while in the latter, such an attitude
is the one they most spontaneously assume. One Substance, extricating
itself by finding at last a true form,—such is the process, once begun!
And no one *part* is either "lost" or "saved" in any other sense than that
it either arrests or furthers the transmission through itself to others of
God's life-giving tides.

This probably sounds to most ears thin and cold and mythical enough,
—the "Divine-Natural Humanity" especially, with its abolition of selfishness, appearing quite as shallow and insipid a dream as any other paradise
excogitated by imaginative man. This is the inevitable result of trying to
express didactically and articulately, in the form of a story, what in its
origin is more like an intuition, sentiment, or attitude of the soul. The
matter shall be immediately thickened and filled out to the reader's
understanding by quotations from Mr. James himself, touching succes-
sively the various elements of the scheme. But if I may be permitted an
opinion here, I should say that in no such successive shape as this did the

scheme have *authority* over Mr. James's own mind. I fancy that his belief in its truth was strongest when the dumb sense of human life, sickened and baffled as it is forever by the strange unnatural fever in its breast of unreality and dearth struggling with infinite fulness and possession, became a sort of voice within him, and cried out, "This *must* stop! The good, the good, is really *there*, and *must* see to its own! Who is its own? Is it this querulous usurping, jealous *me*, sickened of defeat and done to death, and glad never to raise its head again? Never more! It is some sweeter, larger, more innocent and generous receptacle of life than that cadaverous and lying thing can ever be.[6] Let *that* but be removed, and the other may come in. And there must be a way to remove it, for God himself is there, and cannot be frustrated forever of his aim,—least of all by such an obstacle as that! He must *somehow*, and by eternal necessity he *shall*, bring the kingdom of heaven about!"

I may as well say here, once for all, that the kingdom of heaven postulated in this deep and simple way, and then more articulately formulated as the "Divine-Natural Humanity," remained to the end a mere postulate or programme in my father's pages, and never received at his hands any concrete filling out. It was what *must* come to be, if God truly exist,—an assumption we *owe* to his power and his love, and that any man with a sense of God's reality will scorn to hesitate to make. That, moreover, the kingdom was to be made of no other stuff than the actual stuff of human nature, was but another tribute,—a tribute of manly loyalty to the real divinity of the Good existing in the human bosom now. In his earlier years, between 1842 and 1850, when Mr. James's ideas were being settled by the reading of Swedenborg, he also became interested in the socialistic fermentations then so rife, and in particular in the writings of Fourier. His first two works shadow forth the Divine-Natural Humanity as about to be born, through the yoking of the passions into harmonious social service, by the growth of socialistic organization, in place of the old régime of Church and State, among men. Since then, there have been many disappointments, in which he shared; and although Fourier's system was never displaced from his mind as at least a provisional representation of possible redeemed life, I think that at the last he cared little to dispute about matters of detail, being willing to cast the whole burden upon God, who would be sure to order it rightly when all the conditions were fulfilled. . . .

A word of comment after so much exposition may not be out of place. Common-sense theism, the popular religion of our European race, has, through all its apparent variations, remained esssentially faithful to pluralism, one might almost say to polytheism. Neither Judaism nor Christianity could tend to alter this result, or make us generally see the world in any other light than as a collection of beings which, however they might have arisen, are now severally and substantively there, and the important thing about whom is their practical relations with each other. God, the Devil, Christ, the Saints, and we, are some of these beings. Whatever monistic and pantheistic metaphysics may have crept into the history of Christianity has been confined to epochs, sects, and individuals. For the great mass of men, the practical fact of pluralism has been a sufficient basis for the religious life, and the ultra-phenomenal unity has been nothing more than a lip-formula.

And *naïve* as in the eyes of metaphysics such a view may seem, finite and short of vision and lacking dignity from the intellectual point of view, no philosopher, however subtle, can afford to treat it with disdain; unless, perhaps, he be ready to say that the spirit of Europe is all wrong, and that of Asia right. God, treated as a principle among others,—*primus inter pares* ["first among his peers"],—has warmth and blood and personality; is a concrete being whom it does not take a scholar to love and make sacrifices and die for, as history shows. Being almost like a personage in a drama, the lightning of dramatic interest can play from him and about him, and rivet human regard.

The "One and Only Being," however, the Universal Substance, the Soul and Spirit of Things, the First Principle of monistic metaphysics, call it by names as theological and reverential as we will, always seems, it must be confessed, a pale, abstract, and impersonal conception compared with that of the eternal living God, worshipped by the incalculable majority of our race. Such a monistic principle never can be worshipped by a majority of our race until the race's mental constitution change.

Now, the great peculiarity of Mr. James's conception of God is, that it is monistic enough to satisfy the philosopher, and yet warm and living and dramatic enough to speak to the heart of the common pluralistic man. This double character seems to make of this conception an entirely fresh and original contribution to religious thought. I call it monistic enough to satisfy the metaphysician, for although Mr. James's system is anything but a *bald* monism, yet it makes of God the one and only *active* principle; and that is practically all that monism demands. Our experience makes us, it is true, acquainted with an *other* of God, in our own selfhood; but for Mr. James, that other, that selfhood, has no positive existence, being really *naught*, a provisional phantom-soul breathed by God's love into mere logical negation. And that a monism, thus mitigated, can speak to the common heart, a perusal of those pages in which Mr. James portrays creation on God's part as an infinite passion of self-surrender to his opposite, will convince any reader. Anthropomorphism and metaphysics seem for the first time in these pages to go harmoniously hand in hand. The same sun that lights up the frozen summits of abstraction, lights up life's teeming plain,—and no chasm, but an open highway lies between.

The extraordinary power and richness of this conception of the Deity ought, one would say, to make Mr. James's writings indispensable to students of religious thought. Within their compass, each old element receives a fresh expression, each old issue a startling turn. It is hard to believe, that, when they are better known, they will not come to be counted among the few truly original theological works which our language owns. So that even those who think that no theological thought can be *conclusive* will, for this reason, perhaps, not refuse to them a lasting place in literature.

Their most serious enemy will be the *philosophic* pluralist. The naïf practical pluralism of popular religion ought, as I have said, to have no quarrel with the monism they teach. There is however a pluralism hardened by reflection, and deliberate; a pluralism which, in face of the old mystery of the One and the Many, has vainly sought peace in identification, and ended by taking sides against the One. It seems to me that the deepest of all philosophic differences is that between this pluralism and all forms of monism whatever. Apart from analytic and intellectual arguments, pluralism is a view to which we all practically incline when in the full and successful exercise of our moral energy. The life we then feel tingling through us vouches sufficiently for itself, and nothing tempts us to refer it to a higher source. Being, as we are, a match for whatever evils actually confront us, we rather prefer to think of them as endowed with reality, and as being absolutely alien, but, we hope, subjugable powers. Of the day of our possible impotency we take no thought; and we care not to make such a synthesis of our weakness and our strength, and of the good and evil fortunes of the world, as will reduce them all to fractions, with a common denominator, of some less fluctuating Unity, enclosing some less partial and more certain form of Good. The feeling of *action*, in short, makes us turn a deaf ear to the thought of *being;* and this deafness and insensibility may be said to form an integral part of what in popular phrase is known as "healthy-mindedness." Any absolute moralism must needs be such a healthy-minded pluralism, and in a pluralistic philosophy the healthy-minded moralist will always feel himself at home.

But healthy-mindedness is not the whole of life; and the *morbid* view, as one by contrast may call it, asks for a philosophy very different from that of absolute moralism. To suggest personal will and effort to one "all sicklied o'er" with the sense of weakness, of helpless failure, and of fear, is to suggest the most horrible of things to him. What he craves is to be consoled in his very impotence, to feel that the Powers of the Universe recognize and secure him, all passive and failing as he is. Well, we are all *potentially* such sick men. The sanest and best of us are of one clay with lunatics and prison-inmates. And whenever we feel this, such a sense of the vanity of our voluntary career comes over us, that all our morality appears but as a plaster hiding a sore it can never cure, and all our well-doing as the hollowest substitute for that well-*being* that our lives ought to be grounded in, but, alas! are not. This well-being is the object of the *religious* demand,—a demand so penetrating and unassuageable that no consciousness of such occasional and outward well-doing as befalls the human lot can ever give it satisfaction. On the other hand, to satisfy the religious demand is to deny the demands of the moralist. The latter wishes to feel the empirical goods and evils, on the recognition of which his activity proceeds, to be *real* goods and evils, with their distinction absolutely preserved. So that of religion and moralism, the morbid and the healthy view, it may be said that what is meat to the one is the other's poison. Any absolute moralism is a pluralism; any absolute religion is a monism. It shows the depth of Mr. James's religious insight that he first and last and always made moralism the target of his hottest attack, and pitted religion and it against each other as enemies, of whom one must die utterly, if the other is to live in genuine form. The accord of moralism and religion is superficial, their discord radical. Only the deepest thinkers on both sides see that one must go. Popular opinion gets over the difficulty by compromise and contradiction, and the shifting, according to its convenience, of its point of view. Such inconsistency cannot be called a solution of the matter, though it practically seems to work with most men well enough. Must not the more radical ways of thinking, after all, appeal to the same umpire of practice for corroboration of their more consistent views? Is the religious tendency or the moralistic tendency on the whole the most serviceable to man's life, taking the latter in the largest way? By their fruits ye shall know them. *Solvitur ambulando* [literally, "deal with it as it comes"]; for the *decision* we must perhaps await the day of judgment. Meanwhile, the battle is about us, and we are its combatants, steadfast or vacillating, as the case may be. It will be a hot fight indeed if the friends of philosophic moralism should bring to the service of their ideal, so different from that of my father, a spirit even remotely resembling the lifelong devotion of his faithful heart.

NOTES

1. J. A. Kellogg, *Philosophy of Henry James: A Digest* (New York: John W. Lovell Co., 1883).

2. J. Milsand, *Luther et le Serf-Arbitre* (Paris: Fischbacher, 1884). Passim.

3. Empirically, we know that we are creatures with a lack, a destitution, a death, an ultimate helplessness. Which of us but sometimes "lifts a pallid face in prayer to God, lest some hideous calamity engulf his fairest hopes? . . . We are all without real selfhood, without the selfhood which comes from God alone. We have only a showy and fallacious one . . . which is wholly inadequate to guarantee us against calamity. We shiver in every breeze, and stand aghast at every cloud that passes over the sun. When our ships go down at sea, what shrieks we hear from blanched and frenzied lips peopling the melancholy main, perturbing the sombre and sympathetic air for months afterwards! When our children die, and take back to heaven the brimming innocence which our corrupt manhood feels no use for, and therefore knows not how to shelter; when our friends drop off; when our property exhales; when our reason totters on its throne, and menaces us with a downfall,—who then is strong? Who in fact, if we were left in these cases for a moment to himself,—that is, if he were not steadied in his own despite by the mere life of routine and tradition,—but would be ready to renounce God and perish? So too our *ennui* and prevalent disgust of life, which lead so many suffering souls every year to suicide, which drive so many tender and yearning and angel-freighted natures to drink, to gambling, to fierce and ruinous excess of all sorts,—what are these things but the tacit avowal

(audible enough, however, to God!) that we are nothing at all and vanity; that we are absolutely without help in ourselves; and that we can never be blessed and tranquil until God take compassion on us, and conjoin us livingly and immortally with himself?"—*Christianity the Logic of Creation*, p. 133.

4. This is why I said one might call the system pantheistic. Mr. James denounces pantheism, however; for he supposes it to exclude a dualism even of *logical* elements, and to represent the Divine as manifesting itself in phenomena by a simple outward movement without subsequent recoil. It is a matter of verbal definition after all. One might say that the gist of his differences, both with pantheism and with ordinary theism, is that while the latter represent creation to be essentially the formation of Two out of an original One, to Mr. James it is something more like the union into One of an original Two.

5. "That is to say, the only hindrance to men's believing in God as a creator is their inability to believe in *themselves* as created. Self-consciousness, the sentiment of personality, the feeling I have of life in myself, absolute and underived from any other save in a natural way, is so subtly and powerfully atheistic, that, no matter how loyally I may be taught to insist upon creation as a mere traditional or legendary fact, I never feel inclined personally to believe in it, save as the fruit of some profound intellectual humiliation or hopeless inward vexation of spirit. My inward *afflatus* from this cause is so great, I am conscious of such superabounding personal life, that I am satisfied, for my own part at least, that my sense of selfhood must in some subtle exquisite way find itself wounded to death—find itself *become death* in fact, *the only death I am capable of believing in*—before any genuine spiritual resuscitation is at all practicable for me."—*Society the Redeemed Form of Man*, p. 185.

6. "Just in proportion, accordingly, as a man's spiritual knowledge improves, will his contempt for himself, as an unmixed spiritual tramp and irredeemable vagabond, increase and abound. We might very well bear with an uninstructed or inexperienced child, who, shut up to the companionship of its doll, constructed all of sawdust and prunella, looks upon it as spiritually alive; but one has no patience with an experienced, instructed man or churchman, who undergoes precisely the same hallucination with regard to his own worthless doll of a selfhood,—which is destitute even of so much as a sawdust and prunella reality,—and conceives that the Divine being has nothing better to do than literally to bestow divine and immortal life upon that dead, corrupt, and stinking thing."—*New Church Independent*, September, 1879, p. 413.

21

HENRY JAMES

Henry James left a record of his own impressions
of his father in *Notes of a Son and Brother* which
he composed toward the end of his life. What
distinguishes the impressions of the novelist from
those of the philosopher is the particular perception
each had of his father. Though both are addressing
themselves to the nature of their father's spiritual
insight and experience, William is striving for what
might be called its substance, the ideas which shaped
it and gave it sufficient intellectual outline to be
compared and contrasted with other systems of belief,
whereas Henry is seeking to express what might be
called its sensibility, the qualities which determined
its ethos and generated its tone. Who can say which is
the more illuminating, the more essential, the more
definitive? In any case, reading these two impressions
together, those William recorded less than three years
after his father's death and those Henry wrote almost
twenty years later, tends to confirm a suspicion that
the one without the other provides only half the truth,
that to know what the elder James's ideas were without
knowing how he experienced them is not to know the
ideas he experienced.

The following selection is taken from Henry James's
Notes of a Son and Brother (New York, 1914), 155–72.

These returns to that first year or two at Newport contribute meanwhile to filling out as nothing in the present pages has yet done for me
that vision of our father's unsurpassable patience and independence, in
the interest of the convictions he cherished and the expression of them, as
richly emphatic as it was scantly heded, to which he daily gave himself.
We took his "writing" infinitely for granted—we had always so taken it,
and the sense of him, each long morning, at his study table either with

bent considering brow or with a half-spent and checked intensity, a lapse backward in his chair and a musing lift of perhaps troubled and baffled eyes, seems to me the most constant fact, the most closely interwoven and underlying, among all our breaks and variations. He applied himself there with a regularity and a piety as little subject to sighing abatements or betrayed fears as if he had been working under pressure for his bread and ours and the question were too urgent for his daring to doubt. This play of his remarkable genius brought him in fact throughout the long years no ghost of a reward in the form of pence, and could proceed to publicity, as it repeatedly did, not only by the copious and resigned sacrifice of such calculations, but by his meeting in every single case all the expenses of the process. The untired impulse to this devotion figured for us, comprehensively and familiarly, as "Father's Ideas," of the force and truth of which in his own view we were always so respectfully, even though at times so bewilderedly and confoundedly persuaded, that we felt there was nothing in his exhibition of life that they didn't or couldn't account for. They pervaded and supported his existence, and very considerably our own; but what comes back to me, to the production of a tenderness and an admiration scarce to be expressed, is the fact that though we thus easily and naturally lived with them and indeed, as to their more general effects, the colour and savour they gave to his talk, breathed them in and enjoyed both their quickening and their embarrassing presence, to say nothing of their almost never less than amusing, we were left as free and unattacked by them as if they had been so many droppings of gold and silver coin on tables and chimney-pieces, to be "taken" or not according to our sense and delicacy, that is our felt need and felt honour. The combination in him of his different vivacities, his living interest in his philosophy, his living interest in us and his living superiority to all greed of authority, all overreaching or overemphasising "success," at least in the heated short run, gave his character a magnanimity by which it was impossible to us not to profit in all sorts of responsive and in fact quite luxurious ways. It was a luxury, I to-day see, to have all the benefit of his intellectual and spiritual, his religious, his philosophic and his social passion, without ever feeling the pressure of it to our direct irritation or discomfort. It would perhaps more truly figure the relation in which he left us to these things to have likened our opportunities rather to so many scattered glasses of the liquor of faith, poured-out cups stood about for our either sipping or draining down or leaving alone, in the measure of our thirst, our curiosity or our strength of head and heart. If there was much leaving alone in us—and I freely confess that, so far as the taking any of it all "straight" went, my lips rarely adventured—this was doubtless because we drank so largely at the source itself, the personally overflowing and irrigating. What it then comes to, for my present vision, was that he treated us most of all on the whole, as he in fact treated everything, by his saving imagination—which set us, and the more as we were naturally so inclined, the example of living as much as we might in some such light of our own. If we had been asked

in our younger time for instance what *were* our father's ideas, or to give
an example of one of them, I think we should promptly have answered (I
should myself have hastened to do so) that the principal was a devoted
attachment to the writings of Swedenborg; as to whom we were to remember betimes, with intimate appreciation, that in reply to somebody's plea
of not finding him credible our parent had pronounced him, on the contrary, fairly "insipid with veracity." We liked that partly, I think, because
it disposed in a manner, that is in favour of our detachment, of the great
Emanuel, but when I remember the part played, so close beside us, by
this latter's copious revelation, I feel almost ashamed for my own incuri-
ous conduct. The part played consisted to a large extent in the vast, even
though incomplete, array of Swedenborg's works, the old faded covers
of which, anciently red, actually apt to be loose, and backed with labels
of impressive, though to my sense somewhat sinister London imprint,
Arcana Coelestia, Heaven and Hell and other such matters—they all had,
as from other days, a sort of black emphasis of dignity—ranged themselves before us wherever, and however briefly, we disposed ourselves,
forming even for short journeys the base of our father's travelling library
and perhaps at some seasons therewith the accepted strain on our mother's
patience. I recall them as inveterately part of our very luggage, requiring
proportionate receptacles; I recall them as, in a number considerable even
when reduced, part of their proprietor's own most particular dependence
on his leaving home, during our more agitated years, for those speculative
visits to possible better places (than whatever place of the moment) from
which, as I have elsewhere mentioned, he was apt to return under premature, under passionate nostalgic, reaction. The Swedenborgs were
promptly out again on their customary shelves or sometimes more im-
provised perches, and it was somehow not till we had assured ourselves
of this that we felt *that* incident closed.

Nothing could have exceeded at the same time our general sense—
unless I all discreetly again confine myself to the spare record of my
own—for our good fortune in never having been, even when most helpless,
dragged by any approach to a faint jerk over the threshold of the inhabited temple. It stood there in the centre of our family life, into which
its doors of fine austere bronze opened straight; we passed and repassed
them when we didn't more consciously go round and behind; we took for
granted vague grand things within, but we never paused to peer or penetrate, and none the less never had the so natural and wistful, perhaps even
the so properly resentful, "Oh I say, do look in a moment for manners
if for nothing else!" called after us as we went. Our admirable mother
sat on the steps at least and caught reverberations of the inward mystic
choir; but there were positive contemporary moments when I well-nigh
became aware, I think, of something graceless, something not to the credit
of my aspiring "intellectual life," or of whatever small pretensions to
seriousness I might have begun to nourish, in the anything but heroic im-
punity of my inattention. William, later on, made up for this not a little,
redeeming so, to a large extent, as he grew older, our filial honour in the

matter of a decent sympathy, if not of a noble curiosity: distinct to me even are certain echoes of passages between our father and his eldest son that I assisted at, more or less indirectly and wonderingly, as at intellectual "scenes," gathering from them portents of my brother's independent range of speculation, agitations of thought and announcements of difference, which could but have represented, far beyond anything I should ever have to show, a gained and to a considerable degree an enjoyed, confessedly an interested, acquaintance with the paternal philosophic *penetralia* ["insights"]. That particular impression refers indeed to hours which at the point I have reached had not yet struck; but I am touched even now, after all the years, with something exquisite in my half-grasped premonitory vision of their belonging, these belated discussions that were but the flowering of the first germs of such *other*, doubtless already such opposed, perceptions and conclusions, to that order of thin consolations and broken rewards which long figured as the most and the best of what was to have been waited for on our companion's part without the escape of a plaint. Yet I feel I may claim that our awareness of all that was so serenely dispensed with—to call it missed would have been quite to falsify the story and reflect meanly on the spirit—never in the least brutally lapsed from admiration, however unuttered the sentiment itself, after the fashion of raw youth; it is in fact quite distinct to me that, had there been danger of this, there came to us from our mother's lips at intervals long enough to emphasise the final sincerity and beauty a fairly sacred reminder of that strain of almost solely self-nourished equanimity, or in other words insuperable gaiety, in her life's comrade, which she had never seen give way. This was the very gaiety that kept through the years coming out for us—to the point of inviting free jokes and other light familiarities from us at its expense. The happiest household pleasantry invested our legend of our mother's fond habit of address, "Your father's *ideas*, you know—!" which was always the signal for our embracing her with the last responsive finality (and, for the full pleasure of it, in his presence). Nothing indeed so much as his presence encouraged the licence, as I may truly call it, of the legend—that is of our treatment *en famille* of any reference to the attested public weight of his labours; which, I hasten to add, was much too esoteric a ground of geniality, a dear old family joke, not to be kept, for its value, to ourselves. But there comes back to me the impression of his appearing on occasion quite moved to the exuberance of cheer—as a form of refreshment he could draw on for a stronger and brighter spurt, I mean—by such an apology for resonance of reputation as our harmless, our of course utterly edgeless, profanity represented. It might have been for him, by a happy stretch, a sign that the world *did* know—taking us for the moment, in our selfish young babble, as a part of the noise of the world. Nothing, at the same time, could alter the truth of his case, or can at least alter it to me now: he had, intellectually, convictionally, passionally speaking, a selfless detachment, a lack of what is called the eye for effect—always I mean of the

elated and interested order—which I can but marvel at in the light of the
rare aptitude of his means to his end, and in that of the beauty of both,
though the stamp was doubtless most vivid, for so differing, so gropingly
"esthetic" a mind as my own, in his unfailingly personal and admirable
style. We knew he had thoroughly his own "unconventional" form, which,
by the unspeakable law of youth, we managed to feel the distinction of
as not platitudinous even while we a bit sneakingly felt it as quotable, on
possible occasions, against our presence of mind; the great thing was at
all events that we couldn't live with him without the sense that if his
books resembled his talk and his character—as we moreover felt they
couldn't help almost violently doing—they might want for this, that or the
other which kept the conventional true to its type, but could as little fail
to flush with the strong colour, colour so remarkably given and not taken,
projected and not reflected, colour of thought and faith and moral and
expressional atmosphere, as they could leave us without that felt side-
wind of their strong composition which made after all so much of the air
we breathed and was in the last resort the gage of something perpetually
fine going on.

It is not too much to say, I think, that our religious education, so far
as we had any, consisted wholly in that loose yet enlightening impression:
I say so far as we had any in spite of my very definitely holding that it
would absolutely not have been possible to us, in the measure of our
sensibility, to breathe more the air of that reference to an order of goodness and power greater than any this world by itself can show which we
understand as the religious spirit. Wondrous to me, as I consider again,
that my father's possession of this spirit, in a degree that made it more
deeply one with his life than I can conceive another or a different case
of its being, should have been unaccompanied with a single one of the
outward or formal, the theological, devotional, ritual, or even implicitly
pietistic signs by which we usually know it. The fact of course was that
his religion was nothing if not a philosophy, extraordinarily complex and
worked out and original, intensely personal as an exposition, yet not only
susceptible of application, but clamorous for it, to the whole field of
consciousness, nature and society, history, knowledge, all human relations
and questions, every pulse of the process of our destiny. Of this vast and
interesting conception, as striking an expression of the religious spirit
surely as ever was put forth, his eldest son has given an account[1]—so far
as this was possible at once with brevity and with full comprehension—
that I should have been unable even to dream of aspiring to, and in the
masterly clearness and justice of which the opportunity of the son blends
with that of the critic, each character acting in perfect felicity, after a
fashion of which I know elsewhere no such fine example. It conveys the
whole sense of our father's philosophic passion, which was theologic, by
my direct impression of it, to a degree fairly outdistancing all theologies;
representing its weight, reproducing its utterance, placing it in the eye
of the world, and making for it the strong and single claim it suggests,

in a manner that leaves nothing to be added to the subject. I am not concerned with the intrinsic meaning of these things here, and should not be even had they touched me more directly, or more converted me from what I can best call, to my doubtless scant honour, a total otherness of contemplation, during the years when my privilege was greatest and my situation for inquiry and response amplest; but the active, not to say the obvious, moral of them, in all our younger time, was that a life of the most richly consequent flowed straight out of them, that in this life, the most abundantly, and above all naturally, communicated *as* life that it was possible to imagine, we had an absolutely equal share, and that in time I was to live to go back with wonder and admiration to the quantity of secreted thought in our daily medium, the quality of intellectual passion, the force of cogitation and aspiration, as to the explanation both of a thousand surface incoherences and a thousand felt felicities. A religion that was so systematically a philosophy, a philosophy that was so sweepingly a religion, being together, by their necessity, as I have said, an intensity of relation to the actual, the consciousness so determined was furnished forth in a way that met by itself the whole question of the attitude of "worship" for instance; as I have attempted a little to show that it met, with a beautiful good faith and the easiest sufficiency, every other when such came up: those of education, acquisition, material vindication, what is called success generally. In the beauty of the whole thing, again, I lose myself—by which I mean in the fact that we were all the while partaking, to our most intimate benefit, of an influence of direction and enlargement attended with scarce a single consecrated form and which would have made many of these, had we been exposed to intrusion from them, absurdly irrelevant. My father liked in our quite younger period to read us chapters from the New Testament and the Old, and I hope we liked to listen to them—though I recall their seeming dreary from their association with school practice; but that was the sole approach to a challenge of our complete freedom of inward, not less than our natural ingenuity of outward, experience. No other explicit address to us in the name of the Divine could, I see, have been made with any congruity—in face of the fact that invitations issued in all the vividest social terms, terms of living appreciation, of spiritual perception, of "human fellowship," to use the expression that was perhaps oftenest on his lips and his pen alike, were the very substance of the food supplied in the parental nest.

The freedom from pressure that we enjoyed in every direction, all those immunities and exemptions that had been, in protracted childhood, positively embarrassing to us, as I have already noted, before the framework, ecclesiastical and mercantile, squared at us as with reprobation from other households, where it seemed so to conduce to their range of resource— these things consorted with our yet being yearned over or prescribed for, by every implication, after a fashion that was to make the social organisation of such invidious homes, under my subsequent observation of life, affect me as so much bleak penury or domestic desert where these things of the spirit, these genialities of faith were concerned. Well do I remember, none the less, how I was troubled all along just by this particular crookedness of our being so extremely religious without having, as it were, anything in the least classified or striking to show for it; so that the measure of other-worldliness pervading our premises was rather a waste, though at the same time oddly enough a congestion—projecting outwardly as it did no single one of those usual symptoms of propriety any of which, gathered at a venture from the general prospect, might by my sense have served: I shouldn't have been particular, I thought, as to the selection. Religion was a matter, by this imagination, to be worked off much more than to be worked in, and I fear my real vague sentiment to have been but that life would under the common equipment be somehow more amusing; and this even though, as I don't forget, there was not an item of the detail of devotional practice that we had been so much as allowed to divine. I scarce know why I should have wanted anything more amusing, as most of our coevals would have regarded it, than that we had from as far back as I could remember indulged in no shade of an approach to "keeping Sunday"; which is one of the reasons why to speak as if piety could have borne for us any sense but the tender human, or to speak at all of devotion, unction, initiation, even of the vaguest, into the exercises or professions, as among our attributes, would falsify altogether our mere fortune of a general liberty of living, of making ourselves as brightly at home as might be, in that "spiritual world" which we were in the habit of hearing as freely alluded to as we heard the prospect of dinner or the call of the postman. The oddity of my own case, as I make it out so far as it involved a confused criticism, was that my small uneasy mind, bulging and tightening in the wrong, or at least in unnatural and unexpected, places, like a little jacket ill cut or ill sewn, attached its gaping view, as I have already more than enough noted, to things and persons, objects and aspects, frivolities all, I dare say I was willing to grant, compared with whatever manifestations of the serious, these being by need, apparently, the abstract; and that in fine I should have been thankful for a state of faith, a conviction of the Divine, an interpretation of the universe—anything one might have made bold to call it—which would have supplied more features or appearances. Feeling myself "after" persons so much more than after anything slse—to recur to that side of my earliest and most constant consciousness which might have been judged most deplorable—I take it that I found the sphere of our more nobly supposititious habitation too imperceptibly peopled; whereas the religious life of every other family that could boast of any such (and what family didn't boast?) affected my fancy as with a social and material crowdedness. That faculty alone was affected—this I hasten to add; no directness of experience ever stirred for me; it being the case in the first place that I scarce remember, as to all our young time, the crossing of our threshold by any faint shade of an ecclesiastical presence, or the lightest encounter with any such elsewhere, and equally of the essence, over and above, that the clerical race, the preeminently restrictive tribe, as I apprehended them, couldn't very well have agreed less with the general colour of my fondest vision: if it be not indeed more correct to say that I was reduced to *supposing* they couldn't. We knew in truth nothing whatever about them, a fact that, as I recover it, also flushes for me with its fine awkwardness—the social scene in general handsomely bristling with them to the rueful view I sketch, and they yet remaining for us, or at any rate for myself, such creatures of pure hearsay that when late in my teens, and in particular after my twentieth year, I began to see them portrayed by George Eliot and Anthony Trollope the effect was a disclosure of a new and romantic species. Strange beyond my present power to account for it this anomaly that amid a civilisation replete with "ministers"—for we at least knew the word—actively, competitively, indeed as would often appear quite violently, ministering, so little sense of a brush against approved examples was ever to attend me that I had finally to draw my nearest sufficiency of a true image from pictures of a social order largely alien to our own. All of which, at the same time, I allow myself to add, didn't mitigate the simple fact of my felt—my indeed so luxuriously permitted—detachment of sensibility from everything, everything, that is, in the way of great relations, as to which our father's emphasis was richest. *There* was the dim dissociation, there my comparative poverty, or call it even frivolity, of instinct: I gaped imaginatively, as it were, to such a different set of relations. I couldn't have framed stories that would have succeeded in involving the least of the relations that seemed most present to *him;* while those most present to myself, that is more complementary to whatever it was I thought of as humanly most interesting, attaching, inviting, were the ones his schemes of importances seemed virtually to do without. Didn't I discern in this from the first a kind of implied snub to the significance of mine?—so that, in the blest absence of "pressure" which I just sought here passingly to celebrate, I could brood to my heart's content on the so conceivable alternative of a field of exposure crammed with those objective appearances that my faculty seemed alone fitted to grasp. In which there was ever the small torment of the fact—though I don't quite see to-day why it should not have been of a purely pleasant irritation—that what our parent most overflowed with was just the brave contradiction or opposition between all his parts, a thing which made for perfect variety, which he carried ever so easily and brightly, and which would have put one no less in the wrong had one accused him of knowing only the abstract (as I was so complacently and invidiously disposed to name it) than if one had foolishly remarked on his living and concluding without it. But I have already made clear his great mixed range—which of course couldn't *not* have been the sign of a mind conceiving our very own breathing humanity in its every fibre the absolute expression of a resident Divinity. No element of character, no spontaneity of life, but instantly seized his attention and incurred his greeting and his comment; which things could never possibly have been so genially alert and expert—as I have, again, before this, superabundantly recorded—if it had not fairly fed on active observation and contact. He could answer one with the radiant when one challenged him with the obscure, just as he could respond with the general when one pulled at the particular; and I needn't repeat that this made for us, during all our time, anything but a starved actuality.

NOTES

1. *Literary Remains of Henry James* (Boston, 1885). The portrait accompanying the volume gave us, alas, but the scantest satisfaction.

CHRONOLOGY OF THE LIFE
OF HENRY JAMES, SENIOR

1811   Born in Albany, New York, on June 3

1830   Graduated from Union College, Schenectady, New York

1835–38 Attended Princeton Theological Seminary

1837   Visited England and was exposed to Sandemanianism

1838   Edited Sandeman's *Letters on Theron and Aspasio*

1840   Married Mary Robertson Walsh and completed *Remarks on the Apostolic Gospel*

1842   William James, born January 11

1843   Henry James, Junior, born April 15

1844   Visited England again, experienced spiritual crisis, was introduced to Swedenborg's writings, and met J. J. Garth Wilkinson

1845   Birth of Garth Wilkinson James

1846   Birth of Robertson James. *What Constitutes the State*

1847   *Tracts for the New Times*

1848   Birth of Alice James

1850   *Moralism and Christianity*

1852   *Lectures and Miscellanies*

1853   *Love, Marriage, and Divorce*

1854   *The Church of Christ not an Ecclesiasticism*

1855   *The Nature of Evil*

1857   *Christianity the Logic of Creation*

1861   *The Social Significance of Our Institutions*

1863   *Substance and Shadow*

1869   *The Secret of Swedenborg*

1879   *Society the Redeemed Form of Man*

1882   Death of Mary Walsh James (January 29) and of Henry James, Senior (December 18)

1884   *The Literary Remains of the Late Henry James*, edited, with an introduction, by William James.